PAUL SLANSKY

A FIRESIDE BOOK PUBLISHED BY SIMON & SCHUSTER INC.

NEW YORK   LONDON   TORONTO   SYDNEY   TOKYO   SINGAPORE

THE CLOTHES HAVE
NO EMPEROR

89-14137

A CHRONICLE OF

THE AMERICAN '80S

FIRESIDE
Simon & Schuster Building
Rockefeller Center
1230 Avenue of the Americas
New York, New York 10020

FIRESIDE and colophon are registered trademarks
of Simon & Schuster Inc.

Designed by Bonni Leon

Manufactured in the United States of America

10 9 8 7 6 5 4   Pbk.

Library of Congress Cataloging in Publication
Data

Slansky, Paul.
    The clothes have no emperor : a chronicle of
the American '80s /
    Paul Slansky.
        p.   cm.
    "A Fireside Book."
    1. United States—Politics and government—
1981—1989—Miscellanea.
    2. Reagan, Ronald—Miscellanea.   I. Title.
E876.S53   1989
973.927—dc20   89-37139
                                             CIP

ISBN 0-671-67339-4 Pbk.

For everyone who noticed

"What kind of governor would you be?"

"I don't know. I've never played a governor."

—Ronald Reagan answering a reporter's query during his 1966 campaign for the California statehouse

This book is a work of self-defense.

It is the response of one observer who realized that his perception of the truth—an actor is playing the President—was a distinctly unpopular one. An observer who saw his nation's history being fictionalized as it occurred—an actor is playing the President!—while the ratings race turned media "watchdogs" into accomplices, bit players in the hit TV show the Presidency had become. An observer whose very sanity was threatened by the ease with which illusion—*an actor is playing the President!*—was embraced as reality.

I did not find the President's ignorance charming. I was unwarmed by his genial head-waggling, unreassured by his stern frowns of manly purpose, uncheered by his hearty waves as he strolled to and from his limos and choppers and jets.

His smooth purr did not soothe me. His nostalgic fables about an America that never was did not inspire me. And his canned one-liners, perversely celebrated as "wit" ("If I'd gotten a hand like that in Hollywood, I never would have left") definitely did not amuse me.

The voting majority, humbled by its recent presidential choices, was thrilled to have elected someone who at least looked the part, but all I could see was the emptiness of his suit. To me, the President was a pitchman who seemed not to exist when the camera light was off, a front man so personally invisible that he'd actually called his autobiography *Where's the Rest of Me?*, an aging star who'd spent way too much of his time watching his own movies, like Norma Desmond in *Sunset Boulevard*.

Astonished that so few seemed to share my vision, I was compelled to document it. Armed with scissors, file folders, yellow highlight pens and a bank of VCRs, I embarked on an eight-year quest, gathering evidence to prove my case: AN ACTOR IS PLAYING THE PRESIDENT!

I began reading four, then six, then eight papers a day (and five, then 10, then 20 magazines a week), seeking out the absurd and the outrageous, clipping and filing everything that confirmed my sense that standards were falling across the political, social and cultural landscapes. I became a media prospector, mining vast acres of ink in search of the perfect details and telling quotes that held the golden nuggets of truth. I began a video file, recording the evening newscasts—first one network, then two, then three—and dubbing the key sound-bites onto meticulously logged master tapes. The events of the decade were like a surreal novel unfolding in the media, and I found myself scrambling to get it all down, compiling a memory for a nation that clearly didn't want one.

The Clothes Have No Emperor is the result—a presentation of the Reagan years as I saw them, an invitation to historians to set the record straight while Nancy is around to see it, and a call to vigilance as we set about choosing who will lead us into the next millennium.

Yes, *The President Reagan Show* is off the air now, but a similar entertainment—*Dan Quayle's Playhouse*—is waiting in the wings. As we head into the '90s, the powers that be are working overtime—with the complicity, once again, of segments of the media that surely know better—to lull us into thinking that our Vice President is "growing" into his office and will soon be ready for bigger things.

Do not assume that this lightweight can never be elected to the White House. Back in the '60s, we knew the very notion of "President Reagan" was preposterous.

Paul Slansky
New York
July 1989

"Politics is just like show business. You have a hell of an opening, coast for a while, and then have a hell of a close."
—Ronald Reagan to aide Stuart Spencer, 1966

"Nancy knows not only her own lines but everybody else's. She picks up the cue her terrified classmates forget to give, improvises speeches for all and sundry. Just a part of the game for Nancy."
—1939 high school yearbook describing the former Nancy Davis in the lead role of her senior class play, *First Lady*

At 10:10 A.M. on Election Day 1980, Ronald Reagan and his wife, Nancy, arrived at their Pacific Palisades, California, polling place. Reporters shouted questions at the candidate, who smiled and said, "I can't answer till I get on my mark."

Though his victory seemed likely, he refused to predict it. "You know me," he said, smiling as he placed himself squarely on the taped cross showing where he was supposed to stand. "I'm too superstitious to answer anything like that."

His wife nudged him and quietly said, "Cautiously optimistic."

"Yes," said Reagan, smiling. "I'm cautiously optimistic."

As they left, he was asked whom he voted for. He smiled and said, "Nancy."

NOVEMBER 1980

In which life goes to the movies

11/4   At 8:15 P.M. EST, with 5% of the vote counted, NBC declares former Hollywood actor Ronald Reagan the 40th President of the United States.

When it's all over, Reagan has won 43,901,812 to 35,483,820 in the popular vote, 489–49 in the electoral college, and the Democrats have lost the Senate for the first time since 1954. Among the losers are veteran liberals Frank Church, George McGovern, John Culver, Gaylord Nelson and Birch Bayh, who is defeated by two-term congressman J. Danforth Quayle.

"I'm not bitter," says President Carter, who concedes before the polls in the west have closed. "Rosalynn is, but I'm not." Adds Rosalynn, "I'm bitter enough for all of us."

11/5   "I don't believe it! I don't believe it!"
—Nancy Reagan greeting the Bushes for a post-election lunch

"Well, what do we do now?"
—Vice President–elect George Bush to President-elect Reagan

11/6   Nancy Reagan—whose husband calls her "Mommy"—reveals how she learned the results of the election. "Ronnie had just gotten out of the shower and he was standing in his robe," she says, "and I had just gotten out of the bath and I was standing in my robe, and we had the television on, naturally, when NBC projected him the winner. We turned to each other and said, 'Somehow this doesn't seem to be the way it's supposed to be.' "

11/10   Dan Rather gets into a dispute with Chicago cab driver Eugene Phillips, who has gotten lost following the newsman's directions. When he tries to get out without paying, the cabbie—unaware of his passenger's identity—drives off in search of a cop. Rather sticks his head and shoulders out the window, waves his arms and shouts that he is being kidnapped. The police, for some reason, choose to take the side of the powerful network star, and Phillips is charged with disorderly conduct.

CBS says it will pay the $12.55 fare.

11/12   New York mayor Ed Koch tells a radio audience that he, "like everyone else," once tried marijuana. He claims not to have liked it.

11/14   Despite President-elect Reagan's claim that no personnel decisions have been made, his transition team announces two key appointments: Bush campaign head James A. Baker III as chief of staff, and longtime aide Edwin Meese III as White House counselor with Cabinet rank.

11/15   NBC receives over 400 calls from viewers complaining about the premiere of the new version of *Saturday Night Live,* produced by former talent booker Jean Doumanian. "It was just haplessly pointless tastelessness," writes *Washington Post* TV critic Tom Shales of the witticisms about drugs, Jews and homosexuals, "the kind of Cro-Magnon comedy that might have appealed to the thuggish Droogies of *A Clockwork Orange.*"

The show will maintain this level of humor for three months, at which point a cast member will finally just come right out and say "fuck" on the air. NBC will decide it has seen enough and fire Doumanian.

11/18   Flocking to the Cinema I theater for the hot-ticket screening of Michael Cimino's $36 million western, *Heaven's Gate,* New York's media elite finds itself enduring a 219-minute exercise in pretentious self-indulgence.

"Why aren't they drinking the champagne?" Cimino asks at intermission. Explains a publicist, with some glee, "Because they hate the movie, Michael."

11/19   "*Heaven's Gate* fails so completely that you might suspect Mr. Cimino sold his soul to the devil to obtain the success of *The Deer Hunter,* and the devil has just come around to collect. . . . For all the time and money that went into it, it's jerry-built, a ship that slides straight to the bottom at its christening. . . .*Heaven's Gate* is something quite rare in movies these days—an unqualified disaster."
—Vincent Canby, *The New York Times*

■

"You know what comes between me and my Calvins? Nothing."
—Brooke Shields, 15, in a jeans ad banned by CBS

11/20   President-elect Reagan arrives at the White House to receive a job briefing from President Carter, who later reveals that Reagan asked few questions and took no notes, asking instead for a copy of Carter's presentation.

■

Nancy Reagan tells *The Washington Post* that she and her husband are going to set an example for "a return to a higher sense of morality" when they move into the White House. "It kind of filters down from the top somehow," she explains.

■

United Artists cancels the Los Angeles premiere of *Heaven's Gate* and announces the withdrawal of the film from release pending serious recutting.

11/21   An early morning fire breaks out in the MGM Grand Hotel in Las Vegas, killing 84 and injuring more than 700.

■

After eight months of saturation hype, more than 41 million of America's nearly 78 million households tune in to *Dallas* to learn that Sue Ellen's sister Kristin shot J. R. Ewing. The episode receives a 53.3 rating—the highest in TV history.

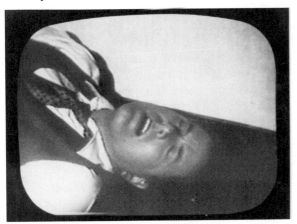

11/23   "Running the government is like running General Motors. It's twice General Motors or three times General Motors—but it's General Motors. . . . The Cabinet secretaries will be like the presidents of Chevrolet and Pontiac. . . . Chevrolet competes with Pontiac. Competition is good. But their competition stops at what is good for General Motors."
—Reagan crony Alfred Bloomingdale

11/24   Amidst a swirl of rumors about his alleged homosexuality, Ronald Prescott Reagan, 22—son of the President-elect, though not, in fact, "Junior"—heads down to Manhattan Supreme Court to marry his girlfriend Doria Palmieri, 29.

"I'm very happy," says Nancy Reagan in California, though *The New York Times* describes her demeanor as "notably subdued."

11/25   "*No más!* No more! No more box!"
—Roberto Duran—who has pigged out on two steaks and is now suffering stomach cramps—surrendering the welterweight crown to Sugar Ray Leonard in the eighth round of their rematch in New Orleans

11/27   At halftime during its Thanksgiving football game, CBS broadcasts an interview with Ronald Reagan in which the President-elect reminisces about his days as a radio sportscaster and recalls his penchant for enhancing events by "making things up."

11/28   President-elect Reagan goes to Beverly Hills for a haircut at Drucker's Barber Shop. Owner Harry Drucker says he has been cutting Reagan's hair exactly the same way for 40 years, describing it as "a traditional haircut, a conservative haircut. . . . It isn't a hippie-type haircut."

And no, he says, Reagan does not dye his hair.

DECEMBER 1980

In which the voice of a generation is stilled

12/2   Government forces in El Salvador shoot four US churchwomen to death.

12/6   "When you help the shepherd, you're helping the sheep."
—TV evangelist Jim Bakker to disciple Jessica Hahn in a Florida motel room

12/8   After lurking outside New York's Dakota apartments for several days, Mark David Chapman gets John Lennon to autograph a copy of his new album, *Double Fantasy*, as he and Yoko Ono leave for the recording studio. When they return, Chapman shows his gratitude by pumping four bullets into Lennon's back and left shoulder. Though he is rushed to the hospital in a police car, the former Beatle dies within minutes.

"Do you know what you just did?" asks the doorman. Says Chapman calmly, "I just shot John Lennon."

12/10 Radio commentator Paul Harvey scoffs at the renewed calls for gun control in the wake of John Lennon's murder. "Well, now, wait a minute," he says. "Death has claimed a lot of rock musicians prematurely, and none with guns. Keith Moon and Janis Joplin and Jimi Hendrix OD'd on drugs, and Elvis Presley and Brian Jones and John Bonham. . . . Plane crashes killed Jim Croce and Otis Redding and Buddy Holly, Ritchie Valens, Ronnie Van Zant. In fact, Lennon at 40 lived much longer than most of those."

So, it turns out he was really kind of lucky.

12/11 Rupert Murdoch's *New York Post* favors its readers with a front-page morgue photo of John Lennon.

■

President-elect Reagan's transition team announces eight major appointments—including Donald T. Regan (Secretary of the Treasury), David A. Stockman (Budget Director), Caspar W. Weinberger (Secretary of Defense), William French Smith (Attorney General) and William J. Casey (Director of the CIA).

Reagan, who not only doesn't attend the half-hour ceremony but can't even be bothered to watch all of it on TV, releases a statement calling this group "the exact combination to create the new beginning the American people expect and deserve."

■

Nancy Reagan reveals that she keeps a gun in a drawer near her bed. "Ronnie was away a lot, you know," she explains, "and I was alone in that house." And what kind of gun is it? She laughs. "It's just a tiny little gun."

12/12 The day after being named the nation's highest law enforcement officer, William French Smith travels to Rancho Mirage, California, to attend a 65th birthday party for Frank Sinatra.

■

Denying a report that Nancy Reagan "can't understand" why the Carters don't move into Blair House during the transition to give her a head start on redecorating the White House, a spokesperson explains that the First Lady-in-waiting merely suggested that she might do that favor for the next First Family.

Says one Carter aide, "I wouldn't be surprised if we have to fend off the moving vans."

12/15 Teamsters president Jackie Presser is named to the Reagan transition team.

12/16 Two more Cabinet appointments are announced in Washington: Alexander Haig (State) and Raymond Donovan (Labor). Meanwhile, in Beverly Hills, President-elect Reagan visits his tailor and stops by Drucker's for another haircut.

12/17 Bernice Brown, wife of former California governor Pat Brown, says that after her husband was defeated by Ronald Reagan in 1966, Nancy's secretary called to ask them to move out of the governor's mansion several days early. "They said they needed extra time," she says, "to wash windows and wax floors and all that."

■

Longtime Reagan aide and Nancy devotee Michael Deaver is named deputy White House chief of staff while, in Los Angeles, the President-elect picks up a bag full of veal and beef slabs from his butcher.

12/18   REAGAN ON THE SIDELINES
HE OFTEN SEEMS REMOTE FROM TRANSITION
   —*The Washington Post*

12/19   REAGAN 'IS REALLY RUNNING THINGS,' MEESE TELLS PRESS
   —*The Washington Post*

12/22   Four more Reagan appointments are announced in Washington, including Jeane Kirkpatrick (UN) and James Watt (Interior). In California, the President-elect visits his ear doctor.

■

John Lennon's "(Just Like) Starting Over" begins a five-week stay on top of the *Billboard* Hot 100, and *Double Fantasy* begins an eight-week run as the nation's best-selling LP.

12/26   REAGAN INTERESTED IN SPEEDING DEVELOPMENT OF SPACE-BASED LASER
   —*The Washington Post*

12/28   "I don't think you pay ransom for people that have been kidnapped by barbarians."
   —President-elect Reagan dismissing Iran's conditions for the release of the 52 American hostages

12/30   President-elect Reagan gets yet another haircut.

12/31   Nancy Reagan is reported to be insisting that whoever is hired as her husband's press secretary must be "reasonably good-looking."

■

In Evergreen, Colorado, a young man named John W. Hinckley, Jr., depressed over the murder of John Lennon, sits alone in his parents' house, drinking peach brandy and recording a New Year's Eve message. "I don't know what's gonna happen this year. It's just gonna be insanity," he says. "Jodie is the only thing that matters now. Anything that I might do in 1981 would be solely for Jodie Foster's sake. . . . It's time for me to go to bed. It's after midnight. It's the New Year, 1981. Hallelujah!"

1981

1/4   Writing about the Sinatra birthday bash, columnist William Safire points out that maybe it wasn't such a good idea for Attorney General–designate William French Smith to have attended a salute to "a man obviously proud to be close to notorious hoodlums."

The President-elect's reaction? "Yeah, I know. We've heard those things about Frank for years, and we just hope none of them are true."

1/6   President-elect Reagan—himself!—announces the appointment of pudgy, balding James Brady as White House press secretary. Asked if Brady's visuals have been approved by Nancy, the usually genial Reagan gets testy.

"I am getting to be an irate husband at some of the things I am reading," he says of his wife's astonishingly poor PR, "none of which are true."

■

Mark David Chapman pleads not guilty by reason of insanity to the charge of murdering John Lennon.

1/9   With his departure for Washington imminent, President-elect Reagan squeezes in one last haircut at Drucker's.

1/12   TV PREMIERE: *Dynasty*. With *Dallas* firmly entrenched at the top of the Nielsen ratings, ABC premieres its own prime time soap— produced by schlockmeister Aaron (*Charlie's Angels*) Spelling—about a rich multi-generational oil family, the Carringtons of Denver, who share the Ewings' idiosyncrasy of all living in the same house. Unlike the critically under-appreciated *Dallas*—which, thanks largely to Larry Hagman's hilarious portrayal of J.R., can also be enjoyed as a satire of corporate America—*Dynasty* is merely a celebration of wealth, a campy wallow in which the absurd plots and inane dialogue are incidental to the garish fashions. It becomes a huge hit.

1/13   "I cannot conceive now of any circumstances . . . which . . . would result in my not being able to provide this committee with the information it requires."

—William Casey underestimating his own imagination at his confirmation hearing to be CIA Director

■

President-elect Reagan is presented with a huge jar of jellybeans at a farewell ceremony in Los Angeles. Reminiscing about passing the jellybean jar around the table during his days as governor, he says, "You can tell a lot about a fellow's character, if a fellow just picks out one color or grabs a handful."

Just *what* one can tell from this is left unrevealed.

1/15   TV PREMIERE: *Hill Street Blues*. Desperate to climb out of its ratings hole, NBC gambles on an upscale cop show that so dazzles the critics that the network has no choice but to give it time to find an audience. Its portrayal of an upper-middle-class vision of the street—and the hot sex between stars Daniel J. Travanti and Veronica Hamel—makes the show the favorite of everyone who hates TV.

Ed Meese—who relaxes by listening to the police band on his radio and collects pig figurines as a tribute to police—expresses his preference for *Adam-12*.

1/17 The most expensive inaugural celebration in American history—an $11 million, four-day parade of white ties, limousines and mink that prompts Reagan partisan Barry Goldwater to complain about such an "ostentatious" display "at a time when most people can't hack it"—gets underway in Washington.

1/18 "Friends have urged me to run for governor in Nevada. Others have told me to try for the US Senate. And I'm thinking about both."
—Las Vegas saloon singer Wayne Newton, taking a break from coordinating the entertainment at the inaugural balls to speculate on his political future

1/19 President Carter appears in the White House briefing room at 4:56 A.M. to announce "an agreement with Iran that will result, I believe, in the freedom of our American hostages."

Criticizing the deal, a Reagan aide declares, "This administration will not negotiate with barbarians or terrorists."

■

"I'm so proud that you're First Lady, Nancy/And so pleased that I'm sort of a chum/ The next eight years will be fancy/As fancy as they come."
—Frank Sinatra at the inaugural gala that he organized, produced and directed, revising "Nancy with the Laughing Face" as "Nancy with the Reagan Face"

1/20 Just before 9 A.M. Michael Deaver, stunned that the President-elect is still sleeping, enters his bedroom to remind him that he's "going to be inaugurated." Says Reagan, "Does that mean I have to get up?"

At noon, promising an "era of national renewal," Ronald Wilson Reagan becomes the oldest man to take the oath of office as President of the United States. As he completes his speech, the 52 hostages held in Teheran for 444 days begin their journey home.

Later, President Reagan visits Tip O'Neill's office, where the House Speaker shows him a desk that was used by Grover Cleveland. Reagan claims to have portrayed him in a movie. O'Neill points out that Reagan in fact played Grover Cleveland Alexander, the baseball player, not Grover Cleveland, the President.

1/21   At his first Cabinet meeting, President Reagan is asked if he intends to issue an expected Executive Order on cost-cutting. He shrugs. Then, noticing Budget Director David Stockman nodding emphatically, he adds, "I have a smiling fellow at the end of the table who tells me we do."

■

On his first full day on the job as National Security Adviser, Richard Allen receives $1,000 and a pair of Seiko watches from Japanese journalists as a tip for arranging an interview with Nancy Reagan.

■

New Yorker Bernhard Goetz is assaulted by three youths who try to steal $1,000 worth of electronics equipment. Goetz subsequently applies for, and is denied, a gun permit.

1/23   A Bit of History, the nation's first museum honoring Richard M. Nixon—well, actually it's more of a roadside coffee shop housing some Nixon memorabilia—opens in San Clemente. "We call it 'A Bit of History,'" explains manager Peter Mitchell, "because, of all the history in the United States, this is just a little bit."

1/26   Peter McCoy, Nancy Reagan's chief of staff, complains that the Oval Office furniture is threadbare. "And," he adds, with some pique, "in my office, we have to have mousetraps. Mousetraps! Why doesn't somebody write an article about that?"

1/27   Welcoming the hostages home, President Reagan puts the world on notice that the US will deal with any such future incidents quite severely. "Our policy," he declares, "will be one of swift and effective retribution." When the band strikes up "Hail to the Chief," Reagan puts his hand over his heart. "Oh!" he says. "I thought this was the national anthem."

Summing up the event, Dan Rather misquotes from the end of *The Wizard of Oz*: "Gee, it's great to be back home."

1/28   At his first press conference as Secretary of State, Al Haig refers to himself as the "vicar" of foreign policy.

1/29   "Their goal must be the promotion of world revolution and a one-world Socialist or Communist state. . . . They reserve unto themselves the right to commit any crime, to lie, to cheat, in order to attain that."
—President Reagan at his first press conference, setting the tone for his dialogue with the Soviets

FEBRUARY 1981

In which the administration shows off its experts

2/2   At his hearing to become undersecretary of state, Reagan crony William Clark is subjected to a current-events quiz. Is he familiar with the struggles within the British Labour Party? He is not. Does he know which European nations don't want US nuclear weapons on their soil? He does not. Can he name the prime minister of South Africa? "No, sir, I cannot." The prime minister of Zimbabwe? "It would be a guess."

Despite his stupefying ignorance of these matters, he is confirmed.

2/5   Testifying before Congress, James Watt is asked if he agrees that natural resources must be preserved for future generations. Yes, he says, but he can't help adding, "I do not know how many future generations we can count on before the Lord returns."

■

On the eve of her husband's 70th birthday party, Nancy Reagan flies her manicurist, Jessica Vartoughian, in from Los Angeles.

2/6 "It's just the 31st anniversary of my 39th birthday."
—President Reagan on turning 70

2/11 Labor Secretary Ray Donovan eases requirements for the labeling of hazardous chemicals in the workplace.

2/18 President Reagan warns a joint session of Congress that the national debt is approaching $1 trillion. And how big is that? "A trillion dollars," he explains, "would be a stack of $1,000 bills 67 miles high."

2/21 REAGAN CHOPS WOOD AS TOP AIDES PREPARE TO SELL HIS BUDGET CUTS
—*The New York Times*

2/23 The drug ordeal of Mackenzie & Papa John Phillips
How they kicked their $1 million habit one day at a time
—*People*

2/24 Jean Harris is convicted of second-degree murder in the shooting of Dr. Herman Tarnower, the Scarsdale Diet Doctor. She gets 15 years to life.

2/25 Appearing on *Donahue* to plug her nude layout in *Playboy*, Rita Jenrette—in the process of divorcing Abscam-tainted congressman John Jenrette—finds herself fielding a phone call from her husband, who accuses her of emptying his checking account. "I'm trying to get my $35,000 back that she took," he says.
"Oh, really?" she shoots back. "Well, I'd like my $30,000 worth of silver that you removed from the house, and every stick of furniture, and everything else you took out of the house."
Donahue observes that "it looks like a messy divorce coming up." Rita agrees.

MARCH 1981

In which the President is shot by a young man who confuses movies with real life

3/3 In an interview with Walter Cronkite, President Reagan cites a 1938 speech by FDR in which he "called on the free world to quarantine Nazi Germany." Roosevelt in fact made no such speech.

3/5 "Well, the 'tiny little gun' disappeared quite a long time ago. I had the 'tiny little gun' when my husband was away a great deal of the time and I was alone and I was advised to have the 'tiny little gun.' "
—Nancy Reagan revealing that she is an ex-owner of diminutive weaponry

3/6 "Jodie Foster Love, just wait. I'll rescue you very soon. Please cooperate. J.W.H."
—Text of a letter hand-delivered at 1 A.M. to actress Jodie Foster's Yale dormitory

"Jodie, Goodbye! I love you six trillion times. Don't you maybe like me just a little bit? . . . It would make all of this worthwhile. John Hinckley, of course."
Text of a letter hand-delivered three hours later

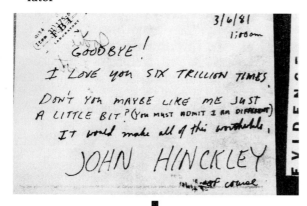

■

REAGAN IS MOVING TO END PROGRAM THAT PAYS FOR LEGAL AID TO THE POOR
—*The New York Times*

■

Washington Post gossip columnist Maxine Cheshire reports that lobbyist and recent *Playboy* model Paula Parkinson—who last year shared a vacation home with three House members—has videotaped several others in her bedroom. A spokesman for Sen. Dan Quayle (R–IN) says that though the then-congressman was a guest at that Florida golfing weekend, he "doesn't remember anyone by the name of Paula Parkinson."
Adds Quayle's wife, Marilyn, "Anyone who knows Dan Quayle knows he would rather play golf than have sex any day."

■

President Reagan holds his second press conference—the first in American history for which the order of the questioners has been determined by the President drawing names out of a jellybean jar. Many of the unchosen—among them, reporters from NBC, ABC and AP—boycott the event, and the system is quickly abandoned.

■

"And that's the way it is, Friday, March 6th, 1981. I'll be away on assignment and Dan Rather will be sitting in here for the next few years. Good night."
—Avuncular Walter Cronkite anchoring his last evening newscast after being retired early by CBS, to be replaced by a nervously intense man who has been given an $8 million contract to prevent him from moving to ABC, and therefore must have a job worth all that money

3/7 Disneyland records the first homicide in its 26-year history: an 18-year-old is stabbed to death in Tomorrowland.

3/16 President Reagan stuns *Los Angeles Times* theater critic Dan Sullivan by calling and asking him to plug his friend Buddy Ebsen's play, *Turn to the Right*. Sullivan takes the opportunity to berate Reagan for cutting funding for the arts, suggesting there might be some boondoggles in the Defense Department.
Yes, replies the President, $4 billion worth, "and we've caught them!"

3/17 Hosting a party for the Special Olympics committee, Henry Kissinger thanks Warner Brothers "for making the story of my life in *Superman* and following it up with *Superman II*."

3/18 THE GALLUP POLL
REAGAN APPROVAL RATING TRAILS EARLIER PRESIDENTS'
—*The Washington Post*

■

"If I didn't own them, somebody else would. . . . It's much ado about nothing."
—White House aide Lyn Nofziger, unrepentant in the face of charges that three Baltimore slums he owns should have been boarded up months ago

HAIGSPEAK

Secretary of State Alexander Haig won the 1981 Doublespeak Award from a group of English teachers. Among the phrases that earned him his victory:

"I'll have to caveat my response, Senator."

"careful caution"

"saddle myself with a statistical fence"

"posthostage-return attitude"

"nuance-al differences"

"epistemologicallywise"

"definitizing an answer"

"This is not an experience I haven't been through before."

3/20   The State Department explains that Alexander Haig was simply expressing "one theory" when he suggested that the four American nuns shot to death in El Salvador might have been killed while trying to "run a roadblock."

3/23   *Dallas'* sugary Victoria Principal spices up her newly single life with Andy Gibb
—*People*

3/24   President Reagan puts George Bush in charge of the administration's "crisis management" team, making Al Haig—whose high opinion of his own abilities is exceeded only by his contempt for Bush's—very unhappy.

3/30   Yoko Ono's "Walking on Thin Ice"—the record John Lennon was working on the night he was killed—peaks on *Billboard*'s Hot 100 at number 58.

∎

Following a speech at the Washington Hilton, President Reagan is shot in the chest by John W. Hinckley, Jr.—though he doesn't notice for a while. Three others are also injured, including press secretary James Brady, who survives a bullet to the brain after being reported dead on all three networks.

When the President sees Nancy at the hospital, he reportedly says, "Honey, I forgot to duck," a line originally spoken by Jack Dempsey to his wife after being beaten by Gene Tunney in 1926. As he enters the operating room, the President reportedly asks the surgeons, "Please tell me you're Republicans." A bullet is removed from his left lung.

When he comes out of anesthesia, he reportedly begins scribbling humorous notes to the nurses: "All in all, I'd rather be in Philadelphia." "Send me to L.A., where I can see the air I'm breathing." "Does Nancy know about us?"

During the operation, Al Haig rushes to the White House briefing room where, trembling and with his voice cracking, he seeks to reassure our allies that the government continues to function: "As of now, I am in control here, in the White House, pending return of the Vice President."

Afterward, Defense Secretary Caspar Weinberger confronts Haig and suggests he has misstated the line of succession. "Look," says Haig, "you better go home and read your Constitution, *buddy*. That's the way it is."

In Hollywood, the Academy Awards presentation is postponed for 24 hours.

3/31 An ABC News/*Washington Post* poll shows that President Reagan's popularity rating went up 11 points after he was shot.

∎

Letters found in his Washington hotel room suggest that John Hinckley, 25, might have been trying to impress actress Jodie Foster, with whom he had become obsessed after repeated viewings of Martin Scorsese's *Taxi Driver*, in which she played a 12-year old whore.

At the Academy Awards ceremony, Robert De Niro wins an Oscar for his performance as Jake LaMotta in Scorsese's *Raging Bull*, only to find that reporters are far more interested in discussing Travis Bickle, the character he played in *Taxi Driver*.

FROM THE PEN OF JOHN W. HINCKLEY, JR.

"Dear Jodie, Don't they make a darling couple? Nancy is downright sexy. One day you and I will occupy the White House and the peasants will drool with envy. Until then, please do your best to remain a virgin. You are a virgin, aren't you? Love, John."

—Unmailed postcard with portrait of the Reagans

"Jodie, I would abandon this idea of getting Reagan in a second if I could only win your heart and live out the rest of my life with you. . . . I just cannot wait any longer to impress you . . ."

—Unmailed letter written hours before the shooting

1981

APRIL 1981

In which the President recovers nicely

4/1   CNN airs a videotape of psychic Tamara Rand "predicting" the Reagan shooting on a Las Vegas talk show reportedly taped on January 6. Rand said she felt Reagan was in danger "at the end of March" from "a thud" in the "chest area" caused by "shots all over the place" from the gun of a "fair-haired" young man named something like "Jack Humley."

4/3   President Reagan poses with Nancy at the hospital. The photo released to the press is carefully cropped to hide the IV tubes hooked up to his left arm.

Actor John Gavin—Janet Leigh's boyfriend in *Psycho*—is named US ambassador to Mexico.

4/5   Talk show host Dick Maurice admits that Tamara Rand's astonishing prediction of the Reagan assassination attempt was actually taped the day after the shooting. Still, she had it pegged pretty close.

4/13   *Washington Post* reporter Janet Cooke wins the Pulitzer Prize for her story about an eight-year-old heroin addict. Unfortunately, it turns out that she made the story up.

4/15   Former FBI officials W. Mark Felt and Edward S. Miller, convicted of authorizing illegal break-ins during the Nixon years, are pardoned by President Reagan, who claims they served the nation "with great distinction."

4/24   "I think it's a terrifically made picture. I don't think Cimino hurt the film one iota by cutting it."
—United Artists vice president Jerry Esbin on the streamlined 148-minute version of *Heaven's Gate*, opening in over 800 theaters

4/25   Maureen Reagan, 40, marries her third husband, 28-year-old Dennis Revell, in Los Angeles. The couple exchange self-penned vows: "I love you because you're going to let me be me."
At the last minute, President Reagan sends word that he and Nancy will be unable to attend, thus avoiding the eagerly anticipated encounter between them and Maureen's mom, Jane Wyman.

4/27   "It's as if somebody called every household in the country and said, 'There will be a curse on your family if you go see this picture.'"
—Jerry Esbin on *Heaven's Gate*'s pathetic $1.3 million opening weekend gross

4/30   A *New York Times*/CBS News poll reports that only 25% of the public knows that El Salvador is in Central America, with 28% placing it in South America. Others think it's "around Israel" and in "Louisiana, near Baton Rouge."

MAY 1981

In which the Pope disrupts the Nation's viewing habits

5/1   Billie Jean King admits having had a lesbian relationship with Marilyn Barnett, a former employee who has filed a palimony suit against the married tennis pro. Says King of her admission, which could result in sharply curtailed endorsement income, "I had to say it. You have to live with yourself."

5/4   FARRAH
    She glitters again on TV, but the real drama is her romance with rowdy Ryan O'Neal
    —*People*

5/9   C.I.A. SEEKS LAW FOR SURPRISE SEARCHES OF NEWSROOMS
    —*The New York Times*

5/10   REAGAN WANTS TO ABOLISH CONSUMER PRODUCT AGENCY
    —*The Washington Post*

5/11   Reggae singer Bob Marley dies at 36 of brain and lung cancer.
    ■
    Ed Meese—staking out territory as the administration's most right-wing law 'n' order man—calls the American Civil Liberties Union "a criminals' lobby."
    ■
    Kim Carnes' "Bette Davis Eyes" begins nine weeks as America's favorite song.

5/13   TV viewers jam the switchboards of stations across America to complain that their soap operas and game shows have been preempted by coverage of the shooting of Pope John Paul II.

5/14   A bitter Michael Reagan says he'll resign from his job at a military supply firm after a letter he wrote on March 24—in which he invoked his father's name on a business solicitation—becomes public.
    "It's just so silly," he says. "Somebody else can write a letter to the military bases . . . and say, 'Hey, I think Ronald Reagan's a great President.' I write a letter and say my Dad's a great President and I have the press on my doorstep."
    And did Dad have any advice for his adopted son? "Don't write any letters."

5/15   TV PREMIERE: *SCTV Network 90.* NBC hires the most talented comedy group in the history of television to create the smartest satire ever broadcast, then makes sure no one will see it by airing it in the middle of the night.

5/17   "His vision, now as then, has a compelling simplicity about it."
    —Honorary degree awarded to President Reagan by Notre Dame, where he first uttered "Win one for the Gipper" 41 years earlier while filming *Knute Rockne—All American*

5/21 WHITE HOUSE SEEKS EASED BRIBERY ACT

SAYS 1977 LAW INHIBITS BUSINESS ABROAD BY U.S. CORPORATIONS
—*The New York Times*

■

The US casts one of only three votes against a World Health Organization ethics code preventing the sale of American infant formulas to Third World countries, where their use with contaminated water has killed thousands.

5/25 PRESIDENT CHOPS WOOD AND DOES PAPER WORK
—*The New York Times*

5/27 John W. Hinckley, Jr., tries to kill himself by taking an overdose of Tylenol.

5/31 *Newsweek* publishes a rare cover story on art, "The Revival of Realism," illustrating it with a realistic painting of a bare-breasted woman.

JUNE 1981

In which some curious symptoms are observed

6/2 Barbara Walters asks Katharine Hepburn and Lauren Bacall what kinds of trees they would be if they were trees.

6/5 The Centers for Disease Control in Atlanta issues a report about unexplained outbreaks of a kind of pneumonia that usually affects only cancer patients. All five cases described—as well as six others under study—are homosexual men in their 20s or 30s. "The best we can say," says epidemiologist Wayne Shandera, "is that somehow the pneumonia appears to be related to gay life-style."

■

Ernest W. Lefever—whose belief that the US should take a soft line when dealing with friendly rightist dictatorships has earned him serious Senate opposition—withdraws from consideration as assistant secretary of state for human rights.

6/12 Baseball's first-ever mid-season strike begins.

■

President Reagan fails to recognize his only black Cabinet member, Housing Secretary Samuel Pierce, at a White House reception for big-city mayors. "How are you, Mr. Mayor?" he greets him. "I'm glad to meet you. How are things in your city?"

6/13 At 12:30 A.M. a venerable television tradition—giving madman Charles Manson air time in an effort to boost ratings—is born, as NBC devotes 90 minutes to an interview conducted by Tom Snyder at California's Vacaville prison. The show is produced by former Nixon media man Roger Ailes.

Among the burning questions answered: Was Manson a heavy drug user? "No, I smoked a little grass, and I've taken some acid, mescaline, psilocybin, peyote, mushrooms, but actually take dope? No. I wouldn't take anything that I feel would hurt me."

6/16 President Reagan holds his third press conference, where he responds to questions on:

- The Israeli attack on Iraq—"I can't answer that"
- Israel's refusal to sign the Nuclear Non-proliferation Treaty—"Well, I haven't given very much thought to that particular question there"
- Pakistan's refusal to sign the treaty—"I won't answer the last part of the question"
- Israeli threats against Lebanon—"Well, this one's going to be one, I'm afraid, that I can't answer now"
- The tactics of political action committees—"I don't really know how to answer that."

As for skepticism about his administration's grasp of foreign affairs, the President declares, "I'm satisfied that we do have a foreign policy."

6/22 Mark David Chapman changes his plea to guilty in the murder of John Lennon. He gets 20 years to life.

6/23 New York mayor Ed Koch turns down a $7,500 offer to perform a Saturday night stand-up comedy routine at the Nevele hotel in the Catskills.

6/28 REAGAN'S AIDES SAY A BALANCED BUDGET IS POSSIBLE BY 1984
  —*The New York Times*

6/29 "I regard voting as the most sacred right of free men and women."
  —President Reagan who, mouthed pieties aside, refuses to commit to supporting an extension of the Voting Rights Act

6/30 "We love your adherence to democratic principle, and to the democratic processes."
  —George Bush offering an exuberant toast to newly re-inaugurated President Ferdinand Marcos, whose fondness for democracy is less celebrated by those who know him better

JULY 1981

In which the first woman goes to the Supreme Court and the First Lady goes to a wedding

7/2 In a letter to a *New York Times* reporter, John W. Hinckley, Jr., refers to his "historical deed" as "an unprecedented demonstration of love. . . . Does Jodie Foster appreciate what I've done? . . . Everybody but everybody knows about John and Jodie. . . . Jodie and I will always be together, in life and in death."

7/3 The Centers for Disease Control in Atlanta issues a report documenting 26 cases—eight of them fatal—of a rare skin cancer called Kaposi's sarcoma. All the patients are male homosexuals.

7/6 Is She Too Sexy for TV?
  Morgan Fairchild of *Flamingo Road* is what the Moral Majority is shouting about
  —*People*

  ■

  Nancy Reagan, 60, celebrates her 58th birthday.

7/7 Socialite Claus von Bulow is indicted in Newport, Rhode Island, for two attempts at murdering his diabetic wife, Sunny—who has been in a coma since last December—by injecting her with insulin.

  ■

  President Reagan nominates Arizona judge Sandra Day O'Connor to be the first woman on the Supreme Court.

7/8 Jerry Falwell suggests that Sandra Day O'Connor's opposition to abortion might not be sufficiently rabid to please him. Responds Sen. Barry Goldwater, "I think that every good Christian ought to kick Falwell right in the ass!"
  O'Connor is confirmed by the Senate, 99–0.

7/14 Max Hugel—appointed by William Casey to run the CIA's covert operations—resigns amidst allegations of fraud in connection with certain of his financial transactions in the early '70s.

7/15 President Reagan dismisses stock fraud charges against William Casey as "old news."

7/16 "I would like to see us do less of the really rotten shows."
—Newly appointed NBC chairman Grant Tinker suggesting a strategy to get the network out of the ratings cellar

7/17 Wayne B. Williams, 23, is indicted for the murder of two of the 28 young blacks killed in Atlanta over the past two years. Williams, himself black, came to police attention when he was spotted driving slowly over a bridge from which a body was believed to have been dumped.

■

With 1,500 people attending a dance in the lobby of Kansas City's Hyatt Regency Hotel, a third floor "sky bridge" walkway collapses onto the walkway below. Both land on the lobby crowd, killing 113.

7/18 Norman Mailer's literary protégé Jack Henry Abbott, a convicted bank robber who has been living in Manhattan on a work-release program, gets into an early-morning argument at an East Village restaurant and stabs a young man to death.
The next day, *The New York Times* calls his collected letters from jail, *In the Belly of the Beast*, "the most fiercely visionary book of its kind in the American repertoire of prison literature . . . awesome, brilliant." Columnist Murray Kempton suggests Abbott could be the first fugitive to surrender to *The New York Review of Books*.

7/23 "Heck, no. I'm going to leave this to you experts. I'm not going to get involved in details."
—President Reagan declining Treasury Secretary Donald Regan's invitation to join the negotiating session at which his tax-cut bill is being shaped

7/25 REPORTS BY CASEY ARE SAID TO OMIT STOCK HOLDING AND A $10,000 GIFT
—*The New York Times*

7/26 The Heimlich maneuver saves the life of New York mayor Ed Koch after he almost chokes to death in Chinatown's Sun Lok Yee restaurant, where waiters say he was talking non-stop while stuffing pork into his mouth. Not wishing to alienate Jewish voters, Koch claims a piece of sautéed watercress caused the problem.

7/28 Nancy Reagan—giddy to be in London for the Royal Wedding—announces, "I'm off to see the King and Queen," though there hasn't been a King of England in 27 years. The British press detests her on sight. "Maybe she'll fall again," writes one paper of the First Lady's propensity for toppling over, "and break her hair."

7/29 Prince Charles weds Lady Diana Spencer, who calls him "Philip Charles Arthur George" instead of "Charles Philip Arthur George" while taking her vows. He, in turn, forgets the word "worldly" while pledging to share his goods with her.

7/30   REAGAN TAX CUT, 25% OVER 3 YEARS, IS VOTED BY WIDE MARGINS IN THE HOUSE AND SENATE
    PRESIDENT BECOMES MASTER OF CONGRESS
    —*The New York Times*

7/31   REAGAN IMMIGRATION PLAN
    ABSENCE OF A METHOD TO DISTINGUISH ALIENS FROM CITIZENS RAISES QUESTIONS ON OUTLOOK
    —*The New York Times*

■

Major league baseball players end their 50-day walkout—the longest in the history of professional sports. In an effort to renew the interest of fans whose teams were doing poorly, a "second season" is established, with an extra set of playoffs.

AUGUST 1981

In which the President takes a much-needed break

8/1   TV PREMIERE: MTV. With the public's attention span shrinking by the second, cable's first 24-hour music channel establishes the four-minute rock video—essentially a commercial for an album—as the hot new art form. Fast cuts, slow motion and artsy black-and-white photography—all selling sex and violence—define the visual style of the decade, spreading to movies, prime time series, advertising and magazines.

8/4   Marine Corps Major Oliver L. North is assigned to White House duty with the National Security Council.

8/5   The Reagan administration begins sending dismissal notices to over 5,000 striking members of the Professional Air Traffic Controllers Union (PATCO). By week's end, the union is broken.

8/6   WHITE HOUSE SEEKS TO LOOSEN STANDARDS UNDER CLEAN AIR ACT
    —*The Washington Post*

8/10   Limited public response results in the closing of the Nixon museum. Says manager Peter Mitchell, "If nothing else, it's been a good stopping point for people to use the restrooms between L.A. and San Diego."

8/13   President Reagan takes time out from a 28-day California vacation to sign the largest budget and tax cuts in history into law. When his dog wanders by, a reporter asks its name.
    "Lassie," the President replies, then corrects himself. "Millie!" he says. "Millie. Millie's her name."

8/18   Jerry Lewis appears on *Donahue* to defend telethons. When a woman says she finds the format "kind of repulsive," he responds by implying that his critic is anti-Semitic, saying, "I've got to get you an autographed photograph of Eva Braun."

8/19   Ed Meese sees no need to wake President Reagan just to tell him the Navy has shot down two Libyan jets. Defending Meese's decision, Reagan explains, "If our planes are shot down, yes, they'd wake me up right away. If the other fellows were shot down, why wake me up?"

■

At Malcolm Forbes' 62nd birthday party, Henry Kissinger is asked if he's read D. M. Thomas' novel *The White Hotel*. "I don't read books," he replies. "I write them."

8/31 "He acted like there was nothing else in the world he had to do, nothing else on his mind."
—Former movie actor Rex Allen, who spent 45 minutes with President Reagan after presenting him with four pairs of free boots

"There are times when you really need him to do some work, and all he wants to do is tell stories about his movie days."
—Unnamed White House aide on President Reagan's detachment from his job

SEPTEMBER 1981

In which it is suggested that less money be spent on school lunches and more on fancy dinnerware

9/4 NBC, which has consistently failed to provide David Brinkley with a forum appropriate for his talents, announces that the veteran newsman has retired. He is quickly hired by ABC News president Roone Arledge, who gives him a weekly Sunday morning show that instantly establishes itself as the class of the field.

■

The Agriculture Department proposes cutting the size of school lunches and offering tofu, yogurt, cottage cheese or peanuts as viable meat substitutes. In addition, condiments such as ketchup and pickle relish would be reclassified as vegetables.

9/7 John W. Hinckley, Jr., writes to a *Washington Post* reporter, pointing out that his travels were necessary to further his relationship with Jodie Foster, and requesting that he not be referred to as a "drifter" in the future.

■

Dudley Moore
With his smash(ed) hit *Arthur*, he's the season's king of comedy and sexy Susan Anton's ace of hearts
—*People*

■

TV PREMIERE: *The People's Court*. Retired judge Joseph Wapner presides over small claims cases whose litigants have agreed to have their disputes heard on TV.

9/11 Nancy Reagan defends her decision to spend $209,508 in donated funds on a 4,732-piece china set. "The White House really badly, badly needs china," she explains. "It's badly needed."

9/14 TV PREMIERE: *Entertainment Tonight*. With show business and gossip increasingly setting the tone for the nation's affairs—and with Hollywood's creative energy focusing less on the product and more on the deal—this nightly half hour provides volumes of nonessential data (movie grosses, TV ratings, record sales) that, in happier times, people knew enough not to care too much about. The show inspires the term "infotainment." Asks comedian Harry Shearer, "Why not 'entermation'?"

9/15 President Reagan says he is "as committed today as on the first day I took office to balancing the budget."

9/16 Sugar Ray Leonard retains his welterweight title by knocking out Thomas Hearns in the 14th round of their Las Vegas bout. Asked about his opponent afterward, the champ says, "He proved he's not just a fighter but a marketable commodity. He can do commercials."

9/18 NOW PLAYING: *Mommie Dearest.* Faye Dunaway *is* Joan Crawford! "No wire hangers—ever!"

9/21 White House Secret Service agent John A. Bachmann, Jr., 29, is arrested for robbing a local bank.

9/23 President Reagan plays host to Sugar Ray Leonard and his wife. "We're very proud," says the President, "to have Sugar Ray and Mrs. Ray here."

9/25 President Reagan —untroubled by the drop in stock prices "because I don't have any"—announces that he has withdrawn the proposal to cut school lunches. He suggests that a dissident faction in the Agriculture Department might have come up with the idea as a form of "bureaucratic sabotage."

Just to set the record straight, aide James Johnson explains, "It would be a mistake to say that ketchup per se was classified as a vegetable. Ketchup in combination with other things was classified as a vegetable." And what things would ketchup have to combine with to be considered a full-blown vegetable? "French fries or hamburgers."

■

With "Start Me Up" heading up the singles chart and *Tattoo You* the top-selling album, the Rolling Stones kick off their sixth triennial American tour—the first to boast a corporate sponsor (Jovan scents)—in Philadelphia's JFK Stadium.

OCTOBER 1981

In which another world leader is shot, though not to impress Jodie Foster

10/1 At his first press conference in 15 weeks, President Reagan denies that his administration has a "millionaires on parade" style. As for the fancy new set of White House china, well, "Nancy's taken a bit of a bum rap on that."

10/2 At a White House briefing with Caspar Weinberger, President Reagan is asked how his MX missiles will be deployed. "I don't know but what maybe you haven't gotten into the area that I'm gonna turn over to the, heh heh, to the Secretary of Defense," he says sheepishly.

"The silos will be hardened," Weinberger says, then nods approvingly as Reagan volunteers, "Yes, I could say this. The plan also includes the hardening of silos."

10/4 The Cincinnati Reds end the strike-marred season with the best overall record in baseball. Unfortunately, they finish in second place in each half-season and fail to qualify for the playoffs.

10/5 *Newsweek* publishes a written interview with John W. Hinckley, Jr. "In closing," he writes, "I would like to say hello to Ms. Foster and ask her one small question: Will you marry me, Jodie?"

Meanwhile, *Time* publishes a letter in which the would-be assassin finally explains his fondness for the actress. "From head to toe, every square inch of Jodie is what attracts me," he writes. "Jodie's got the look I crave. What else can I say?"

10/6　Hours after Egyptian president Anwar Sadat is shot to death, Hollywood producers Sandy Frank and David Levy—who have long wanted to make a TV movie about him—alert the media that they are stepping up their efforts. "Now the story has a definite ending," says Levy. "The lack of an ending was what was stopping it from being made."

10/11　Opening for the Rolling Stones at the Los Angeles Coliseum, a short, skinny black musician named Prince—wearing only bikini briefs—is forced to leave the stage when the overwhelmingly white audience begins throwing garbage at him.

10/15　During a White House interview with Nancy Reagan, Andy Warhol says he "always thought they should have a lottery where they invite one family to dinner every night because it's so exciting to be here."

Says the First Lady, "There are tours, of course, Andy."

10/19　California state senator John Schmitz tells a TV interviewer that if Reagan's policies fail, "the best we could probably hope for is a military coup or something like that." He explains that he is talking about "a good military coup, not a bad military coup."

10/22　"Now, that's silly. I'd never wear a crown. It messes up your hair."
—Nancy Reagan citing a popular postcard portraying her as a queen, hoping that if she makes fun of herself, everyone else will stop

10/23　The national debt hits $1 trillion. (67 miles!)

10/25　Following the Yankees' loss to the Dodgers in the fifth game of the World Series, owner George Steinbrenner gets into a fight on his Los Angeles hotel elevator with two unidentified men who make derogatory comments about the "animals" who live in New York and the "choke-asses" who play for his team. Though he claims to have "clocked" his taunters, his own souvenirs of the encounter include a swollen lip, a bruised head and a cast on his broken left hand.

The Yankees lose the Series and do not soon qualify for another.

10/26　Richard NEVER SAY DIET Simmons
Shape up, Donahue! This guy's zany show is TV's unlikeliest hit—and he's just as outrageous at home
—*People*

10/29　SENATE, 52–48, SUPPORTS REAGAN ON AWACS JET SALE TO SAUDIS
PRESIDENT ELATED
—*The New York Times*

NOVEMBER 1981

In which some chickens come home to roost and the President co-stars with a turkey

11/9   Liz & Luke & Laura

An advance peek at TV's wedding of the year (and look who's crashing)
—*People*

11/10   President Reagan elicits hoots of laughter at his fifth press conference when he says of his constantly feuding aides, "There is no bickering or backstabbing going on. We're a very happy group."

As he leaves, Lesley Stahl holds up a copy of the just-out *Atlantic Monthly* featuring William Greider's article "The Education of David

Stockman," in which the chatty Budget Director:

- Admits, "None of us really understands what's going on with all these numbers"
- Acknowledges that supply-side economics "was always a Trojan horse to bring down the top rate"
- Says of the Reagan tax bill, "Do you realize the greed that came to the forefront? The hogs were really feeding."

Is the President aware of this article? He is not.

11/12   "My visit to the Oval Office for lunch with the President was more in the nature of a visit to the woodshed after supper. . . . He was not happy about the way this has developed—and properly so."

—David Stockman describing his crow-eating lunch with President Reagan, who blames the whole flap on the media

11/13   "This house belongs to all Americans, and I want it to be something of which they can be proud."

—Nancy Reagan showing off her $1 million White House redecoration—funded by tax-deductible donations—to *Architectural Digest*, which is then forbidden to release any of its photos to the general news media

■

The White House announces that the Justice Department is investigating a $1,000 payment given to National Security Adviser Richard Allen by a Japanese magazine after he helped arrange a brief post-inaugural interview with Nancy Reagan.

"I didn't accept it. I received it," says Allen, who explains that "it would have been an embarrassment" to the Japanese to have returned the money.

Asked if Allen will stay on the job, President Reagan says, "On the basis of what I know, yes." Nancy Reagan, however, is said to be furious that she has been dragged into the story.

■

"When I hear people talking about money, it's usually people who don't have any."
—GOP finance chairman Richard DeVos, dismissing charges that Reagan economic policies are unfair

11/15 John W. Hinckley, Jr., suffers minor neck injuries during a failed attempt to hang himself with an army field jacket.

11/16 With the exercise craze peaking, Olivia Newton-John's "Physical" begins a 10-week run as the nation's Number One song.

11/17 "It's impossible/Making love in a Toyota/It's impossible."
—Robert Goulet, apparently mistaking the White House for a Vegas saloon while performing at a state dinner for the president of Venezuela

11/18 President Reagan receives the annual White House turkey, which upstages him by squawking and flapping its wings madly. Not to be outdone, the President recalls a Thanksgiving long ago: he was carving a turkey, noticed what seemed to be blood oozing from it, assumed the bird was undercooked, then realized he had sliced open his thumb. Everyone laughs.

11/20 *Washington Post* columnist Judy Mann writes that Nancy Reagan, who is "in the position to champion causes that will improve the quality of life for Americans," has so far merely "used the position to improve the quality of life for those in the White House."
The First Lady is said to find this criticism more upsetting than any since a 1980 article referred to her "piano" legs—which, according to an aide, caused her to go "into a sort of coma for three days."

11/23 President Reagan vetoes a stopgap spending bill, thus forcing the federal government—for the first time in history—to temporarily shut down. Says House Speaker Tip O'Neill, "He knows less about the budget than any president in my lifetime. He can't even carry on a conversation about the budget. It's an absolute and utter disgrace."

11/25 DOWN IN THE POLLS
23% GIVE MRS. REAGAN "UNFAVORABLE" RATING
—*The Washington Post*

11/27 Barbara Walters asks President Reagan what kind of father he was. "I don't really know," he says. "I tried very hard, and worked at, spending time with the family." And what adjectives would he use to describe himself? "Soft touch, I really am . . . sometimes I'm stubborn, I hope not unnecessarily so, but [long pause] I—I can't answer that question, I wouldn't know how to do it."
He is, however, able to describe his academic record: "I never knew anything above Cs."
And what kind of tree would he be? She doesn't ask.

11/29 With James Baker and Michael Deaver reportedly agreeing with Nancy Reagan that he must be removed, Richard Allen takes a leave of absence while the investigation continues. "I fully expect to resume my duties," he says, embarking on a doomed attempt to save himself by going on TV and taking his case directly to the people, who couldn't care less.

■

Social secretary Muffie Brandon reveals that the White House is experiencing "a terrible tablecloth crisis." Says Brandon, "One set of tablecloths, to my complete and utter horror, went out to the dry cleaner and shrunk."

11/30 "I don't think that we have a crisis here. I think we'll manage. I don't see this as a frightening thing."
—Sheila Tate, Nancy Reagan's press secretary, downplaying the tablecloth alarm

President Reagan tells a $2,500-per-ticket GOP fundraiser in Cincinnati about a letter from a blind supporter. "He wrote in Braille," the President claims, "to tell me that if cutting his pension would help get this country back on its feet, he'd like to have me cut his pension." The altruistic soul's identity is never revealed.

NATALIE WOOD IS FOUND DROWNED ON YACHT VISIT TO SANTA CATALINA
—*The New York Times*

DECEMBER 1981

In which the President gives the Nation a Christmas present

12/2   Following a four-month investigation into William Casey's business dealings, the Senate Intelligence Committee declares that the CIA Director is not "unfit to serve."

"Maybe I should go down to the press briefing room and clutch my hands to my chest?"
—President Reagan, who earlier in the day was reported to have died, at Ed Meese's 50th birthday party

12/4   TV PREMIERE: *Falcon Crest*. CBS's newest prime time soap, set in the Northern California vineyards, provides Ronald Reagan's first wife, Jane Wyman, with the role of an evil, manipulative power broker, who seems to be patterned after his second wife.

12/5   REAGAN WIDENS INTELLIGENCE ROLE; GIVES C.I.A. DOMESTIC SPY POWER
—*The New York Times*

12/8   Joking about Muammar Qaddafi's alleged threats to have him assassinated, President Reagan ends a budget meeting by turning to his Vice President and saying, "Hey, by the way, George, I don't know how you feel about it, but I think I'll just call Qaddafi and meet him out there on the Mall." Everyone laughs.

12/14   A *Newsweek* poll shows that 62% of the American people feel that Nancy Reagan "puts too much emphasis on style and elegance" during hard times, with 61% thinking her "less sympathetic to the problems of the poor and underprivileged" than her predecessors.

"Mr. Reagan has the White House. I have Arlington."
—James Watt justifying his decision to hold two private cocktail parties at Arlington Cemetery's Lee Mansion at the taxpayers' expense

12/16   Asked by a TV news crew about possible irregularities in his relations with the Nixon White House, Chief Justice Warren Burger lunges forward and knocks the camera to the ground. He later claims he was provoked when the lens "hit me in the chin," though

HERE'S WHAT THE CRITICS ARE SAYING ABOUT PRESIDENT REAGAN

"God, he's a bore. And a bad actor. Besides, he has a low order of intelligence. With a certain cunning. And not animal cunning. Human cunning. Animal cunning is too fine an expression for him. He's inflated, he's egotistical. He's one of those people who thinks he is right. And he's not right. He's not right about anything."
—Director John Huston to *Rolling Stone*

"Ronnie was not a big star. He didn't carry enough weight. To think that the guy became President is really kind of funny."
—Actress Viveca Lindfors to *People*

"An amiable dunce."
—Former Defense Secretary Clark Clifford at a Georgetown dinner party

"That incoherent cretin."
—British Labour Party member Andrew Faulds during a House of Commons debate

videotape of the incident shows that the equipment never touched him.

12/17   At his sixth press conference, President Reagan is asked if he agrees with his Justice Department's efforts to overturn the Supreme Court's *Webber* ruling, which allows unions and management to enter into voluntary affirmative action agreements. The President says he "can't bring that to mind as to what it pertains to and what it calls for." When a reporter explains it to him, he says he supports the decision, though White House aides later say he thinks it should be overturned.

12/20 REAGAN OFFICIALS SEEK TO EASE RULES ON NURSING HOMES

PROPOSALS INCLUDE REPEAL OF REGULATIONS ON SANITATION, SAFETY AND CONTAGION
  —*The New York Times*

■

White House PR guru Michael Deaver says he can't get by on his $60,000 government salary.

■

On *60 Minutes*, Mike Wallace asks his friend Nancy Reagan about her image as someone who, despite "the requisite visit to the drug rehabilitation center" or "the requisite amount of time . . . spent on foster grandparents," really only cares about "style and fashion and her rich friends."

"Well, it's not true, of course," she says. "It's just—it's just not true."

Mike does not argue.

12/22 As Christmas approaches, President Reagan authorizes the distribution of 30 million pounds of surplus cheese to the poor. According to a government official, the cheese is well over a year old and has reached "critical inventory situation." Translation: it's moldy.

■

During a PBS interview, President Reagan—who has previously noted that elements of FDR's New Deal resembled fascism—claims that New Deal proponents actually "espoused" fascism. Roosevelt biographer Arthur M. Schlesinger, Jr., calls this "a gross distortion of history."

12/23 Asked to comment on his wife's higher-than-usual disapproval rating, President Reagan says, "I just heard earlier today—and maybe Larry can tell me if this is true—I just heard that some poll or something has revealed that she's the most popular woman in the world."

White House spokesman Larry Speakes says he has seen no such poll.

"I tell you," says the President, "if it isn't true, it should be. I'm on her side."

12/27 Supreme Court Justice William Rehnquist—who has, for several months, been taking substantial doses of Placidyl to relieve intense back pain—checks into George Washington Hospital for treatment of side effects, including speech so severely slurred that he was frequently incoherent in court and, according to a hospital spokesman, his "hearing things and seeing things that other people did not hear and see."

12/29 Special prosecutor Leon Silverman begins an investigation into allegations against Labor Secretary Raymond Donovan regarding a union payoff by his former New Jersey firm, Schiavone Construction. Rejecting suggestions that he resign, Donovan says, "I have paid a large entrance fee to this city, and I intend to stay for the double feature."

1 Defense Department official Thomas K. Jones suggested that all one needs to do to survive nuclear attack is "Dig a hole, cover it with a couple of doors and then throw three feet of dirt on top. . . . If there are enough shovels to go around, everybody's going to make it." What's wrong with his theory?
  a What if you don't have a backyard?
  b Even if you do have a yard, how protective could dirt really be?
  c Even if dirt will do the trick, who's going to shovel it on top for you?
  d All of the above

2 "Smoking kills. If you're killed, you've lost a very important part of your life." Who said it?
  a C. Everett Koop
  b Yul Brynner
  c Brooke Shields
  d Nancy Reagan

3 Which of these actually appeared on TV?
  a *Shrink Rap*, a nightly half hour featuring celebrities and their therapists
  b *The Making of* The Making of *Raiders of the Lost Ark*, a behind-the-scenes look at the behind-the-scenes look at the year's most popular film
  c *The Harlem Globetrotters on Gilligan's Island*, a TV movie starring Bob Denver
  d *They Eeeaaaaarrrrnnnn It*, a TV movie about life at a brokerage house based on John Houseman's Smith Barney commercial

4 What book did Mark David Chapman have in his possession when he was arrested?
  a John Lennon's *A Spaniard in the Works*
  b James Nourse's *The Simple Solution to Rubik's Cube*
  c J. D. Salinger's *The Catcher in the Rye*
  d Yoko Ono's *Grapefruit*

5 What did readers of Albert Goldman's biography learn about Elvis Presley?
  a He once camped out at his mother's grave for six days
  b He once ate 12 pounds of bacon at one sitting
  c He liked to watch teenage girls wrestle in white panties
  d He slept with Brian Epstein

6 Complete President Reagan's oft-repeated platitude: "There is nothing so good for the inside of a man as _____ ."
  a a warm meal
  b the outside of a horse
  c a strong colonic
  d going down to the drugstore and looking at the magazines. I can't do that anymore

7 What was a department store mogul reported to have once said to Rupert Murdoch when he asked why the store doesn't advertise in his tawdry *New York Post*?
  a "People leave it in the subway."
  b "I prefer Zingo players to Wingo players."
  c "The *Times* suits my needs perfectly, thank you very much."
  d "But, Rupert, your readers are my shoplifters."

8 Which film was famous for its 'ludes scene?
  a *Reds*
  b *Chariots of Fire*
  c *Modern Romance*
  d *Rollover*

9 Three of these statements apply to Nancy Reagan. Which describes Maureen?
  a She revealed that she eats bananas in bed—though she prefers apples—so the "crunch crunch" doesn't wake her husband
  b She appeared in an ad for acne lotion
  c She inquired about the possibility of prosecuting a student who wrote in his college newspaper that he hoped the President would die of his gunshot wound
  d She went on to be named the woman most men aged 25–34 would like to date

ANSWERS
1-d, 2-c, 3-c, 4-c, 5-c, 6-b, 7-d, 8-c, 9-b

1982

In which the First Lady gets a great deal on clothes

1/4   Despite being exonerated of any law-breaking, Richard Allen—who made the mistake of getting on Nancy Reagan's bad side—is forced to resign. The President hails his integrity, then appoints noted foreign policy non-expert William Clark to succeed him.

1/8   The White House announces that President Reagan—who often wonders why people think he's anti–civil rights—has signed off on Ed Meese's plan to grant tax-exempt status to South Carolina's Bob Jones University and other schools that practice racial discrimination.

1/12   President Reagan explains that there must have been some kind of "misunderstanding" regarding his efforts to grant tax exemptions to segregated schools, since he is "unalterably opposed to racial discrimination in any form."

1/13   Government clerk Lenny Skutnik dives into the frigid Potomac River to rescue a drowning stewardess from Air Florida Flight 90, which has crashed on takeoff from Washington's National Airport. He is later rewarded by getting to sit next to Nancy Reagan at the State of the Union address, where President Reagan—increasingly perceived as America's emcee—introduces him from the audience.

1/14   President Reagan tells a business luncheon in New York about a Massachusetts resident in his 80s who supposedly sent in his Social Security check "to be used for reducing the national debt." As usual, no proof is offered.

1/15   President Reagan phones *The Washington Post* to explain that when his new policy toward segregated schools was announced, he "didn't know at the time that there was a legal case pending." CBS quickly obtains a memo in which intervention in the Bob Jones University case was specifically requested, and on which Reagan had written, "I think we should."

■

Press secretary Sheila Tate says that Nancy Reagan "has derived no personal benefit" from her acceptance of thousands of dollars worth of clothing from American designers, explaining that the First Lady's sole motive is to help the national fashion industry.

Unless, of course, one considers getting fabulous clothes for free a benefit.

1/18   Following his testimony for the defense at the murder trial of Jack Henry Abbott, Norman Mailer is asked what would happen if Abbott got out of jail and committed yet another murder. "Culture is worth a little risk," he replies. "I am willing to gamble with certain elements in society to save this man's talent."

1/19   Coca-Cola announces an agreement to buy Columbia Pictures for $750 million. Objects bearing the Coke logo soon begin appearing with increasing frequency in the studio's films, along with dialogue like "Would you like a Diet Coke?" Eventually, entire scenes are played out in front of Coke machines.

■

At his seventh press conference, President Reagan:

● Claims there are "a million people more working than there were in 1980," though statistics show that 100,000 *fewer* people are employed

- Contends his attempt to grant tax-exempt status to segregated schools was an attempt to correct "a procedure that we thought had no basis in law," though the Supreme Court had clearly upheld a ruling barring such exemptions a decade earlier
- Claims he has received a letter from Pope John Paul II in which he "approves what we've done so far" regarding US sanctions against the USSR, though the sanctions were not mentioned in the papal message
- Responds to a question about the 17% black unemployment rate by pointing out that "in this time of great unemployment," Sunday's paper had "24 full pages of . . . employers looking for employees," though most of the jobs available—computer operator, for example, or cellular immunologist—require special training, for which his administration has cut funds by over 30%
- Misstates facts about California's abortion law and an Arizona program to aid the elderly
- Responds to a question about private charity by observing, "I also happen to be someone who believes in tithing—the giving of a tenth," though his latest tax returns show charitable contributions amounting to 1.4%.

1/20 "This is a very impressive gathering. When I walked in I thought I was back in the studio on the set of *High Society*."
   —President Reagan at a dinner honoring the first anniversary of his inauguration

1/23 CBS broadcasts *The Uncounted Enemy: A Vietnam Deception*, which charges that Gen. William Westmoreland oversaw the intentional underestimation of enemy forces to improve the perception of how things were going. The general files a libel suit.

1/27 Meeting with a group of television executives, President Reagan volunteers that seeing himself "on the late, late show" is like "looking at the son I never knew I had"—an odd statement from a man who actually has two sons he rarely sees.

1/30 The Hollywood Foreign Press Association bestows its Golden Globe Award for New Star of the Year in a Motion Picture to Pia Zadora for her performance in *Butterfly*.

FEBRUARY 1982

In which the President offers a unique perspective on the truth

2/2 TV PREMIERE: *Late Night with David Letterman*. A precursor of the all-form, no-content comedy of the decade, the NBC program establishes itself as America's hippest show at a time when hipness means utter detachment. The host and his almost exclusively male staff make fun of TV as if they aren't part of it—indeed, as if they are above it—though, when you come right down to it, there they are doing stupid things on television.

2/6 A *Los Angeles Times* profile of California industrialist and Reagan crony Justin Dart opens with a scene in which Dart exchanges warm pleasantries with fellow airline passenger Gerald Ford, then returns to his seat and tells a reporter, "Jerry's a nice man, but he's not very smart. Actually, our seatmate is a dumb bastard."

2/9 George Bush denies that he ever used the phrase "voodoo economics" and challenges "anybody to find it." NBC's Ken Bode promptly broadcasts the 1980 tape.

■

Henry Kissinger enters Massachusetts General Hospital for a coronary bypass. "My doctors have come to two conclusions," he says. "One, that I do have a heart; second, that it is in need of repair."

2/10 Presidential aide Joseph W. Canzeri resigns in the wake of charges that he received exceptionally favorable terms on a $400,000 home loan and that he double-billed $800 in expenses.

2/16 "She really just got tired of people misinterpreting what she was doing."
—Aide telling the public that Nancy Reagan will no longer accept free clothing "on loan" from top designers

2/17 "Lee Majors has decided to give the house to Farrah. We have an exclusive interview with Lee Majors at 11."
—Newsman John Schubeck updating Los Angeles *Quincy* viewers on a breaking story

2/18 At his eighth press conference, President Reagan makes four major misstatements about the history of Vietnam and erroneously claims to support the government of Nicaragua. He concludes by complaining about "all those mistakes you said that I made" at last month's news conference, claiming "the score was five to one in my favor."

2/20 Defending New York mayor Ed Koch's decision to break his 1981 promise that he would "never" seek the governorship of New York, political consultant David Garth says, "I don't believe that the people really believe that he didn't believe that when he said it."

2/22 SUZANNE SOMERS
She lost a job, 22 pounds and her *Three's Company* friends, but she's back with a special and a series on the way
—*People*

2/23 Ed Koch—whose campaign for New York governor has not been helped by a *Playboy* interview in which he claimed that "it's wasting your life" to live in the "sterile" suburbs—insists that he was merely being "jocular" when he scoffed at rural rubes who "have to drive 20 miles to buy a gingham dress or a Sears, Roebuck suit." He goes on to lose the Democratic primary to underdog Mario Cuomo, who is elected in November.

2/24 Addressing the Voice of America's 40th birthday celebration, President Reagan reminisces about making up exciting details while announcing baseball games from wire copy.

"Now, I submit to you that I told the truth," he says of his enhanced version of a routine shortstop-to-first ground out. "I don't know whether he really ran over toward second base and made a one-hand stab or whether he just squatted down and took the ball when it came to him. But the truth got there and, in other words, it can be attractively packaged."

No one questions his premise that embellishing the truth does not compromise it.

2/27 Still proclaiming his innocence, Wayne B. Williams is found guilty of two of Atlanta's 28 child murders and gets two consecutive life terms.

■

The Congressional Budget Office finds that taxpayers earning under $10,000 lost an average of $240 from last year's tax cuts, while those earning over $80,000 gained an average of $15,130.

MARCH 1982

In which a comic figure makes a tragic exit and a tragic figure makes a comic entrance

3/1 Sen. Bob Packwood (R-OR) reveals that President Reagan frequently offers up transpar-

ently fictional anecdotes as if they were real. "We've got a $120 billion deficit coming," says Packwood, "and the President says, 'You know, a young man went into a grocery store and he had an orange in one hand and a bottle of vodka in the other, and he paid for the orange with food stamps and he took the change and paid for the vodka. That's what's wrong.' And we just shake our heads."

■

In a speech to the Civil Defense Association, Ed Meese describes nuclear war as "something that may not be desirable."

3/5 John Belushi dies alone in a Hollywood hotel room. LAPD lieutenant Dan Cooke reports that the 33-year-old comedian's death "appeared to have been from natural causes." And what about those apparent needle marks in the crooks of his arms? Cooke explains that they were caused by "blood settling."

3/8   LIZ AND DICK AGAIN!

After a loving London reunion, Taylor is coy—but Burton still carries the torch
—*People*

■

The Go-Go's' "We Got the Beat" begins a nine-week stay in the Top Ten.

3/10   Coroner Thomas Noguchi reveals that John Belushi didn't die of natural causes—he'd been drinking and shooting cocaine and heroin in amounts that "would have killed anybody."

Meanwhile, the "mystery woman" who was with him before he died is identified as show business hanger-on Cathy Evelyn Smith. Police say they have no reason to suspect her of any criminal involvement.

3/16   "Is it news that some fellow out in South Succotash someplace has just been laid off, that he should be interviewed nationwide?"
—President Reagan—whose Presidency is based on the premise that people believe what they see on TV—complaining about coverage of the nation's economic suffering

■

A jury convicts Claus von Bulow of twice trying to kill his now-comatose wife Sunny by injecting her with insulin. The verdict will be appealed.

3/18   *20/20* airs an interview with a none-too-healthy-looking Cathy Evelyn Smith, who reveals why John Belushi was imbibing alcohol on her last night with him. "He was working on a screenplay that had to do with vintage wine-making," she explains, "so he was drinking wine."

When reporter Tom Jarriel asks about rumors that she's a heroin dealer, her lawyer Robert Sheahan interrupts. "Tom, Tom," he says patronizingly, "she doesn't even have a business license."

3/24   Agriculture official Mary C. Jarratt tells Congress her department has been unable to document President Reagan's horror stories

of food stamp abuse, pointing out that the change from a food stamp purchase is limited to 99 cents. "It's not possible to buy a bottle of vodka with 99 cents," she says. Deputy White House press secretary Peter Roussel says Reagan wouldn't tell these stories "unless he thought they were accurate."

3/27   At the Gridiron Dinner—an annual Washington event at which the powers that be in politics and the media gather to congratulate each other on how inside they all are—Nancy Reagan takes the stage dressed as a bag lady and pokes fun at her clothes-horse image. "Secondhand clothes/I'm wearing secondhand clothes," she warbles, "I sure hope Ed Meese sews." Everyone laughs, and it is understood by all concerned that she has done her penance and will now be granted a fresh start.

4/2 Argentina invades Great Britain's Falkland Islands. Hours later, UN ambassador Jeane Kirkpatrick attends a dinner at the Argentine embassy.

4/4 "If Mr. Reagan thinks he has to cut social spending to help right the economy, others might disagree, but he has earned the right to try. What he is not entitled to do is to cut spending for the poor and then claim that he is *increasing* it."
—*New York Times* editorial

■

2ND-YEAR SLUMP
REAGAN'S POPULARITY NOSEDIVES IN A FAMILIAR PRESIDENTIAL PATTERN
—*The Washington Post*

4/5 Asked about the situation in the Falkland Islands—to which a British fleet is currently en route—President Reagan refuses to choose between one of America's strongest allies and the South American junta that invaded that ally's territory. "We're friends of both sides," he says.

■

Tom Brokaw and Roger Mudd take over from John Chancellor as co-anchors of the *NBC Nightly News*. "Brokaw and Mudd," predicts *Today* producer Steve Friedman, "are going to be the Huntley and Brinkley of the '80s."

4/8 Following two days of official meetings that were hastily scheduled so it wouldn't look as if they were just taking a Caribbean vacation, the Reagans arrive in Barbados for a four-day visit with actress Claudette Colbert.

4/15 "The statisticians in Washington have funny ways of counting."
—President Reagan explaining to Illinois

high school students why, although the Bureau of Labor Statistics reported a rise in unemployment, he believes the jobless rate has in fact declined

■

"England was always very proud of the fact that the English police did not have to carry guns. . . . In England, if a criminal carried a gun, even though he didn't use it, he was not tried for burglary or theft or whatever he was doing. He was tried for first-degree murder and hung if he was found guilty."
—President Reagan citing a favorite example of British jurisprudence

4/16 "Well, it's a good story, though. It made the point, didn't it?"
—White House spokesman Larry Speakes on being informed that President Reagan's fable about British gun law is "just not true"

4/21 Henry Kissinger speaks at the opening of the Beverly Hills corporate headquarters of the Progressive Savings and Loan Association. Says president Lon Harmon, "I was surprised that he was available."

4/22 The Reagan administration complains that the CBS documentary *People Like Us*—a Bill Moyers report on four people who have slipped through the President's alleged "safety net"—constituted a "below-the-belt" attack on its economic policies. The network rejects a government request for a prime time half hour "to present our side."

4/27 California assemblyman Phillip D. Wyman proposes a bill in the state legislature requiring record companies to post warning labels on albums that contain backward-recorded messages singing the praises of Satan. No such law is enacted.

4/30 President Reagan describes the Falkland Islands war as a "dispute over the sovereignty of that little ice-cold bunch of land down there."

MAY 1982

In which the President displays a shaky grasp of matters nuclear

5/6   Los Angeles police chief Daryl Gates explains that a disproportionate number of blacks have been injured or killed by police choke holds because "in some blacks . . . the veins or arteries do not open up as fast as they do in normal people."

5/10   Taking questions from students at a Chicago high school, President Reagan explains why his revised tax exemption policy could not possibly have been intended to benefit segregated schools. "I didn't know there were any," he says. "Maybe I should have"—*Maybe?*—"but I didn't."

At the end, he warns the kids to make sure he hasn't told any lies. "Don't let me get away with it," he says. "Check me out. Make sure that what I told you checks out and is true. Don't be the sucker generation."

■

Stevie Wonder proves that, given the right collaborator, even he can make a wretched record as his duet with Paul McCartney, "Ebony and Ivory," begins a seven-week run as the nation's most popular song.

■

Dr. John J. Hopper, Jr., the Colorado psychiatrist who was treating John W. Hinckley, Jr., during his last five months of freedom, testifies that he had never observed any signs of mental illness in his patient.

■

"If Robert Kennedy were alive today, he would not countenance singling me out for this kind of treatment."
—Sirhan Sirhan in a bold—and unsuccessful—bid for parole

5/12   John W. Hinckley, Jr.'s, defense team presents Jodie Foster's videotaped deposition, in which she says she had never seen her admirer, had not encouraged his phone calls and had thrown away his letters. When she declares, "I don't have any relationship with John Hinckley," the defendant storms out of the courtroom.

5/13   At his 10th press conference, President Reagan—on record as thinking that trees cause more pollution than cars—voices his equally bizarre belief that, while "there is no recall" for missiles fired from silos, "those that are carried in bombers, those that are carried in ships of one kind or another, or submersibles . . . can be recalled if there has been a miscalculation." No one challenges the premise.

5/17   Jane Fonda
Talk about a workout! Her exercise book is the No. 1 best-seller and she's hustling votes for husband TOM HAYDEN
—*People*

5/18   Rev. Sun Myung Moon is convicted of tax evasion. He gets 18 months.

5/19   "She said she just liked money."
—Florida police officer describing the confession to four burglaries by an 11-year-old girl

5/21   Discussing Soviet weaponry at a National Security Council meeting, President Reagan asks CIA deputy director Bobby Inman, "Isn't the SS-19 their biggest missile?"
No, says Inman, "that's the SS-18."
"So," says the President, "they've even switched the numbers on their missiles in order to confuse us!"
Inman explains that the numbers are assigned by US intelligence.

5/26   After viewing the circus with his family in New York, Richard Nixon goes backstage to shake hands with the clowns. "Great! Absolutely great! Really funny!" he tells them. Later, asked what he liked best, Nixon says, "I really enjoy the clowns."

5/29 REAGAN AIDE APOLOGIZES FOR PUERTO RICAN REMARKS
—*The New York Times*

JUNE 1982

In which the President says hello to the Pope and goodbye to the vicar

---

6/1 Richard Nixon predicts that the Democratic nominee in 1984 will be "Kennedy, of course." As for Mondale, "No way. . . . Mondale—blah!—he just doesn't come over. . . . No, Kennedy is going to be the nominee."

6/4 "Can't you get him out of that suit?"
—Photographer alerting a White House aide to the distaste of the press corps for the glen plaid outfit President Reagan has been wearing all over Europe

"I like that suit."
—President Reagan rejecting the criticism

6/7 President Reagan's overscheduling on his European trip catches up with him as he briefly falls asleep during a Vatican meeting with the Pope. Though it seems for a moment as if he might tumble out of his chair, the forward jerk of his head awakens him.

Nancy sees to it that plenty of rest time is booked into all future trips.

6/8 In the wake of an embarrassing mix-up at the UN regarding a US vote on the Falkland Islands war, Jeane Kirkpatrick describes the nation's foreign policy as "stumbling from issue to issue almost on a Mad Hatter basis."

Says Secretary of State Haig, "Do I think US foreign policy is inept? . . . At times it is. At times it's not. At times it's even brilliant. At times it's rather stupid. It would be very hard to ask me to label it."

England wins the war.

6/11 NOW PLAYING: The redundantly titled *E.T. the Extra-Terrestrial*. "It's not only the film of the summer," swoons *Los Angeles Times* critic Sheila Benson, "it may be the film of the decade and possibly the double decade." Steven Spielberg's ultimate fairy tale assures America that the universe is not only tameable but downright cute—"E.T. phone home!" A grateful nation makes it the highest-grossing film of all time, giving the director *carte blanche* to mass-produce sentimental kiddie movies that, combined with the slob humor epitomized by *Police Academy* and the teen angst of the John Hughes oeuvre, render movie theaters increasingly off limits to thinking adults.

6/12   An estimated 750,000 supporters of a nuclear freeze gather in New York's Central Park in the largest disarmament demonstration in US history. President Reagan opines that the Commies are behind it.

6/17   Interior Secretary James Watt warns the Israeli ambassador that if "liberals of the Jewish community" oppose his plans for off-shore drilling, "they will weaken our ability to be a good friend of Israel."

6/20   Caspar Weinberger explains the Pentagon's position on a "protracted" nuclear war: "We don't believe a nuclear war can be won," but "we are planning to prevail if we are attacked." The difference between winning and prevailing is not explored.

6/21   John W. Hinckley, Jr., is found not guilty by reason of insanity. He is committed to St. Elizabeths Hospital in Washington, D.C., for an indefinite stay.

6/25   "With great regret, I have accepted the resignation of Secretary of State Al Haig. I am nominating as his successor—and he has accepted—George Shultz to replace him."
    —President Reagan surprising Al Haig, whose threats to quit (three times before he was even confirmed) had become a regular feature of his tenure, but who had not actually submitted a letter of resignation

6/26   John W. Hinckley, Jr., makes the first of a series of phone calls to a *Washington Post* reporter. He says he feels no remorse about shooting Reagan—"I helped his Presidency. . . . After I shot him, his polls went up 20 percent"—but is sorry about James Brady. "I just honestly wish I could go back before that shooting," he says, "and let him move two inches out of the way."

6/28   Special prosecutor Leon Silverman reports that his six-month investigation of Ray-

mond Donovan has produced "insufficient evidence to prosecute" the Labor Secretary, though he pointedly adds, "I do not use words like *exoneration.*"

■

OH, BOY!
For Diana's 7-pound, 1½-ounce prince, the palace plans a future fit for a king
    —*People*

■

The *National Enquirer* runs an interview with Cathy Evelyn Smith, the last person to see John Belushi alive, who—not realizing she's talking to someone from the press—reveals that she injected a "speedball" of cocaine and heroin that was the *"coup de grace"* that killed him. Though the case had been closed, this most unfortunate indiscretion leads to her conviction for second-degree murder.

6/30   At his 11th press conference, President Reagan:

- Says of sanctions against Argentina, "I can't give you an answer on that"
- Says of the Israeli invasion of Lebanon, "This is a question, again, where I have to beg your tolerance of me"
- Says of the mysterious departure of Al Haig, "Once again you ask a question upon which when I accepted his resignation I made a statement that I would have no further comments on that or take no questions on it."

■

"We were taking speed and drinking cold drinks. We picked up our rifles and started shooting. I don't know why we did it."
    —Phillip Wayne Kelley, 19, explaining how it came to pass that he and a friend killed three strangers in rural Tennessee

■

With 35 states having approved it—three short of ratification—time runs out on the Equal Rights Amendment.

7/1   Rev. Sun Myung Moon performs what his Unification Church calls the "largest wedding ceremony in human history" by marrying 2,075 couples—most of them strangers to each other, and many with no common language—at Madison Square Garden.

7/2   Larry Walters, 33, of Los Angeles rigs 42 weather balloons to his girlfriend's aluminum lawn chair, fills them with helium and soars to 16,000 feet on a 45-minute flight that he aborts—when he gets too cold—by popping the balloons with a pellet pistol. Though his aircraft becomes entangled in power lines, Walters lands safely 20 miles from his starting point.

7/6   Nancy Reagan, 61, celebrates her 59th birthday.

7/8   Ailing Reagan crony Alfred Bloomingdale's 29-year-old mistress, Vicki Morgan, files a $5 million palimony suit against him after being informed that she has received the last of her monthly $18,000 checks. She claims he promised to support her for life.

7/14   The Maryland Poison Control Center reports that 79 people have mistaken their free mailbox samples of the lemon-scented dishwashing liquid Sunlight for lemon juice. Says a Lever Brothers spokesman, "Any kind of cleaning product we introduce has a certain amount of ingestion."

7/15   Supreme Court Justice Byron White is attacked in Salt Lake City by a large bearded man who punches him in the head while shouting, "That busing and pornography just doesn't go!" The assailant, Newton C. Estes, explains that he went after White because he "is causing four-letter words to come in my living room through my television set. I don't know how else to get it to stop except to go direct to the source."

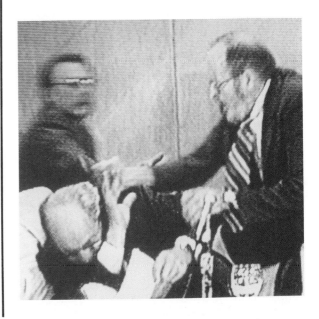

SAY WATT?

"I think he's an environmentalist himself, as I think I am."
—President-elect Reagan on his Interior Secretary–designate

"We will mine more, drill more, cut more timber."
—James Watt summarizing his plans

"I never use the words Democrats and Republicans. It's liberals and Americans."
—James Watt revealing one of his semantic rules

"Maybe we can get Mrs. Reagan to wear a coyote coat."
—James Watt expressing his opinion that coyotes should be killed off

"I speak in black-and-white terms without much gray in my life. I see problems without the complexity that is confusing to a lot of people."
—James Watt explaining that he sees things "in simple terms"

"A left-wing cult dedicated to bringing down the type of government I believe in."
—James Watt describing environmentalists

"I think Americans now have the best Secretary of the Interior they've ever had."
—James Watt defending his policies on *Nightline*

■

Van Gordon Sauter, whose tenure as CBS News president has seen a distinct softening in the network's news coverage, issues an eight-page memo that, in effect, apologizes for the documentary on William Westmoreland after a *TV Guide* article charges that the "often arbitrary and unfair" broadcast was riddled with "inaccuracies, distortions and violations of journalistic standards." Lost in the media brouhaha is the key fact that the show's central premise—that Westmoreland was less than forthright about enemy troop strength—has not been seriously challenged.

7/19 Survivor's *Rocky III* theme "Eye of the Tiger"—the very definition of soulless corporate rock 'n' roll—begins a six-week stay on the top of the chart.

7/21 James Watt announces his five-year plan to open a billion acres of US coastline to oil and gas drilling.

7/23 "Lower! Lower! Lower!"
—Director John Landis on the set of *Twilight Zone—The Movie*, ordering the descent of a helicopter that is disabled by special effects bombs and crashes onto actor Vic Morrow and two illegally employed Vietnamese children, killing all of them in a particularly gruesome manner

7/24 "The operator insisted it was Washington, D.C. I thought he was crazy so I hung up."
—Robert German, 76, on his phone call from President Reagan, who read that he was disappointed that he didn't get to take a photo when the President was in St. Louis

7/25 "Tragedy can strike in an instant, but film is immortal. Vic lives forever. Just before the last take, Vic took me aside to thank me for the opportunity to play this role."
—John Landis delivering a singularly memorable eulogy to Vic Morrow

7/28 Caught off guard at his 12th press conference by Sarah McClendon's question about "sex harassment of women" working in government, President Reagan waggles his head and says, "Now, Sarah, just a minute here with the discussion or we'll be getting an R rating." Though many reporters find this inane quip amusing, Sarah definitely does not.

■

Vicki Morgan files a $5 million lawsuit against Betsy Bloomingdale—Nancy Reagan's legendary "best friend"—for cutting off her monthly checks. She explains that one of her duties with Betsy's Alfred was "to act as a therapist to help Bloomingdale overcome his Marquis de Sade complex."

7/29 Asked why he was invited to the White House dinner for Indian prime minister Indira Gandhi, Wayne Newton says, "I'm an American Indian. I guess that's a connection."

AUGUST 1982

In which the President plays host to foreign leaders, yet admits to a growing sense of isolation

8/2 In order to convey the Administration's crackdown on Israel over its attacks on Beirut, the White House points out the difference between a February 1981 photo which shows President Reagan sitting next to Israeli Foreign Minister Yitzhak Shamir and laughing, and to-day's photo, in which Reagan frowns at him from across a table.

Later, the President goes to Iowa and poses with a boar.

8/4 While on the air, Dan Rather gets a call from President Reagan, who complains about reporting of his policies toward Taiwan. Rather, who tells viewers about the call afterward, says the President "spoke his mind but didn't raise his voice. . . . Hope he won't hesitate to call again."

8/11 President Reagan tells *Time*'s Hugh Sidey that he sometimes feels trapped in the

White House. "You glance out the window and the people are walking around Pennsylvania Avenue and you say, 'I could never say I am going to run down to the drugstore and get some magazines,'" he says. "I can't do that any more."

8/12 Postal Service official Jerry Jones tells Congress that mail will still be delivered "to the extent possible under the circumstances" in the event of nuclear war.

"There won't be a lot of people left to read and write those letters," observes Rep. Edward Markey (D-MA).

"But," says Jones, "those that are will get their mail."

8/16 "Elvis official autopsy table for sale, best offer."

—Ad appearing in two Memphis dailies on the fifth anniversary of his death, though hospital spokesmen deny that this particular souvenir is available

■

ALL ABOUT E.T.

The untold story of his voice, his hands, the hidden dwarfs and other movie magic
—*People*

8/17 "Ladies and gentlemen, Chairman Moe of Liberia is our visitor here today, and we're very proud to have him."

—President Reagan introducing Liberian head of state Samuel K. Doe

8/20 On the same day that Nancy Reagan's adoptive father dies of heart failure, Alfred Bloomingdale succumbs to cancer. Observes Vicki Morgan of Betsy's decision to inter her husband before his death is announced, "She buried him like a dog."

8/23 JILL ST. JOHN

She's helping ROBERT WAGNER build a new life after Natalie
—*People*

SEPTEMBER 1982

In which the President displays a shaky grasp of matters biological

9/4 "South Succotash, with its population of nearly 11 million, must be a considerable place."

—AFL-CIO president Lane Kirkland on the unemployment figures

9/6 Nearing the end of his annual Labor Day Muscular Dystrophy telethon, Jerry Lewis lashes out at those who have dared to question the purity of his motives. "Why am I a criminal?" he demands. "What we are doing here is great work. . . . We've only been at peace 557 days in the last 17,000 years. Had they had telethons, we'd have had peace, I'm sure. Is that idealistic? Is that old-fashioned, mid-Victorian? Is that stupid? Is that rhetoric? No! That's what I believe."

The 15-minute diatribe—the kind of thing telethon fans look for after Jerry's been up for 20 or so hours—turns out to be the last of its kind. By next year, following his heart attack, much of the show is pre-taped to give him plenty of nap time, and the raw edge that made the spectacle so compelling is gone.

9/10 *The Washington Post* reports that of President Reagan's first 72 nominees to the judiciary, 68 are white males.

9/14 Defending his support of anti-abortion legislation, President Reagan says, "I think the fact that children have been prematurely born even down to the three-month stage and have lived to, the record shows, to grow up and be normal human beings, that ought to be enough for all of us."

Later, aide Peter Roussel acknowledges that the record shows nothing of the kind: the youngest surviving fetus was four-and-a-half months old. (A three-month-old fetus is, at most, three-and-a-half inches long.)

Was Reagan aware of this? "He knew," says Roussel, "but he said three instead of four and a half."

■

Princess Grace of Monaco dies of injuries sustained when the car she was riding in with her 17-year-old daughter Stephanie plunged down a 45-foot embankment.

9/15 The first issue of *USA Today* shows up in TV-shaped vending machines in Washington. News of Lebanese president-elect Bashir Gemayel's assassination appears on page nine. The daily quickly becomes known as "Mc-Paper."

9/16 REAGAN ASSERTS BLACKS WERE HURT BY PROGRAMS OF THE GREAT SOCIETY
—*The New York Times*

9/21 Football's first-ever mid-season strike begins. It lasts 57 days—the longest in the history of professional sports.

9/22 *The Reader's Digest Bible*—a condensed version reduced by 40% from the original—is published. "We weren't sure we could do it," says editor John T. Beaudouin, "but after we studied the text and found it repetitive, we thought we could."

9/27 A sworn deposition by Alfred Bloomingdale's ex-mistress Vicki Morgan—in which she describes the Reagan friend as a "drooling" sadist with a fondness for binding and beating nude women and making them crawl on the floor—is made public. Recalling her first sexual encounter with him in 1970, Morgan said, "Alfred had a look in his eyes, believe me when I say this, that scared me to death."

9/28 Unnamed sources reveal that officials at St. Elizabeths Hospital recently intercepted a letter from John W. Hinckley, Jr., to an unidentified woman in the Middle West asking if she would help him kill Jodie Foster.

■

At his 13th press conference, President Reagan is asked if any of the blame for the recession is his. "Yes," he says, "because for many years I was a Democrat."

9/30 Seven people die in the Chicago area when they take capsules of Extra-Strength Tylenol that had been laced with cyanide. "The victims never had a chance," says Dr. Thomas Kim. "Death was certain within minutes."

■

Two days after President Reagan commits the Marines to an indefinite stay in Lebanon, David L. Reagan (no relation) becomes the first Marine to be killed in the conflict.

OCTOBER 1982

In which a maverick auto executive makes his biggest deal yet

10/4 President Reagan suggests—and not, by any means, for the first time—that since he sees big help-wanted sections in the Sunday papers, unemployment must be caused by a lot of lazy people who'd just rather not work.

Veterans Administration chief Robert P. Nimmo—recently in the news for having spent over $50,000 in government funds to redecorate his office—resigns.

Addressing an Ohio veterans' group, President Reagan discusses plans to strengthen three military divisions in Western Europe, "two of which are in Geneva, and one, I believe, still in Switzerland."

10/7 "Somebody goofed."
—Jerry Falwell on the massacre of Palestinian refugees in Beirut

10/8 President Reagan signs a bill to boost US exports while posing on a California pier in front of a huge container ship that turns out to be full of Japanese exports.

10/9 During a sound check for his weekly radio address, President Reagan refers to the Polish government as "a bunch of no-good lousy bums."

JOBLESS RATE IS UP TO 10.1% IN MONTH, WORST IN 42 YEARS
11 MILLION ARE IDLE
DEMOCRATS BUOYED; G.O.P. IS CONCERNED
—*The New York Times*

10/10 The House Commerce Committee judges the Environmental Protection Agency's efforts to enforce the laws "dangerously deficient."

10/11 Campaigning in Texas, President Reagan says that he recently inquired as to what Pac-Man is, "and somebody told me it was a round thing that gobbles up money. I thought that was Tip O'Neill." The crowd roars.

"You can't drink yourself sober, you can't spend yourself rich, and you can't pump the prime without priming the pump. You know something? I said that backwards. . . . You can't prime the pump without pumping the prime . . ."
—President Reagan getting confused in Texas

Viewers of New York's *Live at Five* find out who won this year's "Nobel Peace Prize in Medicine."

10/12 "You don't tell us how to stage the news, and we don't tell you how to report it."
—Larry Speakes to the press

10/14 A palimony suit is filed against Liberace by former chauffeur Scott Thorson, 23, who claims to have been the pianist's lover for six years. "We lived together as man and wife," Thorson tells the *National Enquirer*. "He promised me half of almost everything he owns. He even offered to adopt me as his own son. Then, without warning, he cut me off. That's why I'm suing him for almost $380 million."
He also reveals that Liberace called him "Boober."

10/18 "Now we are trying to get unemployment to go up, and I think we are going to succeed."
—President Reagan getting confused during a GOP fundraising speech

10/19 "It's better than gold. Gold weighs more than that, for God's sake."
—Financially strapped auto manufacturer

John De Lorean in a Los Angeles hotel room, reacting to a suitcase full of cocaine, unaware that he's celebrating with undercover FBI agents who are about to arrest him

■

During a White House meeting with Arab leaders, President Reagan turns to the Lebanese foreign minister. "You know," he says, "your nose looks just like Danny Thomas's." The Arabs exchange nervous glances.

10/26   "Listen, it's been fun. Those inmates in San Quentin were fascinating."
—Greg Jackson ending the premiere of ABC's destined-to-be-short-lived post-*Nightline* news hour, *The Last Word*, which featured an interview with two convicted burglars who advised viewers to leave the lights on when they're away from home

10/28   "Wait till I go home and tell Nancy I played Las Vegas with Wayne Newton and Bob Goulet."
—President Reagan addressing an "Up with America" rally at which the two Vegas saloon singers perform

10/29   John De Lorean—charged with conspiracy to possess and distribute cocaine—is released on $10 million bail.

10/31   Accusing his foes of "cruel scare tactics," President Reagan attacks the "big spenders" for causing inflation, adding, "They even drove prayer out of our nation's classrooms." A White House aide refuses to clarify whom Reagan is talking about, saying only, "They know who they are."

■

PERVASIVE USE OF COCAINE IS REPORTED IN HOLLYWOOD
—*The New York Times*

■

America's nuclear policy is debated on *The Last Word* by noted non-experts Paul Newman and Charlton Heston.

11/2   KABC-TV newsman Chuck Henry tells his election night audience in Los Angeles that the Senate race between Jerry Brown and San Diego mayor Pete Wilson—which Brown loses—has been "shrill and *shrident.*"

11/3   The GOP loses a net total of 26 House seats, seven governorships, and six state legislative houses in the mid-term election.
"We feel very good about what has happened," says President Reagan incongruously.
Observes Ed Meese, "There was nothing to suggest a need to change the basic course."

11/9   President Reagan is asked if he'll be visiting the new Vietnam Veterans Memorial. "I can't tell until somebody tells me," he says. "I never know where I'm going."

11/11 "It would be a user fee."
—President Reagan explaining that his proposed five-cent-a-gallon gasoline tax would not be a tax at all

■

The White House announces that President Reagan was awakened at 3:35 A.M. to be informed of the death of Leonid Brezhnev. George Bush attends the funeral.

11/15 GOVERNMENT RESTRICTING FLOW OF INFORMATION TO THE PUBLIC
—*The New York Times*

11/20 "My fellow Americans, I've talked to you on a number of occasions about economic problems and opportunities our nation faces and I am prepared to tell you, it's a hell of a mess."
—President Reagan, continuing his tradition of quipping during a sound check, where his small live audience pretty much has to laugh, him being the President and all

11/22 "The MX is the right missile at the right time."
—President Reagan in a nationally televised speech in which he renames the deadly weapon "the Peacekeeper," prompting Dallas columnist Molly Ivins to wonder if it will be armed with "Peaceheads"

■

THE DIARY OF CRISTINA DE LOREAN
Telling the kids Daddy was in jail was only the beginning
—*People*

■

Michael Jackson and Paul McCartney's insufferable "The Girl Is Mine"—"the doggone girl is mine"—begins a ten-week stay in the Top Ten.

11/23 The annual White House turkey is presented to President Reagan. As it did last year, this reminds him of the time he gashed his thumb while carving a similar bird, and he does not hesitate to tell the story again.

11/25 Larry Speakes chooses Thanksgiving as the ideal moment to announce that the White House is considering a proposal (conceived by Ed Meese) to tax unemployment benefits. This, says Speakes, would "make unemployment less attractive."

11/26 Ed Meese denies that taxing unemployment benefits has been seriously considered, though he can't help adding, "We do know that generally when unemployment benefits end, most people find jobs very quickly."

■

Six months to the day after going to the circus in New York, Richard Nixon attends one in New Jersey where, once again, he indulges his compulsion to be photographed amidst a group of clowns.

HERE'S WHAT THE CRITICS ARE SAYING ABOUT NANCY REAGAN

"She has a stare that could melt a building."
—Former Reagan aide Jim Lake

"Many times Nancy will react to a problem by wanting to do away with the person who created it."
—Michael Deaver

"Nancy . . . glassy-eyed and overdressed, always looks as if she has just been struck by lightning in a limousine."
—Mark Crispin Miller in *The New Republic*

DECEMBER 1982

In which the President visits foreign lands, yet admits to a growing sense of isolation

12/1 Richard Nixon's prediction notwithstanding, Sen. Ted Kennedy—in the process of divorcing Joan—announces his non-candidacy for the 1984 presidential nomination.

■

At a dinner welcoming him to Brazil, President Reagan calls for a toast to his host, President João Figueiredo, and "the people of Bolivia." In an effort to recover, he explains that Bolivia is "where we're going next," though Colombia is next on the itinerary and no stops in Bolivia are planned.

12/4 President Reagan returns home from his five-day trip to Latin America. "Well, I learned a lot," he tells reporters. "You'd be surprised. They're all individual countries."

An aide is sent out to explain that the President certainly didn't mean to imply that *he* was surprised by this.

■

U.S. JOBLESS RATE CLIMBS TO 10.8%, A POSTWAR RECORD
11.9 MILLION OUT OF WORK
—*The New York Times*

12/6 Marvin Gaye's comeback hit, "Sexual Healing," begins a ten-week stay in the Top Ten.

12/9 "Sometimes I look out there at Pennsylvania Avenue and see people bustling along, and it suddenly dawns on me that probably never again can I just say, 'Hey, I'm going down to the drugstore to look at the magazines.' "
—President Reagan discussing his feelings of confinement with a *People* reporter

12/13 JOAN COLLINS
Her sexy past over, *Dynasty*'s bombshell explodes divorce rumors
—*People*

12/15 Literary agent Bill Adler announces that *The Deaver Diet*, recounting the White House aide's 35-pound weight loss, will be published in early 1984. Adler says the book will

HERE'S WHAT THE CRITICS ARE SAYING ABOUT PRESIDENT REAGAN

"Ronald Reagan is merely an anthology of the worst of American popular culture, edited for television."
—Cultural critic Mark Crispin Miller in *The New Republic*

"Look at the Reagan of the 1930s: a no-talent jerk with looks, charm, and a line of blarney who talks himself into one cushy job after another. . . . Then come the 1950s. In return for his manful anti-communistical efforts in the screen actors' union, the pimps, procurers, and purveyors of popular culture who own stage, screen and radio arrange for him to be paid off with a job selling General Electric toasters on TV and smarmy right-wing politics on the chicken-croquette circuit. How humiliating to think of this unlettered, self-assured bumpkin being our president."
—Nicholas von Hoffman in *Harper's*

"The Great Prevaricator."
—Democratic party chairman Charles Manatt

consist of 75% diet, 20% exercise and 5% "inspiration."

12/16   The House cites EPA chief Anne Gorsuch (known by colleagues as the "Ice Queen") for contempt of Congress for her refusal—at President Reagan's insistence—to turn over subpoenaed documents pertaining to her agency's handling of its $1.6 billion toxic waste cleanup fund.

■

"I sometimes look out the window at Pennsylvania Avenue and wonder what it would be like to be able to just walk down the street to the corner drugstore and look at the magazines. I can't do that anymore."
—President Reagan spontaneously conveying one of his regrets to *The Washington Post*

12/18   "I sometimes look out the window at Pennsylvania Avenue and wonder what it would be like to be able to just walk down the street to the corner drugstore and look at the magazines. I can't do that anymore."
—President Reagan sharing a sudden thought with a radio interviewer

12/20   A malignant growth is removed from Nancy Reagan's upper lip.

12/21   Congress passes the Boland Amendment, barring the CIA and Defense Department from funding the overthrow of the Nicaraguan government.

■

"I thought it was Rich Little at first. I didn't know if it was a crank or for real. The more he talked, the more I realized it was him."

—Reginald Andrews describing a phone call from President Reagan thanking him for saving a blind man who had fallen between the cars of a train

12/23   "Frankly, I think I'm constantly amazed that television is as good as it is."

—CBS Entertainment president B. Donald "Bud" Grant—who believes that "the golden age of television is now"—on *CBS Reports: Don't Touch That Dial*, a documentary about why television is as bad as it is

■

President Reagan suggests that the key to solving the unemployment problem could very well be something as simple as hiring unnecessary workers. "If a lot of businesses . . . could hire just one person," he says, "it would be interesting to see how much we can reduce these unemployment rolls."

12/28   The divorce trial of Herbert, Jr., and Roxanne Pulitzer—notable for its tales of kinky sex, drugs and death threats—ends in Palm Beach, Florida. Roxanne (who had turned down a pre-trial settlement offer of a Porsche, $45,000 a year in alimony and child support, four years in her current home and a $200,000 home after that) loses custody of her two children, is ordered out of the family home and is awarded a total of $48,000.

■

Posing on the deck of the battleship *New Jersey*, President Reagan reports that he has "the strange feeling that I'm back on the set filming *Hellcats of the Navy*."

POP QUIZ

Match the English with its Valley Girl equivalent.

1 excellent
2 gross
3 smoking a joint
4 nerd
5 homosexual
  __**a** grody to the max
  __**b** zod
  __**c** rad
  __**d** bud sesh
  __**e** bufu

6 True or false? A Los Angeles police official explained that the reason Robert De Niro and Robin Williams were never questioned in connection with John Belushi's death—though both had been seen with him hours before he died—was that, being superstars, they are difficult to get in touch with.

7 Which new product was most famous for causing extremely foul-smelling flatulence?
  a Donutz, a breakfast cereal that "tastes like real powdered donuts!"
  b Diet Coke
  c Starch blockers, a short-lived weight-loss fad made from kidney bean extract
  d Sunlight dishwashing liquid

8 True or false? Asked to name "a famous Willie," a *Family Feud* contestant said, "Willie the Pooh."

9 True or false? *CBS Morning News* co-anchor Diane Sawyer referred to Barney Clark, the first artificial heart recipient, as "Barney Rubble."

10 How did President Reagan explain his opposition to the Law of the Sea treaty signed by the overwhelming majority of the world's nations?

a "There are holes in it you could sail my ship in *Hellcats of the Navy* through."

b "The fella that's supposed to tell me what I think about things of that kind is out sick today."

c "I kind of thought that when you go out on the high seas you can do what you want."

d "I just don't think we need any treaties about lawn seeding."

11 Three of these statements were made by right-wing harridan Phyllis Schlafly. Which was uttered by *Cosmopolitan* editor Helen Gurley Brown?

a "Sexual harassment on the job is not a problem for virtuous women, except in the rarest of cases. Men hardly ever ask sexual favors of women from whom the certain answer is no."

b "[The atomic bomb is] a marvelous gift that was given to our country by a wise God."

c "There aren't enough men to go around. . . . Every time there's a plane accident, it's 100 men dead . . . and I literally think, 'Why couldn't some *women* have been on that flight?' "

d "Sex education is a principal cause of teenage pregnancy."

Match the newsmaker with his news.

12 Paul Newman

13 Sylvester Stallone

14 Jerry Rubin

15 Ron Reagan

16 Bijan

___**a** Marketed a $10,000 designer pistol

___**b** Marketed a salad dressing

___**c** Forced a statue of himself on the city of Philadelphia

___**d** Was photographed on unemployment line

___**e** Organized "networking" salons at which people on the make could meet and figure out how to use each other

17 Which of these actually appeared on TV?

a *Couples*, a daily half hour featuring real-life spouses so desperate to be on TV that they were willing to receive counseling for their most intimate problems there

b Michael O'Donoghue's comedy opus *The Last Ten Days in Silverman's Bunker*, in which the former NBC president was compared to Hitler

c *Putting On Heirs*, a David Letterman segment in which Larry "Bud" Melman phoned people whose relatives had recently died and told them they'd been cut out of the will

d *Big Sky*, a poorly reviewed half-hour PBS travelogue of Montana edited down from *Heaven's Gate* footage

ANSWERS

1-c, 2-a, 3-d, 4-b, 5-e, 6-True, 7-c, 8-True, 9-False (She called him "Barney Miller"), 10-c, 11-c, 12-b, 13-c, 14-e, 15-d, 16-a, 17-a

JANUARY 1983

In which the President expresses anger, and the newspaper of record explains what he means

1/2   Heading back to Washington from his annual New Year's Eve vacation at the Annenberg estate in Palm Springs, President Reagan stops in flood-ravaged Monroe, Louisiana, to be photographed filling sandbags.

1/3   Michael Jackson's *Thriller* enters the *Billboard* Top Ten, where it will stay for 78 weeks, 37 of them at Number One, becoming the best-selling album in history. If the album cover is any indication, he seems to have gotten a nose job.

1/4   Two shredders are delivered to the offices of the Environmental Protection Agency.

1/9   "The stench of failure hangs over Ronald Reagan's White House."
—*New York Times* editorial

■

Richard Nixon turns 70.

1/10   Health and Human Services Secretary Richard Schweiker proposes a "tattletale rule" that would force federally funded clinics to inform parents when teenage girls receive birth-control devices.

■

"I've had it up to my keister with these leaks!"
—President Reagan complaining about loose-lipped members of his administration, as reported by aide David Gergen, widely believed to be a prime leaker

1/11   *The New York Times* explains that "keister" is a "slang term for rump."

■

Billy Martin—who has been twice hired and twice fired as manager of the New York Yankees by owner George Steinbrenner—is hired again. "I think both of us have learned," says Steinbrenner. "I think this will be for a long time."

1/13   "The Reagan White House has pioneered the New Graft. Instead of selling influence, sell your White House celebrity . . ."
—Columnist William Safire suggesting that perhaps there is something unseemly about White House PR guru Michael Deaver trading on his position to sell a diet book

1/14   President Reagan refers to his chief arms negotiator, Paul H. Nitze, as "Ed Nitze."

1/16   RATING ON REAGAN LAGS AT MIDTERM

GALLUP POLL SAYS PUBLIC FINDS JOB PERFORMANCE IS POORER THAN 4 PREDECESSORS
   —*The New York Times*

1/17   Realizing that he will never be a great dancer, Ron Reagan quits the Joffrey Ballet and shifts his career toward areas where greatness is not required: writing articles for *Playboy* and taping segments for *Good Morning America*.

1/18   "The President and Cap sit around and talk about how workfare got surfers off the beach in California. They have no concept of what is going on."
   —Unnamed aide on President Reagan's failure to comprehend the seriousness of the recession

1/19   "If you want an example of the failures of socialism, don't go to Russia. Come to America, and see the American Indian reservations."
   —James Watt failing to endear himself to native Americans

1/20   In an interview with *Business Week*, James Watt compares environmentalists to Nazis. "Look what happened to Germany in the 1930s," he says. "The dignity of man was subordinated to the powers of Nazism. . . . Those are the forces that this can evolve into."
   Observes Wilderness Society chairman Gaylord Nelson, "I think the secretary has gone bonkers."

   ■

   President Reagan tells reporters about "the ten commandments of Nikolai Lenin . . . the guiding principles of communism," among them "that promises are like pie crust, made to be broken." Soviet scholars claim that no such commandments exist, and point out that Lenin's name was Vladimir.

1/25   "For a White House aide to publish a diet book while jobless totals rise and cheese lines lengthen is a sure setup for Johnny Carson."
   —*New York Times* editorial on *The Deaver Diet*, which is never published

   ■

   "For the last 30 years he's been in a dream world. . . . I think he actually believes that giving more to rich people will make them work harder, whereas the only way to make poor peo-

THE REAGAN ADMINISTRATION TALKS ABOUT THE ECONOMY

"The number of people remaining in poverty is very small and it grows smaller every day."
   —Domestic adviser Martin Anderson

"An increase in the number of people seeking work who did not find it."
   —Larry Speakes on the cause of unemployment

"Just remember, for every person who is out of work, there are nine of us with jobs."
   —President Reagan on the 10% unemployment rate

ple work is to tax their unemployment bene-fits."

—NAACP executive director Benjamin Hooks, unimpressed by President Reagan's understanding of the underclass

1/26 Having traveled to a Boston bar to show solidarity with the working class, President Reagan dismays his handlers by instead urging the abolition of the corporate income tax.

∎

Genaro Garcia, 13, of Los Angeles kills himself with his father's revolver after his TV is taken away from him as punishment for avoiding school.

1/30 Congratulating Redskins coach Joe Gibbs in the inevitable post–Super Bowl phone call, President Reagan pays special tribute to MVP John Riggins. "Would he mind," asks the President, "if I changed my spelling so it had an 'i' and a couple of 'g's in it?" In fact, the President does not change his name.

1/31 "Has anyone stopped to consider that the best way to balance the federal budget is not by taxing people into the poorhouse and it's not by cutting spending to the bone, but by all of us simply trying to live up to the Ten Commandments and the Golden Rule?"

—President Reagan to a convention of religious broadcasters

∎

Penthouse publishes an interview-by-mail with John W. Hinckley, Jr., who declares himself "a poet first and a would-be assassin last" and says he's become a "strong advocate" of gun control.

FEBRUARY 1983

In which the agency created to clean up messes makes a big one

2/1 "Sometimes my dog will get run over,

or my horses get sick."

—Deb of the Year Cornelia Guest revealing what makes her depressed

"I think children are better brought up with a governess. . . . That doesn't mean I never saw them. Of course I saw them. I went fox-hunting with them."

—Cornelia's socialite mom, C.Z., explaining what being a parent means to her

2/2 California senator Alan Cranston, 68, announces his candidacy for the Democratic presidential nomination. Though he eventually dyes his hair in an effort to appear youthful, the unfortunate orange tint fools no one.

2/4 Amid charges of political manipulation of the Environmental Protection Agency's toxic waste cleanup—including "sweetheart" settlements with some of the worst offenders—EPA head Anne Gorsuch demands the resignation of aide Rita Lavelle, who chooses instead to be fired.

Within a week, six congressional subcommittees are poised to investigate allegations of perjury, conflict of interest and destruction of subpoenaed documents in connection with the growing scandal.

∎

During a difficult point in her husband's press conference, Nancy Reagan barges on stage carrying a birthday cake, instantly turning a news event into entertainment. Observes the President erroneously of his upcoming 72nd: "It's just the 31st anniversary of my 39th birthday."

2/13   John W. Hinckley, Jr., fails in his third attempt at suicide, this time by drug overdose. "I would say it was related to a medication taken at St. Elizabeths," a doctor says. "I would say he took an excessive amount."

2/14   KAREN CARPENTER
    Death comes at 32 to the beloved singer after a valiant battle against anorexia nervosa
    —*People*

2/15   "Nobody can be that wrong all that much of the time."
    —EPA chief Anne Gorsuch telling a Senate subcommittee that her troubles are the result of "political harassment"

■

REAGAN MISSTATEMENTS GETTING LESS ATTENTION
    —*The New York Times*

2/16   At his 16th press conference, President Reagan reaffirms his confidence in Anne Gorsuch, complaining that her "splendid record"—which includes having reduced by almost two-thirds the number of environmental cases being referred for prosecution—is "being overlooked in the flurry of accusations."

2/17   Claiming to represent a "new political generation" with "new ideas," Colorado senator Gary Hart declares his candidacy for the Democratic presidential nomination. His advisers remind him to kiss his wife, Lee—from whom he has twice been separated—to demonstrate that they are now, in the words of an aide, "together for good."

2/21   "I am ready to be President of the United States."
    —Former Vice President Walter (Fritz) Mon-

dale announcing his candidacy for the Democratic presidential nomination

2/22   Beleaguered by charges that the EPA has been sluggish in cleaning up hazardous waste sites, Anne Gorsuch—who has gotten married over the weekend and is now Anne Burford—announces that the government will buy out all homeowners and businesses in dioxin-tainted Times Beach, Missouri.

2/23   Former Florida governor Reubin Askew announces his candidacy for the Democratic presidential nomination.

2/24   Three Canadian documentaries, including the Academy Award nominee *If You Love This Planet*, are classified as "political propaganda" by the Justice Department.

2/25   Playwright Tennessee Williams dies in New York after swallowing the cap of a small plastic bottle. New York newsman Storm Field calls him "Tennessee Ernie Williams."

2/27   The Sunday supplement *Parade* prints this query: "After Watergate, wasn't Richard Nixon secretly committed to a mental institution run by Quakers and replaced by the CIA with a Hollywood double? Isn't this the real reason why his wife, Pat, refuses all interviews—because she is afraid reporters will ask about the look-alike she is living with, and she will have to tell?"
    None of this, the reader is assured, is true.

2/28   With 125 million viewers and a 60.2 rating, the finale of *M*A*S*H* replaces the "Who Shot J.R.?" revelation on *Dallas* as the most watched episode of a TV series.

MARCH 1983

In which the President invents an oddly familiar new weapon

3/1   Condé Nast revives its long-dead flagship magazine, *Vanity Fair*. With editor Richard Locke's 18-months-in-the-making first issue a pretentious disaster, an early demise is assumed. Instead, new editor Tina Brown is imported from Britain to glitz it up, and her obsessions—fame, wealth, power and, of course, that tedious Royal Family—turn out to be '80s America's as well. So established does the magazine become as the house organ for the plutocracy that the First Couple are more than happy to pose, waltzing, for its cover.

3/3   Unhappy with TV news coverage of his administration, President Reagan proposes that the networks report only "good news" for a week. "If the ratings go down," he says, "they can go back to bad news." Responds NBC's Paul Greenberg, "We'll cover the news and let him run the country."

3/4   Unemployed roofer Cecil Andrews calls an Anniston, Alabama, TV newsroom, urging that a crew be sent to the town square "to see somebody set himself on fire." Cameraman Ronald Simmons and sound man Gary Harris alert the police and head for the scene, where Andrews—soaked in lighter fluid—waits while they set up their equipment. They roll 37 seconds of tape as he sets fire to his left thigh and, quickly changing his mind, screams for them to "put it out!" Harris tries but can't, and Andrews—in flames—runs across the square, where a volunteer fireman douses the fire. Andrews is hospitalized with second- and third-degree burns over half his body.
    Says Simmons afterward, "My job is to record events as they happen."

3/5   "There is today in the United States as much forest as there was when Washington was at Valley Forge."
    —President Reagan revealing a little-known "fact" to Oregon lumbermen

3/6   At Big Dan's Tavern in New Bedford, Massachusetts, a woman is gang-raped on a pool table. A crowd looks on appreciatively.

3/8   President Reagan tells a national convention of evangelicals that the Soviet Union is "the focus of evil in the modern world . . . an evil empire." Says historian Henry Steele Commager: "It was the worst presidential speech in American history, and I've read them all."

3/9   President Reagan accepts Anne Burford's resignation, telling her she can leave the EPA with her "head held high."

3/11   "I don't think they'll be happy until the White House looks like a bird's nest."
    —President Reagan accusing Burford critics of "environmental extremism"

3/15   Deputy national security adviser Thomas C. Reed resigns after it is reported that inside information enabled him to turn a $427,000 profit on a $3,125 investment.

3/19   "Let me tell you a true story about a boy we'll call Charlie. He was only 14 and he was burned out on marijuana. . . . One day, when his little sister wouldn't steal some money for him to go and buy some more drugs, he brutally beat her. The real truth is there's no such thing as soft drugs or hard drugs. All drugs are dumb. . . . Don't end up another Charlie."
    —Nancy Reagan—image fully transformed from vapid society dame to caring anti-drug crusader—appearing as herself on NBC's *Diff'rent Strokes*

3/22 "The President, in one of the rare times I have seen him really disgusted, threw his glasses down and said he's had it up to his keister with the banking industry."
—Bob Dole describing the activity at a GOP leadership meeting

3/23 *The New York Times* again explains that "keister" is a "slang term for rump."

■

In what will become known as his "Star Wars" speech, President Reagan proposes a space-based defense system to blast incoming missiles out of the sky, just like in the movies. Just like one movie in particular: the 1940 film *Murder in the Air*, whose hero, Secret Service agent Brass Bancroft (played by Ronald Reagan), gets involved with "the Inertia Projector," a death ray that can shoot down planes.

3/24 President Reagan meets with a group of GOP congresswomen who urge him to stay out of the debate if the Equal Rights Amendment is revived.
"How would you like to trade?" he says. "I've got some amendments I'm very interested in, too. What about trading for making abortion illegal?"
Says a witness, "You could hear people gasping all over the room."

3/28 "This President spends more time taking care with his words than any of his predecessors. . . . His success indicates it's been a good investment. The man has a reputation as a great communicator."
—White House aide David Gergen

■

Chicagoan Willie Bradley, 34, is stabbed to death by his girlfriend Verona Berkley, 42, during a dispute over whether to watch a basketball game (his choice) or *The Thorn Birds*.

APRIL 1983

In which the big story may be too good to be true

4/4 After two-and-a-half months of repair-related delays, the space shuttle *Challenger* takes off on its first flight.

4/5 James Watt bans rock music from the upcoming Fourth of July celebration at the Washington Mall because it attracts "the wrong element." Though the words "Beach" and "Boys" do not pass his lips, the story somehow becomes that Watt has attacked the Beach Boys.

4/7 In the face of support for the unmaligned Beach Boys from George Bush and Nancy Reagan, James Watt rescinds his rock music ban. As a souvenir of his gaffe, President Reagan presents him with a plaster foot with a bullet hole.

■

To celebrate the 50th anniversary of the premiere of *King Kong*, a 50-foot gorilla balloon is affixed to the tower of the Empire State Build-

ing. It tears during inflation and hangs limply from the building's spire like a huge plastic garbage bag.

4/11   The Motion Picture Academy's Spielberg shut-out continues as *Gandhi*—not *E.T.*—wins all the major Oscars. Columnist Joe Morgenstern writes, "Gandhi was everything the voting members of the academy would like to be: moral, tan and thin."

4/12   Democrat Harold Washington is elected the first black mayor of Chicago.

4/14   President Reagan is asked if his administration is trying to overthrow the San-

dinistas in Nicaragua. "No," he says, "because that would be violating the law."

4/15   NOW PLAYING: *Flashdance*—basically *Saturday Night Fever* with a female lead. The film, the first designed to be seen in four-minute pieces on MTV, is notable for starting the bare-shouldered sweatshirt look and for providing producer Don Simpson and his partner, Jerry Bruckheimer, with the formula—no plot, emotion or character development but plenty of fast cuts set to blaring, soulless rock music—that brings them even greater success with *Beverly Hills Cop* and *Top Gun*.

■

HEADLESS BODY IN TOPLESS BAR
—*New York Post*

4/18   South Carolina senator Ernest (Fritz) Hollings becomes the second "Fritz" in the race for the Democratic presidential nomination.

■

Seventeen Americans and 46 Lebanese are killed when a truck bomb plows into the US embassy in Beirut.

4/21   Ohio senator John Glenn announces his candidacy for the Democratic presidential nomination, becoming the first former astronaut—he orbited Earth three times in 1962—to seek the office.

4/22   The West German magazine *Stern* announces "the journalistic scoop of the post–World War II period": the discovery of 62 volumes of Adolf Hitler's secret diaries—reportedly hidden in a hayloft for 35 years—that portray him as virtually unaware of the Holocaust. Says reporter Leo Pesch, "It was like reading notes left behind by a dull accountant."
    But, are they genuine? Hitler scholar Hugh Trevor-Roper verifies their authenticity, declaring, "I'm staking my reputation on it."

4/26   "We think there is a parallel between

federal involvement in education and the decline in profit over recent years."
—President Reagan making an impenetrable point to *USA Today*

4/27   President Reagan asks Congress for $600 million for his Central American policies, pointing out—as if it had some relevance—that this "is less than one-tenth of what Americans will spend this year on coin-operated video games."

MAY 1983

In which a bright young star does something clever with his feet, and the President does something silly with his hands

5/1   Nancy Reagan receives an honorary doctorate of law from California's Pepperdine University, which also gave one to her husband while he was governor.

Asks Nancy, "Do you think we'll have to call each other doctor from now on?" Everyone laughs.

5/4   "Don't you fellows have to vote?"
—President Reagan, unaware that the three Republican congressmen visiting him were defeated six months ago

■

Six reporters question President Reagan in the Oval Office while the rest of the press corps listens over a PA system. The President lauds the Nicaraguan contras as "freedom fighters" and observes that nuclear weapons "can't help but have an effect on the population as a whole."

5/5   Reporter Lou Cannon infuriates the White House by revealing that journalists listening to the Reagan interview in the briefing room reacted by "occasionally breaking into laughter or making puzzled comments about the President's answers."

5/6   The Hitler diaries are revealed to be a hoax. Among the discrepancies noted: the paper, glue, ink and parts of the covers were all made after the war. Handwriting expert Kenneth Rendell tells *Newsweek* they "were not only forgeries, they were bad forgeries." *Stern* publisher Henri Nannen says, "We have some reason to be ashamed," and Hugh Trevor-Roper—he of the vanishing reputation—says, "I'm extremely sorry."

5/11   Deputy commerce secretary Guy W. Fiske resigns after it is disclosed that he was interviewing for a job as president of a communications satellite company at the same time he was involved in the decision to sell the government's weather satellites to private industry.

5/16   Performing "Billie Jean" on NBC's *Motown 25th Anniversary* special, Michael Jackson suddenly begins dancing backward across the stage and, with this move, becomes the biggest star of the decade.

5/18   During a speech to the White House News Photographers dinner, President Reagan sticks his thumbs in his ears and wiggles his

fingers. Says the leader of the free world, "I've been waiting years to do this."

5/25 HIGH COURT REJECTS TAX BENE-FITS FOR SEGREGATED SCHOOLS
—*The Washington Post*

5/26 THREE FIRED FROM CIVIL RIGHTS UNIT
    NEW CHOICES SHARE REAGAN OPPO-SITION TO RACIAL QUOTAS
—*The Washington Post*

5/28 "I put them aside and spent the evening with Julie Andrews."
—President Reagan telling aides that, rather than reading his briefing books, he spent the eve of the Williamsburg economic summit watching *The Sound of Music*

JUNE 1983

In which the secret of the President's debating success is revealed

---

6/7 "It was really funny. I was sitting there so worried about throw weight, and Reagan sud-

denly asks us if we've seen *WarGames*."
—Unnamed congressman describing a White House meeting about arms control at which the President revealed that averting a movie nuclear catastrophe was far more interesting to him than the nuts and bolts of preventing a real-life one

6/9 In his book, *Gambling with History,* *Time* correspondent Laurence Barrett reveals that Reagan campaign aides had "filched" the Carter camp's briefing papers to help prepare their candidate for the 1980 debate. The irrepressible David Stockman turns out to have been Barrett's source.

■

Addressing a forum in Minnesota, President Reagan is asked how the federal government plans to respond to a report on education that he has "approved . . . in its entirety." He is unable to provide anything more specific than that he is "going to have meetings," and finally turns to Education Secretary T. H. Bell for help. "Could you fill in what I left out?" the President asks Bell. "I won't be offended."

6/10 "It embarrasses all of us as Americans to have to point out that the President of the United States is not telling the truth. . . . I want to believe that he doesn't know any better. I want to believe that those who furnish him those spurious statistics are the culprits and that the President of the United States is innocently making these statements, not aware of their total untruth."
—House Majority Leader Jim Wright on President Reagan's claim that he has increased federal aid to education

6/16 Ariela Gross, a 17-year-old New Jersey student, meets with President Reagan to present him with a petition supporting a nuclear freeze. She reports that the President "expressed the belief that there must be something wrong with the freeze if the Soviets want it."

6/18 The space shuttle *Challenger* lifts off

in one of the smoothest launches yet, carrying among its crew of five physicist Sally Ride, the first US woman in space.

6/20 "This time they'll be 'feet people' and not 'boat people.' "
—President Reagan warning that congressional rejection of his Central American policies could result in "a tidal wave of refugees . . . swarming into our country"

6/24 On the day *Twilight Zone—The Movie* opens, John Landis is arraigned for involuntary manslaughter in the deaths of Vic Morrow and two Vietnamese children.

■

Dismissing the whole Carter briefing book affair as "much ado about nothing," President Reagan expresses doubt that "there ever was a briefing book as such." As to how his aides could have no memory of receiving the book— if it did exist—he says, "Look, ask me what paper came to my desk last week and I couldn't tell you."

6/28 At his 18th press conference, President Reagan:

- Defends the ethics of his campaign's having accepted the Carter material—"Well, my answer is that it probably wasn't too much different from the press rushing into print with the Pentagon Papers"
- Supports William Casey's professed ignorance of its existence—"I can understand his very well not having paid any attention. He wasn't going to wade through a stack of papers. They didn't come in a binder or a cover or anything"
- Observes, lest he be perceived as a bit morally lax, "there shouldn't be unethical things in a campaign."

■

A 35-by-100-foot chunk of the Connecticut Turnpike—along with two cars and two tractor-trailers driving on it—falls 70 feet into the Mianus River, killing three.

6/29 President Reagan suggests that one cause of the decline in public education is the schools' efforts to comply with court-ordered desegregation.

■

President Reagan appears on a TV tribute to James Bond, where he speaks about the fictional secret agent as if he were a real human. "James Bond is a man of honor," says the President, "a symbol of real value to the free world." Says Tip O'Neill aide Chris Matthews, "This is the kind of thing we all thought Reagan would be doing if he had *lost* the '80 election."

JULY 1983

In which the First Lady's best friend's dead husband's ex-mistress meets her fate

7/1 A *New York Times*/CBS News poll reveals that 25% of the American public knows

that the Reagan administration supports the government in El Salvador, and 13% knows it opposes the government in Nicaragua, with a mere 8%—comprised mainly of people hostile to these positions—aware of both.

7/4   Rev. Jerry Falwell says that AIDS—which he calls a "gay plague"—is God's way of "spanking" us.

■

The Police's "Every Breath You Take" begins an eight-week stay at the top of the singles chart.

7/5   "It would be totally uncharacteristic and quite incredible that I would hand anybody a book I knew to be from the Carter campaign and say this might be helpful to the debate."
—William Casey denying James Baker's accusation that he was the source of the Carter briefing book, binder or no binder

7/6   Nancy Reagan, 62, celebrates her 60th birthday.

7/7   Vicki Morgan, 30, is bludgeoned to death with a baseball bat. Her roommate, Marvin Pancoast—whom she met four years ago when they were both patients at a mental hospital—confesses to the murder.
"Vicki was special," Pancoast recalls fondly. "You just couldn't get enough of her."

7/11   Lawyer Robert K. Steinberg announces that he has videotapes of Vicki Morgan's group sexual encounters with two other women and six "friends and appointees" of the Reagan administration—among them, of course, Alfred ("The Drooler") Bloomingdale.
The next day, he claims the tapes have been stolen.

7/18   John W. Hinckley, Jr., mails a letter to *The New York Times*. "I would like to tell everyone concerned that I'm not the least bit dangerous," he writes. "I'm just a harmless mental patient who wouldn't hurt a fly, Presi-

dent Reagan or Jodie Foster. My suicidal days are over so I'm not even a threat to myself."

7/20   ABC newsman Frank Reynolds, 59, dies of viral hepatitis. Peter Jennings takes over as evening news anchor.

■

House Majority Leader Jim Wright recalls a conversation in which President Reagan voiced his suspicions about student loans: " 'Well, Jim, I don't know,' he said. 'They tell me that a lot of these kids are taking out these loans and putting them in CDs [certificates of deposit] and not even going to college.' "

7/21   Samantha Smith, an 11-year-old Maine schoolgirl whose letter to Yuri Andropov

urging him not to start a war led to a two-week visit to the Soviet Union, holds a press conference in Moscow. Does she still fear that Andropov might launch a nuclear attack? She smiles and says, "Oh, no."

7/26 Congress, with an authorization of $2.6 billion, says "Yes!" to the Peacekeeper.

■

At his 19th press conference, President Reagan is asked why there are no women on his 12-man commission on Central America. "Maybe," he suggests, "it's because we're doing so much and appointing so many that we're no longer seeking a token or something."

■

Roger Mudd is dropped as co-anchor of NBC's nightly newscast. Tom Brokaw—whose cuteness apparently outweighs his inability to pronounce all 26 letters of the alphabet—continues as a solo act.

■

Reagan appointee Thomas Ellis acknowledges at a Senate hearing that he belongs to an all-white country club, was a recent guest of the government of South Africa (where he has extensive holdings) and served as director of a group that financed research on the genetic inferiority of blacks. Still, he says, "I do not believe in my heart that I'm a racist." He withdraws his name two days later.

■

Mick Jagger turns 40.

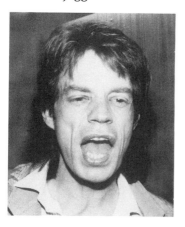

7/28 Agriculture Secretary John Block and his wife arrive at a Washington Safeway to demonstrate that a family of four can live on a food stamp budget of $58 a week.

But, isn't this shopping excursion a publicity stunt? "No," says Block, as cameras roll. "I think it has got a genuine purpose, too."

■

Robert Paul Yarrington, who collected $210,000 in 1980 for the loss of his left foot in a motorcycle accident, is convicted of insurance fraud in San Jose. It turns out that he hired two friends to stage the accident and hack off his foot with a hatchet.

AUGUST 1983

In which the President's protective coating is remarked on

8/2 Rep. Pat Schroeder (D-CO) says that Reagan is "perfecting the Teflon-coated Presidency . . . nothing sticks to him. He is responsible for nothing—civil rights, Central America, the Middle East, the economy, the environment. He is just the master of ceremonies at someone else's dinner."

■

Claiming to be "perplexed" by continuing accounts of Americans going hungry, President Reagan establishes a Task Force on Food Assistance to explain it to him.

8/3 POVERTY RATE ROSE TO 15% IN '82, HIGHEST LEVEL SINCE MID-1960'S
—*The New York Times*

■

President Reagan tells a convention of women's clubs, "If it wasn't for women, us men would still be walking around in skin suits carrying clubs." The gals are not amused.

8/4 Rita Lavelle is indicted for perjury in connection with her congressional testimony about the toxic waste cleanup fund.

8/5 In an era of increasing mergers and takeovers, US District Judge Harold H. Greene approves the break-up of AT&T—the largest court-ordered dismantling of a company since 1911.

8/13 Addressing a church group in Anaheim, James Watt compares those who fail to speak out against abortion to "the forces that created the Holocaust" by offering no resistance to Hitler.

8/21 Philippine dissident Benigno Aquino returns to Manila. As he leaves the plane, he is immediately shot to death.

8/22 Barbara Honegger resigns her job at the Justice Department after writing an op-ed piece for *The Washington Post* in which she calls Reagan's policies toward women "a sham." She is described by a department spokesman as a "low-level Munchkin."

8/24 Traveling from Miami to New York, Amtrak's Silver Meteor strikes and kills a woman in Georgia, slams into an abandoned pick-up truck in South Carolina, and derails after smashing into a disabled tractor-trailer truck in North Carolina. "The train was just plagued by a set of very unusual accidents," says a Seaboard Railroad spokesman, adding that "bad things only come in threes."

On the return trip, the train crushes the car of a North Carolina motorist who tries to run a crossing.

8/25 Barbara Honegger holds a news conference to display a photograph of herself with President Reagan. "They called me a Munchkin," she says. "This is me with the Wizard of Oz."

8/29 Eurythmics' "Sweet Dreams (Are Made of This)" hits the top of the chart.

SEPTEMBER 1983

In which the First Lady gets alarmingly small

9/1 A Soviet fighter mistakenly shoots down Korean Air Lines Flight 007 after it strays into Soviet airspace, killing 269, including right-wing congressman Larry McDonald (D-GA). George Shultz calls Tip O'Neill to tell him about the incident.

"What does the President think about this?" asks O'Neill.

"We'll tell him when he wakes up," says Shultz.

Dan Rather returns instantly from his vacation upon hearing the news and—after CBS shows him on horseback at the ranch as the crisis unfolds—so does President Reagan.

9/5 TV PREMIERE: *Thicke of the Night*, a late-night talk show starring seriously bland Canadian Alan Thicke. "I was watching the show at home," says its host, whose producer, Fred Silverman, has predicted that he will wipe out Johnny Carson, "and after 25 minutes I had to get some fresh air. I walked into the kitchen and literally fainted from anxiety from what I was seeing."

Carson survives the onslaught, and Thicke goes on to play the father in a hit sitcom.

9/6 Two more US Marines are killed in Lebanon.

9/8 "I think it's great. Now when I whisper sweet nothings in his ear, I know that he'll hear me."

—Nancy Reagan on her husband's new hearing aid

9/13 George McGovern, who amassed 17 electoral votes in 1972, announces his candidacy for the Democratic presidential nomination. "You have to do what you have to do," he says, "and I have to do this."

9/15 President Reagan wears his new hearing aid at a state dinner, prompting fashion-conscious guest Merv Griffin to exclaim, "I think everybody's running out to get them whether they need them or not." In fact, there is no surge in the purchase of unnecessary hearing aids.

9/16 TV PREMIERE: *Webster*. Not content to let NBC corner the market on sitcoms about miniature black children being raised by white folks, ABC builds a show around 40-inch-tall Emmanuel Lewis, who is soon being carried around by Michael Jackson as if he were a pet.

9/17 Vanessa Williams (Miss New York) becomes the first black Miss America.

9/19 Press secretary Sheila Tate acknowledges that Nancy Reagan—whose recent weight loss has become the subject of considerable speculation—is down from a size 6 to a size 4. She denies that the First Lady is ill.

9/21 James Watt describes the makeup of his coal-leasing commission to a group of lobbyists. "We have every kind of mix you can have," he says. "I have a black, I have a woman, two Jews and a cripple." As a public furor erupts, a spokesman explains that Watt "was attempting to convey that this is a very broadly based commission."

9/22 Despite James Watt's hastily written letter of apology to President Reagan, Bob Dole joins the swelling ranks of those calling for Watt's resignation. "I don't mind him shooting himself in the foot," says Dole, "but I don't think he should be wounding the President and the Republican party in the process."

9/23 National Kidney Foundation president Dr. David A. Ogden decries as "immoral and unethical" a plan by Virginia doctor H. Barry Jacobs to buy kidneys from poor people—among them, residents of Third World nations—and sell them to wealthier people who need kidney transplants.

■

NOW PLAYING: *The Big Chill*. Though the superficial script is far outclassed by the ensemble cast, Lawrence Kasdan's semi-remake of John Sayles' *Return of the Secaucus Seven* is the first big studio American film to show '60s activists questioning their '80s values. As such, "Big Chill Generation" enjoys a brief vogue as a hip sobriquet for baby boomers, until a simpler, two-syllable label is invented. In an era of movie music dreck like Michael Sembello's "Maniac," the '60s soundtrack alone brings people into theaters.

9/27 "If I thought he was bigoted or prejudiced, he wouldn't be part of our administration."
—President Reagan defending James Watt

■

Polio victim Bob Brostrom arrives at the White House on crutches to present 120,000 pieces of mail supporting James Watt. If Watt loses his job for saying "cripple," argues Brostrom, then hospitals for "crippled children" should change their names.

■

Addressing a GOP fundraising dinner in Washington, Henry Kissinger—unable to abandon the Superman shtick—bemoans the difficulties of commuting "from Krypton."

9/29 Society gossip columnist Suzy reports that Nancy Reagan is down to a size 2.

OCTOBER 1983

In which the President retaliates for his humiliation at the hands of one small nation by invading another

10/4 At a meeting with congressmen to discuss arms reduction, President Reagan—in office for almost three years—says he has only recently learned that most of the USSR's nuclear arsenal is land-based. This elementary information is essential to any rational thinking about disarmament.

10/9 Claiming that his "usefulness" to President Reagan "has come to an end," James Watt resigns. "The press tried to paint my hat black," he says of his troubled tenure, "but I had enough self-image to know the hat was white." He later assumes a crucifixion pose for photographers.

■

Ed Koch—a strong contender for the title "America's Fattest Mayor"—eats so much food and drinks so much wine at the Italian restaurant Parma that he faints in the men's room.

10/11 "I'd tell them to 'just say no.' " —Nancy Reagan, introducing the magic words that will make the nation's drug problem go away

10/13 Senate Majority Leader Howard Baker is informed that President Reagan has appointed noted environmental non-expert William Clark to be the new Secretary of the Interior. "You're kidding," says Baker. "Now tell me who it really is."

10/15 Eddie Murphy gets his first HBO special. Viewers expecting the sassy, beguiling kid from *Saturday Night Live* instead find an obnoxious homophobe whose idea of funny is a fantasy of Ralph Kramden and Ed Norton engaging in anal sex. As it happens, endless repetitions of the word "faggot" and jokes about "that AIDS shit" are far less amusing than Murphy thinks and, though it hardly interferes with his stardom, the show loses him some fans that he'll never get back.

10/16 Larry Flynt takes out a full-page ad in the nation's major newspapers to announce his candidacy for the Presidency. Explaining that he is running as a Republican because he is "wealthy, white" and "pornographic," he pledges to "outdo James Watt. I promise to have a black, a woman, two Jews, a cripple, a homosexual, an Oriental . . . *and* a Mexican in my Cabinet."

10/17 President Reagan appoints retired Marine Corps Lt. Col. Robert C. McFarlane as

his third National Security Adviser, and names Rear Adm. John M. Poindexter to the NSC staff.

10/18 President Reagan is asked if he will pressure Turkey to help resolve the problem in Cyprus. "Oh," he says, "I wish the Secretary of State were here."

10/19 "I heard from my cat's lawyer. My cat wants $12,000 a week for Tender Vittles."
—Johnny Carson on his ex-wife-to-be Joanna's demand of $220,000 in monthly support payments

■

Asked at his 20th press conference if he believes that Martin Luther King, Jr., had Communist ties, President Reagan alludes to a court order sealing transcripts of phone taps until 2018, quipping, "We'll know in about 35 years, won't we?"

And what about the safety of the US Marines in Beirut? "We're looking at everything that can be done to try and make their position safer," he says. "We're not sitting idly by."

10/23 A truck bomb at the US barracks in Beirut kills 241 Marines.

■

NBC newscaster Jessica Savitch, 36, drowns—along with her boyfriend—when he mistakenly drives their rented station wagon into a 15-foot-deep canal during a storm.

Five years later, two biographies portray her as an emotionally strung out druggie.

10/24 Los Angeles news anchor Jerry Dunphy, widely believed to have been the inspiration for the character of Ted Baxter, is shot while sitting in his car at the entrance to his studio. As he lies in the street waiting for an ambulance, he reportedly asks photographers, "How do I look?"

He survives the attack.

■

In the face of serious political strife on the island of Grenada, Larry Speakes calls press speculation about a US invasion "preposterous."

10/25 Claiming that US medical students there are in grave danger, President Reagan diverts attention from the Beirut fiasco by launching an invasion of Grenada. Lest there be any doubt about presidential involvement in this decision, photographs are released showing a pajama-clad Reagan—up at 5:15 A.M.!—being briefed on the situation.

Curiously, reporters are prevented from covering the event.

10/26 American medical students from Grenada kiss the tarmac upon landing in South Carolina. Scoffs school bursar Gary Solin, "Our safety was never in danger. We were used by this government as an excuse to invade Grenada." President Reagan says US troops "got there just in time" to prevent a Cuban takeover.

10/31 "He only works three to three and a half hours a day. He doesn't do his homework. He doesn't read his briefing papers. It's sinful that this man is President of the United States."
—Tip O'Neill on Ronald Reagan

NOVEMBER 1983

In which the President is threatened by a movie

11/2   President Reagan signs a bill making Martin Luther King, Jr.'s, birthday a national holiday. When the crowd sings "We Shall Overcome," the President does not join in.

11/3   Rev. Jesse Jackson announces his candidacy for the Democratic presidential nomination, claiming that he wants to "restore a moral tone" to the national discourse.

■

President Reagan explains that the action he ordered in Grenada was not an invasion but was, rather, a "rescue mission." As for a UN resolution deploring this action, "It didn't upset my breakfast at all."

■

"Be sure to wear clean, hole-less socks, as you will be required to remove your shoes before entering."
—Memo from Nancy Reagan to reporters covering her upcoming visit to a Tokyo art exhibit

11/7   *The New York Times* reports a city plan to improve the lives of South Bronx residents by pasting vinyl decals—featuring cheery images of curtains, shades, shutters and plants —on the boarded-up windows of abandoned tenements. Says a housing official, "Perception is reality."

■

For the second time in four months, George Bush breaks a Senate tie by voting to resume the production of nerve gas.

HERE'S WHAT THE CRITICS ARE SAYING ABOUT PRESIDENT REAGAN

"The first President I shook hands with was Calvin Coolidge. In those days the President would shake hands with any high school class that arrived in Washington. There was so little for him to do. Reagan is very similar to Coolidge."
—I. F. Stone

"I would never refuse an assignment unless it completely repelled me. In 1980, a national magazine asked me to go to Santa Barbara to photograph the President at his ranch. Well, I hate Santa Barbara and, far worse, I hate Reagan. I can't ignore my feelings and just make a pretty picture."
—Photographer/environmentalist Ansel Adams in the *Playboy* interview

"This President is treated by both the press and foreign leaders as if he were a child. . . . It is major news when he honors a political or economic discussion with a germane remark and not an anecdote about his Hollywood days."
—Columnist Richard Cohen

11/8   Democrat W. Wilson Goode becomes the first black mayor of Philadelphia.

11/10   President Reagan phones George Bush's mother, Dorothy, to assure her that her boy did the right thing by voting in favor of chemical weapons. "He didn't talk about nerve gas," says Ma Bush, "but I knew what the idea was."

11/12   Reporter William Coist reveals that South Bronx residents have suggested the expansion of the decal program "to provide designer clothing decals to place over . . . tattered apparel," along with "large Mercedes-Benz decals to strap to their sides" and "decals of strip sirloin for them to eat."

11/14   President Reagan tours the demilitarized zone between North and South Korea. With a camera crew recording the event for a re-election campaign film, he says of a North Korean "propaganda village" on the border, "It looks just like a Hollywood backlot, and it isn't any more important."

On the flight home, Nancy is filmed cuddling two South Korean children she is bringing to the US for heart surgery.

11/20   One hundred million people see the town of Lawrence, Kansas, destroyed in *The Day After*, an ABC movie about the aftermath of a nuclear attack. The administration—terrified that the film might remind people how scared they are of President Reagan's hostility to arms control—trots out George Shultz afterward to assure viewers there isn't going to be a war.

11/21   President Reagan receives the annual White House Thanksgiving turkey. "You're looking at the press a lot like I do sometimes," he says to the bird, "with your mouth wide open and a total misunderstanding of everything they're asking."

11/22   Navy Secretary John Lehman announces changes in procurement techniques designed to eliminate expenditures like $780 for a screwdriver and $67.20 for an oil filter clamp.

NORMALLY THEY'RE THREE CENTS EACH, BUT FOR YOU . . .

Item	Regular price	Pentagon price
Diodes	4 cents	$110.00
Bolts	67 cents	$17.59
Nut	13 cents	$2,043.00
Flat washer	$3.00	$387.00
Coffee brewer	$2,500.00	$7,622.00
Toilet seat	under $20.00	$640.09
Duckbill pliers	under $9.00	$748.00
Allen wrench	12 cents	$9,606.00
Plastic cap for stool leg	17 cents	$1,118.00

11/30   Parents across America flock to toy departments, where they assault each other over limited supplies of the season's inexplicably hot Christmas item, Cabbage Patch Dolls.

DECEMBER 1983

In which the President fondly recalls a few World War II films

12/1   Rita Lavelle is convicted of three counts of perjury and of obstructing a congressional investigation. She gets six months and a $10,000 fine.

■

At the Golden Nugget, Frank Sinatra tells South Korean blackjack dealer Kyong Kim to "go back to China" when she refuses to break New Jersey rules and deal his cards face down from her hand, rather than face up from a mechanical "shoe." She accedes to his wishes when he threatens never to sing at the hotel again—and to have her fired—if she doesn't.

12/2   Michael Jackson's 14-minute "Thriller" video premieres on MTV. "I have something I want to tell you," he says to a young girl in the clip, prior to turning into a werewolf. "I'm not like other guys."

12/3   Concrete barricades are erected in front of the White House to prevent truck bombers from cruising in as easily as they seem to in Beirut.

■

"There is no question that many well-intentioned Great Society–type programs contributed to family break-ups, welfare dependency and a large increase in births out of wedlock."
—President Reagan blaming the problems of the poor on anti-poverty programs

■

"She's a great lady. When I say she's a woman, I'm talking about people who are superior to men. Please don't print what I just said."
—US Information Agency chief Charles Z. Wick, who has just claimed that Margaret Thatcher opposed the invasion of Grenada because she's "a woman"

12/4   "Move over, Jane Fonda, here comes the Ronald Reagan workout plan."
—President Reagan, describing his exercise regimen in *Parade*, where he appears on the cover pumping iron

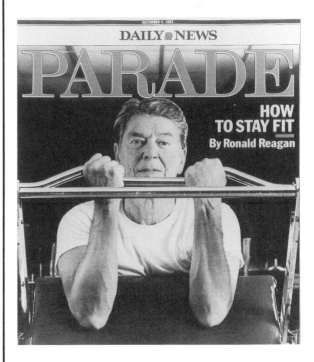

12/6   The Israeli newspaper *Maariv* reports that during a meeting with Prime Minister Yitzhak Shamir, President Reagan—who spent World War II making training films in Hollywood—claimed to have served as a photographer in an army unit filming the horrors of Nazi death camps. Shamir says Reagan also claimed to have saved a copy in case there was ever any question as to whether things had really been so bad. When asked just that question by a family member, Shamir quotes him as saying, "This is the time for which I saved the film, and I showed it to a group of people who couldn't believe their eyes."

■

"[Not] until now has there ever been a time in which so many of the prophecies are coming together. There have been times in the past when people thought the end of the world was coming, and so forth, but never anything like this."
—President Reagan revealing a disturbing view about the "coming of Armageddon"

12/8   Continuing his tradition of holiday season insensitivity, a well-fed Ed Meese scoffs at the notion that the administration's policies are unnecessarily cruel to the poor. "I don't know of any authoritative figures that there are hungry children," he declares. "I've heard a lot of anecdotal stuff, but I haven't heard any authoritative figures. . . . I think some people are going to soup kitchens voluntarily. I know we've had considerable information that people go to soup kitchens because the food is free and that that's easier than paying for it. . . . I think that they have money."

12/10   George Bush meets secretly with Manuel Noriega at the Panama City Airport. They discuss allegations of money-laundering and drug-dealing against the Panamanian general—allegations the Vice President later claims to be unaware of.

12/11   "As long as one American is hungry . . . then we have unfinished business in this country."
William Safire suggesting a more sensitive response to the hunger problem

12/12   "As long as there is one person in this country who is hungry, that's one person too many, and something must be done about it."
—President Reagan responding to the hunger problem

■

Introducing this year's White House Santa, Mr. T, as "a man who I admire a lot," Nancy Reagan plops herself in his lap and plants a kiss on the top of his head.

■

"A B-17 coming back across the channel from a raid over Europe, badly shot up by anti-aircraft. `. . . The young ball-turret gunner was wounded, and they couldn't get him out of the turret there while flying.

"But over the channel, the plane began to lose altitude, and the commander had to order

his men to bail out. And as the men started to leave the plane, the last one to leave—the boy, understandably, knowing he was being left behind to go down with the plane, cried out in terror—the last man to leave the plane saw the commander sit down on the floor. He took the boy's hand and said, 'Never mind, son, we'll ride it down together.' Congressional Medal of Honor posthumously awarded."
—President Reagan addressing the Congressional Medal of Honor Society

12/15   Ed Meese tells the National Press Club that literature's classic miser, Ebenezer Scrooge, to whom he has recently been compared, suffered from "bad press in his time. If you really look at the facts, he didn't exploit Bob Cratchit." Explains Meese, "Bob Cratchit was paid 10 shillings a week, which was a very good wage at the time. . . . Bob, in fact, had good cause to be happy with his situation. He lived in a house, not a tenement. His wife didn't have to work. . . . He was able to afford the traditional Christmas dinner of roast goose and plum pudding. . . . So let's be fair to Scrooge. He had his faults, but he wasn't unfair to anyone."

12/16   "Did he really say that? I can't believe he said that. . . . Dickens is saying that the poor deserve to live not on the margins, but with comfort and love and with freedom and medical attention. I mean, isn't that the very point about Tiny Tim? . . . He desperately needs a doctor and can't get to one because his family is so poor. . . . He's dying because he can't get medical care. . . . Boy, I'm really getting angry now. I can't believe these people."
—University of Pennsylvania Victorian literature scholar Nina Auerbach on the Meese interpretation of A Christmas Carol

■

Billy Martin is fired by George Steinbrenner for the third time.

■

Columnist Lars-Erik Nelson—after check-

ing the citations on all 434 Congressional Medals of Honor awarded during World War II—reveals that not one of them matches the story President Reagan told the other day. "It's not true," writes Nelson. "It didn't happen. It's a Reagan story. . . . The President of the United States went before an audience of 300 real Congressional Medal of Honor winners and told them about a make-believe Medal of Honor winner."

Responds Larry Speakes, "If you tell the same story five times, it's true."

12/20   At his 21st press conference, President Reagan claims that El Salvador has "a 400-year history of military dictatorships," though the first military regime didn't take power until 1931.

12/21   The Washington Post reports that the White House is feverishly searching the Medal of Honor files in an effort to verify President Reagan's story. Says a researcher, "We will find it." They never do.

■

Gerald and Betty Ford and Henry Kissinger make "special guest star" appearances on Dynasty. Kissinger plays his scene with Joan Collins, who coos, "Henry, hello!"

"Hello, Alexis, good to see you," he replies, as they engage in a seemingly interminable handshake.

"I haven't seen you since Portofino," she says, adding lewdly, "It was fun."

He is identified in the credits as "Dr. Henry Kissinger."

12/24   At a Chicago celebration for the 12th anniversary of his organization Operation PUSH, Jesse Jackson hops into Mr. T's lap, though he does not kiss his head.

12/26   "I've never done it without telling."
—Charles Z. Wick denying he ever secretly recorded telephone conversations

OUT OF THE MOUTHS OF ROCK STARS

"I wanted them to remember me."
—Ozzy Osbourne explaining why he took a moment at a CBS Records marketing meeting to bite off the head of a dead dove

"I'm not a snob. Ask anybody. Well, anybody who matters."
—Simon LeBon of Duran Duran

"We're the American youth. And youth is about sex, drugs, pizza and more sex."
—Nikki Sixx of Mötley Crüe

12/27 "I often advised the caller that I was recording the conversation or a portion of it, but in haste I did not do this consistently."
—Charles Z. Wick telling *The New York Times* that, upon reflection, perhaps he does recall having done a little secret taping

12/28 Dr. George Graham, a member of the President's Task Force on Food Assistance, says he doubts that "anyone in their right mind believes that there is a massive hunger problem." He further claims that black children are "probably the best-nourished group in the United States."

■

Lars-Erik Nelson reports that a reader saw a scene very similar to President Reagan's Medal of Honor story in the 1944 movie *Wing and a Prayer*. "Adding to the confusion," writes Nelson, "Dana Andrews at one point reprimands a glory-seeking young pilot with the words: 'This isn't Hollywood.' . . . You could understand that some in the audience might confuse reality with fiction."

1 "He and the Boss were together, and neither of them could figure out if France was a member of NATO or not." Who was being described?
- **a** Dan Rather and Van Gordon Sauter
- **b** Clarence Clemons and Bruce Springsteen
- **c** Charles Z. Wick and President Reagan
- **d** President Reagan and Nancy Reagan

2 Which member of the administration returned from Africa and reported that "some of them have marvelous minds, those black people over there"?
- **a** Ed Meese
- **b** James Watt
- **c** Charles Z. Wick
- **d** Clarence Pendleton

3 Which movie was supposed to help elect John Glenn to the Presidency but didn't?
- **a** *An Officer and a Gentleman*
- **b** *My Dinner with Andre*
- **c** *Tootsie*
- **d** *The Right Stuff*

Match the newsmaker with his/her news.
4 Daniel Crane
5 Gerry Studds
6 Shirley MacLaine
7 Joan Rivers
8 David Byrne
9 Richard Gere
- __**a** Author of book about past lives
- __**b** Wore big suit on stage
- __**c** Congressman censured by House for affair with 17-year-old female page
- __**d** Congressman censured by House for affair with 17-year-old male page
- __**e** Said when Elizabeth Taylor pierced her ears, "gravy came out"
- __**f** Bared buttocks in yet another film

10 Which of these actually appeared on TV?
- **a** *Brad!*, a prime time special starring *Saturday Night Live*'s Brad Hall
- **b** *Maneral*, an action drama about a suave professor of mineralogy who possesses the ability to turn himself into a rock
- **c** *Lie Detector*, featuring F. Lee Bailey interrogating people hooked up to a polygraph machine
- **d** *I'm Lavelle, She's Gorsuch—No, Wait—She's Burford*, a sitcom about two gals who get into all kinds of scrapes at the Environmental Protection Agency

11 Which journalist was revealed to have secretly helped coach Ronald Reagan for his 1980 debate with Jimmy Carter, and to have told TV viewers afterward that Reagan's "game plan worked well"?
- **a** Robert Novak
- **b** George Will
- **c** R. Emmett Tyrell
- **d** William Safire

12 "We misread the tea leaves." Who said it?
- **a** Time Inc. vice president Kelso F. Sutton explaining the company's decision to fold the five-month-old *TV-Cable Week*, with losses estimated at $47 million
- **b** NBC entertainment chief Brandon Tartikoff admitting that *Manimal* isn't going to knock off *Dallas* after all
- **c** Unnamed Bloomingdale's buyer explaining the failure of the store's "street couture"—a kind of bag lady chic—to really catch on
- **d** *Esquire* editor Philip Moffitt admitting that an awful lot of people thought the "Esquire Register" was a big bore

13 Which TV character observed, "Once you give up integrity, the rest is a piece of cake"?
- **a** Alex Keaton
- **b** Alexis Carrington Colby
- **c** Diane Chambers
- **d** J. R. Ewing

ANSWERS

1-c, 2-c, 3-d, 4-c, 5-d, 6-a, 7-e, 8-b, 9-f, 10-c, 11-b, 12-a, 13-d

JANUARY 1984

In which the Nation's hottest star catches fire

1/4 Deputy defense secretary Paul Thayer resigns amid charges of insider trading. He eventually serves 19 months for perjury and obstruction of justice.

1/5 Dallas resident Larry Boff dials the city's emergency number to get an ambulance for his stepmother, who is having trouble breathing.

"Can I speak with her, please?" asks nurse Billie Myrick.

"No, you can't," he says. "She seems incoherent."

"Why is she incoherent?" asks Myrick.

"How the hell do I know?" says Boff.

"Sir," says Myrick, "don't curse me."

The argument goes on like this for eight minutes, and by the time an ambulance is sent, Boff's mother has expired. "She's dead now," he tells Myrick. "Thank you, ma'am!"

1/6 Homophobe Dan White—who claimed that his 1978 killing of San Francisco mayor George Moscone and supervisor Harvey Milk was caused by his junk food diet (the "Twinkie defense")—is released from jail. He asphyxiates himself 21 months later.

■

President Reagan says he has no intention of asking for Charles Z. Wick's resignation just because he secretly taped a few phone calls.

■

TV PREMIERE: *The New Show.* After more than three years away from weekly television, former *Saturday Night Live* producer Lorne Michaels returns to NBC with a prime time comedy hour. Unfortunately, neither he nor his writers have anything really new to say, and the show serves mainly to provide the brilliant Dave Thomas and Catherine O'Hara an opportunity to appear in the kind of lame sketches they skewered so savagely on *SCTV.* It dies before spring.

1/8 RADIO PREMIERE: *Hellcats of the White House.* With most American comics perversely uninterested in the stunning material being provided by the Reagan administration, Harry Shearer, host of the Los Angeles radio hour *Le Show,* introduces the smartest political satire of the decade, a serial portraying life with the First Couple from their point of view—that it's all a '40s movie. Set within their small circle of friends and aides, the President constantly lapses into anecdotage while the First Lady can be heard undergoing "industrial-strength mechanically aided cosmetic work."

1/9 At a preliminary hearing requested by the defendants in the *Twilight Zone* case, John Landis—in court because an accident on his set killed three people, decapitating two of them—openly mocks the prosecutor.

■

DEATH OF A BEACH BOY

The drowning of DENNIS WILSON at 39 ends the act of America's most troubled supergroup

—*People,* which underestimates the ability of the surviving members to keep singing those same old songs

■

Charles Z. Wick celebrates Richard Nixon's 71st birthday by apologizing for secretly taping "a small percentage" of his phone conversations.

1/10 REAGAN TASK FORCE FINDS NO EVIDENCE OF GREAT HUNGER
—*The Washington Post*

1/11 Columnist Lars-Erik Nelson suggests another source for the Medal of Honor story: an apocryphal item in the April 1944 issue of *Reader's Digest*, a magazine known to be a lifelong Reagan favorite. "The bomber had been almost ripped apart by German cannon," it read. "The ball turret gunner was badly wounded and stuck in the blister on the underside of the fuselage. Crewmen worked frantically to extricate the youngster, but there was nothing they could do. They began to jump. The terror-stricken lad screamed in fear as he saw what was happening. The last man to jump heard the remaining crewman, a gunner, say, 'Take it easy, kid. We'll take this ride together.' "

1/15 The eight Democratic candidates take part in a three-hour Dartmouth debate moderated by Ted Koppel and Phil Donahue. Among the highlights:

- John Glenn accuses Walter Mondale of speaking "gobbledygook"
- Mondale calls Glenn's statement "baloney"
- Gary Hart says the nation needs "new ideas"
- Jesse Jackson declares, "If you deal with text out of context, you have a pretext," and no one asks what it means.

Says pollster Pat Caddell afterward, "I felt uncomfortable having the candidates hold up their hands like they were children trying to get the attention of Phil Donahue. It's too symbolic of what's happening to our politics."

1/16 A testy Gary Hart—"the candidate with new ideas," as his campaign literature describes him—admits that he was born in 1936 and not, as he has been claiming for years, 1937. "It's whenever the records say," he says. "It's

not a big deal." He later explains that the discrepancy stems from some "lighthearted" family controversy about his mother's age, though his uncle, Ralph Hartpence, doubts Gary's mother—by all accounts a severe, humorless woman—"had anything to do with it."

Doubt is also cast on the candidate's claim that the 1961 change in the family name from Hartpence to Hart was initiated by his parents. Uncle Ralph thinks Gary foresaw a political career for himself and wanted to embark upon it without his childhood nickname, "Hot Pants," coming back to haunt him.

■

"Just suppose with me for a moment that an Ivan and an Anya could find themselves, oh, say, in a waiting room, or sharing a shelter from the rain or a storm with a Jim and Sally, and there was no language barrier. . . . Before they parted company, they would probably have touched on ambitions and hobbies and what they wanted for their children and problems of making ends meet. And as they went their separate ways, maybe Anya would be saying to Ivan, 'Wasn't she nice? She also teaches music.' Or Jim would be telling Sally what Ivan did or didn't like about his boss. They might even have decided they were all going to get together for dinner some evening soon."
—President Reagan, switching from his "evil empire" rhetoric to a more folksy "we're all just people" approach as he prepares for his re-election campaign

■

Cher
She's gay and gritty in *Silkwood*, but off-screen she still loves glamour, glitz and guys who can kiss
—*People*

1/17 The Supreme Court rules 5–4 that recording TV broadcasts with a VCR is legal, sparing the government a serious enforcement dilemma.

1/20 During a White House meeting about acid rain, President Reagan repeatedly calls

EPA chief William Ruckelshaus "Don." Chief of staff James Baker finally slips the President a note telling him to stop.

1/22 "You've given me some problems. I have already had a call from Moscow. They think that Marcus Allen is a new secret weapon and they insist that we dismantle him."
—President Reagan injecting inane Soviet-bashing into his inevitable post–Super Bowl call congratulating Raiders coach Tom Flores

1/23 President Reagan nominates Ed Meese as the new head of the Justice Department. Observes Sen. Howard Metzenbaum (D-OH), "William French Smith has not been a distinguished attorney general, but this is getting ridiculous."
Meese says he "will try to do as outstanding a job as Bill Smith did."

1/25 At an off-the-record breakfast with *Washington Post* reporter Milton Coleman, Jesse Jackson refers to Jews as "Hymie" and calls New York "Hymietown."

1/27 "You find yourself remembering what it was like when on the spur of the moment you could just yell to your wife that you were going down to the drugstore and get a magazine. You can't do that anymore."
—President Reagan telling *Time* a story he hasn't told the magazine in more than 17 months

■

Michael Jackson suffers second- and third-degree burns on his scalp when a smoke-bomb canister explodes during the filming of a Pepsi ad. He insists on keeping his trademark white glove on as he's wheeled into the hospital, where doctors say reconstructive surgery will likely be required.
Meanwhile, Doubleday announces it will publish the 25-year-old singer's autobiography, to be edited by Jacqueline Onassis.

1/29 Claiming that his "work is not fin-

ished," President Reagan announces that, yes, he's running again, and so's Bush.

1/31 Defending himself against charges of callousness on *Good Morning America*, President Reagan argues that you can't help those who simply will not be helped. "One problem that we've had, even in the best of times," says the President, "is the people who are sleeping on the grates, the homeless who are homeless, you might say, by choice." Does David Hartman ask him to explain the idea of someone *choosing* homelessness? Of course not.

FEBRUARY 1984

In which the Reverend retracts a denial

2/2 "The White House is engaging in a new form of McCarthyism—Charlie McCarthyism."
—Tip O'Neill aide Chris Matthews on the propensity for underlings to speak for the President

■

"He may be ready to surrender, but I'm not."
—President Reagan attacking Tip O'Neill's advocacy of a pullout from Beirut

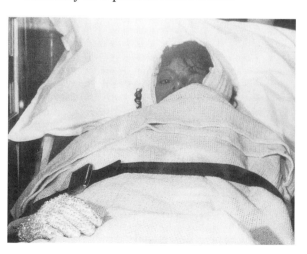

■

"If you could add together the power of prayer of the people just in this room, what would be its megatonnage?"
—President Reagan posing an unanswerable question at a national prayer breakfast

2/6   President Reagan celebrates his 73rd birthday—"the 34th anniversary of my 39th birthday"—in his hometown of Dixon, Illinois. "It's great to be back home," he says. "And, you know, if our old house on Hennepin Avenue looked as good in 1924 as it does now, I might never have left." Everyone laughs.

2/7   President Reagan announces plans to get the Marines out of Beirut and onto offshore ships, describing the retreat as "decisive new steps." Explains Larry Speakes, "We don't consider this a withdrawal but more of a redeployment."

■

"I think Michael Jackson is a national treasure. I like the way he dresses, the way he looks, the way he does everything. This is a far-out man."
—Fashion designer Halston at a party celebrating *Thriller*'s entry into the *Guinness Book of World Records*

2/12   "Can a handicapped person run the nation? One is now!"
—Jesse Jackson, dismissing the notion that a disabled person could not be President

2/13   *The Washington Post* reports that Jesse Jackson, in private conversations, "has referred to Jews as 'Hymie' and to New York as 'Hymietown.'" Milton Coleman is quickly identified as the source.

■

Cyndi Lauper's "Girls Just Want to Have Fun" begins eight weeks in the Top Ten. Though her intelligence and humor are welcome additions to the rock scene, the wrestling revival she drags along with her is not.

2/14   George Bush attends the funeral of Soviet leader Yuri Andropov.

2/16   Welcoming Nazi hunter Simon Wiesenthal and Rabbi Marvin Hier to the White House, President Reagan again claims, according to Hier, to have "photographed Nazi atrocities while he was with the Signal Corps." When reporters question this account, James Baker elicits from Reagan the clarification that he "never left the country" during the war and "never told anyone that he did." As to how Shamir and Hier—in two separate meetings—could have come away with the same wrong story, Baker has no explanation.

2/17   While an aide 30 feet away briefs reporters on the pullout of Marines from Lebanon, President Reagan fulfills the duties of his office by arm-wrestling for the cameras with the publisher of a body-building magazine.

2/19   "It simply is not true, and I think that the accuser ought to come forth."
—Jesse Jackson responding, with some indignance, to reports that he referred to Jews disparagingly

2/20 REAGAN REPORTED IN DARK ON TALKS
SECURITY AIDE SAYS PRESIDENT WAS UNAWARE OF CONTACTS U.S. HAD WITH P.L.O.
—*The New York Times*

∎

Walter Mondale wins the Iowa caucus with 45% of the vote, three times the total of runner-up Gary Hart, who nonetheless treats his showing as a huge victory.

2/22 "The only difference between a board of directors . . . and our Cabinet meetings is when it comes time for decision we don't take a vote. The decision is mine."
—President Reagan defending himself against the media-created "fiction" that "I sit back and then somebody tells me what to do"

2/23 "Our country stands before two paths . . . our past and our future . . . one path . . . the course of the old . . . other path . . . new leadership . . . new generation of leadership . . . new generation of leadership . . . new generation of leadership . . . new generation of leadership . . . new strategies . . . new generation of leadership . . . new ways . . . new help . . . new generation of leadership . . . new job skills . . . new tax . . . new generation of leadership . . . new generation of leadership . . . new generation of leadership . . . new generation of leadership . . . new path . . . as Robert Kennedy told us . . ."
—Excerpts from the basic Gary Hart campaign speech

∎

"They tell me I'm the most powerful man in the world. I don't believe that. Over there in that White House someplace, there's a fellow that puts a piece of paper on my desk every day that tells me what I'm going to be doing every 15 minutes. *He's* the most powerful man in the world."
—President Reagan on an unidentified aide

∎

At a debate in New Hampshire, Jesse Jackson tells moderator Barbara Walters he has "no recollection" of using the terms "Hymie" or "Hymietown."

∎

CNN provides live national coverage of the Massachusetts trial of six men accused of last year's pool-table gang rape. Four are convicted.

2/25 Introducing Jesse Jackson in Chicago, Black Muslim minister Louis Farrakhan tells "the Jewish people" that when they attack Jackson, they attack his supporters as well. "If you harm this brother," he says, "I warn you in the name of Allah, this will be the last one you do harm." Asked for his reaction, Jackson says, "Ask Farrakhan about his own introduction."

∎

"I'm here! It's me! It's Mayor Koch! I'm here!"
—New York mayor Ed Koch at the Berlin Wall, announcing his presence to East German soldiers

2/26 "That he was governor. That he went up to the moon. You know—he's well known."
—New Hampshire voter Sheila Brace explaining her support for John Glenn, who was neither a governor nor a visitor to the moon

∎

Questioned by Lesley Stahl about the confusion over his age, Gary Hart declares, "I was born in 1936." Why, then, do his official and campaign biographies say 1937? "I can't account for every piece of paper that's been written by my campaign or anyone else." So, it turns out it wasn't his fault at all.

Later, he takes part in an axe-hurling contest. Though he misses his target several times, the clip seen on the evening news—validating his aura of momentum—shows his single bull's-eye.

∎

Jesse Jackson appears at a Manchester synagogue to say that, yes, now that he thinks about it, he does recall referring to Jews as "Hymie" and New York as "Hymietown," though it "was not done in the spirit of meanness."

2/28 With his two Pepsi commercials premiering on the awards telecast—*sans* hair ignition footage—Michael Jackson wins a record eight Grammys. For variety, he removes his shades during one of his acceptance speeches, explaining that "Katharine Hepburn, who's a dear friend, said I should."

Observes Eurythmics singer Annie Lennox, "He's a little too much of a commodity at the moment."

■

The newly discovered voting bloc "Young Urban Professionals"—made up largely of upwardly mobile baby boomers eager to abandon idealism for materialism—gives Gary Hart a surprise 10-point victory over Walter Mondale in New Hampshire. Fritz Hollings (4%), Alan Cranston (2%) and Reubin Askew (1%) withdraw from the race. Says Johnny Carson of the winner, "I like his slogan: 'Vote for me, I have Kennedy hair.' "

Meanwhile, having finally "come of age" as consumers, the '60s kids—now known, and not to their liking, as "yuppies"—continue to define the cultural ethos, the signposts of which include Amstel Light, Day Timers, New Age music, designer ice cream, bottled water, running shoes, call-waiting, aspartame, designer fiction, detoxification and rented movies for the VCR.

MARCH 1984

In which the candidate of new ideas loses some momentum

3/2 "When Democratic voters start displaying their volatility, we can choose one of two explanations: they are moved by excitement or by ennui. The evidence of New Hampshire powerfully suggests that they are bored. Its Democrats were already tired of Mondale, who is the husband type, and they turned in their weariness to Hart, who seems the boyfriend type."
—Columnist Murray Kempton

HARTMANIA

"I like his new ideas thing."
—Robert E. Box, retired Alabama minister/college teacher

"I like the way he looks. I just think he might be good. Who knows?"
—New York garment district worker

"The greatest candidate to run for President in my lifetime."
—Former Speaker of the House Carl Albert

"Hart. John Hart. I like him."
—Voter speaking on National Public Radio

"He's doing the things that ought to be done, whatever that is."
—Woman in Gilley's country-and-western nightclub in Houston

"I'm really excited about him. He's got new ways of doing things."
—Vermont motel manager Margaret Ann Reilly

"He does have new ideas, even though I can't remember exactly what they are. Maybe I'm just on the bandwagon, but everybody seems to like him."
—Illinois high school senior John Shepherd

HARTPHOBIA

"A coldhearted wretch who lacks compassion."
—Rival candidate Walter Mondale

"If you want to know what I think, he reminds me of Nixon. He can't even get his name and age straight."
—Mondale supporter Martina Jackson on whether Hart more closely resembles Carter or JFK

"His Newness."
—Press nickname for the candidate

■
NOW PLAYING: *This Is Spinal Tap*, the funniest rock movie ever made, about a heavy metal band so loud its amps go "to 11." The film spawns a live tour by actors/writers Christopher Guest, Michael McKean and Harry Shearer—who perform all their "hits," including "Hell Hole," "Sex Farm," "Big Bottom" and "Tonight I'm Gonna Rock You Tonight."

3/4   Gary Hart defeats Walter Mondale in the Maine caucus and, the next day, in the Vermont primary.

■
The Reagans celebrate their 32nd wedding anniversary.

3/6   Attacking the President for saying things about him "when he knows them to be

NANCY REAGAN TALKS ABOUT HER WEDDING ANNIVERSARY

"It seems like 29 minutes."
—Nancy Reagan on the occasion of her 29th wedding anniversary

"It feels like 30 minutes."
—Nancy Reagan on the occasion of her 30th wedding anniversary

"I cannot believe it's been 32 years. It seems like 32 minutes."
—Nancy Reagan on the occasion of her 32nd wedding anniversary

untrue," Jimmy Carter observes, "President Reagan doesn't always check the facts before he makes statements, and the press accepts this as kind of amusing."

■

"I think I'll put in an amendment to build a chapel at Camp David so he could go to church."
—Tip O'Neill on President Reagan's school prayer legislation

"The President is not doing anything he hasn't done for 30 years."
—Larry Speakes denying that Reagan is using religion for political gain

■

DEVELOPER SAYS HE DISCUSSED JOB AFTER HELPING SELL MEESE'S HOUSE
—The Washington Post

3/7 APPOINTEE TELLS OF LOANS ARRANGED FOR MEESE
—The New York Times

3/9 Defending his failure to attend church, President Reagan piously observes, "Frankly, I miss it very much. But I represent too much of a threat to too many other people for me to be able to go to church." But, why does he not hold services in the White House, as previous Presidents have done? No one asks.

■

Roger Mudd reports that "the Gary Hart name and age controversy has become rich, raw material for the political joke circuit." He points out that if other Presidents had abbreviated their names, we would have had "Lyndon B. John," "Richard M. Nix" and "Calvin Cool."

3/11 On a radio broadcast from Chicago, Black Muslim minister Louis Farrakhan tells reporter Milton Coleman, "One day soon we will punish you with death" for reporting Jesse Jackson's "Hymie/Hymietown" usage. He later denies this is in any way intended as a threat.

■

During a debate in Atlanta, Gary Hart is asked what he would do as President if a Czechoslovak passenger jet heading toward Strategic Air Command bases ignored US warnings to turn back. "If the people they looked in and saw had uniforms on, I would shoot the aircraft down," he says. "If they were civilians, I would just let them keep going."

Observes John Glenn—experienced in jet fighter combat—to appreciative chuckles, "You don't go peeking in the windows to see if they have uniforms on."

Later, Mondale gets his licks in, telling Hart, "When I hear your new ideas, I'm reminded of that ad, 'Where's the beef?'" This adoption of the slogan from a popular hamburger commercial proves so devastating that Mondale jokes he should fire his speechwriters and researchers and "hire somebody from Hee-Haw."

3/13 Attorney General–designate Edwin Meese admits that he "inadvertently failed to list" a $15,000 interest-free loan from a man who later received a federal job (as did his wife, his son and several other Meese friends who had helped him out financially) in his financial disclosure statements. He explains that "it never occurred to me that an interest-free loan was a thing of value."

■

Gary Hart wins six Super Tuesday contests (Florida, Massachusetts, Rhode Island, Nevada, Oklahoma and Washington) though the media —eager to keep the race alive—interprets Mondale's ability to avoid a shutout (he wins Georgia and Alabama) as a victory of sorts.

On NBC, Roger Mudd asks Hart, "Why do you imitate John Kennedy so much?" Hart says he doesn't. Undeterred, Mudd shifts to a different brother. "Will you do your Teddy Kennedy imitation for me now?" he asks. "I've heard it's hilarious." Hart, unamused, declines.

3/14 YOUTH ROBS WOMAN TRAPPED UNDERNEATH BUS IN TRENTON OF $2,000
—*The New York Times*

■

George McGovern—whose high-road appeal to the public's "conscience" won him the improbable admiration of Richard Nixon, but not nearly enough votes—withdraws from the race.

■

The Twentieth Century–Fox Licensing Corporation announces plans to market a line of *Dynasty* products, including a *Dynasty* fur collection, Forever Krystle perfume, "*Dynasty* blue" tuxedos, *Dynasty* jewelry, *Dynasty* lingerie, *Dynasty* hosiery, *Dynasty* shoes, *Dynasty* blouses, *Dynasty* linens, *Dynasty* wall coverings, *Dynasty* china and a *Dynasty* board game. Says president Chuck Ashman, "By Christmas you will be able to dress like Krystle, Alexis, Blake or Jeff . . . do your home in the Carrington motif, and even smell like one of them."

3/15 SENATOR'S START
HOME TOWN IN KANSAS REMEMBERS GARY HART, THEN GARY HARTPENCE
HIS MOTHER AND HER CHURCH GAVE AUSTERE BACKDROP FOR A SERIOUS, QUIET BOY
A PURLOINED CHEMISTRY TEST
—*The Wall Street Journal*

■

An indignant Gary Hart attacks Walter Mondale for airing ads in Illinois that raise the issues of Hart's age and name changes. He apologizes two hours later after learning that no such spots have been broadcast.

3/16 John Glenn withdraws from the presidential race.

■

CIA station chief William Buckley is kidnapped in Beirut. He dies in captivity 15 months later.

3/17 Gary Hart apologizes for a TV spot attacking Cook County Democratic chairman Edward Vrdolyak. Though Hart claims the ad has been pulled, a series of failed communications keeps it on the air all weekend. "Here's a person who wants to be President of the United States," observes Mondale, "and he can't get an ad off television." Hart—who expected to win Illinois—loses by six points, and his aura of invincibility evaporates.

3/22 "The standard for the Attorney General nominee should not be: can he prove he is not a felon?"
—Sen. Joseph Biden (D-DE) expressing his doubts about the Meese nomination

3/23 Gary Hart addresses the continuing questions about his background. "When I tell the truth, I expect my word to be taken as truth," he says testily. "Obviously, if I don't tell the truth and people can prove it, that's a very disastrous thing."

3/25 MEESE SAYS HE NEVER CONSIDERED THAT LOAN MIGHT LOOK IMPROPER
—*The New York Times*

3/27 Gary Hart wins in Connecticut, but no one really notices because attention is focused on next week's primary in New York.

3/28 Disapproving of artificial means to prolong life in an increasingly overcrowded world, Colorado governor Richard D. Lamm says—perhaps too bluntly—that terminally ill elderly people have a "duty to die and get out of the way."

3/29 "When I throw my glasses, they know I'm angry."
—President Reagan explaining how his aides can tell he's upset—besides, of course, when he talks about his "keister"

3/30 TV PREMIERE: *Lifestyles of the Rich and Famous.* Host Robin Leach visits the homes of fabulously wealthy people and asks them questions like, "Liberace, are you a gentle man living in a crazy world?"

APRIL 1984

In which the First Couple goes souvenir shopping

4/1 On the eve of his 45th birthday, Marvin Gaye—in the midst of a significant career comeback—gets into a fight with his father, who shoots him to death.

4/2 Rep. George Hansen (R-ID)—charged with filing false financial statements—becomes the first congressman convicted under the 1978 Ethics in Government Act.

■

"We have taken that question out of the game because it is distasteful in this country."
—Selchow and Righter executive John Nason confirming that the question, "How many months pregnant was Nancy Davis when she walked down the aisle with Ronald Reagan?" has been removed from the American version of Trivial Pursuit (the answer: two and a half)

4/3 COUNSEL IS NAMED FOR MEESE INQUIRY
JACOB STEIN, LAWYER IN CAPITAL AND TEACHER, IS DESIGNATED
—*The New York Times*

■

Walter Mondale beats Gary Hart, 45% to 27%, in the New York primary, with Jesse Jackson at 26%, his best showing to date.

4/4 President Reagan is asked about the perception that his administration helps the rich at the expense of the poor. "Oh, I'm concerned about it," he says. "It's a political problem if people believe it, but there's absolutely no truth in it."

4/5 "The deaths lie on him and the defeat in Lebanon lies on him and him alone. . . . The trouble with this fellow is he tries to be tough rather than smart."
—Tip O'Neill rejecting President Reagan's claim that congressional criticism of US policy encouraged terrorist attacks

4/6 During a manhunt for Christopher Wilder, sought in connection with the murder of several females across the nation, CBS airs a video-dating application by the suspect. "I want to date," Wilder says on the three-year-old tape. "I want to socially meet and enjoy the company of a number of women."
He is killed by police a week later.

■

MEESE APPARENTLY FAILED TO REPORT REIMBURSEMENTS
—*The Washington Post*

■

The Wall Street Journal reports direct CIA involvement in the mining of Nicaraguan harbors.

4/8 Jesse Jackson calls Louis Farrakhan's threats against reporter Milton Coleman "a bit inciting and distasteful," but refuses to repudiate the Muslim leader. "My approach," he says, "is to separate the sinner from the sin."

■

Richard Nixon returns to television in a series of interviews, conducted by former aide Frank Gannon, for which CBS paid $500,000. Among the highlights:

- His acknowledgment that it's the media's responsibility to examine the President "with a microscope . . . but when they use a proctoscope it's going too far."
- His description of his 1974 call to George Wallace, trying—and failing—to get him to exert influence over a Democrat on the House Judiciary Committee. "As I hung up the phone, I knew it was all over," he says. "I turned to Al Haig. I said, 'Well, there goes the presidency!' "
- His claim that being "the most vilified man" in American politics "didn't bother me that much, but believe me, it bothered my family."

Writes Ward Just in his novel *American Blues* of the ex-President's ongoing exposure of his bizarre psyche, "I realized suddenly that Nixon was the generational link. . . . I had no doubt that he would last the century, my grandchildren could watch him on *Meet the Press* . . ."

4/9 Barry Goldwater writes to William Casey protesting the mining of Nicaraguan harbors. "It gets down to one, little, simple phrase: I am pissed off!" he says. "This is an act violating international law. It is an act of war."

■

One day after his administration announced it will not recognize the World Court's jurisdiction over the mining of Nicaraguan harbors, President Reagan proclaims May 1 as "Law Day USA." Says the President, "Without law, there can be no freedom, only chaos and disorder."

■

The *National Enquirer* reports that John W. Hinckley, Jr., "has found love behind the walls of his mental hospital" and is romantically involved with Leslie deVeau, a 40-year-old Washington socialite who shotgunned her daughter to death, then lost an arm in a suicide attempt. Or, as the *New York Post* puts it, "HINCKLEY HAS HOTS FOR ONE-ARMED SOCIALITE KID-KILLER."

■

With his first film, *Terms of Endearment*, director James L. Brooks achieves what has always eluded Steven Spielberg: he wins a lot of Oscars for a critically acclaimed film that made $100 million.

4/10 "Thanks as well to Secretary of Agriculture John Black for his fine leadership."
—President Reagan expressing gratitude to John Block as he signs a farm bill

■

Walter Mondale wins the Pennsylvania primary.

4/11 *The Chicago Tribune* reports that in the same speech containing his threat to Milton Coleman, Louis Farrakhan called Hitler "a very great man," though, to be sure, "wickedly great."

■

Reagan daughter Patti Davis, 31, announces her engagement to 25-year-old yoga instructor Paul Grilley in Los Angeles. The White House reports that the First Lady is "very happy."

4/13 "The beef is here tonight!"
—Jerry Falwell introducing President Reagan at a fundamentalist rally

4/16 It's a guy, it's a girl—IT'S BOY GEORGE!
Joke, freak or pop genius—kids are getting his message . . .
—*People*

4/22 Sensing that the nomination is slipping away, Gary Hart claims Walter Mondale is evading campaign financing laws by accepting the benefits of "hundreds of thousands of dollars of political action committee money." Though this is perfectly legal, Hart begins a Nixonian effort to plant the idea in the public mind that it's not, incorporating the chant "Give the money back, Walter!" into his basic speech.

■

The Reagans embark on a four-day journey

to China, with rest stops in Honolulu and Guam to minimize the chances of untimely napping.

■

"I think I really wanted to write my biography more to be able to mention that Jack Kennedy and I were friends than anything else."
—Jerry Lewis in *Parade*

4/23 John Landis and two co-workers are indicted on three counts for "the involuntary manslaughter of the actors Vic Morrow, Renee Chen and My-ca Le." The director says he finds it "disheartening" that "being innocent is not enough."

4/25 James Baker III is asked if he's ever been to a Communist country. "Well," he replies, "I've been to Massachusetts."

4/26 William Casey apologizes to the Senate Intelligence Committee for keeping the Nicaraguan mining a secret.

■

ROBERT KENNEDY'S SON DAVID FOUND DEAD IN HOTEL
—*The New York Times*

4/27 Nancy Reagan presents a Peking zoo with a check for $13,077 raised in America to help China's starving pandas. Jesse Jackson notes that senior citizens in the US are "eating cat and dog food" while the First Family is "over there feeding Communist pandas."

■

Citing tainted evidence, the Rhode Island Supreme Court overturns Claus von Bulow's attempted-murder convictions and orders a new trial. "I'm quietly grateful," says von Bulow emotionlessly, "but nobody is going to see any demonstrative celebration."

4/29 The Reagans travel to Xi'an, where they pose at an excavation site among a group of 2,200-year-old life-size statues. They then visit a hastily created "free market" where local citizens pretend to inspect the merchandise as if they were really shopping. President Reagan says the market—created solely for the purpose of being photographed and instantly dismantled—shows that capitalism in China is "flourishing."

4/30 Students at Shanghai's University of Fudan ask President Reagan which experiences best prepared him for his current career. "You'd be surprised," he tells them, "how much being a good actor pays off."

■

The *National Enquirer* points out that Gary Hart's new signature—yes, he's changed that, too—bears a disturbing resemblance to Richard Nixon's. "Both Hart and Nixon use large capital letters, indicative of a massive ego and overpowering ambition," says handwriting expert Robert Wasserman, who says both signatures are very hard to read. "Indecipherable signatures reveal that the person has something to hide," he adds, noting that Nixon's had become "very unreadable" by the time he reached the White House. "If Hart was a used car salesman and I saw his signature on a contract, I'd be worried."

MAY 1984

In which the President meets the Nation's hottest star

5/1 "He thought they were the Smith Brothers."
—Larry Speakes on President Reagan's reaction to Peking wall posters of Stalin, Lenin, Marx and Engels

■

Walter Mondale wins the Tennessee primary.

5/8 Gary Hart—on the verge of being written off—wins the Ohio and Indiana primaries.

5/9 Richard Nixon's comeback continues as he is warmly received at the annual meeting of the American Society of Newspaper Editors, where he predicts that Mondale won't pick a female running mate. Says the renowned political seer, "He's going to take either Bentsen or Hart."

5/12 During a white-water river trip in Oregon, Gary Hart has to be talked out of trying to run a particularly hazardous rapid. Explains the would-be most powerful man on the planet, "I love danger!"

■

The number two man at the Housing Department, Philip Abrams, expresses doubt that Hispanics live in crowded homes because of poverty. "I don't think so," he says. "I'm told that they don't mind and they prefer, some prefer, doubling up. . . . It's a cultural preference, I'm told."

5/14 Declaring, "Well, isn't this a thriller?" President Reagan presents Michael Jackson with an award for allowing "Beat It" to be used in anti–drunk driving ads. Jackson later avoids gawking adult fans by locking himself in a White House men's room.

5/15   Gary Hart wins a 2–1 victory over Walter Mondale in the Nebraska primary.

■

The Senate Foreign Relations Committee rejects the nomination of Leslie Lenkowsky to be deputy director of the US Information Agency because of his involvement in, and lying about, the blacklisting of 95 prominent Americans of a non-right-wing persuasion—among them Walter Cronkite and Coretta Scott King—from the USIA's overseas speaking program.

5/16   Experimental comedian Andy Kaufman—best known for his role in *Taxi* and his wrestling with women—dies at 35 of lung cancer. Many fans assume he's just kidding.

5/17   Walter Mondale announces that he is creating an escrow account to refund $400,000 in PAC contributions.

5/18   Gary Hart says a refund of $400,000 "is not enough."
"You mean it didn't satisfy him?" says Mondale. "That comes as a shock. Gosh, I thought it would satisfy him."

■

President Reagan has his first complete physical examination in over two years. A small polyp in his colon is found to be benign.

5/22   Asked about the possibility of secret funds going to the contras, President Reagan declares, "Nothing of that kind could take place without the knowledge of Congress."

5/25   Gary Hart tells supporters at a Los Angeles fundraiser that he has just been reunited—after what he implies was a painful campaign-induced separation—with his wife, Lee. "She campaigns in California," he says enviously, "and I campaign in New Jersey."
"I got to hold a koala bear," says Lee.
"I won't tell you what I got to hold," Hart chuckles, oblivious to how these jokes will play back east. "Samples from a toxic waste dump."

5/28   "I was just talking about the hazards of commuting coast-to-coast. That's all I said. The people of New Jersey are more intelligent than that. They know a remark made in jest and lightheartedly, about having to commute coast-to-coast to see my wife, was not meant disparagingly about this state."
—Gary Hart in a damage control mode

JUNE 1984

In which the defacing of a national monument is proposed

6/3   During a debate in Burbank, Jesse Jackson uses his closing statement to tweak the press, telling a story about an imaginary boat ride with the Pope, during which his holy cap blows off. "He reached for it and he could not get it," says Jackson. "And of course what happened was Jesse Jackson got up and walked across the water and got the cap and brought it back. And the Pope expressed his thanks to me. And the press was in the next boat and they saw this entire event. Headlines next day: 'Jesse Can't Swim.' "

6/4   MERIT BOARD CHIEF SAID TO HELP FRIEND OF MEESE GET JOB
—*The Washington Post*

■

The battle over an explosive new book about JOHN BELUSHI
Feeling betrayed, his widow, Judy, confronts author Bob Woodward
—*People*

6/5   Though he ekes out a five-point victory in California—where the Hollywood community has gone incomprehensibly ga-ga over him—Gary Hart is soundly beaten by Walter Mondale in New Jersey, with Jesse Jackson a close third.

6/6   "I will be the nominee of the Democratic Party."
—Walter Mondale claiming to have the 1,967 delegates he needs

"Welcome to overtime. . . . The one thing that can be said about this nomination contest is that it is not over."
—Gary Hart

■

The *Los Angeles Times* reports that Teamsters president Jackie Presser has been an FBI informer since the 1970s. Surprisingly, he is not killed.

■

Sen. Roger Jepsen (R-IA)—a staunch member of the Christian right—acknowledges membership in a private spa that was later shut down as a house of prostitution. Claiming he thought it was a health club, he says he only went once, realized his error and never returned. Though the 1977 incident occurred before his "commitment to Christ," he loses his re-election bid.

■

In the PR coup of Michael Deaver's career, President Reagan commemorates the 40th anniversary of D-Day on the site of the Normandy invasion as campaign cameras roll. "These are the boys of Pointe du Hoc," he says of the veterans sitting before him. "These are the men who took the cliffs. These are the champions who helped free a continent. These are the heroes who helped end a war." As he leaves, a veteran shouts out, "Welcome aboard, Ronnie. You're 40 years late."

6/10   President Reagan complains about daughter Patti's liberal comments about marijuana usage and pre-marital cohabitation. "I'm just sorry that spanking is out of fashion now," he says, though it is unclear when spanking a child in her 30s was in fashion.

6/11   Jerry Lewis begins a one-week trial as a talk show host. "I just wish the best wish I could ever wish for you," Lewis—who played a smarmy character like this in Martin Scorsese's brilliant *The King of Comedy*—tells his audience. "To have people in show business as your friends."
The show is not extended beyond its tryout.

6/12   Discussing US-Soviet relations with GOP leaders, President Reagan announces, "If they want to keep their Mickey Mouse system, that's okay."
"It's a change in his view," says an official. "It's not an evil empire. It's a Mickey Mouse system."

■

Sharon Porto, a witness at the Marvin Pancoast murder trial, testifies that Vicki Morgan had been planning to write a book in which she would "name a lot of government people" she had been involved with. Says Porto, "Meese was one name I heard."
Pancoast is convicted.

6/13   Close Meese pal Herbert Ellingwood is reported to have created a "talent bank" to place fundamentalist Christians in civil service and political positions.

6/14   At his 25th press conference, President Reagan claims that his tax policies—which have produced a windfall for the wealthy—"have been more beneficial" to the poor "than to anyone else." Though this would seem to be a difficult claim to get away with, no one challenges him.

■

Bloomingdale's advertises the availability of its own one-size-fits-all, Michael Jackson–inspired rhinestone-studded white glove—"Only one glove, of course, will do for those who know what's hot and sassy"—at $9.95 each.

6/15 Some of the pundits and insiders have said, 'Why don't you quit?' Well, let me tell you something I told my friends in Colorado: I don't quit."
—Gary Hart, sounding less Kennedyesque and more Nixonian by the day

6/16 Due to a videotape mix-up, attendees at the Cattle Baron's Ball in Dallas watch Ronald Reagan tell them, "Good evening. I'm delighted to have this opportunity to speak before the Washington Charity Dinner of 1984."

6/17 Eight days after winning the Belmont Stakes (and, six weeks earlier, the Kentucky Derby), Swale finishes a routine gallop and returns to his stable, where he suddenly drops dead. Says attending veterinarian Robert Fritz, "Sometimes horses die on you, and you never know why."

6/18 *Born in the U.S.A.* begins an 84-week run in the Top Ten, turning Bruce Springsteen—whose populist songs about hard times are perversely misinterpreted by many fans as celebrations of Reaganism—into America's preeminent rock star, with even as unlikely a fawner as George Will gushing about him in print.

6/19 Denver radio talk show host Alan Berg—whose broadcast philosophy has been, "I stick it to the audience and they love it"—is shot to death outside his home. Two members of The Order, a neo-Nazi group, get 150 years for the murder.

6/24 Louis Farrakhan attacks Judaism as a "gutter religion," though he insists he said no such thing. A media consensus forms that he actually might have called it a "dirty" religion, and this, for some reason, is perceived as not having been so bad.

6/26 Hart aide Kathy Bushkin attacks as "outrageous" a *Vanity Fair* article in which writer Gail Sheehy reported the candidate's relationship with Marilyn Youngbird—a "radiant divorcee" whom he allegedly called his "spiritual adviser"—and described a 1979 Comanche "sunrise ceremony" at which, according to Youngbird, "they brushed the front and back of our bodies with eagle feathers. It was sensual, oh yes."
Did Hart have an affair with the woman? Bushkin is "sure he hasn't."

6/27 "Your policies are not in the least anti-black or anti-poor. As a matter of fact, it's my opinion that your fight against inflation, your war on the drug traffic, your tough stand against street crime, your effort in revitalizing the nation's economy, are all of great importance to us poor people and us black people in America."
—Letter allegedly received by President Reagan from a 39-year-old black man whose identity, as is so often the case with these epistles of unsolicited support, goes unrevealed

6/28 With no apparent upside to his association with Louis Farrakhan, Jesse Jackson finally breaks with him, denouncing his latest remarks as "reprehensible and morally indefensible."

6/30   Walter Mondale appears before the National Organization for Women's convention in Miami, where he endures a lengthy audience chant of such slogans as "What do we want? A woman VP! When do we want it? NOW!" This insures that if he does select a female running mate, he will appear to have caved in to pressure.

■

"It's very possible that this meeting will lead to further discussions about joint projects. . . . They like each other and that's important. They respect each other and that's even more important."
— Spokesman for Pia *(Butterfly)* Zadora suggesting that a dinner meeting she and her husband had with Bo *(Bo-lero)* Derek and her husband might bear artistic fruit

■

GOP chairman Frank Fahrenkopf suggests the addition of President Reagan's likeness to Mount Rushmore, saying he "can't think of any President more deserving" of joining the ranks of Washington, Jefferson, Lincoln and Teddy Roosevelt.

THE PIA ZADORA DECADE

"I don't know, people say I'm a sex symbol, but I think I'm an actress."
— Pia Zadora, star of *Butterfly* and *The Lonely Lady*

"I think *Lonely Lady* is trashy, but I think it *does* make a statement."
— Pia Zadora on the promotion beat

"And this broad's smart. You wouldn't believe her IQ. It's fantastically high."
— Pia Zadora's much older, extremely wealthy husband, Meshulam Riklis, who pays for making the movies

JULY 1984

In which the President and his opponent make some surprising choices

7/2   President Reagan appoints scandal-tainted Anne Burford as chairman of the National Advisory Committee on Oceans and Atmosphere, declaring himself "very pleased to have her back in the Administration."

■

Prince's "When Doves Cry" begins a five-week run as the nation's Number One song.

7/6   Gary Hart tells *The Denver Post* that Walter Mondale's vice presidential selection process—in which he has interviewed three women, two blacks, one Hispanic and one wealthy Texan—is "a little like pandering." Says a Mondale aide, "I can't believe he keeps saying these things."

■

The Jacksons' Victory Tour gets underway in Kansas City. The ticket policy—requiring fans to send $120 for a chance at buying four tickets of indeterminate location, with those not chosen having to wait weeks for refunds—is so unpopular that Michael has to announce its abandonment and, as an extra PR gesture, the donation of all his proceeds to charity. His brothers, whose last chance to cash in on him is this tour, make no such altruistic pledge.

■

Nancy Reagan, 63, celebrates her 61st birthday.

7/8 Boy George and Jerry Falwell appear on *Face the Nation* to discuss androgyny.

7/10 President Reagan claims that his environmental record is "one of the best kept secrets" of his Presidency. When a reporter asks where Anne Burford fits into that record, Larry Speakes steps forward and orders the lights turned off. Reagan, believed by many to be the most powerful man on the planet, stands behind his aide, saying, "My guardian says I can't talk."

7/12 Ice cream vendor Ebenezer Obomanu calls for help after being shot on his route in Chicago. His cries attract 100 youths who help themselves to his wares while leaving him bleeding in the street for over an hour.

■

At the Minnesota statehouse, Walter Mondale introduces Rep. Geraldine Ferraro, who represents the "Archie Bunker" district in Queens, New York as his running mate. "This is an exciting choice," he says, surprised by the intensity of the applause. "Let me say that again. This is an exciting choice!"

Performing an environmental photo opportunity in Kentucky, President Reagan offers his first comment on the nomination—that it's no more historic than his naming Sandra Day O'Connor to the Supreme Court—from inside a cave.

7/13 Geraldine Ferraro kicks off her campaign by attacking President Reagan's false piety. "The President walks around calling himself a good Christian," she says. "I don't for one minute believe it, because the policies are so terribly unfair."

7/14 The Mondale momentum screeches to a halt as the candidate—desperate for southern votes—names Georgian Bert Lance, one of the most scandal-tainted figures from the Carter administration, as the new party chairman. As William Winpisinger, president of the Machinists union, puts it, every last bit of "garbage" had been cleaned out of the Democrats' yard when Mondale showed up and "dropped a load of manure on the front doorstep."

7/15 Walter Mondale says he will retain current party chairman Charles Manatt. Instead of dropping Bert Lance completely, he names him to head his campaign, guaranteeing two more weeks of When-Is-Lance-Leaving? stories.

7/16 New York governor Mario Cuomo gets the Democratic convention underway in San Francisco with a keynote speech stunning for its eloquence and sense of outrage.

"There is despair, Mr. President," he says, "in the faces that you don't see, in the places that you don't visit in your shining city." He warns what Reagan's re-election will mean: "If July brings back Anne Gorsuch Burford, what can we expect of December?" He focuses squarely on the Supreme Court—a key issue that Democrats are usually too wimpy to push—urging his audience to contemplate a judiciary "fashioned by the man who believes in having government mandate people's religion and morality. The man who believes that trees pollute the environment, the man that believes that the laws against discrimination against people go too far . . ."

By the time he gets to the part about watching his immigrant father's feet bleed, most of his audience is wondering why Mondale is the candidate.

7/17 Jesse Jackson ends months of speculation ("What Does Jesse Want?") by adopting a tone of contrition in his speech to the convention. (He wants to run for President again.)

"If there were occasions when my grape turned into a raisin and my joy bell lost its resonance, please forgive me," he says. "Charge it to my head, not to my heart."

Meanwhile, Gary Hart continues to predict his own victory.

7/18 In San Diego, James Oliver Huberty straps an arsenal to his body, tells his wife, "I'm going to hunt humans," and strolls down the block to the local McDonald's where, while his radio blares out Scandal's "The Warrior"—"Shootin' at the walls of heartache/Bang bang/I am the warrior"—he kills 21 people and wounds 19 (a record body count for one man in one day) before being slain by police.

■

Following Gary Hart's address to the convention—a stale, vaguely sour address in which he warns, "This is one Hart you won't leave in San Francisco"—Walter Mondale is nominated for President.

7/19 "Mr. Reagan will raise taxes, and so will I. He won't tell you. I just did."
—Walter Mondale accepting the nomination, exhibiting an honesty he will not be rewarded for

7/20 Wandering around the Moscone Center as the convention is dismantled, 86-year-old Sally Bowers reminisces about all the "inspirational" speakers, "especially the governor of New York, Kimona. Is that his name?" Collector Howard Raab says he's looking for a button for "the guy from Albany—Camel, Como, what's his name?"

■

Vanessa Williams, the first black Miss America, is ordered to relinquish her title after *Penthouse* publishes old nude photos of her in sexually explicit poses with another woman. Publisher Bob Guccione declares himself "a little bit tired of being the heavy in this instance. I didn't take her clothes off. She did."

7/21 In Vermont, James Fixx—author of *The Complete Book of Running* and a tireless proponent of the theory that this exercise increases life expectancy—dies at 52 of a heart attack while jogging.

■

Walter Mondale takes advantage of his convention momentum by going fishing for five days.

7/23 The *National Examiner* reports that Richard Nixon was grooming Elvis Presley for the Presidency. "If it hadn't been for his tragic and untimely death," writes the tabloid, "the king of rock 'n' roll might be sitting in the Oval Office today."

■

Gossip columnist Taki—who in 1978 wrote a column condemning cocaine use—is arrested at London's Heathrow Airport with 25 grams of the drug in his pocket.

7/24 Declaring a small polyp found in President Reagan's large intestine "something you don't have to worry about," Dr. Daniel Ruge says the President—whom he calls "one of the healthiest people I know"—is unlikely to have another complete physical exam for "two or three years."

■

At his 26th press conference, President Reagan claims that "not one single fact or figure" backs up Democratic "demagogucry" that his budget cuts have hurt the poor. The next morning, a congressional study reports that cuts in welfare have pushed more than 500,000 people—the majority of them children—into poverty.

7/25 "The national Democratic leadership is going so far left, they've left America."
—President Reagan campaigning in Austin

7/26 The Federal Communications Commission raises the number of TV stations one company can own from seven to 12. "Bigness isn't necessarily badness," says chairman Mark Fowler. "Sometimes it is goodness."

■

Flying to a rally in New Jersey, President Reagan declines Sam Donaldson's joking invitation to view the *Penthouse* spread of Vanessa Williams. "I don't look at those kind of pictures," says the President. "I'm a good boy."

7/27 Anne Burford dismisses the job she has been appointed to as insignificant. "It's a nothing-burger," she says. "They meet three times a year. They don't do anything. It's a joke." Having so blurted, she has no choice but to have her nomination withdrawn.

7/28 "Set your sights high, and then go for it. For yourselves, for your families, for your country and—will you forgive me if I just be a little presumptuous?—do it for the Gipper."
—President Reagan delivering a pep talk to US Olympic athletes who go on to dominate the games, to the delight of jingoistic commentators

"Celebrating the 23rd Olympiad of the modern era, I declare open the Olympic Games of Los Angeles."
—President Reagan reversing the two clauses he had to remember

7/30 Prince's *Purple Rain*—which, unbeknownst to many parents, contains a song with lyrics about masturbation—begins a 24-week reign as the nation's best-selling album.

7/31 Asked whether he believes President Reagan is a "good Christian," Mario Cuomo says, "I don't think we ought to judge one another's soul. I'm not going to judge Ronald Reagan and ask, 'Why did you leave your first wife? Was that a Christian thing to do? Have you seen your grandchild?' I don't want to judge his soul or his conscience. . . . I'm not going to debate Ronald Reagan on whether he's a hypocrite."

As to whether Bert Lance should leave the Mondale campaign, Cuomo says, "It won't make any difference. He's a walnut in the batter of eternity."

AUGUST 1984

In which the Nation gets a glimpse behind the curtain

8/1 Stymied by a reporter's question about arms control during a Santa Barbara photo op, President Reagan stands silently for several seconds, grunting and shrugging, until Nancy, beside him, lowers her head and mutters, "Doing everything we can."

Says the leader of the free world, instantly, "We're doing everything we can."

8/2 Bert Lance submits his resignation as general chairman of the Mondale campaign.

1984

Olympics guru Peter Ueberroth acknowledges receipt of a letter from the International Olympic Committee protesting ABC's mindlessly flag-waving coverage of the games.

8/3 The Census Bureau reports that 35.3 million Americans were living in poverty in 1983—an 18-year-high rate of 15.2% of the population.

8/5 Reviewing the Nancy-feeds-Ronnie-his-line incident, *New York Times* reporter Francis X. Clines writes of the vacationing President, "Subjects such as the Soviet Union seem to haunt Mr. Reagan the way vows to read Proust dog other Americans at leisure."

Notes *Village Voice* press critic Geoffrey Stokes, "This may be the only time in history in which the words 'Mr. Reagan' and 'read Proust' will appear in the same sentence." Humorist Veronica Geng promptly writes a *New Yorker* piece in which those words appear in every sentence.

8/8 George Bush denies that he and President Reagan have been having difficulty coordinating their positions on a tax increase. "Absolutely not," he says. "There's no difference between me and the president on taxes. No more nit-picking. 'Zip-a-Dee-Doo-Dah.' Now it's off to the races."

8/9 On the 10th anniversary of Richard Nixon's resignation, former Nixon speech writer Benjamin J. Stein writes a *Washington Post* op-ed column called "Was Watergate Really Such a Big Deal?" Stein thinks not.

"Really, who now knows what Watergate was about? What was all the shouting about?" he writes. "If whatever Nixon did was so obscure that no one can even remember what he did any longer . . . how drastic could it have been? . . . If the nation chased a President out of office for the only time in 200 years *and no one clearly remembers why,* something went drastically wrong . . ."

Writes the *Post* in an editorial, "Not to put too fine a point on it, we think we can remember."

The US wins the gold medal in the first synchronized swimming competition, the silliest event in the history of the Olympics.

8/10 Halfway through the eagerly anticipated women's 3,000-meter final, US runner Mary Decker trips over British (formerly South African) runner Zola Budd's bare feet, landing in the infield where she remains, with a pulled muscle in her hip, until the race is over. (Budd finishes seventh.)

"Zola Budd tried to cut in without being actually ahead," she tells reporters afterward, though there is some dispute as to who was at fault. "Her foot caught me and to avoid pushing her, I fell. . . . I don't think there was any question she was in the way." Lest anyone fail to catch her drift, she repeats, "I hold Budd re-

102

sponsible for what happened." Then she begins sobbing and her 290-pound discus-throwing fiance Richard Slaney carries her off.

8/11   President Reagan again indulges his penchant for whimsy during a sound check. "My fellow Americans," he jests, "I'm pleased to tell you today that I've signed legislation that will outlaw Russia forever. We begin bombing in five minutes." Though he gets his expected big laugh from the sycophants in the room, others are less amused.

8/12   With questions about her financial disclosures dominating coverage of her campaign, Geraldine Ferraro says she'll release her income tax returns but has been unable to convince her husband, John Zaccaro, a New York real estate developer, to release his. "You people married to Italian men," she says, "you know what it's like."

8/13   Michael Deaver—for reasons known only to himself—reveals to NBC's Chris Wallace that President Reagan nods off in Cabinet meetings. "I've seen him when he had difficulty staying awake," says Deaver, "but he wasn't the only one in the room that was."

■

Richard Burton
At 58, death ends his greatest performance—a life as lover, rogue and magnificent actor
—*People*

8/14   Patti Davis marries Paul Grilley in a private ceremony at the Bel-Air Hotel in Los Angeles. Her parents attend the wedding.

8/16   John Z. De Lorean is acquitted on charges of cocaine-trafficking in Los Angeles. "I'm so happy!" says his wife, Cristina, who has stood by him throughout his 22-month ordeal. "We won!" A month later she leaves him and goes on to become a successful morning TV personality in Los Angeles.

■

"He was off-handed and with a very big smile he said that he had to go into a Cabinet meeting and that he certainly was not going to bomb Russia in the next five minutes."
—Edgar M. Bronfman describing President Reagan's mirthful departure from a meeting with Jewish leaders

■

"I was really talking low. I must have been on his good side or he had that gizmo turned up, or whatever. But I wasn't prompting him. I was talking to myself out of sheer frustration."
—Nancy Reagan denying that she fed her husband his line at the ranch, though it's clear from the tape that she did just that

8/17   "She was talking to herself. . . . She didn't even know I could hear. I guess I had the button turned up."
—President Reagan, annoyed at reports that his wife "is the power behind the throne, directing me or something"

8/19   Geraldine Ferraro explains that her husband, John—who has released his tax returns after all—"did nothing wrong" by borrowing $100,000 from the funds of an incapacitated woman whose estate he was overseeing because he "never knew it was improper."

■

Asked to respond to Mondale's charge that his bombing joke had made the world uneasy, President Reagan blames the media. "Isn't it funny?" he says. "If the press had kept their mouth shut, no one would have known I said it." No one points out that if *he'd* kept his mouth shut, they couldn't have reported it.

8/20   "President Reagan is a symbol to a generation *happy* with itself!"
—Steve Clark, chairman of the Young Republicans National Federation

■

With Mario Cuomo as his guest, Phil Donahue sticks his mike in a woman's face and says,

"Now, don't think about it, answer me right away. Who are you going to vote for?" "Reagan!" she says, as the audience cheers.

Observes Cuomo, "That's what you get when you don't think about it."

■

"It's a pain in the ass to explain. . . . No ERA, and no exception for rape and incest. On women's issues, it's a stinkeroo."

—Sen. Lowell Weicker, the GOP's last liberal, bitching about the GOP platform

■

The Republican convention gets underway in Dallas with a contemptuous speech by Jeane Kirkpatrick (who refers derisively to the "San Francisco Democrats") and a lackluster keynote address by US treasurer Katherine Ortega. Denying that her selection was an attempt to pander to women, one GOP official explains, "Ortega wasn't chosen because she's a woman. She was chosen because she's a Hispanic."

8/21 With her tax returns finally public, Geraldine Ferraro holds a 90-minute news conference in New York to put the controversy about her finances behind her. By confidently rebutting many of the charges—and good-humoredly acknowledging the unrebuttable ones —she does what she set out to do, even getting applause from her inquisitors at the end.

■

"I'm conservative but I'm not a nut about it."

—George Bush defining himself in Dallas

■

"WOMEN FOR REAGON"
—Placard spotted in Dallas

8/22 "You could call them Fritz and Tits because then there'd be three boobs in the White House. . . . Geraldine Ferraro! Big deal, let's put a woman in the White House. May I just tell you something? Can we talk here for a second? Its no big deal to have a woman in the White House. John F. Kennedy had a thousand of them."

—Joan Rivers entertaining a GOP women's

luncheon in Dallas—at Nancy Reagan's request

■

"I was looking at all this financial disclosure, and it looks like Edith and Archie have turned out to be Pamela and Averell Harriman, *dahling.*"

—An exquisitely bitchy George Bush on Geraldine Ferraro's finances

■

"All I know is that I cannot get him to take a nap."

—Nancy Reagan defending her husband's determined wakefulness to Dan Rather, who fails to ask if this means she thinks her good friend Mike Deaver was lying

■

"The Reagan administration has done more for the needy than any in all history."

—Sen. Paul Laxalt placing the President's name in nomination

■

"Let's make it one more for the Gipper!"
—Nancy Reagan to the convention, while a huge TV screen above the podium shows her

RONALD REAGAN *IS* THE PRESIDENT OF THE UNITED STATES

"A kind of 18-minute Pepsi commercial with Reagan as Pepsi . . . Flashprez . . . What a Feeling!"
—TV critic Tom Shales on the campaign film that introduces President Reagan to the convention

"It's got an energy about it. It's got a vitality about it. It's got a *truth* about it."
—Phil Dusenberry—who produced the Michael Jackson Pepsi spots—assessing his Reagan film

"It is a bit slick, positively slick, and people may think that it's not full of the substance that they would like to see in a documentary, but I think that's more the contemporary treatment that we've applied to it."
—Media adviser Doug Watts on the film

"It's not that everybody agrees with what you're doing, but there's a certain *respect* for the United States of America. And it's loud, and it's clear, and I run into that all over the country. . . . They might argue with ya on one or two things if you gave 'em a chance, but *it's back*. You get the feeling the country's movin' again. A certain pride level."
—George Bush fawning over Reagan in the film

"I hope that people out there recognize what a wonderful bunch of young people we've got in the military now. When they see someone in the street in uniform, I hope they'll go up and say hello, and maybe tell them they're a little proud."
—President Reagan in the film

"There ain't no doubt I love this land/ God bless the U-S-A!"
—Lee Greenwood singing the beer commercial–influenced 1984 Reagan theme song

"I feel more patriotic towards my country. I feel more proud to be an American."
—Black youth in the film

"I think he's just doggone honest. It's remarkable. He's been on television, what have I heard, 26 times? Talking to us about what he's doing? Now, that's—he's not doing that for any other reason than to make it *real clear*. And if anybody has any question about where he's headed, it's their fault. Maybe they don't have a television."
—Young woman in the film, dripping with contempt for anyone who would go TV-less in the age of such a telegenic leader

husband in his hotel suite watching her on TV, inspiring her to wave frantically at him, and him—after some prompting—to wave back

■

"They're like Jack and Jackie. They're role models for grace and elegance."
—California representative Bobbi Fiedler on the Reagans

■

"The hall is full of people who want to run in 1988. I think we could probably count a dozen or more. If they're all laid end to end, we promise you we'll bring you a picture of it."
—David Brinkley

8/23   "Isn't the real truth that they are intolerant of religion? They refuse to tolerate its importance in our lives."
—President Reagan at a Dallas prayer breakfast, attacking those nitpickers who insist on separating politics and religion

■

". . . accept your nomination . . . clearest political choice . . . them . . . high interest rates . . . spending bill . . . tax . . . teen-age drug use, out-of-wedlock births and crime . . . schools deteriorated . . . allies mistrusted us . . .
"Since January 20th, 1981 . . . not one inch of soil . . . fallen to the Communists . . . pessimism is ended . . . more confident than ever . . . strongest economic growth . . . lowest inflation rates . . . fastest rate of job creation . . . highest level of business investment . . . on the move again . . . new eras of opportunity . . . prosperity that will finally last . . .
"Balanced budget amendment . . . line-item veto . . . voluntary prayer amendment . . . the Lord back in the schoolrooms . . . drugs and violence out . . .
"Equality of all men and women . . . shining city on a hill . . . Olympic torch . . . celebration . . . thank you, God bless you, and God bless America!"
—President Reagan accepting renomination

8/25   Johnny Carson's second wife, Joanne,

finds her friend Truman Capote—no stranger to drugs and alcohol—dead in the guest bedroom of her Bel Air home. She says he'd been obsessed with finishing his long-awaited novel *Answered Prayers*, though nothing close to a complete manuscript is ever found.

8/27   President Reagan announces a search for a teacher to be the first citizen in space. "When that shuttle lifts off," says the man who has presided over drastic cuts in education funding, "all of America will be reminded of the crucial role teachers and education play in the life of our nation."

■

Former battered wife Tina Turner enjoys rock's comeback of the decade as "What's Love Got to Do with It" begins a three-week run at Number One.

SEPTEMBER 1984

In which the President discusses the perils of home decorating

9/3   Walter Mondale's campaign kicks off in New York City, where he marches in the Labor Day parade at such an early hour that crowds are non-existent.
Later, at a picture-perfect southern California rally, President Reagan debuts his macho campaign slogan: "You ain't seen nothin' yet."

9/5   Michael Jackson's personal manager Frank DiLeo announces "once and for all" that his client is not gay. Warning that legal action will be taken against any future such insinuations, he reads a written statement from Jackson: "NO! I've never taken hormones to maintain my high voice. "NO! I've never had my cheekbones altered in any way. NO! I've never had cosmetic surgery on my eyes. YES! One day in the future I plan to get married and have a family. Any statements to the contrary are simply untrue."

■

Campaigning in Portland, Oregon, Geraldine Ferraro holds the umbrella for Walter Mondale, who checks his notes while local candidate Barbara Roberts gets drenched.

9/6 Dallas Rev. W. A. Criswell, who recently delivered the closing benediction at the GOP convention, says he thinks "this thing of separation of church and state is a figment of some infidel's imagination."

9/9 "I absolutely believe President Reagan when he says he does not want to establish a state religion—that would require him to attend services."
—Sen. Daniel Moynihan on *This Week with David Brinkley*

9/10 Obviously irritated that his slippery position on abortion has become an issue, George Bush refuses to answer any more questions on the subject, citing "my right as an American to remain silent."

9/12 "There are an awful lot of things I don't remember."
—George Bush denying that his failure to recall his previous support for abortion poses a credibility problem

■

"The main difference between us and the other side is, we see an America where every day is the Fourth of July, and they see an America where every day is April 15th."
—President Reagan campaigning in New York

9/13 *The Wall Street Journal* publishes an opinion-page piece speculating on Geraldine Ferraro's dead father-in-law's possible mob connections.

■

"The other side's promises are a little like Minnie Pearl's hat. They both have big price tags hanging from them."
—President Reagan campaigning at the Grand Ole Opry

■

"We are in a different phase now, trying to merge the thesis and the antithesis into a synthesis without doing violence to either."
—Jesse Jackson "explaining" his support for Walter Mondale

9/16 TV PREMIERE: *Miami Vice.* The first mainstream series to take advantage of the violence and action of rock videos, the NBC show—set in the glamorous cocaine underworld—looks great (hot cars, hot colors, hot clothes), sounds great (TV stereo is coming into its own) and moves fast. So what if nothing really happens? Don Johnson's facial stubble and lack of socks sets a major fashion trend, while Philip Michael Thomas becomes known for his huge ego.

9/17 George Bush continues to respond testily to questions about abortion. "My position is like Ronald Reagan's," he says. "Put that down, mark that down. Good. You got it."

9/18 "It wasn't done with that in mind. It was done because there are people out there that need help."
—President Reagan, denying that his generous new farm policy has any connection to the upcoming election

∎

Campaigning against Elliot Richardson for the GOP Senate nomination in Massachusetts, Ray Shamie—who wins, but then loses the election—explains the difference between himself and his opponent with refreshing candor. "Elliot believes government can do good things for people," he says. "I don't."

9/19 "Only in 1984 could anyone who was part of Democrats for Nixon in 1960 go around parading himself as the new JFK."
—Ted Kennedy on President Reagan's constant quoting of President Kennedy

∎

"America's future rests in a thousand dreams inside our hearts. It rests in the message of hope in the songs of a man so many young Americans admire: New Jersey's own Bruce Springsteen. And helping you make those dreams come true is what this job of mine is all about."
—President Reagan attempting to add America's hottest rock star to his pantheon of co-opted heroes

9/20 A suicide bomber drives into the US embassy annex in Beirut, killing two Americans. It is the third such incident in 19 months.

∎

Independent counsel Jacob A. Stein says his six-month investigation of Ed Meese has found "no basis" for prosecution, adding that

HERE'S WHAT THE CRITICS ARE SAYING ABOUT PRESIDENT REAGAN

"Ronald Reagan is the most breathtaking new thinker around."
—Rep. Newt Gingrich (R-GA)

"Those without a sense of irony about American politics may find it hard to believe that a man of such limited vision, mediocre intellect and narrow comprehension can cut a figure of world-historical importance."
—Editorial in *The Nation* following President Reagan's re-election

"He rubs me the wrong way. He's laughing too much. And he's joking. And he thinks he's funny, and he's not."
—Toledo voter Norma Rerucha

"It takes deep bravery to be fearless about one's own hypocrisy. Politicians of average duplicity cower at being found out. Not Reagan."
—Columnist Colman McCarthy

"The President is like some sort of child monarch of old, surrounded by advisers, cut off from the people."
—Columnist Richard Cohen

"I think it's rubbish—he's always been gaga."
—*New Republic* editor Michael Kinsley on the sudden emergence of the "age issue"

THE REAGAN CAMPAIGN TALKS ABOUT ITS ADS

"I heard you were selling soap so I thought you might like to meet the bar."
—President Reagan to his advertising team

"It's warm. Warm and fuzzy—but a good fuzzy."
—Ron Travisano on his Reagan foreign policy spot, which features kids getting haircuts

"We'll have this nice couple in an ordinary house. Something good will happen to them, and the guy will say, 'Hey, honey, now that we've got so much money, let's go out for a steak.' But in the Hispanic version we'll have the guy say, 'Let's go out for a taco.' "
—Media adviser Doug Watts explaining Reagan ethnic ad strategy

his limited mandate prevents him from commenting on "Mr. Meese's ethics and the propriety of his conduct." President Reagan pledges to renominate him if re-elected, saying, "I know he'll be a truly distinguished Attorney General."

■

TV PREMIERE: *The Cosby Show*. NBC establishes itself as the decade's dominant network by starring America's most overexposed shill in a retrograde sitcom that, with a white cast, could have shared air time with Ronald Reagan in the mid-1950s. With the lives of blacks portrayed as no different from those of whites, the show magically solves the nation's racial problems and, at its peak, becomes the highest-rated series in 20 years.

■

"The Sandinistas came in. They overthrew Somoza, killed him and overthrew him. Killed him, threw him out."
—George Bush displaying ignorance about the fate of Somoza, who fled Nicaragua when he was overthrown and was later assassinated in Paraguay

9/21 "The President was mentioning my name the other day, and I kinda got to wondering what his favorite album musta been. I don't think it was the *Nebraska* album."
—Bruce Springsteen entertaining his Pittsburgh audience with a snide comment about Reagan, yet not endorsing Mondale, either

■

The Reagans accept the invitation of seven-year-old black child Rudolph Lee-Hines to have dinner at his home. They present their host with a jar of jellybeans.

9/22 "I'm serious—they'll both do the same thing, and I think it's important how he presents himself."
—College freshman John Smith explaining that the advantage of Ronald Reagan over Walter Mondale is that he's "better dressed"

9/23 "Anyone that's ever had their kitchen done over knows that it never gets done as soon as you wish it would."
—President Reagan justifying the incomplete security measures at the US embassy annex in Beirut, where an iron gate was lying on the ground awaiting installation

"Anyone that's ever had their kitchen done over knows that the process is nothing at all like trying to stop somebody from driving a truckload of explosives into your house."
—Columnist Russell Baker

9/24 "I believe that the future is far nearer than most of us would dare hope."
—President Reagan addressing the UN

■

DI'S PRIDE AND JOY
Move over, William—little Prince Henry is checking into the royal nursery
—*People*

9/25 "Do you know what wins elections? It's who puts money into this and who takes money out. And the one good reason why Ronald Reagan is going to be re-elected is because he's putting something in here and the other people are taking money out."
—George Bush whipping out his wallet at a campaign rally

9/26 "I was up in New England the other day, campaigning in Vermont, and I said, 'It's nice to be here in Vermont when the sap is running,' and one of the pickets stood up and said, 'Stop talking about Mondale like that.'"
—George Bush campaigning in Indiana

■

President Reagan explains to a group of Ohio college students that the US wants good relations with the USSR "because peace in America is such an attractive way to live that a war is a terrible interruption."

■

President Reagan explains that the latest Beirut bombing was actually the fault of Jimmy Carter, who he claims presided over "the near-destruction of our intelligence capability." Carter, unable to hide his contempt, notes Reagan's repeated efforts "to blame his every mistake and failure on me and others who served before him."

9/28 Soviet Foreign Minister Andrei Gromyko takes Nancy Reagan aside during a White House reception and says, "Every night, whisper 'peace' in your husband's ear." The First Lady reportedly responds, "I'll also whisper it in your ear." No further details on these sleeping arrangements are forthcoming.

9/30 In an editorial signed by owner Walter H. Annenberg—at whose Palm Springs estate the Reagans have seen in the New Year for the past quarter century—*TV Guide* urges its readers to re-elect the President.

OCTOBER 1984

In which the President finally acts his age

10/1 Patti Davis begins work in a small role on the daily prime time syndicated soap opera, *Rituals*.

10/2 DONOVAN INDICTED AND GIVEN A LEAVE TO DEFEND HIMSELF
BUSINESS DEALINGS CITED
LABOR SECRETARY SAYS CRIMINAL INVESTIGATION IN THE BRONX IS 'OBVIOUSLY PARTISAN'
—*The New York Times*

■

"Make no mistake about it, this President is in charge. He is in touch, he is a strong leader. I saw it when he met with Gromyko the other day. I was there."
—George Bush boasting that President Reagan actually participated in a conversation with a foreign dignitary

"When baffled by a third terrorist attack in Lebanon, Reagan clumsily talks about kitchen remodeling and blames a fictitious cutback in U.S. government intelligence operations. This is his own government he is talking about. He has not a clue how it works."
—Columnist Lars-Erik Nelson

10/3 Complaining that he'd been "singled out" and "taken to the cleaners," George Bush acknowledges that he recently paid $198,000 in back taxes and interest after an audit of his 1981 tax return. And why hadn't he revealed this before, especially in light of Ferraro's problems? "You didn't ask me about it."

■

A House Intelligence Committee report finds "no logical explanation" for the lapse in security at the embassy in Beirut, since State Department and embassy officials had plenty of reason to suspect that a bombing attempt was not only possible but probable.

■

President Reagan takes part in a dress rehearsal for Sunday's debate, with David Stockman playing the part of a very aggressive Walter Mondale—so aggressive that he provokes Reagan into shouting, "Shut up!" Afterward, the President tells him, "You better send me some flowers, because you've been nasty to me."

10/4 "I'm legally and every other way, emotionally, entitled to be what I want to be and that's what I want to be and that's what I am."
—George Bush explaining why he considers himself a Texan even though he was born in Massachusetts, grew up in Connecticut, lives in Washington and pays taxes in Maine

10/5 Larry Speakes is asked if President Reagan has read the House report on the latest Beirut truck bombing. "I don't think he's read the report in detail," he says. "It's five-and-a-half pages, double-spaced."

An ABC News/*Washington Post* poll shows President Reagan ahead of Walter Mondale by a margin of 55%–37%, with a lead of at least ten points in 47 states.

■

Unaware that her *NBC News Digest* segment is airing four minutes early, Jennifer McLogan is televised combing her hair in front of a mirror and complaining about how it looks.

10/6 John Zaccaro tells *Redbook* he intends to sit in on Cabinet meetings if his wife is elected Vice President. "I think I would insist on being there," he says. "Even if they didn't like it, I would sit in."

■

President Reagan—who has not had a press conference in over 10 weeks—says that if reelected, his administration "will continue to be as responsive as possible to the public through the media."

10/7 "I don't like a guy who admits he will raise taxes."
—Ohio medical student Lee Szykowny explaining her rejection of Walter Mondale

■

In their first debate in Louisville, Walter Mondale clearly beats President Reagan, who terrifies viewers by demonstrating how he answers questions when his wife isn't standing next to him. In the course of 90 minutes, the President:

● Talks about a law he signed in California as if it had been signed by his Democratic predecessor
● Reprises his hit line, "There you go again," only to have it thrown back in his face by Mondale, who knows he won't be able to resist repeating it and is ready with a stinging rejoinder
● Blanks out completely in the middle of an answer, stalling for a mini-eternity—"The system is still where it was with regard to the . . . uh . . . the . . . uh . . . the . . . uh . . . the . . . uh . . ."—until he comes up, who

knows how, with the missing word, "progressivity"

- Claims that the increase in poverty "is a lower rate of increase than it was in the preceding years before we got here," though in fact it is higher
- Explains that a good bit of the defense budget goes for "food and wardrobe," becoming the first US President to so refer to military uniforms
- Admits, as he prepares to deliver his closing statement, "I'm all confused now."

Afterward, a frantic Nancy Reagan confronts White House aides, demanding, "What have you done to Ronnie?"

10/8 Barbara Bush points out that, unlike Geraldine Ferraro, she makes no pretense of playing down the family wealth, adding, "No poor boy stuff like that $4 million—I can't say it, but it rhymes with rich." She later fails to convince reporters that the unspoken word was "witch." Meanwhile, Ferraro asks an aide, "Why is that nice old lady calling me a bitch?"

■

The Burning Bed, an NBC TV movie starring Farrah Fawcett as a battered wife who torches her husband's gas-soaked bed, provokes unfortunate reactions from three viewers: a battered wife in Chicago shoots her husband, a Massachusetts man beats his wife senseless and a Milwaukee man sets fire to his.

10/9 FITNESS ISSUE
NEW QUESTION IN RACE: IS OLDEST U.S. PRESIDENT NOW SHOWING HIS AGE?
REAGAN DEBATE PERFORMANCE INVITES OPEN SPECULATION ON HIS ABILITY TO SERVE
CHOPPED LOGS, SAWING WOOD
—The *Wall Street Journal* heralding a tidal wave of stories in which the media misdirects its attention to the President's age, rather than to the more pertinent area of his intelligence

"I'll challenge him to an arm wrestle any time."
—President Reagan attempting to shift the focus from his brain to his biceps

"I think they both looked tired at the end. Mondale's makeup was beginning to drip."
—Maureen Reagan assessing the debate at a White House luncheon
■

After a week on the show—during which she repeatedly failed to make her morning call, complained about her makeup and wardrobe and refused to pose for publicity shots—Patti Davis is fired from *Rituals*.

10/10 "She's too bitchy."
—Bush aide Peter Teeley assessing the Ferraro personality
■

"I'm here for drugs."
—Nancy Reagan admonishing reporters not to ask political questions at a Georgia press conference announcing a drug-awareness program

Still defensive about his debate performance, President Reagan says, "With regard to the age issue and everything, if I had as much makeup on as he did, I'd have looked younger, too." He goes on to make the surprising claim that he not only went makeup-free during the debate, but "I never did wear it. I didn't wear it when I was in pictures."

10/11 "Well, frankly, I know I made him up."
—G.E. *Theater* makeup artist Howard Smit, who, like *Death Valley Days* makeup man Del Acevedo, suggests that President Reagan misremembers the distant past

"He came by and shook hands afterward. . . . It certainly looked like more than just a tan."
—Debate panelist James Weighart, suggesting that Reagan misremembers the immediate past

"I believe he was wearing makeup at the Waterbury rally, no question about it."
—Mayor Edward Bergin recalling a recent presidential visit to Connecticut

■

REAGAN 'MENTALLY ALERT,' DOCTOR SAYS
WHITE HOUSE SEEKS TO BLUNT HEALTH ISSUE
—*The Washington Post*

■

"He was brutalized by a briefing process that didn't make any sense. The man was absolutely smothered by extraneous material."
—Sen. Paul Laxalt, citing overpreparation as the cause of President Reagan's dismal debate performance

"Since when is it considered cruel and unusual punishment to expect the President to learn the facts he needs to govern?"
—Geraldine Ferraro

■

Geraldine Ferraro and George Bush debate in Philadelphia, with Ferraro putting on a surprisingly low-key performance and Bush an alarmingly animated one. Since the culture values noise and movement over quiet reason, the instant media analysis gives him the victory, though it's hard to find anything he said to earn it. Quite the contrary:

"Almost every place you can point, contrary to Mr. Mondale's—I gotta be careful here—but contrary of how he goes around just saying everything bad. If somebody sees a silver lining, he finds a big black cloud out there. I mean, right on, whine on, harvest moon!"
—George Bush failing to display the calm stability one looks for in a world leader

"Let me help you with the difference, Mrs. Ferraro, between Iran and the embassy in Lebanon. . . . We went to Lebanon to give peace a chance . . . and we did. We saw the formation of a government of reconciliation and for somebody to suggest, as our two opponents have, that these men died in shame—they better not tell the parents of those young Marines."
—George Bush introducing the fatuous charge that Mondale and Ferraro have dishonored the memories of the slain Marines by attacking administration policies responsible for their deaths

"Let me just say, first of all, that I almost resent, Vice President Bush, your patronizing attitude that you have to teach me about foreign policy. . . . And let me say further that no one has ever said that those young men who were killed through the negligence of this administration and others ever died in shame."
—Geraldine Ferraro, not quite confident enough to own her resentment

"I don't think it's winnable. I was quoted wrong, obviously, 'cause I never thought that."
—George Bush denying that he told journalist Robert Scheer that he thought nuclear war is "winnable," though Scheer has him on a 1980 tape saying just that

"I wish everybody could have seen that one—the President, giving the facts to Gromyko in all of these nuclear meetings. *Excellent*, right on top of that subject matter. And I'll bet you that Gromyko went back to the Soviet Union saying, 'Hey, listen, this President is calling the shots. We'd better move.' "

—George Bush, treating the President's alleged ability to engage a foreign leader in a discussion as an accomplishment worthy of special praise

10/12　"We tried to kick a little ass last night. Whoops! Oh, God, he heard me! Turn that thing off!"

—George Bush whispering his analysis of the debate to a New Jersey longshoreman, then noticing that his remark has been picked up by a live mike

■

"Let's see if I've got one for me."

—Last words of TV actor Jon-Erik Hexum who, seriously underestimating the damage potential of a blank cartridge from a .44 Magnum, jokingly fires one into his head

10/14　"Whatever it is they know about Reagan, it is certainly something they don't want us to find out."

—David Broder on the President's overly protective aides

10/15　"What am I supposed to order?"

—President Reagan to an aide at a McDonald's campaign stop in Tuscaloosa

■

"Now, think about that for a minute. You fire the missiles. They come out of the submarine holes. They go through the water. They go through the air for several thousand miles. And then you decide you didn't want to fire them. So they stop. And then like a movie rolling backwards, the missile backs up, goes down through the water and back to the submarine holes."

—Walter Mondale encouraging voters to contemplate the fact that the man with his

finger on the button said nuclear missiles launched from submarines can be called back, though Reagan now claims he "never said any such thing"

■

The Associated Press reports the existence of a CIA-prepared manual advising Nicaraguan rebels how to blackmail unwilling citizens into supporting their cause, how to arrange the deaths of fellow rebels to create martyrs and how to kidnap and kill (or, as the manual puts it, "neutralize") government officials.

10/16　George Bush pulls out a dictionary in his ludicrous effort to prove that the Democratic ticket maligned the murdered Marines. " 'Humiliation: shame, disgrace and degradation,' " he crows. "Webster's equates humiliation with . . . deep shame. . . . Accusing young men of dying without a purpose and for no reason is, in the lexicon of the American people, a shame. . . . I said our opponents suggested our Marines died in shame. That was and is an accurate statement of the case."

Mondale suggests that Bush "doesn't have the manhood to apologize."

10/18   Defending George Bush's assertion that Mondale and Ferraro had implied that the 241 Marines killed in Beirut had "died in shame," press secretary Peter Teeley says, "You can say anything you want during a debate, and 80 million people hear it." And what if the print media can prove that he lied? "So what? Maybe 200 people read it or 2,000 or 20,000."

■

A senior administration official says President Reagan did not know about the assassination manual until "after it appeared in the newspaper yesterday."

■

The *New York Post* reports that Sheila Devin, who has been charged with promoting prostitution by running a $1,000-a-night call girl ring, is really Sydney Biddle Barrows, a *Mayflower* descendant to be known forevermore as the "Mayflower Madam."

10/19   "The idea that the public has come to feel that they have a vested interest in protecting him is fascinating to me."
—CBS's Lesley Stahl on negative reaction to news reports critical of President Reagan

■

"Wouldn't it be much more honest if Mondale bluntly accused Reagan of being an addled, confused old coot? I'm sure he believes it, as do many Democrats. That's really their main campaign message. So why not just get it out in the open?"
—Columnist Mike Royko

■

"Why aren't we talking about these hos-

tages? . . . Why is it allowed to stand when Ronald Reagan says America won't have hostages again? . . . Are we bored with hostages now?"
—Lucille Levin, wife of one of the three Americans kidnapped by Lebanese terrorists in March, bemoaning the media's failure to remind the public of how tough the President talked when he took office

10/20   "I don't know which possibility is worse . . . a President who doesn't know what his government is doing or a President knowing of this illegal action and approving it."
—Walter Mondale on President Reagan's professed ignorance of the CIA manual

10/21   At the second Reagan/Mondale debate in Kansas City, the President successfully delivers an obviously rehearsed one-liner—"I will not make age an issue in this campaign. I am not going to exploit for political purposes my opponent's youth and inexperience"—and thereby puts an end to fears about his recently displayed senility.

So determined are voters to ignore his flaws that not even his observation that Armageddon could come "the day after tomorrow" (a comment that prompts Nancy to gasp, "Oh, no!") or his almost incoherent closing statement (something about a time capsule and a drive down the Pacific Coast Highway) can dissuade them.

10/22   A TIE GOES TO THE GIPPER
IN A CLOSE DEBATE, MONDALE SCORES POINTS BUT REAGAN PROTECTS HIS LEAD
—*Time*

■

REAGAN WINS A DRAW
MONDALE LANDS SOME PUNCHES, BUT DOESN'T SCORE THE KNOCKOUT HE WAS HOPING FOR
—*Newsweek*

10/23   The Christic Institute releases a statement from close to 100 religious leaders who find President Reagan's belief in the imminence of Armageddon "profoundly disturbing."

10/24 "Everybody who has ever thought for more than two minutes about the nuclear dilemma knew that. If you didn't know that, you didn't know what the subject even was."
—*The Washington Post,* scoffing at President Reagan's debate claim that Soviet dependence on land-based missiles came as a surprise to many in his administration

■

"You can't call them back! You can't call them back! You can't call them back!"
—Hecklers scoffing at President Reagan's notion about recalling nuclear missiles

■

"If I could find a way to dress up in his tax program, I could scare the devil out of people on Halloween."
—President Reagan campaigning in Ohio

10/25 "Mondale don't know nothing, and not only that, but the woman running against you, I don't know her name and I don't want to know her name."
—George Bush supporter greeting the candidate

■

CIA Director William Casey writes Congress to explain that the "thrust and purpose" of the CIA manual was to improve the effectiveness of the Nicaraguan rebels in "face-to-face communication."

■

"I read every comic strip in the paper."
—President Reagan, who had no time to read the five-and-a-half-page report on the latest Beirut bombing

10/26 Dr. Leonard Bailey of the Loma Linda University Medical Center transplants the heart of a seven-month-old baboon into a 12-day-old infant known as "Baby Fae." She survives for 20 more days.

■

"I think Mr. Mondale in this last few weeks

has been the most negative guy that I ever heard. The election is this, the Great Communicator against the Great Depressor and our man, our President, is going to make it. . . . We are going for the gold."
—George Bush campaigning in Kentucky

10/27 "Let me assure you of one thing: the United States under this administration will never—*never*—let terrorism or fear of terrorism determine its foreign policy."
—George Bush

10/28 "Mr. Reagan's ignorance about the Soviet Union and his air-headed rhetoric on the issues of foreign policy and arms control have reached the limit of tolerance and have become an embarrassment to the U.S. and a danger to world peace."
—*The Chicago Tribune* endorsing—yes, endorsing—the President

10/29 *Doonesbury* news reporter Roland Hedley, Jr., announces this is the day George Bush "will formally place his embattled manhood in a blind trust."

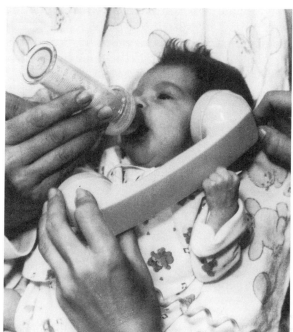

HERE'S WHAT THE CRITICS ARE SAYING ABOUT GEORGE BUSH

"Should we send some Valium up to the podium?"
—San Francisco voter at a Bush rally

"He has so manfully converted himself into the model of a vice president that the very sight of him sets the beholder to praying for the good health of the President. . . . By will, energy, and the suppression of every impulse of shame, he has transformed himself into an Ivy League cheerleader, the perfect gentleman on his way to being the perfect idiot."
—Columnist Murray Kempton

"Sort of a Boy Scout with a hormone imbalance."
—GOP analyst Kevin Phillips

"He is the only American statesman whose portrait is an authentic classic of Western Art, being of course by Paul Klee and entitled *The Twittering Machine*."
—Murray Kempton

"Every woman's first husband."
—Barbara Ehrenreich and Jane O'Reilly in *The Wall Street Journal*

"He seems to reveal himself, as all viewers of *Dallas* will long since have noted, as the Cliff Barnes of American politics—blustering, opportunistic, craven and hopelessly ineffective all at once."
—*Washington Post* editorial

■
60 Minutes' DIANE SAWYER
Her career is tough on her love life (though she's dated Beatty)—the dilemma is marriage and kids
—*People*

10/31 India's prime minister Indira Gandhi is shot to death at her home by two Sikh members of her personal bodyguard.

NOVEMBER 1984

In which the series is renewed, and a bit player demands a bigger part

11/1 "I'm for Mr. Reagan—blindly."
—George Bush campaigning in New York

"He said he supports the President blindly. I think that's about the best way to do it."
—Walter Mondale

11/2 "Under this President's strong and principled leadership, America is back with pride, patriotism and prosperity. We're Number One, and there's a lot of idiots who don't know that."
—George Bush responding to hecklers at a New Jersey rally

■
After a last meal of Cheez Doodles and Coca-Cola, 51-year-old Velma Barfield is executed in North Carolina for murdering her boyfriend by poisoning his beer. Nine minutes after she is declared dead, her body is brought to a waiting ambulance, where a donor-transplant

team tries in vain to restart her heart in order to save her kidneys. Announces the *New York Post*: "GRANNY EXECUTED IN HER PINK PAJAMAS."

11/3   President Reagan explains that the word "neutralize" in the CIA manual—which he, of course, has not read—merely meant "remove from office," not "assassinate." And how does one remove an unwanted official? "You just say to the fellow that is sitting there in the office, 'You're not in the office anymore.'"

11/4   President Reagan, whose last press conference was in July, claims that if you counted up all the questions he took on his way on and off Air Force One—just since Labor Day!—it would add up to *six* news conferences. "I think that that sort of belies the fact that I'm in a cocoon," he says, "and that I am not available to the media."

■

Activist Mitch Snyder ends his 51-day hunger strike in exchange for the administration's promise to renovate a squalid, rat-infested 800-bed homeless shelter. An official insists that the White House decision had nothing to do with the fact that a story about Snyder was about to run on *60 Minutes*.

11/5   Nancy Reagan gets out of her Sacramento hotel bed to get a blanket and, not realizing the bed is on a raised platform, pitches forward and bashes her head on a chair, forming an egg-sized lump at her hairline. She remains wobbly for days.

■

"Just look at the choice. Gerry Ferraro or George Bush. It's a choice between someone who's grown during the campaign and someone who's shrunk."
—Walter Mondale on the last day of the campaign in Los Angeles

■

"And now, for the last time in the campaign that I can say it, because I know it drives a certain candidate up the wall, I'm going to say

it, and that is, you ain't seen nothin' yet."
—President Reagan addressing his last rally in San Diego

11/6   With a still woozy Nancy Reagan losing her balance at their California polling place, the First Couple cast their ballots. Asked whom he's just voted for, the President smiles, bobs his head and says, "I can't remember his name."

Though Reagan declines to predict it—"I'm cautiously optimistic," he says—Dan Rather announces his re-election at 8:01 P.M. EST. His 525 electoral votes are the most ever won, his 49 states (he loses DC and Minnesota) tie Nixon's 1972 landslide and he takes the popular vote by 59% (54,450,603) to Walter Mondale's 41% (37,573,671).

In Los Angeles, the President—his glassy-eyed wife beside him—declares victory. "America's best days lie ahead," he says, "and you know—you'll forgive me—I'm gonna do it just one more time: You ain't seen nothin' yet!'"

11/7   "Robert Redford. Maybe Walter Cronkite."
—Mondale speech writer Martin Kaplan on who could have beaten Reagan

11/9   The Ethiopian famine, which has been worsening for years, finally catches the attention of the network newscasts.

11/10   The White House announces that two Reagan-ordered investigations have concluded that there was "no violation" of the law when the CIA manual was written for the Nicaraguan rebels.

11/12   Rock's reclusive PRINCE
A rare look inside the secret world of his Royal Badness
—*People*

11/16   The annual White House turkey is presented to President Reagan. As have many of his predecessors, he flaps his wings wildly in the President's face.

11/21 Nancy Reagan tells columnist Betty Beale that the First Couple and adopted son Michael have been experiencing a three-year "estrangement," which explains why the pro-family President has never set eyes on his 19-month-old granddaughter Ashley.

Responds Michael, "I never realized we were estranged. Maybe strange, but not estranged."

11/22 Michael Reagan says that the family rift is "not an estrangement as much . . . as a jealousy Nancy might have toward me and my family, you know, being the son of another marriage." The White House retaliates by citing a family friend's suggestion that Michael "needs some guidance," and rumors circulate that he might be, among other things, a kleptomaniac. Michael calls this "defamation of character," comparing himself to "one of the guys in the Cabinet they're trying to ease out."

11/25 William Schroeder, 52, becomes the second recipient of an artificial heart. He survives for 620 days, though the several strokes he suffers seriously impair the quality of his life.

11/26 John W. Hinckley, Jr., writes to *Newsweek* proposing that he—as a "political prisoner"—be exchanged for internally exiled Soviet dissident Andrei Sakharov. "I would be much safer and happier in the U.S.S.R.," he says. "I think exchanging Hinckley for Sakharov is a fair trade."

11/27 "Hopefully we can get this whole thing solved, but not in the press."
—Michael Reagan appearing on *Today* after being interviewed by *The Washington Post*

"I just want to see this whole thing taken care of, really, in an above-board type of way, outside of the press."
—Michael Reagan minutes later on the *CBS Morning News*

11/28 "He thinks he can keep dumping on us. Now we're fighting back. . . . He's been estranged from all of us."
—Maureen Reagan intruding into the feud

11/29 "Sam, I'm not gonna take any questions in this photo opportunity here. I'm just thinkin' of lookin' pretty for the cameras."
—President Reagan to Sam Donaldson, who had the temerity to ask a question during a picture-taking session

DECEMBER 1984

In which an overwrought New Yorker acts out underground

12/3 "Five Minutes," Bootsy Collins and Jerry Harrison's funk single—with a vocal track comprised of bits and pieces from the President's hilarious bombing joke—begins a 10-week run on the *Billboard* dance chart.

■

A gas leak at a Union Carbide pesticides plant in Bhopal, India, kills 2,000 people in one night, with an eventual death toll of 3,329.

12/4 Jerry Falwell testifies at his $45 million libel trial against Larry Flynt that he "felt like weeping" when he saw a parody ad in *Hustler* quoting him as claiming that he "always got sloshed" before preaching, and that he'd lost his virginity to his mother in an outhouse. Interrogating Flynt in a videotaped deposition, Falwell's lawyer, Norman R. Grutman, asks if he'd intended to harm his client's integrity.

Replies Flynt, "To assassinate it."

12/5 NOW PLAYING: *Beverly Hills Cop.* Producers Don Simpson and Jerry Bruckheimer prove that if you start a movie with a zillion car crashes, blast soulless rock on the soundtrack and hire the nation's favorite black comic to do a bunch of his characters, you can make a lot of money.

12/6 The President meets with six-year-old Kristin Ellis, the March of Dimes poster child. He gives her a jar of jellybeans, and she gives him a black, 12-pound sheep dog puppy. The dog, named Lucky, becomes a regular feature on weekend newscasts as she drags Nancy Reagan across the White House lawn to and from the Camp David helicopter.

12/9 Returning to the White House from a Camp David weekend, President Reagan is asked if there have been any new developments on the Kuwaiti jet hijacked in Iran.

He hesitates. "Nothing new on Iran, no," mutters Nancy.

"No," says the President.

12/13 At the White House Christmas tree lighting ceremony, President Reagan says, "I've talked myself into the Christmas spirit. I'm going to give a gift right now. I'm not going to light the tree, I'm going to let Nancy do it." There follows several seconds of confusion as they are unable to locate the switch. "Where's the button?" asks the President. "Where do we go?" They are told.

12/17 *People* points out that though President Reagan, unlike his predecessors, seems as young as he did when he took office, chief of staff James Baker has visibly aged.

The magazine also reports that it has run 73 photos and 33,205 words on Michael Jackson in 1984.

■

Madonna's "Like a Virgin" begins a six-week run as the nation's favorite song. The singer's kinky sexual image—underwear-as-outerwear topped off with crucifix accessories—comes as a relief to rock fans put off by the fey posturing of Boy George and the asexuality of Michael Jackson.

Her next single, "Material Girl," proves her to be in sync with the national zeitgeist and, with legions of Madonna-Wanna-Be's adopting her look, she realizes her ambition to become the female star of the decade.

12/22 Four black youths are joined in a New York subway car by a tall, skinny white man with thick glasses. As he later tells the story, one of them asks for five dollars, which scares him so much he pulls out his unlicensed gun and shoots all four—firing an extra shot into the back of one, paralyzing him for life—before escaping into the underground tunnels.

12/28 At a fence-mending session with son Michael, the Reagans set eyes on their 20-month-old granddaughter Ashley for the first time. "It was a nice visit," says Nancy afterward. "There are no differences. All is resolved. Everybody loves each other and this is a wonderful way to start the new year."

12/31 Claiming to have acted in self-defense—even though his victims were "armed" only with screwdrivers—Bernhard Goetz, a 37-year-old Manhattan electronics specialist, surrenders to police in Concord, New Hampshire, where he confesses to being the "DEATH WISH SUBWAY GUNMAN."

"I wanted to kill those guys, I wanted to maim those guys, I wanted to make them suffer in every way I could," he says, practically foaming at the mouth. "If I had more bullets I would have shot 'em all, again and again. . . . I was gonna gouge one of the guys' eyes out with my keys afterwards. You can't understand this. I know you can't understand this. That's fine."

He three times suggests to police that they "put a bullet in my head."

POP QUIZ

1 Which mini-series featured the classic line, "Which one of you bitches is my mother?"
a V
b Hollywood Wives
c Lace
d The Winds of War

2 Three of these were earnest films about people struggling to save their farms. Which one was a mindless exercise in right-wing paranoia involving a Soviet invasion of the US?
a Country
b Places in the Heart
c Red Dawn
d The River

3 True or false? The National Transportation Safety Board referred to plane crashes as "controlled flights into terrain."

4 Who is Edwin Thomas?
a The man who arranged for the sale of Ed Meese's San Diego home, and who was then named Undersecretary of the Interior
b The chairman of the bank that kept loaning Ed Meese money even though he was 15 months behind in his mortgage payments, and who was then named an alternate US delegate to the UN
c The man who arranged $60,000 in loans for Ed Meese, and who was then appointed to the US Postal Service Board of Governors
d The man who loaned Ed Meese's wife, Ursula, $15,000 interest free to buy Biotech stock, and who was then named to head the San Francisco office of the General Services Administration

5 Which movie featured a scene in which a man's heart was pulled out of his chest?
a *The Terminator*
b *Ghostbusters*
c *Indiana Jones and the Temple of Doom*
d *Splash*

6 Which of these actually appeared on TV?
a *Ich Bin Ein Schmuck,* a *60 Minutes* segment about New York mayor Ed Koch's trip to the Berlin Wall
b *Apocryphal Now,* a devastating ABC News exposé of President Reagan's hard-to-prove war stories
c *Of Meese and Memory,* a CBS documentary examining the suspicious number of things the Attorney General–designate has forgotten
d A scene from *Hellcats of the Navy* at the Republican convention

7 What controversy disrupted academic life at New Jersey's Bound Brook High School?
a Should students be allowed to listen to their Walkmans in class?
b Should students be allowed to wear a single white glove in imitation of Michael Jackson?
c Should break dancing be allowed on school property?
d Why were students killing themselves?

8 What was the point of the Reagan ad featuring the bear in the woods?
a We have to protect the environment
b We have to be afraid of the Soviets
c Homeless people don't have it so bad
d We have to make sure animals don't escape from zoos

Match the newsmaker with his/her news.
9 Mollie Wilmot
10 Lee Iacocca
11 R. Foster Winans
12 Michael Kinsley
13 Clara Peller
14 Carl Lewis
15 Ed Koch
___**a** "Wrote" book-length self-justification disguised as best-selling autobiography
___**b** Leaked inside information obtained through job at *The Wall Street Journal* to male lover
___**c** Said "Where's the beef?" before Walter Mondale did
___**d** Explained that a "gaffe" occurs "not when a politician lies, but when he tells the truth"
___**e** Found that a huge freighter crashed through the sea wall of Palm Beach domicile, where it stayed for months
___**f** "Wrote" memoir boasting of inflicting pain on others
___**g** Was first Olympic athlete to sport Grace Jones haircut

ANSWERS
1-c, 2-c, 3-True, 4-d, 5-c, 6-d, 7-b, 8-b, 9-e, 10-a, 11-b, 12-d, 13-c, 14-g, 15-f

JANUARY 1985

In which the President opens the new season with a special episode

1/2   William Clark resigns as Secretary of the Interior, becoming the first of the Reagan inner circle to go home to California.

1/4   DEAVER TO LEAVE WHITE HOUSE POST FOR PRIVATE LIFE
   AIDE CLOSEST TO THE REAGANS CITES THE COST OF LIVING—NO WORD ON SUCCESSOR
   —*The New York Times*

1/7   Nancy Reagan tells *Time* she has deliberately altered "the gaze" she uses to stare raptly at her husband "because there was so much talk about it and it was kind of ridiculed."

■

   Announcing, "I found you someone your own age to play with," Michael Deaver informs President Reagan that White House chief of staff James Baker and Treasury Secretary Donald Regan have decided to swap jobs. The President nods amiably.

1/8   Richard Nixon is reported to be in "excruciating pain" suffering from "the worst case of shingles" his doctor has ever seen.

1/9   President Reagan concludes his 27th press conference—his first in almost six months—by urging reporters to "get together and find some way in which I don't have to leave so many hands in the air." No one dares suggest increasing the frequency of such events.

■

   With unlikely hero Bernhard Goetz back home, WNBC-TV airs an exclusive interview with the waitress who served him lunch in a New Jersey diner. "*What* did he have to eat?" the reporter asks breathlessly. "A turkey sandwich on whole wheat toast with lettuce and tomato," comes the reply, "and a glass of orange juice."

1/10   One of Bernhard Goetz's victims explains that the screwdrivers he and his friends were carrying were intended not to intimidate subway riders, but to rob arcade game machines.

1/13   President Reagan is reported to have recently spent part of a Sunday reading a 17-page briefing paper on arms control. And, as if that wasn't enough, he even "made a large number of marginal notations."

1/14   Nancy Reagan insists that new reports of her husband's disengagement are "absolutely untrue." And what of the Regan/Baker job swap, worked out without Presidential consultation? "Yes," she says, "but he was the one who made the decision to accept it. He could have said no."

■

   Former Miss America Phyllis George—who has no discernible journalistic experience—becomes co-anchor of the *CBS Morning News*. "So far," she says after her first hour, "I've enjoyed it."

1/17   Sen. Alfonse D'Amato (R-NY)—no stranger to pandering—expresses solidarity with Bernhard Goetz. "I'm afraid to get in that subway system even when I'm with my bodyguard," he says, "and my bodyguard is afraid."

■

   With Frank Sinatra in town to produce and direct the inaugural galas, *The Washington Post* runs a piece recapping the sleazy glories of the Rat Pack. When reporters try to interview him later, he is not a happy man. "You read the *Post* this afternoon?" he snarls, eyes blazing and index finger waving. "You're all dead, every one of you. You're all dead."

1/20 Not content to have his inauguration televised, President Reagan's aides inject him into the Super Bowl coin toss. The live feed linking him to Stanford is open ten minutes before he goes on the air, enabling satellite dish owners to spy on the leader of the free world as he:

- Practices the coin flip three times—"It is heads. . . . It is tails"—so he's prepared for all possibilities
- Reveals a really neat idea a friend of his had—"Frank Sinatra had a recommendation, instead of tossing the coin, what would have been a lot better. You'd have had me outdoors throwing out the ball. I would have thrown it—a little artwork of maybe a ball going across a map—and out there, one of them catching a ball, as if it's gone all the way across the United States. How about that?"
- Stands immobile, almost deflated, as the minutes tick by, as if he doesn't quite exist when the camera's not on.

Finally, he gets his cue and—suddenly animated—he flips the coin. "It is tails!" he announces, adding some banality about how all the players should do their best. The network cuts away and, somewhat forlornly, he resumes the less satisfying non-televised portion of his life.

1/21 With the inaugural parade cancelled due to extreme cold, several high school bands perform for the Reagans at an indoor arena, where Nancy forgets to introduce her "roommate," then overreacts to this omission in Edvard Munch–like horror.

1/24 The jury in Israeli official Ariel Sharon's libel trial against *Time*—which accused him of encouraging the 1982 massacre of Palestinians in Lebanon—rules that while the magazine did indeed print a false and defamatory paragraph, it did so unknowingly and is not guilty. Both sides claim victory.

1/25 A grand jury indicts Bernhard Goetz for illegal possession of a weapon. Charges of attempted murder are not brought.

1/28 Michael Jackson joins dozens of the top names in pop music at a Hollywood sound studio to record the anti-famine anthem "We Are the World," which he wrote with Lionel Richie. When the video is released, Jackson is the only singer whose solos have been reshot so he can be seen singing all alone.

■

MEL GIBSON
THE SEXIEST MAN ALIVE
—*People*

■

Lawyers for Ed Meese—renominated to be Attorney General—reveal that the Office of Government Ethics found him in violation of federal ethical standards.

1/30 "If there were any doubt in my mind that four years from now you could look back

and say, 'Ed Meese has fulfilled the standards that I've set for this office,' then I would retire right now and withdraw."
—Ed Meese assuring the Judiciary Committee that his days of playing fast and loose with ethics are behind him

■

Joining the exodus of first-term appointees, UN ambassador Jeane Kirkpatrick tells President Reagan she's leaving, too.

■

Redskins star John Riggins gets drunk at a Washington dinner. "Come on, Sandy baby, loosen up," he tells his tablemate, Justice Sandra Day O'Connor. "You're too tight." He then goes to sleep on the floor, snoring loudly during a speech by George Bush.

FEBRUARY 1985

In which the Nation gets a new top cop

2/4 Addressing a convention of religious broadcasters, President Reagan defends his arms build-up, citing Luke 14:31 to verify that "the scriptures are on our side in this." Then, for the benefit of the Jews in the audience, he describes how much he liked looking out over Lafayette Park at "the huge menorah, celebrating the Passover season."

■

Sen. William Cohen (R-ME) and Sen. William Roth (R-DE) reveal that the Navy has been paying $640 each for toilet seats that sell to consumers for $25.

2/5 "Birthday? Oh, you mean the 35th anniversary of my 39th birthday?"
—President Reagan on his upcoming 74th

2/6 "Salad Bars: A Hidden Killer."
—Sweeps-month local news exposé on New York's WABC-TV

2/13 President Reagan defends offshore drilling to a Santa Barbara reporter. "You've got that whole expanse of ocean," he says. "It isn't as if you were looking at the ocean through a little frame, and now somebody put something in the way." And, anyway, he has a solution. "We've got a lot of freighters . . . up in mothball. Why don't we bring down some and anchor them between the shore and the oil derrick? And then the people would see a ship, and they wouldn't find anything wrong with that at all."

■

Actor Sean Penn has his first date with Madonna, whom he met on the set of her "Material Girl" video.

2/15 NOW PLAYING: *Lost in America*. Albert Brooks (who wrote the film with Monica Johnson before anyone ever heard of Gary Hartpence) presents the first—and definitive— yuppie satire, about a successful couple in their mid-30s who decide to drop out of society *à la Easy Rider* and look for America in a luxury Winnebago. Brooks' "nest egg" speech is the funniest movie rant of the '80s.

2/17 Pursuing the strategy many urged him to adopt during the Vietnam War, William Westmoreland withdraws his libel suit against CBS and declares victory. He later contends that the naked girl shown running down the road in a famous Vietnam War–era photo had not been napalmed, but had been burned by a hibachi.

2/21 At his 28th press conference, President Reagan says he is not seeking the overthrow of the Sandinista regime—he'd be satisfied "if they'd say 'uncle' " to the contras and abdicate.

2/22 "By accepting unsecured loans from a man he later helped appoint to a federal position; by accepting a promotion in the Army Reserves that smacked of preferential treatment; and by asking that a check he had already deposited be altered after discovering that the original purpose of the check might be illegal, Meese has demonstrated a clear lack of judgment and an appalling indifference to the appearance of impropriety."
— John Glenn in *The Washington Post*, urging Senate rejection of Ed Meese, who is confirmed the next day

2/28 Defending the President's decision to abolish the Small Business Administration, David Stockman is shown a two-year-old tape of Reagan praising the agency. "We at the White House," says Stockman, "have come to enjoy watching old films of the President."

MARCH 1985

In which the President shows how much he's forgotten about the American Revolution

3/1 Desperate to win contra aid, President Reagan says the Nicaraguan rebels are "the moral equal of our Founding Fathers." Historical novelist Howard Fast calls this "an explosion of such incredible ignorance that . . . he is not fit for public office of any kind."

3/6 "Nuclear war would be the greatest tragedy, I think, ever experienced by mankind in the history of mankind."
— President Reagan demonstrating his awareness of just how serious it would be if he pushed the button

■

Geraldine Ferraro's Diet Pepsi ad—for which she is reported to have been paid over $500,000—premieres on *The Fall Guy.*

3/8 A second benign polyp is found in the presidential colon. Says Larry Speakes, "There is no clinical evidence that this kind of polyp ever becomes malignant."

3/13 President Reagan—whose fondness for talking tough is exceeded only by his love of getting laughs—does both as he wraps himself in Clint Eastwood's aura and declares, "I have only one thing to say to the tax increasers: 'Go ahead and make my day.'"

■

George Bush attends the funeral of Soviet leader Konstantin Chernenko.

3/15 Labor Secretary Raymond Donovan resigns after being ordered to stand trial on fraud and larceny charges.

■

"Molinari, you creep! Cut out this crap!"
— Sen. Alfonse D'Amato refusing to believe that the person on the other end of the phone is actually President Reagan

3/18 ABC is purchased by Capital Cities Communications for more than $3.5 billion, the largest non-oil acquisition in corporate history and the first time a network has been sold.

■

"More than twice as many people are fighting in the field right now against the Nicaraguan communist regime as fought against Somoza."
— President Reagan trying to garner support for contra aid

3/19 "Nearly three times as many men are fighting the communists right now as the Sandinistas had fighting Somoza."
— President Reagan trying even harder for contra aid

3/20 Rupert Murdoch enters the movie business, buying 50% of the Twentieth Century–Fox studio.

3/21 *20/20*'s Geraldo Rivera attempts to shed some light on the Bernhard Goetz debate by re-enacting the subway shootings, while Barbara Walters shares Chinese take-out with the gunman in his apartment.

A week later, Goetz—who is being seen, in the wake of reports about his vicious New Hampshire confession, as less a hero than kind of a creep—is indicted for attempted murder, after all.

■

At his 29th press conference, President Reagan explains that he has no intention of visiting a concentration camp site during his upcoming visit to West Germany. To do so, he explains, would impose an unpleasant guilt trip on a nation where there are "very few alive that remember even the war, and certainly none of them who were adults and participating in any way." Though this stunning ignorance of the actuarial tables is displayed to a roomful of reporters, not one challenges it.

3/25 "You like me! Right now! You like me!"
—Sally Field accepting her Best Actress Oscar for *Places in the Heart*

3/26 General Electric—the corporation that, by hiring Ronald Reagan as its spokesman in the '50s, is most responsible for him being where he is today—is indicted on 108 counts of fraud for falsely billing the Pentagon for over $800,000. It pleads guilty.

3/29 NOW PLAYING: *Desperately Seeking Susan*. Director Susan Seidelman's insistence on casting the then-unknown Madonna pays off, as her presence transforms a slick New Wave farce about amnesia into a cultural event and confirms the singer's ultra-superstar status as she mounts her first concert tour. "Into the Groove" becomes the all-time best-selling 12″ dance single.

3/31 "I find the 'drama' of it all some of the hippest and funniest stuff done in America today. . . . Its camp freshness fits perfectly into NBC's late-night mold."
—*Saturday Night Live* producer Dick Ebersol announcing plans to start airing monthly wrestling specials

APRIL 1985

In which the President shows how much he's forgotten about World War II

4/1 EXCLUSIVE: The wedding album of Christie & Billy
A rare interview and personal photos reveal the "chemistry" that bonds Brinkley and her hot rocker, Joel
—*People*

4/2 Nancy Reagan sports a bruise on her chin, reportedly caused by the hyperactive Lucky bashing her with her head during a bath.

4/3 Robert Dornan (R-CA) reveals the "best compliment" he has yet received on the House floor—Henry Hyde (R-IL) said, "If we were Indians in the Plains Wars and you were a cavalry trooper, we would kill you just to drink your blood." This, explains Dornan, was how true warriors showed respect.

4/7 Addressing Easter Sunday worshipers at a Harlem church, Ed Koch claims "it was God that selected me" for the mayoralty of New York.

4/8 Michael Deaver is asked if he has any plans to write a White House memoir. "Never, never," he says. "You can't take a special relationship of trust and then do a kiss-and-tell book."

4/10 Federal officials reveal that the four "unicorns" at the Ringling Bros. circus are goats whose horns have been surgically altered to grow together out of the middle of their heads.

4/11 The White House announces that President Reagan will lay a wreath at the Bitburg, West Germany, military cemetery housing the graves of both American and Nazi soldiers. Oops! Correction: no Americans are buried there.

4/12 Sen. Jake Garn (R-UT) becomes the first lawmaker in space as he joins the crew of the space shuttle *Discovery,* where he serves as a guinea pig for motion-sickness experiments.

4/13 WHITE HOUSE RECONSIDERING REAGAN'S VISIT TO GERMAN WAR GRAVES
—*The New York Times*

4/16 As the contra aid vote approaches, President Reagan claims he "just had a verbal message delivered to me from Pope John Paul, urging us to continue our efforts in Central America." The Vatican quickly issues a denial.

4/17 REAGAN GOING TO DEATH CAMP
—*New York Newsday*

■

"We haven't finished yet."
—Ballet dancer Fernando Bujones to President Reagan, who has stepped on stage with Nancy to thank him

4/18 Michael Deaver—who somehow failed to notice Nazi gravestones last time he was there—is back in West Germany searching for an appropriate concentration camp to add to the President's itinerary. Asks Rep. Pat Schroeder, "What are they looking for? The right light angle?"
Meanwhile, Reagan defends his visit to Bitburg by claiming the German soldiers "were victims, just as surely as the victims in the concentration camps." Says an aide, "Oh my God!"

4/19 Elie Wiesel—fortunate enough to be accepting a medal from the President on the same day *The New York Times* carries the headline "Reagan Likens Nazi War Dead to Concentration Camp Victims"—tells his host, "That place, Mr. President, is not your place. Your place is with the victims of the SS." Reagan puts on his sad face.

■

"[The handicapped] falsely assume that the lottery of life has penalized them at random. This is not so. Nothing comes to an individual that he has not . . . summoned."
—Eileen Marie Gardner, who resigns from President Reagan's Education Department after this quote is exhumed from an article she wrote for the conservative Heritage Foundation

4/22 THE WOMAN WHO CRIED RAPE
Rejected by an Illinois judge, Cathleen Webb tells the full, heart-rending story behind her courtroom lies that sent an "innocent" man to prison
—*People*

4/23 The *Dynasty* craze peaks as the nighttime soap—whose vapid celebration of materialism makes it the quintessential Reagan-era series—becomes America's highest-rated show. With a spinoff starring a hideously toupeed Charlton Heston on the way, the season ends with a cliffhanger so witless—a terrorist massacre at a foreign wedding—that hordes of viewers suddenly find the whole thing moronic and stop watching.

■

Coca-Cola, which has been selling itself as the less sweet alternative to the surging Pepsi, announces that it is changing its formula to make it—sweeter! Coke chairman Roberto Goizueta calls the switch "the surest move ever made."

4/25 HOUSE DECISIVELY DEFEATS ALL PLANS BY BOTH PARTIES TO AID REBELS IN NICARAGUA
  —*The New York Times*

4/26 257 IN THE HOUSE BID KOHL CANCEL CEMETERY EVENT
  —*The New York Times*

4/27 82 SENATORS URGE REAGAN TO CANCEL HIS BITBURG VISIT
  —*The New York Times*

4/28 Billy Martin is hired for the fourth time as Yankee manager. And why does he think he can get along with George Steinbrenner this time? "We're good friends now. We're closer than we've ever been before."

4/29 President Reagan defends the Bitburg visit as "morally right," adding, "I know all the bad things that happened in that war. I was in uniform for four years myself." He does not claim to have filmed the death camps.

MAY 1985

In which the Nation re-affirms its preference for bare-chested grunting

---

5/5 Having atoned in advance with a visit to the Bergen-Belsen death camp, President Reagan spends eight minutes at Bitburg, where cameras are forced to shoot the ceremony from poor angles. He cites a letter from 13-year-old Beth Flom who, he claims, "urged me to lay the wreath at Bitburg cemetery in honor of the fu-

ture of Germany." In fact, she urged him not to go at all. Summing things up, he says, "It's been a wonderful day."

5/7 Nancy Reagan learns the flamenco in Madrid.

MURDOCH TO BUY 7 TV STATIONS; COST $2 BILLION

JOINS FOX CO-PARTNER IN METRO-MEDIA ACCORD
—*The New York Times*

5/8 Opponents of President Reagan's Nicaraguan policies heckle him at the European Parliament. "They haven't been there," he says. "I have." For the record, he has not.

Arriving in Lisbon, President Reagan fails to recognize Portuguese prime minister Mario Soares—whom he has met before—and walks right past him.

Marianne Mele Hall resigns as chairman of the Copyright Royalty Tribunal after it becomes known that a book she worked on in 1982, *Foundations of Sand*, said US blacks "insist on preserving their jungle freedoms, their women, their avoidance of personal responsibility and their abhorrence of the work ethic."

5/10 Having successfully booked the President into a Nazi cemetery and received his diplomat's discount on a BMW, Michael Deaver resigns.

Buddy Ebsen's friend Richard Nixon attends a meeting of the *Barnaby Jones* fan club. "Most clubs are useless, but this one is for fun," says the former President, who liked the show because it "was a good mystery where you knew the good guys from the bad guys." Ebsen says Nixon claims to have seen each episode "at least" three times and committed much of the dialogue to memory.

5/13 A long-running confrontation between Philadelphia police and a radical black cult called MOVE comes to a head when mayor Wilson Goode orders its headquarters bombed. The resulting blaze destroys 61 homes, killing 11. Says one resident, "MOVE in its wildest day never perpetrated anything on our block like what Wilson Goode did."

The mayor defends his strategy as "perfect, except for the fire."

5/15 Following his release from jail after her recantation of her six-year-old rape charge, Gary Dotson and Cathy Crowell Webb make the rounds of the network morning shows.

"What were the first things you said to each other?" asks Joan Lunden on *Good Morning America*.

"Who would you like to see play you in the movie?" asks Jane Pauley on *Today*.

"How about a hug?" asks Phyllis George on the *CBS Morning News*. They decline to embrace.

Explains George later, "I wanted to get the personal side."

5/17 Under some delusion about the career opportunities awaiting him elsewhere, Patrick Duffy appears in his last episode of *Dallas*, in which Bobby, having just spent the night with Pam, is run down and killed by his insanely jealous ex-sister-in-law.

5/20 Private detective John A. Walker is arrested—along with three others, including his brother and son—for conspiring to deliver secret Navy documents to the Soviets. "I'm a celebrity," he declares. "I feel like Eichmann or someone." He gets life.

■

Time Inc. certifies heterosexuality's reclamation of rock, as *People* runs a cover story on Bruce Springsteen's marriage to a model ("Who's the Boss Now?"), while *Time* runs a sultry cover portrait of Madonna ("Why She's Hot").

5/21 MEESE NAMES PANEL TO STUDY HOW TO CONTROL PORNOGRAPHY
—*The New York Times*

5/22 NOW PLAYING: *Rambo: First Blood Part II*. Opening in a record 2,165 theaters, Sylvester Stallone's rewrite of the Vietnam War—"Do we get to win this time?"—grosses $32.5 million in its first six days. Says the star of the increasing monosyllabism of his characters, "I try to eliminate as much dialogue as possible, and I guess *Rambo* is my really best experiment. To me, the most perfect screenplay ever written will be one word."

5/23 President Reagan bestows the Presidential Medal of Freedom—the nation's highest civilian award—on the otherwise rarely paired

Mother Teresa and Frank Sinatra.

5/27 "WITH GREAT PRIDE AND ENTHUSIASM I WISH TO INFORM YOU THAT FILM HAS OPENED SATURDAY 18 MAY.... NEVER A FILM HAS APPEALED TO THE AUDIENCE AS THIS AND NEVER A FILM WAS APPLAUDED DURING SCREENING WITH THIS INTENSITY.... THIS IS DEFINITELY GOING TO BE THE HIGHEST GROSSING FILM IN THE HISTORY OF LEBANON."
—Telegram from the Beirut distributor of *Rambo: First Blood Part II* to the American distributor

5/30 41 ARE KILLED IN BRUSSELS AS BRITONS BATTLE ITALIANS IN A SOCCER RIOT
—*The New York Times*

5/31 MDMA, better known as Ecstasy—a kind of "baby acid" that has become the drug of choice among yuppies desperate for the artificial feeling of well-being it induces—is banned by the government.

6/5   David Stockman observes that if the Securities and Exchange Commission had jurisdiction over the way the executive and legislative branches of government have handled the deficit, "many of us would be in jail."

6/7   NOW PLAYING: *Perfect*. John Travolta's career—already in rickety shape after his *Staying Alive* fiasco with auteur Sylvester Stallone—officially comes to an end with this fatuous celebration of health clubs as the new singles bars. The film is notable for launching the movie career of starstruck *Rolling Stone* editor Jann Wenner, who plays the squat, amoral editor of a once-hip rock publication. Critic Tom Shales calls the film "everything bad about the '80s rolled into one ghastly travesty."

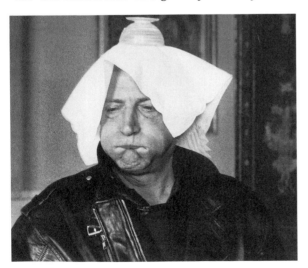

6/10   Claus von Bulow—acquitted at his retrial—tells Barbara Walters he hopes to visit his comatose wife. "I'll have to have someone independent with me," he says, "because, you know, they have said, oh, I might hurt her in the hospital."

A month later, he is seen posing in black leather in *Vanity Fair*, which also features his droll impression of Queen Victoria.

6/11   Nazi war criminal Josef Mengele's son Rolf says a skeleton recently exhumed from a Brazilian grave is indeed that of his father.

6/12   In the wake of Nicaraguan president Daniel Ortega's stupidly timed journey to Moscow, the House reverses itself and votes $27 million in humanitarian aid for the contras. Says Tip O'Neill of President Reagan's obsession with Central America, "He is not going to be happy until he has our Marines and our Rangers down there for a complete victory. He can see himself leading a contingent down Broadway with paper flying out the windows, with a big smile on his face like a kind of Grade-B motion picture actor coming home the conquering hero."

6/14   TWA Flight 847 is hijacked to Beirut by Lebanese Shiites who show they mean business by killing US Marine Robert Dean Stethem, 23, and dumping his body onto the tarmac. With passengers periodically brought forward to meet the press, the 16-day crisis is the first to feature a "hostage spokesman," Texas businessman Allyn Conwell, whose apparent gratitude for his new-found celebrity leads him to express an inappropriate degree of support for his captors' cause.

6/17   A revamped *Us* magazine—presenting what new editor Jann Wenner calls "the wide, wide world of what's hot"—hits the newsstands. Explaining the difference between his all-celebrity publication and its rather more successful rival, Wenner tells a reporter that *People* is "doing the ghetto tree doctor and the nun with herpes." He later says *People* deals with "ghetto nuns and tree surgeons with herpes," explaining that it sounds better the second way.

6/18 William Bradford Reynolds, nominated to the number two post at the Justice Department, apologizes four times to the Senate Judiciary Committee for having been less than candid about his record as head of the Civil Rights Division. "It's not a question of ambiguities," says Sen. Dennis DeConcini (D-AZ). "It's a question of out-and-out bold distortions and untruths that have been told to this committee." His promotion is not approved.

6/19 "Wow. You know, I may turn my head here to Don Regan again. . . . For me to try and off the top of my head bring up some of the other benefits . . . Now, wait a minute."
—President Reagan asking for help after an Indiana businessman erroneously assumes he can explain his own tax plan

"They turned out the lights. That tells me I can't talk anymore."
—President Reagan explaining that he is not allowed to answer any more questions

■

An ABC crew is allowed to interview TWA Flight 847 pilot John Testrake. What does he think will happen if a rescue attempt is made? "I think," says Testrake, speaking from the window of the plane with a gun held to his head, "we would all be dead men."

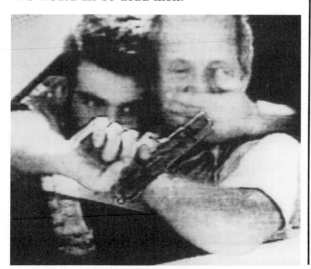

6/25 Henry Kissinger appears on *Nightline* to decry the willingness of the networks to turn over chunks of air time to events orchestrated by the media-savvy TWA terrorists. "If the Nazis had invited networks to Auschwitz to watch people marching off to the gas chambers," he asks, "would it be appropriate news coverage to cover that?"
"Absolutely!" says his stunned friend Ted Koppel. "Can you imagine what the outrage of the world would have been? . . . I can't imagine that you would think otherwise." Kissinger wisely does not pursue his point.

■

Richard Nixon provides an update on his health. "I have fully recovered from the shingles," he says. "There were times when the blisters [on his upper back] would break and I would bleed right through my shirt and suit jackets. I ruined at least four suits."

6/26 NBC announces that actor Mark Lindsay, who had been signed to play John Lennon in a TV movie, has been dropped from the role—at Yoko Ono's insistence—because his real name is Mark Chapman.

6/28 "Good morning, David. Good morning, America."
—Hostage spokesman Allyn Conwell, having a fine time chatting with David Hartman from captivity

6/30 An arrest warrant is issued for Sean Penn in Nashville after he assaults two photographers—beating one with his own camera—while fiancee Madonna looks on. Says one victim, "He went for us like a madman."

■

The 39 hostages—whose captors threw them a farewell party at a seaside hotel—are freed in Beirut.
During a sound check prior to announcing their release, President Reagan says, "Boy, after seeing *Rambo* last night, I know what to do the next time this happens."

Dismissing White House annoyance at the reporting of this latest blurt, ABC bureau chief George Watson says, "He's certainly tempting the hands of electronic fate. The mike is open, the room is completely quiet, everybody in the world is waiting for him to say something, and he says something he doesn't want anybody to hear."

JULY 1985

In which two aging actors make medical headlines

7/4 "What I remember about V-J Day is that Mrs. Nixon and I went to Times Square to celebrate, and I got my pocket picked. Never forgot that! In those days we didn't have a great deal of money. Sort of put a damper on the day."

—Richard Nixon reminiscing to *Time* on the occasion of the 40th anniversary of the end of World War II

■

Yankee fan Joanne Barrett is shot in the wrist during the sixth inning of a game at Yankee Stadium. Police say the shot came from inside the park.

7/6 Nancy Reagan, 64, celebrates her 62nd birthday.

7/8 "We are especially not going to tolerate these attacks from outlaw states run by the strangest collection of misfits, Looney Tunes and squalid criminals since the advent of the Third Reich."

—President Reagan talking tough about terrorism

■

Baptist minister Dwight Wymer begins using a homemade electric stool to teach his Bible students to obey God. He discontinues the tactic when told he will be subject to prosecution if the 12-volt shocks cause any injury.

7/9 David Stockman resigns his position as Budget Director to take a job on Wall Street and write his White House memoir, for which Harper & Row pays him over $2 million.

■

Ed Meese tells the American Bar Association that the authors of the Constitution would find recent Supreme Court decisions affirming the separation of church and state "somewhat bizarre."

7/10 *Playboy* and *Penthouse* both claim to be first on the newsstands with years-old nude photos of Madonna. "I think they're very European," says *Playboy* spokeswoman Elizabeth Norris of her magazine's layout. "She has hair under her arms."

Coca-Cola announces that while it will continue to market the new Coke that everyone hates, it will also bring back the original formula under the brand name "Coca-Cola Classic."

7/12   President Reagan goes to Bethesda Naval Hospital to have the benign polyp found in March removed. His surgeons find yet another polyp, this one pre-cancereous.

Says Nancy to Donald Regan, "Oh, God, Don, not again!"

7/13   Acting President George Bush presides over a seven-hour-and-54-minute mini-administration while a large polyp and two feet of colon are removed from acting President Reagan.

■

Boomtown Rats singer Bob Geldof organizes Live Aid—a 16-hour rock 'n' roll telethon broadcast from London and Philadelphia to 152 countries, and featuring most of the hot acts of the day. The event raises somewhere between $20 and $50 million for Ethiopian famine victims. "Good morning, children of the '80s," says Joan Baez. "This is your Woodstock, and it's long overdue."

Among the bands reuniting for the day are Crosby, Stills, Nash and Young; Led Zeppelin; and Black Sabbath. "Isn't it great to be here?" says Ozzy Osbourne. "Now, here's 'Paranoid.' "

7/15   "The President has cancer."
—Dr. Steven Rosenberg revealing that Reagan's polyp was malignant, though it had not spread

"The polyp had cancer."
—President Reagan

■

An ill-looking Rock Hudson shows up at a Hollywood press conference to help his friend Doris Day promote an upcoming cable show. Ten days later, a hospital in Paris, where the

actor has flown for treatment, announces that he has AIDS.

7/16   Larry Speakes says President Reagan is "champing at the bit" to get back to work. Meanwhile, Nancy—who has decreed that only she and Donald Regan are allowed to visit—brings him a Snoopy jigsaw puzzle.

7/18   President Reagan reacts to his first solid food since surgery by bursting into a recital of "The Cremation of Sam McGee" and "The Shooting of Dan McGrew." Yes, in their entirety.

7/19   George Bush announces that New Hampshire high school teacher Sharon Christa McAuliffe has been chosen as the first "citizen" astronaut. "I'm still kind of floating," she says. "I don't know when I'll come down to earth."

7/22   An arrest warrant is issued in Los Angeles for Ed Meese, who owes $130.50 for an unpaid $10 jaywalking ticket he received in 1980. He pays the fine.

7/29   Despite one of its main engines failing six minutes into its flight—the first malfunction during takeoff in the space shuttle program—the *Challenger* lands safely after an eight-day journey.

7/31   Ryan White, 13, a hemophiliac who contracted AIDS through a blood transfusion, is barred from returning to school in Indiana.

AUGUST 1985

In which the Nation shifts its attention to another part of the presidential anatomy

8/1   With President Reagan sporting a bandage on his nose, Larry Speakes acknowledges that "a small area of irritated skin on the right side of the President's nose was removed." According to presidential physician T. Burton Smith, no biopsy was performed on the "little pimple type of thing." Nancy Reagan reiterates that no biopsy—none!—was performed.

8/5   President Reagan reveals that a biopsy performed on his nose skin proved that the irritation was skin cancer. "I violated all the rules," he says of the pimple. "I picked at it and I squoze it and so forth, and messed myself up a little bit. . . . And then my little friend that I had played with began to come back." While some previous President could conceivably have used the non-word "squoze," it seems certain that none ever referred to a cancerous nose pimple as "my little friend."

■

Ed Meese flies to Arkansas to chop down marijuana stalks for the cameras. Bad weather forces him to settle for posing with a pile of already confiscated plants.

8/6   Larry Speakes—who had minimized the seriousness of the President's nose cancer to the point where he claimed, wrongly, that no anesthesia had been required during its removal—reacts badly when reporters accuse him of misleading them. "If you look very carefully at my words," he says, "you will find that there is a substantial body of accurate information there." Reporters laugh.

8/12   A spokesman for Burt Reynolds announces that, despite ongoing rumors, the actor does not have AIDS.

8/15   *20/20* presents a Geraldo Rivera report on neo-Nazi farmers in the Midwest who blame "Jewish bankers" for their economic woes. During the segment—entitled "Seeds of Hate"—he describes this handful of extremist nuts as an army made up of "ministers of hate" and "preachers of hate" who espouse the "philosophy of hate," a philosophy that he finds "sick" and "malignant." Another nice touch: gunfire crackles on the soundtrack as the groups' violent deeds—including the murder of Alan Berg—are listed.

■

In a speech broadcast worldwide by satel-

POP GOES THE PRESIDENT

"We were being led by a team of people with good intentions and bad ideas, people with all the common sense of Huey, Dewey and Louie."
—President Reagan comparing the Carter administration to Donald Duck's nephews

"You know, when we got to Washington, this country was in the fast lane headed toward economic oblivion. The folks who'd been at the wheel were more reckless than the Dukes of Hazzard."
—Campaigning in Nevada

"The way I see it, if our current tax structure were a TV show, it would either be *Foul-Ups, Bleeps and Blunders* or *Gimme a Break*. If it were a record album, it would be *Gimme Shelter*. If it were a

movie it would be *Revenge of the Nerds* or maybe *Take the Money and Run*. And if the IRS ever wants a theme song, maybe they'll get Sting to do, 'Every breath you take, every move you make, I'll be watching you.'"
—Selling his tax reform program to high school students

"You know, when it comes to this yearly budget process, I keep thinking of that current movie hit, *The Little Shop of Horrors*. Now the budget isn't exactly like the man-eating plant in that movie. It isn't mean, and it isn't green. It doesn't come from outer space. But it does only say one thing: 'Feed me! Feed me! Feed me!'"
—Selling his economic policies

lite, South African leader P. W. Botha rejects any significant tension-easing reforms. President Reagan doesn't bother to watch.

■

Michael Jackson buys publishing rights to the Beatles song catalogue for $47.5 million.

8/16 With TV news helicopters circling overhead, Madonna marries Sean Penn in Malibu. Says Penn of the event weeks later, "I consider myself very human and very moral, and I would have been very excited to see one of those helicopters burn and the bodies inside melt."

8/19 *The New York Times* begins a series exploring baseball's love affair with cocaine. Among the revelations:

- Tim Raines of the Expos would slide into bases head first to protect the vial of coke he carried in his pocket
- Billy Martin searched Yankee players' lockers and bags during games
- Cocaine orders were frequently placed from—and delivered to—the Royals' clubhouse where, according to the dealer, "players talked about baseball while using drugs, and talked about drugs while playing baseball."

Public attention focuses on Pittsburgh, where dealer Curtis Strong—who apparently traveled with the Pirates—is about to stand trial for selling coke to, among others, Dave Parker, Enos Cabell, Lonnie Smith and Keith Hernandez. Strong is convicted.

David Letterman upsets Bryant Gumbel by shouting at him from an NBC window while he tapes a prime time *Today* special in Rockefeller Center. "His sense of humor is horseshit, and I feel sorry for him," says Gumbel, who carries the grudge for years.

YOU REALLY MUST LEARN TO SAY WHAT YOU MEAN, BRYANT

"It's not that I dislike many people. It's just that I don't like many people."

—Bryant Gumbel

"There's something that bothers me about a person who will not blink. I'm serious. Everybody blinks—it's like swallowing—but not Dan. . . . He makes me uncomfortable."

—Bryant Gumbel on Dan Rather

"Jennings is one of those guys who thinks he's a little bit superior."

—On Peter Jennings

". . . Real jerk . . . the worst . . . I feel sorry for him because he has such a glorified opinion of himself."

—On Garrison Keillor

"A damn actor in the White House."

—On President Reagan

"Five minutes with Jeane Kirkpatrick is an eternity."

"There was a great headline in the paper down south the other day . . . 'STALLONE STILL A JERK.' "

"I prefer people less enamored of themselves. I have an aversion to professional celebrities who appear on the cover of *People* every six months, and who run out and do every little cheap gym ad."

—On Cher

"*Everything* Joan does is seen as a step towards something that will benefit her. *Everything.*"

—On Joan Collins

"I'm the guy who did—what's Mick Jagger's girlfriend's name? — I'm the guy who did four parts with her. *You* try that sometime. It's like talking to a window."

—On Jerry Hall

". . . Less a star than he thinks. He's not nice, accommodating, sweet, talkative or cooperative."

—On James Earl Jones

"That buffoon."

—On Mr. T

8/20   Seeking to block economic sanctions against South Africa, Rev. Jerry Falwell calls Bishop Desmond Tutu "a phony" and urges Americans to buy Krugerrands (South African gold coins).

8/22   At the request of the White House, Sylvester Stallone temporarily abandons his plan to present President Reagan with a Rambo poster.

8/24   President Reagan tells an interviewer that the "reformist administration" of South African president P. W. Botha has made significant progress on the racial front. "They have eliminated the segregation that we once had in our own country," says the President, "the type of thing where hotels and restaurants and places of entertainment and so forth were segregated— that has all been eliminated."

8/25   The White House confirms reports that during his oft-recalled days as head of the Screen Actors Guild, President Reagan doubled as an FBI informant (T-10) whose area of expertise was Communist influence in post– World War II Hollywood.

■

"I would consider myself in the forefront of the civil rights movement in the country today.... There is no one who is more adamant in defense of civil rights, no one who is more opposed to discrimination in any form, no one who is more the champion of minorities, and of all citizens for that matter, than I am."
—Ed Meese to David Brinkley, who is too much of a gentleman to laugh in his face

■

Samantha Smith, 13, whose career since her 1983 visit to Moscow has led to an upcoming prime time series starring Robert Wagner, is killed with her father in a Maine plane crash.

8/26   "Not totally, no."
—Larry Speakes on whether President Reagan actually thinks racial segregation has been eliminated in South Africa

8/29   20/20 broadcasts a segment featuring Geraldo Rivera running with the bulls in Pamplona, Spain.

8/30   CBS announces that Phyllis ("How about a hug?") George will no longer be appearing on the CBS Morning News.

SEPTEMBER 1985

In which the Senate confronts an issue of vital unimportance

9/1   Ocean researchers locate the remains of the Titanic, which sank in 1912.

9/2   "I think Harry would be very pleased." —President Reagan in Independence, Missouri, standing in front of a statue of Truman who, he absurdly claims, would smile on his tax cuts for the rich

■

EXCLUSIVE: PRISCILLA PRESLEY breaks her silence to tell the story of her bizarre LIFE WITH ELVIS
—People

9/4   Assessing President Reagan's standing in the latest Gallup poll, Larry Speakes says, with no irony, "He didn't get to 65 points with a song and a dance and a nice smile."

■

Australian media baron Rupert Murdoch— whose recent efforts to buy seven Metromedia TV stations have been blocked by a law limiting foreign ownership of broadcast licenses—becomes a US citizen.

9/7   "It became a television show. There's nothing wrong with it being a television show, but I think it was something more. It used to be this little restaurant you couldn't get into, and

as it expanded, it became the same as the others."
—Lorne Michaels on *Saturday Night Live,* to which he is returning as producer after a five-year hiatus

"Between now and November 8th, I would like it to be the Manhattan Project. Everybody knows they're working on it and that it's important, but nobody knows quite what it is."
—Lorne Michaels explaining his philosophy of leadership

9/8   Theodore Streleski is freed from a California prison after serving seven years for beating a Stanford professor to death with a hammer. Explaining his lack of remorse, he says, "I say Stanford treats students criminally. If I express remorse, I cut the ground out from under that argument. I would not only be a murderer but a dirty lying dog. I am a murderer. I am not a dirty lying dog."

9/9   Promoting his appearance in the movie *When Nature Calls,* G. Gordon Liddy says the story about him eating rats as a child "has grown way out of proportion." Explains Liddy, "I only ate the left hind quarter. Of one rat."

■

Rupert Murdoch begins syndicating what he bills as "a weekly series of columns by the pontiff." The "columns" turn out to be transcriptions of public papal utterances. "For all I know," says one contemptuous editor, "it might be remarks he made ten years ago during a stickball game in Krakow."

■

HAS ROCK GONE TOO FAR?
L.A.'s grisly "Night Stalker" case inflames the debate over sex, violence and devil worship in lyrics and videos. Now parents are taking action
—*People*

■

Nancy Reagan tapes her first rock video,

singing a chorus of an anti-drug song called "Stop the Madness."

9/12   "If I may use a word that people our age will remember, 'Balderdash!' "
—President Reagan responding to Mario Cuomo's criticism on *Meet the Press* that his tax plan will hit the middle class the hardest

"Balderdash? He used that in a movie once. The President has a perfect right to use any words he wants. I have a different lexicon."
—Mario Cuomo responding to the Reagan response

9/16   Dire Straits' "Money for Nothing"— an instant classic satirizing blue-collar envy of the easy life of rock stars—begins three weeks as the Number One song. Many radio stations delete the verse about "the little faggot with the earring and the makeup."

9/17   At his 32nd press conference, President Reagan calls SDI (Star Wars) "a weapon that won't kill people. It'll kill weapons." Asked how much importance he places on getting along with new Soviet leader Mikhail Gorbachev, the President quips, "Well, I wasn't going to give him a friendship ring or anything."

9/18   "I thought that Le Duc Tho had discovered some hidden physical attraction for me. He couldn't keep his hands off me."
—Henry Kissinger revealing a little-known aspect of the Vietnam peace talks

9/19   At the urging of Susan Baker (wife of Treasury Secretary James) and Tipper Gore (wife of Tennessee senator Albert), the Senate Commerce Committee holds a hearing about whether stickers should be placed on albums warning parents about dirty rock lyrics. Says Sen. Paul Trible (R-VA), "I believe this may well be the most important hearing conducted by the Commerce Committee this year."

THE PMRC'S GREATEST HITS

Overheard at the Senate Commerce Committee hearing on dirty rock lyrics:

"Mr. Ling, I'm sorry. Your time has expired."

—Sen. John Danforth (R-MO) cutting off the testimony of Parents Music Resource Center consultant Jeff Ling, who has cited a 15-minute litany of lyrics—including graphic descriptions of perverse sex acts—from mostly obscure albums

"While the wife of the Secretary of the Treasury recites, 'Gonna drive mah love inside you,' and Senator Gore's wife talks about bondage and oral sex at gunpoint on the *CBS Evening News*, people in high places work on a tax bill that is so ridiculous, the only way to sneak it through is to keep the public's mind on something else: porn rock! . . .

"Children in the vulnerable age brackets have a natural love for music. If, as a parent, you believe they should be exposed to something more uplifting than 'Sugar Walls,' support the music appreciation programs in schools."

—Frank Zappa testifying at the hearing

"Let me say, although I disagree with some of the statements that you make, and have made on other occasions, I have been a fan of your music, believe it or not, and I respect you as a true original and tremendously talented musician."

—Sen. Albert Gore (D-TN) to Frank Zappa

"There is nothing on the face of the album which would notify you if the record has pornographic material or material glorifying violence?"

"No, there is nothing that would suggest that to me."

—Exchange between John Danforth and Tipper Gore

"I would say that a buzz saw blade between the guy's legs on the album cover is a good indication that it's not for little Johnny."

—Frank Zappa

"It's an honor to be able to ask questions. I've been a fan for a long time, Mr. Denver."

—Albert Gore to John Denver

"Excuse me, are you gonna tell me you're a big fan of my music as well?"

—Dee Snider of Twisted Sister to Albert Gore, who admits he is "not a fan"

Paul Adao

Sean Penn and Madonna are photographed in New York hiding their heads in their jackets.

9/20 EARTHQUAKE ROCKS MEXICO; HUNDREDS ARE FEARED DEAD AS BUILDINGS FALL AND BURN
CAPITAL BADLY HIT
HOSPITALS ARE THRONGED AS NUMBER OF INJURED IS PUT IN THOUSANDS
—*The New York Times*

9/21 "I never liked him. I don't like him now. And I never will like him."
—Barry Goldwater on Richard Nixon

Four weeks after Samantha Smith's death, ABC airs the first episode of her new series, *Lime Street*. Its pre-credit opening scene ends with a plane crash.

Yankee manager Billy Martin gets into a shoving match with a patron at a Baltimore bar who claims the Yankee manager said his newlywed bride had a "pot belly."

"I didn't say she had a pot belly," explains Martin, indicating another customer at the bar. "I said this woman here had a fat ass."

9/22 Billy Martin winds up with a broken arm and two cracked ribs after a drunken brawl with Yankee pitcher Ed Whitson.

9/26 Sen. Jesse Helms adds an amendment to an appropriations bill forbidding the use of any funds for the benefit of "any cult, organization or other group that has a purpose, or that has any interest in, the promoting of Satanism or witchcraft." It is adopted without debate.

9/29 TV PREMIERE: *Amazing Stories*. Having made movie theaters unsafe for adults with his endless goonies 'n' gremmies, Steven Spielberg invades the nation's living rooms with an anthology series fueled by one more recycling of his exhaustively examined childhood fears. Writes Tom Shales of the first episode—about a "ghost train" that comes crashing through a farmhouse one night—"I hear America asking: 'What was so "amazing" about that?'" NBC is stuck with it for a two-year commitment.

OCTOBER 1985

In which many citizens cancel Mediterranean cruises

10/1 Margaret Heckler—whose messy divorce has put her in bad odor with the First Lady—grimaces beside President Reagan as he announces that she has agreed to leave her post as Health and Human Services Secretary to become ambassador to Ireland. He explains that he "wouldn't have been so eager" to make her an ambassador "if she hadn't done such a good job" in the Cabinet. So why is he removing her from a job she's great at and forcing her to take one she doesn't want? No one asks.

10/2 Rock Hudson dies of AIDS. Shirley (wife of Pat) Boone rushes into his home, grabs his legs and speaks in tongues for a half hour in a futile effort to resurrect him.

10/6 *The New York Times Magazine* runs a cover story on "The Mind of the President," in which it is pointed out that though Reagan "likes to say . . . that he is a 'voracious reader' and 'history buff' . . . neither he nor his friends, when asked, could think of particular history books he had read or historians he liked." Says a White House aide, "You have to treat him as if you were the director and he was the actor, and you tell him what to say and what not to say, and only then does he say the right thing."

■

Arbor House takes out an ad for *The Lost Writings* of George Orwell, who is described as the author of *Animal House*.

10/7 Palestinian terrorists hijack the Mediterranean cruise liner *Achille Lauro*. Before they surrender two days later, they kill wheelchair-bound New Yorker Leon Klinghoffer and throw him overboard. Denying the crime later, leader Mohammed Abul Abbas says, "If someone really died, which I doubt, then for sure it was a matter of a heart attack and the responsibility of the captain." Another Palestinian

suggests that grief-stricken widow Marilyn Klinghoffer murdered her husband for the insurance money.

An autopsy performed after his body washes ashore shows he was shot in the head.

■

"You don't have many suspects who are innocent of a crime. That's contradictory. If a person is innocent of a crime, then he is not a suspect. . . . *Miranda* only helps guilty defendants. Most innocent people are glad to talk to the police. They want to establish their innocence so that they're no longer a suspect."
—Ed Meese, chief law enforcement officer of the nation

■

Maria Shriver's man ARNOLD
Why JFK's niece loves the savviest, silliest strong man in showbiz
—*People*

10/8 President Reagan welcomes Singapore president Lee Kuan Yew and his wife, Mrs. Lee, to the White House. "It gives me great pleasure," he says, "to welcome Prime Minister Lee Kuan Yew and Mrs. Yew to Singapore."

■

Sylvester Stallone has dinner at the White House. "It's always flattering to have the highest person in the land admire your work," he says of the President's incessant nattering about Rambo. And what does Stallone think of the *Achille Lauro* hijacking? "Let's put it this way," he says: "I'm an action actor so I'd like to have a little action."

Also in attendance is first-teacher-in-space-to-be Christa McAuliffe. "He told us a lot of stories about when he was in films," she says of her host. "He also said maybe I could take some papers to grade with me in space."

10/10 On a trip to Chicago to promote his tax reform program, President Reagan stuns reporters by suggesting that PLO leader Yasir Arafat could try the captured *Achille Lauro* hijackers. He is quickly sent out with a retraction.

Hours later, US fighter jets intercept the Egyptian plane carrying the hijackers to freedom and divert it to Italy, where they will be tried.

10/11 President Reagan shows up in the White House briefing room to introduce Robert McFarlane, who will answer questions about the capture of the hijackers. And, since he is again sporting a bandage, he begrudgingly admits he has had yet another skin cancer removed from his nose. "And now," he says, "I can stand before you proudly and say, 'My nose is clean.'"

10/12 Richard Nixon is chosen to arbitrate a dispute between baseball owners and umpires. "The game will not survive," he says, "unless people continue to have confidence in qualified, competent umpires." His efforts are successful.

10/17 Richard Nixon's comeback continues as he addresses a dinner for black GOP businessmen in New York. "I don't think the American people are ready for him to sit down at the dining room table," observes Democratic pollster Harrison Hickman, but "now they're willing to send him a sandwich out in the kitchen."

10/22 Geraldo Rivera—who has made no secret of his displeasure with ABC News president and Ethel Kennedy pal Roone Arledge's cancellation of a *20/20* segment about the JFK/RFK connection to the death of Marilyn Monroe—learns that his 15-year association with the network has come to an end. "That's what happens when you're ahead of your time," he says. "When I die, people will understand."

10/27 Billy Martin is fired by George Steinbrenner for the fourth time, and is replaced by Lou Piniella.

10/31 "We would not deploy . . . until we sit down with the other nations of the world, and those that have nuclear arsenals, and see if we cannot come to an agreement on which there will be deployment only if there is elimination of nuclear weapons."
—President Reagan, seeming to suggest that the Soviets would help decide whether the United States deploys a space weapon system

NOVEMBER 1985

In which the President makes a new friend

11/3 Appearing on *This Week with David Brinkley*, Philippine president Ferdinand Marcos announces his willingness to call a snap election "right now." Says the embattled leader, "I'm ready, I'm ready, I'm ready." Corazon Aquino, widow of a man whose murder Marcos is widely believed to have ordered, emerges as his chief opponent.

11/4 Latest media star "Humphrey," the hump-backed whale that has spent the past three-and-a-half weeks cruising fresh waters, is guided under the Golden Gate Bridge and back out to sea, never to be heard from again.

11/5 Larry Speakes dismisses President Reagan's incoherent rambling about SDI deployment as "presidential imprecision," explaining that he meant to use the word "sharing" instead of "deployment." Oh.

11/6 "It may be said of Brad Reynolds, and President Reagan, decades from today, that they did more to free the nation of policies of prejudice than any other policy-maker since Abraham Lincoln."
—Sen. Orrin Hatch at a dinner honoring the Justice Department's rigid right-wing ideologue

"Brad Reynolds has proved to be nothing less than the most powerful advocate of civil rights in our time."
—Ed Meese paying similarly preposterous tribute

"As a Cub Scout he blew up his Cub Scout leader's outhouse. His interest in incendiaries continued into adolescence, when he threw a bomb into a librarian's car in high school. So when his critics call him a 'bomb thrower,' they are more accurate than they know."
—Madeleine Will, wife of George, surprising Reynolds by revealing some little-known moments from his past

11/7 President Reagan has lunch with six Soviet specialists in preparation for his upcoming summit. A participant reports that though the President was "very affable" and seemed to be listening very intently, he asked no questions.

11/9 Toasting Princess Diana on her first visit to the United States, President Reagan refers to her as "Princess David."

Observes a BBC correspondent, "President Reagan greeted the Prince and Princess wearing a plaid jacket that was remarkably similar to the carpet at Balmoral Castle."

■

"It's like watching old men die."
—Former *Saturday Night Live* writer Michael O'Donoghue on the critically reviled season premiere, which features NBC *wunderkind* Brandon Tartikoff taking urine samples from cast members for drug testing, a piece about the Kennedys having murdered Marilyn Monroe (played by host Madonna), and a sketch in which a gay actor and a junkie actress are afraid of getting AIDS from each other.

"I think the nature of *Saturday Night* is that it's the kind of experience people like only in retrospect. Nobody seems to like it at the time."
—Lorne Michaels responding to the intense critical loathing for his show

11/12 Brandon Stoddard is named president of ABC Entertainment, leaving CBS as the only Brandon-less network.

HERE'S WHAT THE CRITICS ARE SAYING ABOUT PRESIDENT REAGAN

"He's melting. No one's noticed yet, but he *is* melting. We're talking about a semi-solid mass with dark hair. If the Democrats had come out and just said, 'He's melting,' I think they would have done much better. . . . It's going to be a real flood when he finally goes into total liquidation."
—Actress Carrie Fisher

"The task of watering the arid desert between Reagan's ears is a challenging one for his aides."
—Columnist David Broder

■

President Reagan pledges not to keep SDI all to himself. "We will make available to everyone this weapon," he says. "I don't mean we'll give it to them. They're going to have to pay for it—but at cost." In fact, he will have no say about any of this, since he will be out of office long before any space-based weapon could possibly be built.

11/13   "He's just so programmed. We tried to tell him what was in the bill but he doesn't understand. Everyone, including Republicans, were just shaking their heads."
—Rep. Mary Rose Oskar (D-OH) on President Reagan's reaction to the Gramm-Rudman-Hollings balanced budget bill

11/14   "Imagine if people in our nation could see the Bolshoi Ballet again, while Soviet children could see American plays and hear groups like the Beach Boys. And how about Soviet children watching *Sesame Street?*"
—President Reagan proposing a Soviet-American cultural exchange

11/15   Soviet spokesman Georgi Arbatov says that while President Reagan prepared for the summit by watching taped interviews, Mikhail Gorbachev has more traditional methods of study. "He doesn't need 10-minute video clips," Arbatov says. "He has a concentration span." He claims not to know if Gorbachev watched any of Reagan's old movies, adding, "They are B-rated anyway." Responds Reagan—keenly sensitive to underappreciation of his acting achievements—"Well, he's never seen *King's Row.*"

11/17   With his Oregon sex cult dismantled and his 93 Rolls Royces sold off after his arrest for violating US immigration laws, Bhagwan Shree Rajneesh leaves for India. He describes his four years here as "hell," and says Americans are "sub-human."

■

Donald Regan explains why the Geneva ac-

tivities of Nancy Reagan and Raisa Gorbachev will be of special interest to female readers. "They're not . . . going to understand throw-weights," he says, "or what is happening in Afghanistan, or what is happening in human rights. Some women will, but most . . . would rather read the human interest stuff."

The President, meanwhile, is reported to be upset by suggestions that Raisa is more attractive than his Nancy.

11/19   "Is God Punishing Us?"
—Sweeps-month three-part local news series on New York's WNBC-TV featuring footage of the Colombian volcano, Puerto Rican floods, Ethiopian famine, a record number of air crashes and, of course, the AIDS epidemic

■

President Reagan—who has explained that he failed to meet with previous Soviet leaders because "they kept dying on me"—demonstrates his youthfulness by lunging out without an overcoat to greet Mikhail Gorbachev at the start of their two-day summit in Geneva. The two spend almost three hours alone with their interpreters, though a "news blackout" makes their alleged rapport difficult to confirm. The President reportedly urges the Soviet leader to "do one thing for me. Tell Arbatov they weren't all B-movies."

■

Nancy Reagan and Raisa Gorbachev have tea in Geneva. "I found her a very nice lady," says the First Lady afterward. And what did they discuss? "Big city living as against not big city living."

11/25 "Go ahead! Atta boy, Wilfred. You tell 'em, Wilfred. Yes, sir, Wilfred, you let 'em have it."

—President Reagan, saved from having to answer reporters' questions by the screams of the annual White House turkey, this year named Wilfred

11/26 President Reagan tells reporters that his 688-acre ranch—to which the rambunctious Lucky is being exiled—is "dog heaven." When reporters attempt to shift the topic to an upcoming tax bill, the President says, "I'm concentrating on dog heaven."

Upon landing in California, Lucky bids the public farewell by taking a dump on the tarmac.

■

Random House pays $3 million for Edmund Morris' biography of President Reagan, due to be published in 1991.

11/27 NOW PLAYING: *Rocky IV*. Sylvester Stallone shows the first signs that the culture may be leaving him behind, as this neanderthal anti-Soviet screed arrives in theaters mere days after President Reagan made a new friend in Geneva. Stallone's huge blonde girlfriend Brigitte Nielsen plays the wife of the pumped-full-of-steroids Russian boxer who, of course, loses.

DECEMBER 1985

In which the role of the dog is recast

12/1 President Reagan is honored by friends in the entertainment industry at a black-tie event at an NBC studio. Among those paying tribute are Burt Reynolds, Dean Martin, Emmanuel Lewis and Charlton Heston, who tells the President, "To the world, you are America." Reagan reveals his "dream Cabinet," which would have included Secretary of State John Wayne, Defense Secretary Clint Eastwood and Treasury Secretary Jack Benny.

12/2 With record company money going into videos instead of the live tours that are so essential for the growth of young bands, the American music scene becomes stagnant enough to produce a Top Ten populated by Lionel Richie, Mr. Mister, Glenn Frey, Phil Collins, Heart, Eddie Murphy (!) and Starship, whose "We Built This City" may be the worst song of the decade.

■

Rocky's angry mom comes out swinging at his live-in lover . . .

MY SON SLY HAS FALLEN FOR A GOLD-DIGGER
—*Star*

JOAN COLLINS' NEW HUSBAND IS A WIMP SAYS HIS EX-LOVE
—*Star*

12/3 "Fly away, fly away, fly away home. Dan Rather reporting from New York. Thank you for joining us. Good night."

—The increasingly bizarre CBS anchor signing off following a report on duck hunting

12/4 President Reagan says he told Mikhail Gorbachev to "just think how easy his task and mine might be if suddenly there was a threat to this world from some other species from another planet." Should such an event occur, suggests the President—of whom it can accurately be said that he's watched too many movies— "we would find out once and for all that we really are all human beings here on this Earth together."

■

John Poindexter becomes President Reagan's fourth National Security Adviser when Robert McFarlane resigns—apparently because of tension with Don Rogan, who is widely believed to have spread rumors about McFarlane's alleged lack of marital fidelity.

12/6 After a year of the First Lady being dragged around by Lucky, the role of the White House dog is recast with a smaller actor as President Reagan gives Nancy an early Christmas present: a year-old King Charles spaniel.

" 'Oh, honey,' " Larry Speakes quotes Nancy as saying, " 'thank you, thank you, thank you.' "

This bristly, nervous, unhappy-looking animal—she names him Rex—not only shares his predecessor's insistence on leash control, but brings the additional unpleasantness of incessant barking. He is later rumored to have bitten the President more than once. Still, having already used up their quota on pet returns, the Reagans are stuck with him.

12/7 While other administration officials meet at the White House, George Bush attends the Army-Navy football game.

12/9 Financially strapped Iowa farmer Dale Burr, 63, goes on a shooting spree that claims the lives of his wife, a bank president, another farmer and himself. Says a sheriff's deputy of a note found at the Burr home, "He said he couldn't manage his problems anymore."

12/11 George Bush participates in a dinner honoring the memory of *Manchester Union Leader* editor William Loeb, whose loathing for Bush was no secret. Bush goes so far as to read selections from Loeb's vitriolic attacks ("a spoon-fed little rich kid," "incompetent liberal masquerading as a conservative") aloud.

■

General Electric buys RCA (and with it, NBC) for $6.3 billion.

12/12 New Jersey librarian Ann Scarpellino calls Warner Books to point out an error in *First Love: A Young People's Guide to Sexual Information*, co-authored by Dr. Ruth Westheimer. The chapter on contraception says it's "safe" to have sex the week before and the week of ovulation, when the word most certainly should have been "unsafe." The publisher recalls 115,000 copies.

■

REAGAN WIDENS USE OF LIE TESTING ON TOP ADMINISTRATION OFFICIALS
—*The New York Times*

12/13 258 ON U.S. TROOP FLIGHT DIE AS PLANE CRASHES IN GANDER ON WAY HOME FROM MIDEAST
—*The New York Times*

12/15 *60 Minutes* interviews Berkeley professor Michael Rogin, who posits the theory that the President honestly can't tell the difference between movies and reality. The evolution of a Reagan anecdote is traced from the point where he credits it as a movie scene to the point where

WHAT THE PRESIDENT ISN'T

"I'm not a scientist enough to know what they would take to make them that way."

—President Reagan refusing to speculate on the possibility of defensive SDI weapons being used offensively

"I'm not a lawyer, and I don't intend to get into too many legal areas where I might be caught short."

—President Reagan refusing to speculate on which nation the *Achille Lauro* hijackers will be tried in

"I'm not medical. I'm not a lawyer and I'm not medical, either."

—President Reagan refusing to speculate about the recurrence of cancer on his nose

"I'm no linguist, but I have been told that in the Russian language there isn't even a word for freedom."

—President Reagan revealing his ignorance of the Russian word "*svoboda*"

"I'm not an intellectual."

—President Reagan displaying no false modesty

he tells it as if it really happened. Viewer response proves this to be one of the least popular segments in the program's 17-year history.

■

Tom Brokaw hosts NBC's annual "Christmas in Washington" special, at the end of which he can be seen on stage singing carols with the Reagans.

12/16 Sylvester Stallone dismays his mother by marrying Brigitte Nielsen, 22, in Beverly Hills. The couple—fast becoming the Woody and Mia of the moron movie genre—return to the set of their new film, *Cobra*, the next day.

12/18 NOW PLAYING: *The Color Purple*. Overreaching beyond even *his* wildest imagination, Steven Spielberg takes off his beanie and makes his bid for Oscardom with an oafish adaptation of the most popular black feminist novel of the '80s. Though Gene Shalit crows, "It should be against the law not to see *The Color Purple*," the film wins no Academy Awards.

12/19 "The minute in this government I am told that I'm not trusted is the day that I leave."

—George Shultz announcing that he would resign before he'd take a lie detector test

■

Ted Kennedy says he won't be a presidential candidate in 1988.

12/24 REAGAN UNAWARE OF SWEEP OF POLYGRAPH ORDER
—*The Washington Post*

12/28 AIRPORT TERRORISTS KILL 13 AND WOUND 113 AT ISRAELI COUNTERS IN ROME AND VIENNA
4 ATTACKERS KILLED
GUNMEN FIRE INTO CROWDS AND THROW GRENADES NEAR LINES AT EL AL
—*The New York Times*

12/31 Rick Nelson is killed in a plane crash.

1 Complete the perfume ad: "In the kingdom of passion, the ruler is _____ ."
  a Scoundrel. Joan Collins' Scoundrel
  b Uninhibited. Cher's Uninhibited
  c Obsession. Calvin Klein's Obsession
  d Passion. Elizabeth Taylor's Passion

2 "We've got a good shot of her. She's just gotten out of a de-tox treatment clinic. How do you like the cleavage?" At an editorial meeting for which publication were these sentences uttered?
  a *U.S. News and World Report*
  b *USA Today*
  c *Us*
  d *Vanity Fair*

3 True or false? Smokey the Bear was dropped from TV ads for forest fire prevention because "adults in this country no longer take a talking bear seriously."

4 True or false? Many female reporters among the White House press corps began wearing red outfits at news conferences to emulate the First Lady and perhaps attract the President's attention.

Who said what?
  5 John Simon
  6 Bhagwan Shree Rajneesh
  7 Howard Cosell
  8 Bernhard Goetz
  9 Ed Koch
10 Ike Turner
  __**a** "You don't look too bad. Here's another."
  __**b** "Yeah, I hit her, but I didn't hit her more than the average guy beats his wife."
  __ **c** "So many religions look after the poor. Leave the rich to me!"
  __**d** "I have been vilified more than Charles Manson."
  __**e** "Homosexuals in the theater! My God, I can't wait until AIDS gets all of them."

__**f** "My problem is a simple one. I am not capable of blathering pap."

11 Which of these actually appeared on TV?
  a *There He Goes Again*, a documentary examining the record number of overseas trips taken by outgoing Attorney General William French Smith
  b *I Heard That Was Good*, a weekly discussion of movies the panel members haven't seen and books they haven't read
  c *Gorby's Blotch*, a local news sweeps story about the Soviet leader's birthmark
  d *Moonlighting*, a detective series popular among critics who mistook the speedy repetition of dull wisecracks by self-absorbed actors for wit

12 What was *Faces of Death*?
  a An ode to suicide by Ozzy Osbourne
  b A popular videocassette depicting the actual murders of humans and animals
  c A documentary about undertakers
  d The anti-abortion film showing the destruction of a fetus

13 What was *not* endorsed by Mary Lou Retton?
  a Wheaties
  b Ever-Ready batteries
  c Blackglama furs
  d McDonald's

14 True or false? *Rolling Stone* boasted to advertisers that the majority of its readers voted to re-elect President Reagan.

15 In the world of advertising, who was "Herb"?
  a The off-camera neighbor who was always being talked to by that creep Ernest
  b A nerd who never ate at Burger King
  c A mystery man who claimed to have lost 76 pounds and made over $6 million by using and selling Herbalife products
  d The real-life model for Joe Isuzu

16 Who recorded "Bonzo Goes to Bitburg"?
a The Flaming Keisters
b The Waving Idiots
c The Vapid Ignoramuses
d The Ramones

17 Why did President Reagan say he regretted joking at the Gridiron dinner that the US should "keep the grain and export the farmers"?
a "Nancy told me later that the fella just before me told the exact same joke."
b "The plight of our farmers is no laughing matter."
c " 'Cause I didn't get a laugh."
d "I wouldn't want the kids who might want to grow up to be farmers to be afraid we're going to send them to another country."

18 During President Reagan's summer of sickness, what did Donald Regan do that upset Nancy Reagan?
a He sat at the President's Oval Office desk
b He took a helicopter to the hospital while she felt it more appropriate for an employee like him to travel by car
c He put the last piece in the President's Snoopy jigsaw puzzle, a ceremony she felt her husband should have performed
d He told an aide that the President's colon cancer had spread to his nose because he "has his head up his ass"

19 Who said Prince "looks like a dwarf who fell into a vat of pubic hair"?
a Sheena Easton
b Boy George
c Cyndi Lauper
d Whitney Houston

20 Which of Nancy Reagan's friends received two broken ribs from a cab driver who reacted badly to demands that he turn off the radio and drive with two hands?
a Michael Deaver
b George Will

c Mike Wallace
d Jerome Zipkin

Match the newsmaker with his/her news.
21 James Wolcott
22 Linda Evans
23 Uli Derickson
24 Randy Newman
25 Jesse Helms
26 Helene von Damm
27 Pat Robertson
28 Esther Williams

___a Tried to arrange takeover of CBS so conservatives could "become Dan Rather's boss"
___b Accused Brooke Shields of trying to "make a national shrine out of her hymen"
___c Resigned as US ambassador to Austria after earning the wrath of Nancy Reagan
___d Was kissed by Rock Hudson
___e Sold hit song to ABC for use as insufferable fall season promo jingle
___f Criticized comedian Billy Crystal for basing his career on the lampoon of a dead man
___g Heroic figure in TWA hijacking who was initially reported to have helped identify Jewish passengers
___h Told a hurricane to go someplace else, and it did

29 Which Woody Allen film anticipated a leader who was seen waving on TV a lot and whose nose became a cause for some concern?
a *Stardust Memories*
b *Sleeper*
c *Zelig*
d *The Purple Rose of Cairo*

ANSWERS

1-c, 2-c, 3-True, 4-True, 5-e, 6-c, 7-d, 8-a, 9-f, 10-b, 11-d, 12-b, 13-c, 14-True, 15-b, 16-d, 17-c, 18-b, 19-b, 20-d, 21-b, 22-d, 23-g, 24-e, 25-a, 26-c, 27-h, 28-f, 29-b

1986

JANUARY 1986

In which the Nation gets a nasty science lesson

1/7   President Reagan begins his 33rd press conference by calling the Vienna airport "Vietnam International," calls 11-year-old terrorist victim Natasha Simpson "Marsha Simpson" and says Qaddafi is "not only a barbarian but he's flaky."

1/10   Spotting a car weaving along a New York highway, police find Queens borough president Donald Manes at the wheel, bleeding from a slashed wrist and ankle. Manes claims to have been attacked, but the injuries turn out to be self-inflicted.

1/12   Asked by reporter Gabe Pressman about his "wish list" for improving the quality of life in New York, real estate mogul Donald

Trump thinks the big problem is street peddlers. "I see trucks pulling up at 6:30 in the morning and people bringing carts off these trucks right onto Fifth Avenue," says Trump, who seems to think he owns the street just because he built a big ugly building there. "I don't think the politicians really understand how upset the public is when they see a man selling hot dogs and dumping the catsup and mustard all over the sidewalk. . . . How come the law goes after everybody else, but the law doesn't go after the people that are selling nonsense on the street, not paying taxes, ruining the environment, ruining the city, ruining the great streets of the city of New York?"

1/15   President Reagan is asked if he intends to see Halley's Comet. "If it's a choice between sleeping or seeing it," he replies, "I'll wait and see it on television."

1/16   In Macao filming *Shanghai Surprise* with wife Madonna—who plays a 1930s missionary—Sean Penn punches out yet another photographer.

1/17   President Reagan's colon yields three more benign polyps.

1/21   Donald Manes receives a hospital visit from Ed Koch. "I went over to Donny and I hugged Donny and kissed Donny on the forehead," Koch tells reporters, "and I said, 'Don't worry, Donny, everything will be all right.'" Five days later—with investigations into the city's Parking Violations Bureau gearing up—Koch appears on TV to call Donny a "crook" who should be removed from office. Says Koch as the scandal expands into the largest in recent city history, "How could I know? How could anyone have known? No one knew."

1/23 In the tradition of his 1984 accusation that Mondale had slandered the memory of the murdered Marines, George Bush accuses Mario Cuomo of "pitting one American against another" by raising the question of ethnic bigotry in national politics. "Worst of all," Bush claims, "he's telling us to be ashamed to stand up and be proud of this great land." Cuomo, who of course has said nothing of the kind, observes, "There are few things more amusing in the world of politics than watching moderate Republicans charging to the right in pursuit of greater glory."

1/24 George Bush addresses the first meeting of the Liberty Federation, the benign new name for the odious Moral Majority. "America is in crying need of the moral vision you have brought to our political life," he gushes to Jerry Falwell. "What great goals you have!"

■

Church of Scientology founder L. Ron Hubbard dies of a stroke.

1/26 President Reagan sits for a pre–Super Bowl interview with Tom Brokaw, who elicits the "news" that the President—as the leader of *all* the people—feels it would be inappropriate for him "to take sides." He does, however, tell several familiar stories about his college football and sportscasting days.

1/27 The launch of the *Challenger* space shuttle is delayed for the sixth time in six days. Engineers for Morton Thiokol, which builds the solid rocket boosters, express serious concern about whether the critical O-ring seals will hold in the abnormally low Florida temperatures, but their objections are overruled and lift-off is scheduled for the next morning, with Christa McAuliffe's students prepared to watch in class.

1/28 In a bitter early-morning confrontation at the White House, Tip O'Neill attacks President Reagan to his face for spreading "a bunch of baloney" about the reasons for job-

lessness. "I thought you would have grown in five years," he shouts, adding, "I never did believe your story about the Chicago welfare queen."

■

"Roger, go with throttle up."
—*Challenger* commander Francis R. Scobee, 74 seconds into his flight

"Flight controllers here looking very carefully at the situation. [Pause] Obviously a major malfunction."
—NASA public affairs officer describing events

"We all knew if the seals failed, the shuttle would blow up."
—Engineer from Morton Thiokol

"The President was stunned. He said something like, 'Isn't that the one with the teacher on it?' "
—Patrick Buchanan reporting the presidential reaction

"That'll be a tough act for Dad to follow."
—Michael Reagan discussing the impact of the explosion on President Reagan's scheduled State of the Union message, which is delayed a week

■

The Ford Motor Company announces the cancellation of its advertising campaign linking its Aerostar minivan to the space shuttle.

1/30 "The unpleasant sound emitting from Bush as he traipses from one conservative gathering to another is a thin, tinny 'arf'—the sound of a lapdog."
—George Will, repelled by what he perceives as George Bush's grotesque pandering to the far right

"We have to reconsider a strategy that results in major news media figures across the ideological spectrum questioning his character."
—Unnamed Bush aide

FEBRUARY 1986

In which kids do the darndest things

2/4 President Reagan's State of the Union address is moved up to 8 P.M. to avoid interfering with the timely broadcast of the Joan Collins mini-series *Sins* and its chief competition, *Peter the Great*. The speech is notable for its repetition of the words "family" (19 times) and "future" (13 times), and for the President's citing of a line from the film *Back to the Future:* " 'Where we're going, we don't need roads.' " Those who have followed the President's pronouncements on Armageddon find this remark vaguely ominous.

2/6 President Reagan turns 75, prompting not just the familiar joke about the "36th anniversary of my 39th birthday" but the additional insight that 75 is "only 24 Celsius."

2/7 President-for-Life Jean-Claude ("Baby Doc") Duvalier and his wife, Michele, leave Haiti in a hurry.

2/8 Parodying Tom Cruise's *Risky Business* dance as part of his hosting chores on *Saturday Night Live,* Ron Reagan becomes the first presidential offspring ever to dance on national television in his underwear. Observes the President, "Like father, like son."

2/11 With Ferdinand Marcos apparently having stolen the election, President Reagan looks on the bright side, claiming to be "encouraged" by evidence of a "two-party system in the Philippines," even if only one is allowed to win.
    Observes Rep. Stephen Solarz (D-NY), "The suggestion that the opposition should accept with equanimity the fact that the election has been stolen constitutes prima facie evidence that they are smoking hashish in the White House."

2/17 THE REBEL REAGAN
Patti Davis raises a ruckus with her novel about a cold mother and a square father (who just happens to be President)
—*People*

■

Press secretary Elaine Crispen reports that Nancy Reagan has so far had no time to read Patti's novel, *Home Front,* in which a new First Lady tours the White House burbling, "There's just so much history here! Imagine all the people who have been within these walls. But, good grief, I just can't wait to redecorate."

2/18 "As I've said before, you can't fight attack helicopters piloted by Cubans with Band-Aids and mosquito nets."
—President Reagan campaigning for military, not just humanitarian, contra aid

2/20 President Reagan stages a five-hour visit to Grenada, where he is serenaded in a calypso song as "Uncle Reagan." Caspar Weinberger snaps photos without removing his lens cap.

2/21 *The Wall Street Journal* unmasks George Bush as a user of the phrase "deep doo-doo."

■

Geraldine Ferraro's son John Zaccaro, Jr.— known on the Middlebury, Vermont, campus as "the Pharmacist"—is arrested after selling a quarter gram of cocaine to an undercover policewoman. Police say he has been dealing since 1983.

2/24 Michael Deaver—who claims to be "making far more than I ever thought I would" from his new lobbying firm—appears on the cover of *Time* in his black Jaguar talking on a car phone. The cover line reads, "Who Is This Man Calling?" Soon after the magazine hits the stands, Nancy Reagan calls. "Mike, you made a big mistake," she says of this flaunting of success. "I think you're going to regret it."

"If Reagan buys it, I'll even throw in a bed that sleeps six."

—Larry Flynt on the rumor (untrue, it turns out) that the Reagans are considering buying his $4.9 million Bel Air mansion

2/25 Corazon Aquino is sworn in as the new Philippine president in the wake of a citizens' revolt following Ferdinand Marcos' fraudulent election. At Malacanang Palace, Marcos is also sworn in but, having lost control of the military, he and Imelda accept the US offer of sanctuary. They flee to Hawaii with as much money as they can escape with, though they are forced to leave most possessions behind. Among them: 3,000 pairs of Imelda's shoes, hundreds of matching handbags, thousands of dresses and 500 black bras. Says *Women's Wear Daily* publisher John Fairchild, "She spent all this money, but she was never attractively dressed."

2/26 "I don't expect you'll hear me writing any poems to the greater glory of Ronald and Nancy Reagan. Why should I?"

—Robert Penn Warren on the occasion of being named the first US poet laureate

2/28 Though the comment exists on tape, President Reagan denies that he called reporters "sons of bitches" for asking questions at a photo op. Larry Speakes claims Reagan said, "It's sunny and you're rich," though he offers no clue as to what that inane comment would have meant.

Nancy Reagan continues her tradition of kissing the bald heads of large black men by bussing Harlem Globetrotter Curly Neal.

MARCH 1986

In which the President sees red

3/1 "Some of his statements are almost more than a human being can bear."

—Jimmy Carter on President Reagan's habitual lying about the nation's military preparedness when he took office

3/3 President Reagan reveals his ignorance of the condition of Central American roads by claiming that victory for the Sandinistas would create "a privileged sanctuary for terrorists and subversives just two days' driving time from Harlingen, Texas."

"They hope Patti finds writing satisfying."

—Spokesperson Elaine Crispen on the First Couple's reaction to their daughter's literary career

3/5 President Reagan renews his campaign for another $100 million in contra aid. "If we don't want to see the map of Central America covered in a sea of red, eventually lapping at our own borders," he warns, "we must act now." The House votes no.

■

MEESE BACKS DRUG TESTS FOR EMPLOYEES
—*The New York Times*

■

Nancy Reagan withdraws her participation in the anti-drug Concert That Counts because she disapproves of the lyrics of some of the musical acts scheduled to perform.

■

After watching Bruce Springsteen sign autographs on a flight to Los Angeles, Richard Nixon introduces himself to the singer. "I notice that you sign your full name," he says. "And it's such a very long name. When I was vice president, I remember going in to see President Eisenhower while he was signing a stack of letters. He looked at me and said, 'Dick, you're lucky to have a short name.' "

3/6 Two hours before she is scheduled to appear on *The Tonight Show*, Patti Davis—who earlier in her publicity tour had been dropped from her mother's friend Merv Griffin's show—is told that her appearance has been cancelled by the show's guest host, her mother's friend Joan Rivers. When she travels to Washington the next day for an appearance on *Larry King Live*, she does not drop by the White House.

3/11 Hundreds of hours of "home movie" videotapes left behind by the fleeing Marcoses are released by the Aquino government. Among the highlights: several tunes by Imelda (who fancies herself quite the songstress) and a performance by Ferdinand, Jr. (aka "Bong Bong") —sporting a flashing red electronic bow tie— of "We Are the World."

3/12 "I hope she makes a lot of money. I thought it was interesting fiction."
—President Reagan's reaction to his daughter's novel

3/13 With his wife on the phone to his psychiatrist and his daughter following him through the house, a distraught Donald Manes plunges a kitchen knife into his heart. At a luncheon the next day, Ed Koch refers to the suicide as "an enormous tragedy," then moves on to more important matters. "How many here," he asks, "read my first book?"

■

Appearing on *Today*, presumed GOP presidential candidate Jack Kemp—who has been dogged by rumors of homosexual encounters since he worked for Governor Reagan in the '60s—denies "categorically" and "absolutely" that he has ever taken part in anything of the kind.

■

Federal district judge nominee Jefferson B. Sessions is questioned by the Senate Judiciary Committee about some derogatory comments he made about the NAACP and his statement that the Klan was "okay" until he found out that some were "pot smokers."
"I may have said something about the NAACP being un-American or Communist," he admits, "but I meant no harm by it." He is the first of President Reagan's judicial appointments to be denied confirmation.

3/14 "I guess in a way they are counter-revolutionary and God bless them for being that. And I guess that makes them contras and so it makes me a contra, too."
—President Reagan campaigning for contra aid

3/16 President Reagan goes on TV yet again to warn that the Soviets want to make Nicaragua "a second Cuba," or even "a second Libya," right on America's "doorstep." As he speaks, a map of the region shows the nations turning red.

3/17 "A Miami dispatch yesterday . . . described Federal District Judge John J. Sirica incorrectly. He is alive."
—Correction in *The New York Times*

3/18   Thanks to disorganization among Illinois Democrats—and the vaguely foreign-sounding names of their opponents—Mark Fairchild and Janice Hart, two disciples of extremist Lyndon LaRouche, win the party's nominations for lieutenant governor and secretary of state. "We're going to roll our tanks down State Street," declares Hart at their victory press conference, promising "Nuremberg tribunals" for drug dealers and mandatory AIDS testing. They are not elected.

■

William F. Buckley, Jr., suggests in *The New York Times* that everyone found to have AIDS "should be tattooed in the upper forearm, to protect common-needle users, and on the buttocks, to prevent the victimization of other homosexuals." The idea is not widely embraced.

3/21   Four years after it was first discredited, President Reagan resurrects his fable about British gun laws in an interview with *The New York Times*. Do any of the three veteran reporters challenge him? They do not.

■

ABC's *World News Tonight* begins picking a "Person of the Week."

3/22   President Reagan invites Nancy on stage at the Gridiron Dinner to say something nice about the press. She stands silently. "Don't you have just a few kind words?" he asks. "Won't you say something?" Another pause. "I'm thinking," says the First Lady. "I'm thinking." Everyone laughs.

3/24   PATTI'S BOOK RIPS FIRST FAMILY APART
'STAY OUT OF OUR LIVES!' NANCY TELLS HER
'I HATE MY MOTHER,' SAYS PATTI
—*National Enquirer*

■

In an interview broadcast on Oscar night, Barbara Walters talks to the Reagans about their favorite subject: the movies. Discussing fleeting romantic involvements between stars, the President says, "I coined a term for it. Leading lady-itis, leading man-itis. . . . I came here and the first picture, June Travis was the leading lady. . . . And I could see where it *did* happen. The picture ended and—"

"And you said, 'Bye-bye,' " says Nancy.

"And, yeah, I said, 'Bye-bye,' " says the President, whose wife pats his knee and says, "Good boy!"

And which films made the greatest impression on him as a youth? *"Dracula,"* he says, "and, oh—the man that's built by the doctor."

Frankenstein? Walters asks. The President nods. *"Frankenstein."*

■

Falco's "Rock Me Amadeus"—as hideous a cacophony as has ever topped the chart—begins three weeks as the nation's favorite song.

3/27   "I don't see why anyone should put me down for my job. I'm bright. I'm intelligent. I turn letters—*so what?* I also talk. I talk on the show! People know my name on the show!"
—Vanna White defending her role on *Wheel of Fortune*

3/30   Rona Barrett asks Dolly Parton if she would submit to breast reduction in order to get better film parts. "I see myself doing more serious roles," says Parton, "and not having my boobs removed to do it."

3/31   ANDY'S LUV
(and Di's delight) Sarah Ferguson
—*People*

APRIL 1986
In which the situation turns explosive

4/1   DEAVER MET WITH OMB CHIEF ON BEHALF OF B1 CONTRACTOR
—*The Washington Post*

■

The Los Angeles County Board of Supervisors votes to lobby Congress to rename the Angeles National Forest the "Reagan National Forest." Says Sierra Club spokesman Bob Hattoy, "Naming a national forest after Ronald Reagan is like naming a day care center after W. C. Fields."

4/2   After stopping for a snack at a New Jersey Burger King, Richard Nixon leaves a note. "Best Wishes to Burger King, home of the Whopper," he writes. "Love, Richard Nixon."

4/3   Michael Reagan makes his TV acting debut as a politician on the daytime soap opera *Capitol*. He goes on to host his own game show, *Lingo*, which unfortunately is seen only in Canada.

4/4   "I wonder what people thought I was going to do when I left the White House. Be a brain surgeon?"
—Michael Deaver defending himself against charges that he has cashed in on his White House connections with unseemly speed and greed

4/6   Oliver Sacks' *The Man Who Mistook His Wife for a Hat*, an examination of bizarre neurological disorders, begins a 26-week run on the *Times* best-seller list. One highlight is an account of oppositely impaired patients—aphasiacs who can't understand spoken words, but do take in information from extraverbal cues, and tonal agnosiacs who understand the actual words, but miss their emotional content—watching a speech by President Reagan.

"It was the grimaces, the histrionisms, the false gestures and, above all, the false tones and cadences of the voice," writes Sacks, which caused the word-deaf aphasiacs to laugh hysterically at the Great Communicator, while one agnosiac, relying entirely on the actual words, sat in stony silence, concluding that "he is not cogent . . . his word-use is improper" and suspecting that "he has something to conceal."

"Here then," writes Sacks, "was the paradox of the President's speech. We normals—aided, doubtless, by our wish to be fooled, were indeed well and truly fooled . . . And so cunningly was deceptive word-use combined with deceptive tone, that only the brain-damaged remained intact, undeceived."

4/8   Clint Eastwood is elected mayor of Carmel, California, by a 72–27 margin over the incumbent, who is not a famous movie star.

4/9   President Reagan says he rarely quotes William F. Buckley, Jr., "because he uses too big a words."

■

At his 35th press conference, President Reagan defends Michael Deaver against charges of influence peddling. "I have to tell you," says the President of his friend, "Mike has never put the arm on me."

4/10 $1M OR DATE WITH JOAN COLLINS?
MOST TAKE MONEY
—*USA Today*

4/12   Excerpts from David Stockman's memoir, *The Triumph of Politics: Why the Reagan Revolution Failed*, appear in *Newsweek*.

The gist of it is that the President was a little weak on the relationship between taxes and budget deficits. Recalling having to sit through an "embarrassing" 20-minute lecture by the ignorant Reagan, Stockman writes, "What do you do when your President ignores all the palpable, relevant facts and wanders in circles?"

Though the book is rife with devastating anecdotes—one of the best features Caspar Weinberger defending his swollen military budget by showing Reagan cartoon drawings of three soldiers in varying states of preparedness, prompting Stockman to write, "Did he think the White House was on Sesame Street?"—the media focuses instead on the author's alleged betrayal of the President.

■

Sean Penn assaults a male friend of Madonna's—whom he accuses of trying to kiss her—at the trendy Hollywood club Helena's. He later pleads no contest and is sentenced to one year's probation.

4/14 Refuting the popular myth that she spent too much money on herself, Imelda Marcos explains that she was "too busy thinking about electrical power, education, roads, bridges and transportation to shop."

■

Claiming to be retaliating against Libya for its alleged involvement in the bombing of a Berlin disco that killed a US serviceman, President Reagan orders a series of air strikes against what the White House calls "terrorist centers." It is later revealed that the real intent of the bombing was to assassinate Qaddafi, who is not injured, though his infant daughter is killed. In any event, Frank Sinatra must be pleased, since he sends a telegram that reads, "Encore, encore, encore. Francis Albert."

4/15 "I'll go anywhere I wanna go, anytime I wanna go. I had a great time. They had a great golf course."
—Frank Sinatra, feeling no guilt about singing at South Africa's Sun City resort

4/16 A gloating Donald Regan says an old Marine Corps buddy called to suggest that the lyrics to "The Marine Hymn" be changed to "From the halls of Montezuma to what's left of Tripoli."

The President is reported to have told Michael Deaver—whose questionable ethics had been getting a lot of media attention—"Well, Mike, I bombed Libya for you."

4/17 "I don't have too much time for fiction."
—President Reagan claiming not to have read David Stockman's book

4/18 "When you meet the President you ask yourself, 'How did it ever occur to anybody that he should be governor, much less President?'"
—Henry Kissinger addressing a small group of scholars at the Library of Congress, unaware of the presence of a reporter

4/21 "I have yet to see one shred of evidence that supports this patently ridiculous and Orwellian contention."
—Rep. Edward Markey (D-MA) dismissing the administration's claim that a ban on underground testing might somehow encourage other nations to develop their own nuclear weapons

■

Addressing a group of newspaper publishers, Richard Nixon is asked what he thinks were the lessons of Watergate. "Just destroy all the tapes," he says. So convivial is the spirit that the former President even shares a laugh with *Washington Post* publisher Katharine Graham.

■

Geraldo Rivera hosts a live broadcast during which Al Capone's "secret underground vault" is opened for the first time in 50 years. "This is an adventure you and I will take together," he pants. After almost two hours of wallowing in mob lore, he detonates a charge and blows down a wall, revealing . . . dirt and an empty bottle. Rivera—as humiliated as someone utterly shameless can be—strolls off into the night, singing, "Chicago, Chicago, that toddlin' town." The show gets the highest ratings in syndicated TV history.

4/24 The director of the Cannes film festival reports that macho man Sylvester Stallone has decided not to attend the event for fear that he might become a victim of terrorism in the wake of the US attack on Libya.

4/26 Inescapable TV pitchman Jim ("Ernest") Varney does a turn in the White House press room, to the enormous amusement of Larry Speakes.

■

Austrian-born right-winger Arnold Schwarzenegger marries Kennedy niece Maria Shriver at the family compound in Massachusetts. Austrian presidential candidate Kurt Waldheim sends a sculpture of the couple.

At the reception, Teddy Kennedy dances with Grace Jones.

4/28 Abnormally high radiation levels are recorded across Scandinavia, forcing the reluctant Soviets to announce that the world's worst nuclear accident is underway in the Ukraine, where a reactor at the Chernobyl power station is experiencing meltdown. Though a disaster on a holocaust scale is averted, 31 people are killed, 135,000 evacuated and 6 million Kiev residents are faced with tainted water and milk. Long-term damage to health and the environment is impossible to discern. Initial Soviet refusal to give out any information about casualties fuels tabloid speculation about thousands buried in mass graves.

■

Lobbyist Michael Deaver, under investigation by several congressional committees, requests an independent counsel to look into charges that he lined up clients—among them the governments of Canada, South Korea and Puerto Rico—before leaving the White House.

Ed Meese announces that his "longtime association" with Deaver disqualifies him from any further involvement in the case.

MAY 1986

In which a lot of people hold hands

5/3 The University of Maryland announces that hundreds of boxes of papers and memorabilia donated 12 years ago by Spiro Agnew will remain uninspected for three to five more years.

5/4 *Parade* prints this query: "Who is the member of the Reagan Cabinet referred to as 'Fathead'? And which of the Washington lobbyists with great access to the White House is known as 'The Raging Queen'?" The reply: "Sorry, but to answer your two questions would do more harm than good."

5/5 Barbara Bush reveals that when her husband turned 60 two years ago, he resolved never again to eat broccoli, Brussels sprouts, cauliflower or cabbage, And, she adds, "he hasn't."

5/6 Larry Speakes reports that in Tokyo last week, President Reagan told French president François Mitterrand, "Let this be the first day of the rest of our lives." Mitterrand's response is unreported.

■

Having prevented the confirmation of Jefferson Sessions, the Democrats try for two by taking on Reagan appeals court nominee Daniel A. Manion, who cites among his 10 "most significant" cases the defense of a client accused of improperly repairing a Volkswagen Rabbit. Manion—whose career is closely tied to that of his John Bircher father, and whose legal writings are rife with what *The New York Times* describes as "non-standard spelling, grammar and syntax"—is defended by Indiana senator Dan Quayle, who went to law school with him and therefore knows that he "epitomizes what we all like to see in jurisprudence."

■

Michael Jackson signs a $15 million deal with Pepsi that the *Guinness Book of World Records* declares "the biggest commercial sponsorship deal" ever. Other Jackson product on the way: Michael's Pets, a line of stuffed animals, based on his backyard menagerie, that is also being developed as a TV cartoon series.

■

"It was clear that the movie picture business was not fulfilling enough for him. It was obvious he wanted more, his mind was bigger."
—Nancy Reagan on her husband

"This must be an X-rated film!"
—Nancy Reagan on being asked how many nights she and her husband have spent apart

■

Rupert Murdoch's Fox Broadcasting Company announces that its first show will be a late-night hour starring Joan Rivers, who has been Johnny Carson's permanent guest host for three years. Asked what kind of surprises she hopes to spring on her audience, she gives the example of a guest coming on to "admit they were a lesbian." By the time she gets around to calling Carson he has already heard her good news and, furious that she let him hear it first from someone else, hangs up on her without a word.

5/16 Michael Deaver testifies under oath

before the House Energy and Commerce Subcommittee, characterizing attacks on him as "mean-spirited . . . groundless and impertinent" and "an implicit attack on the integrity of the President." He says he has "never traded on my relationship with the President for any client, and I never will"—a comment bound to make many of them wonder what they're paying him for.

■

"As we were driving up, I said something that was totally inane. I said, 'It looks like the goddamn Pentagon.' Natch, it *was* the Pentagon."
—Producer Don Simpson on getting government cooperation for the filming of *Top Gun*, a celebration of fighter pilots that becomes the year's highest-grossing film

"A Top Gun instructor once told me there are only four occupations worthy of a man: actor, rock star, jet fighter pilot or President of the United States."
—Tom Cruise, star of *Top Gun*

■

Patrick Duffy accepts a huge amount of money to return to *Dallas*. The series ends its season with him turning up in Pam's shower, assuring a summer of speculation about who he is—an evil twin? an impostor? Bobby himself, back from wherever he's been recuperating while everyone thought he was dead?—and how he got there.

5/19 Nicholas von Hoffman expresses a healthy skepticism about Nancy Reagan's anti-drug campaign. Noting the First Lady's "dead eyes and death mask smile," the columnist writes, "Can you think of a well-known American with less chance to influence the green-haired, angel-dusted, coke-sniffing teen-agers dancing through the school corridors than this prissy, inanimate lady?"

5/21 President Reagan tells a group of students, "I don't believe that there is anyone that is going hungry in America simply by reason of denial or lack of ability to feed them. It is by people not knowing where or how to get this help." Asked what this observation is based on, Larry Speakes says, "That is his view." Critics note that the Reagan administration eliminated the program that informed needy people of available benefits.

5/22 Bette Davis tells Johnny Carson the only passable performance Ronald Reagan ever gave was as the amputee in *King's Row*. "But," she adds, "you know, take a man's leg off and you've got a lot going for you in those scenes."

■

United Artists chairman Lee Rich and Sylvester Stallone announce that they have signed a six-year, 10-picture deal. According to the star, *Rocky V* could very well be one of those pictures "if we can find the right material. We don't want to do *Rocky vs. the Planet of the Apes*."

5/23 NOW PLAYING: *Cobra*. "You're the disease. I'm the cure," grunts Sylvester Stallone as a cop so tough he wears shades during a shootout in a dark supermarket. Though the film is deemed a sure hit, the psychopathic actions of its hero—who douses one killer with gasoline before igniting him, and impales another on a smelting hook before sending him into a blast furnace—make him a little, well, hard to relate to. It grosses over $60 million, but the suspicion grows stronger that Stallone's moment has finally passed.

CRITICS ACROSS AMERICA ARE RAVING ABOUT *COBRA*

"... Hopped-up, gaseous ... a lurid, ludicrous, exhausting, enervating bloody mess ..."
—Sheila Benson, *Los Angeles Times*

"... Neurotically stupid ..."
—Ralph Novak, *People*

"... This piece of steaming crud ..."
—Glenn Lovell, *San Jose Mercury News*

"... A celebration of an American death squad. ... Unimaginably degraded ..."
—David Denby, *New York*

"... This film shows such contempt for the most basic American values embodied in the concept of a fair trial that Mr. Stallone no longer, even nominally, represents an ideology that is recognizably American ..."
—Nina Darnton, *The New York Times*

"... The foulest, greediest, most anti-American movie in ages. ... He may wear Old Glory as his diaper, but his work soils everything this country claims to stand for. ... Stallone is one of the most contemptible figures in American public life, purveying messages of hatred to make money he'll never need ..."
—John Powers, *L.A. Weekly*

"... Stallone is dynamite ..." —Joel Siegel

5/25 Hands Across America—an attempt by promoter Ken Kragen to raise money for the homeless by creating a coast-to-coast human chain—attracts 5 million participants. Though long gaps break up the 4,152-mile route and considerably less than the hoped-for $50 million in donations is raised, a lot of people still have a good time gawking at celebrities, standing around in the middle of traffic-free streets and singing well-meaning songs.

5/26 Maureen Reagan attacks the media for reporting that her father had initially refused to join the Hands Across America line. "He didn't know he had been invited," she explains.

■

Newsweek—which two weeks ago ran a cover story on the rehabilitation of Richard Nixon ("He's Back")—reports on a new study showing that college-educated single women of 40 "are more likely to be killed by a terrorist" than they are to find a mate. Writes columnist Ellen Goodman of this statistic, "The only news . . . that could terrify more readers would be an amalgam of both stories: 'Richard Nixon's Back, and He Wants to Marry YOU!' "

5/29 Former government prosecutor Whitney North Seymour, Jr., is appointed to investigate conflict-of-interest charges against Michael Deaver.

6/5 Model Marla Hanson, involved in an $850 dispute with her former landlord, Steven Roth, is slashed in the face by two razor-wielding men while Roth looks on. Told later by police that Hanson will need 100 stitches, he replies, "That's her. I'm out $850."

6/8 Kurt Waldheim, whose Nazi past seems to have helped more than hurt, is elected president of Austria.

6/9 DC Comics announces that, as part of its "updating" of *Superman*, Clark Kent will be "more open about his feelings" and "a little more upwardly mobile."

6/11 President Reagan distinguishes himself at his 37th press conference by:

- Responding to a question about abortion with an answer about an unrelated case
- Displaying a certain confusion about whether or not the SALT II treaty exists and about whether or not he plans to order construction of another space shuttle
- Claiming that the government is providing 93 *million meals a day* to hungry Americans.

He later explains that he spent too much time concentrating on which reporters to call on. "Next time," he tells aides, "I'm going to concentrate not on who I'm calling on, but what I'm going to say."

6/16 US intelligence sources reveal that Muammar Qaddafi has become so unbalanced that he dresses in drag and takes mind-altering drugs, prompting the *New York Post* to announce, "MADMAN MOAMMAR NOW A DRUGGIE DRAG QUEEN." The tabloid includes an altered photograph of the Libyan

leader, claiming that, "dressed in drag," he "might look like this."

6/17 Chief Justice Warren Burger gives up his lifetime seat on the Supreme Court to organize the hype for next year's Bicentennial of the Constitution. President Reagan promotes the court's most right-wing Justice, William Rehnquist, to the top spot, and names conservative Antonin Scalia to the vacancy, beginning the remaking of the court that his foes have long feared would be his lasting legacy.

6/19 Two days after being the first draft pick of the Boston Celtics—and one day after signing a multi-million-dollar, 10-year contract to endorse Reeboks, University of Maryland basketball star Len Bias dies of a cocaine overdose. His death, followed eight days later by that of Cleveland Browns safety Don Morris, helps kick off a summer of drug hysteria.

6/20 Two more polyps are removed from President Reagan's large intestine.

■

The editors of *The New York Times* announce their decision that "Ms." has become part of the language and is now allowed to appear in the paper's pages.

6/23 At a ceremony honoring high school scholars, President Reagan reveals that his favorite TV show is *Family Ties*.

■

Citing "unethical," "unprofessional" and "particularly reprehensible" misconduct dating back to the 1960s, a New York State court disbars Roy Cohn, who is dying of what he insists is not AIDS.

6/24 The Senate fails by one vote to defeat Daniel Manion after an arm-waving, red-faced Dan Quayle pressures Kansas Republican Nancy Kassebaum into withdrawing her vote against him. "You know," Quayle tells Ted Koppel, "I'm not so sure that we want all those that graduated number one or number two in their class to be on . . . our federal judiciary. This is a diversified society."

6/25 The House finally caves in and votes 221–209 for military aid to the contras, which leader Adolfo Calero claims could be the turning point in the war. "It will be," he says, "like the light at the end of the tunnel."

6/29 Arch-conservative North Carolina senator John East, 55 and in failing health, asphyxiates himself in his garage.

6/30 President Reagan rejects a Soviet proposal to resume talks on the 1979 SALT II treaty, which he has decided to abandon. Jokes the President, "Too much SALT isn't good for you."

■

With her pro–teen motherhood song "Papa Don't Preach" heading for the top of the singles chart, Madonna releases her third album, *True Blue*. Its dedication: "To my husband, the coolest guy in the universe."

JULY 1986

In which the Nation's top cop publishes a dirty book

7/1 HIGH COURT, 5–4, SAYS STATES HAVE THE RIGHT TO OUTLAW PRIVATE HOMOSEXUAL ACTS
—*The New York Times*

7/2 "You don't have to be a doctor to look at me and know I am dying. I am an out-and-out heroin junkie with an eight-gram-a-day habit."
—Boy George, whose brother says doctors have given the rock star two months to live

7/3 Boy George claims his recent weight loss has been deliberate. "I'm fit enough to run the London Marathon," he says. "Tell my fans I'm fine." He is soon arrested for heroin possession.

■

ABC begins 17½ hours of coverage of Liberty Weekend, a four-day celebration of the centennial of the newly renovated Statue of Liberty. Presiding over the relighting ceremony, President Reagan refers to poet Emma Lazarus (who wrote the dedication a century earlier) as "Emmett Lazarus."

7/4 Caught up in the spirit of Liberty Weekend, Bob Hope jokes that the Statue of Liberty has AIDS, but "nobody knows if she got it from the mouth of the Hudson or the Staten Island fairy."

7/6 Producer David Wolper—who promised that the Statue of Liberty finale would feature "good glitz and glitter"—brings the weekend to an end with a three-hour closing ceremony that includes 200 Elvis impersonators singing "Hound Dog" while scores of jazzercise ladies dance around them.

■

Nancy Reagan, 65, celebrates her 63rd birthday.

■

"my partners and me are/fired to fight/so bloody unchristmas/is the violent night."
—Sean Penn, holding the first public reading of his poetry

7/7 Random House announces that it will publish Nancy Reagan's memoirs in 1989. Says her agent, "She's a no-holds-barred lady."

7/9 Sen. Alfonse D'Amato goes undercover to demonstrate how easy it is to get crack in Manhattan, buys two vials as surveillance cameras roll, then indignantly denies it is an election-year stunt.

■

Standing in front of a bare-breasted statue at the Justice Department, Ed Meese accepts the 1,960-page report from his $500,000 pornography commission. Available in two volumes from the government for $35, the report becomes something of a cult item for its 100-plus-page listing of book, movie and magazine titles (*Teenage Dog Orgy, Cathy's Sore Bottom, Lesbian Foot Lovers—The Movie*) and 200 pages of detailed descriptions and excerpts from said material.

7/16 "Are the women of America prepared to give up all their jewelry?"

—Donald Regan questioning the depth of public support—in particular, female support—for economic sanctions against South Africa

7/19 "What I did was tape on my VCR this week everything I could on the Kennedy wedding, and after this I will switch to the royal wedding on the same tape."

—Kennedy-watcher Maryann Connor outside the Massachusetts church where Caroline Kennedy marries Buckminster Fuller acolyte and self-styled Renaissance man Edwin Schlossberg

7/20 Nancy Reagan arrives in London for the wedding of Prince Andrew and Sarah ("Fergie") Ferguson. How does it feel to be back in England? "Love it," she ad-libs. And is she looking forward to the wedding? "I should say so."

At the wedding, she wears an outfit topped off with a gaucho hat that critic Elvis Mitchell says makes her look like "Zorro's mother."

7/22 Addressing the nation to explain his opposition to sanctions against South Africa, President Reagan refers to it as "South America." Says Bishop Desmond Tutu, "Your President is the pits as far as blacks are concerned . . . I found the speech nauseating."

7/23 "Even with all the tanks and gunships from the Soviet Union, my guess is that the Sandinistas would make it about as far as the shopping center in Pecos before Roger Staubach came out of retirement, teamed up with some off-duty Texas Rangers and the front four of the Dallas Cowboys and pushed the Sandinistas down the river, out across the Gulf and right back to Havana where they belong."

—President Reagan campaigning in Dallas

"I've been asked to come back against the Giants and the Redskins, but not against the Sandinistas."

—Roger Staubach

7/24 *USA Today* presents photographic evidence that Dan Rather is artificially darkening his hair.

7/25 NOW PLAYING: *Heartburn.* Carl Bernstein—the target of Nora Ephron's revenge novel about their failed marriage—becomes the only reporter played by both Dustin Hoffman *and* Jack Nicholson. *Washington Post* critic Rita Kempley says the film version—co-starring Meryl Streep—"has been so waspified you'd think Nora Ephron had married Woodward instead of Bernstein."

7/29 The United States Football League— created out of the perverse notion that what America needs is *more football*—wins its antitrust suit against the NFL, but is awarded only one dollar, considerably shy of the $1.69 billion USFL owners had been counting on to bail out the failing league.

7/30 At his confirmation hearing, William Rehnquist:

- Explains that a 1952 memo he wrote supporting the "separate but equal" doctrine represented not his views, but those of the justice he was clerking for
- Denies having challenged the credentials of minority voters in the early '60s
- Claims to have no recall that his Vermont vacation home came with an unlawful covenant prohibiting its sale to anyone of the "Hebrew race," though a 1974 letter from his lawyer informing him of this is soon discovered.

Senators are left to decide whether the Chief Justice should be a man who somehow forgot that the deed to his house was illegal.

8/1 Four witnesses rebut William Rehnquist's denials of having challenged minority voters at the polls in 1962. "I assure you," testifies San Francisco attorney James Brosnahan, "I *assure* you that if it was *even close* I would be home having my Friday afternoon lunch at Jack's.... I'm telling you my recollection."

■

Touring the Middle East, George Bush makes small talk with Jordanian commander in chief Lt. Gen. Zeid Bin Shaker. "Tell me, general," he says, "how dead is the Dead Sea?"

Replies Shaker, "Very dead, sir."

8/2 Roy Cohn dies at 59 of AIDS.

8/4 Having just announced his administration's election-year effort to seem tough on drugs, President Reagan is asked if this means he is taking over the anti-drug movement from Nancy. Asks the President, grinning like an imbecile, "Do I *look* like an idiot?"

8/7 A Let's-Repeal-the-22nd-Amendment-and-Give-Reagan-a-Third-Term rally is interrupted by a protester who tries to bring everybody down. "Ronald Wilson Reagan is the beast, he's 6-6-6," the man shouts. "Check it out."

8/8 Universal executives Sid Sheinberg and Frank Price are reported to have gotten into a fistfight during an argument about which of them was responsible for letting George Lucas spend $35 million on the *Heaven's Gate* of comedy, *Howard the Duck.*

8/9 President Reagan sets a statesman-like example by submitting a sample of his urine for drug testing. George Bush, oddly enough, does the same.

8/11 The revelation that Andrew Wyeth has been, for 15 years, secretly doing portraits of a blonde model with high cheekbones earns him the covers of *Time* and *Newsweek.*

8/12 A House subcommittee votes to send evidence to Whitney North Seymour, Jr., that Michael Deaver "knowingly and willfully" lied under oath. By the end of the month, the lobbyist has lost $1 million worth of clients who feel his powers of persuasion may have passed their peak.

8/13 The parents of 13-year-old Deanna Young of Orange County, California, are arrested after the girl shows up at the police station with a bag of marijuana, pills and cocaine from their home. Says Nancy Reagan, "She must have loved her parents a great deal. I hope they realize just how much she loves them." The story becomes the subject of an instant bidding war in Hollywood.

■

Nancy Reagan's friend Mary Martin suggests that perhaps the First Lady should avoid seeing her current play, *Legends,* since it contains a hash brownie scene. Sure enough, it is announced the next day that a "schedule conflict" will prevent the Reagans from attending the show.

8/20 Mailman Patrick Sherrill responds to a series of reprimands by showing up at the Edmond, Oklahoma, post office with three pistols and killing 14 people before blowing his own brains out. "There was a lot of blood, a lot of bodies," says a police officer afterward. "With 14 people, you're going to have a lot of blood."

8/21 Surrogate mother Mary Beth Whitehead begins a losing court battle to keep the five-month-old girl—known in court documents as Baby M—that she carried to term for a $10,000 fee.

8/25 *The Wall Street Journal* reports that

the US and Libya "are on a collision course again" and that Qaddafi will soon be taught "another lesson."

8/26 Robert Chambers, 19, tells police how 18-year-old Jennifer Levin came to be lying bruised and strangled to death in Central Park after the two of them left an Upper East Side bar together. "She molested me in the park," says the hulking 6'4" youth of his considerably smaller victim. Though he is charged with second-degree murder, his media coverage is bizarrely sympathetic ("SECRET AGONY OF PREPPIE SUSPECT"), while his victim's treatment ("HOW JENNIFER COURTED DEATH," "WILD SEX KILLED JENNY") implies that she had it coming.

8/29 Sean Penn gets into a scuffle with two photographers after spitting on one of them.

8/30 A week after Soviet physicist Gennadi Zakharov is arrested for spying in New York, American correspondent Nicholas Daniloff is arrested for spying in Moscow. Declares President Reagan, "There will be no trade."

SEPTEMBER 1986

In which the First Lady learns an unpleasant truth, and the President tells a pleasant untruth

9/1 "Surround yourself with the best people you can find, delegate authority, and don't interfere."
—President Reagan, as quoted in a *Fortune* interview for its cover story "What Managers Can Learn from Manager Reagan"

■

Dan Rather begins closing his nightly news broadcast with the word "courage." Says Rather, "It's a good word. I think I'm going to use it for a while." He says he also likes the word "meadow," but doubts he could sign off with it.

9/2 With national drug hysteria peaking, Dan Rather hosts *48 Hours on Crack Street*, a two-hour special on the country's latest cocaine scourge. A Tom Brokaw coke special airs three days later.

Meanwhile, in Indiana, a 13-year-old summons police to his home to confiscate less than an ounce of marijuana and arrest his parents.

9/3 The long-delayed manslaughter trial of John Landis and four others in the *Twilight Zone* case opens in Los Angeles. "These were not deaths in which someone can get up and wipe the bloody-looking catsup off their faces," says prosecutor Lea D'Agostino, whose flair for the macabre extends to displaying photographs of the mutilated victims in her office. "They were very, very real deaths."

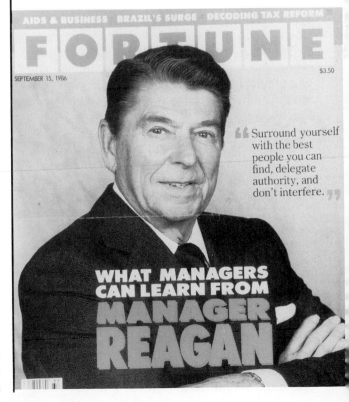

AIDS & BUSINESS · BRAZIL'S SURGE · DECODING TAX REFORM

FORTUNE

SEPTEMBER 15, 1986 $3.50

❝Surround yourself with the best people you can find, delegate authority, and don't interfere.❞

WHAT MANAGERS CAN LEARN FROM MANAGER REAGAN

9/4 "When the chapter on how America won the war on drugs is written, the Reagans' speech is sure to be viewed as a turning point."
—White House announcement of an upcoming anti-drug speech amusingly billed as the Reagans' first "joint address"

9/8 "There will be no trade."
—President Reagan on the continuing Soviet incarceration of Nicholas Daniloff

■

Dan Rather stops saying "courage" after *Newsweek* suggests it's an attempt "to rally shell-shocked troops" at demoralized, financially troubled CBS, which has been the subject of takeover rumors for almost two years. Two days later—with chairman Thomas Wyman admitting having begun secret negotiations to sell to Coca-Cola—control of the network is assumed by its largest stockholder, billionaire Laurence Tisch.

■

Paul Simon's *Graceland* begins a 97-week stay on the *Billboard* LP chart.

9/10 Director John Landis reveals the hitherto-unguessed-at depths of his immaturity when, following the hostile testimony of a witness, he blocks her exit with his outstretched legs and *makes her climb over him!*

9/13 Michael Jackson, seen recently with a gauze mask over his face, attends the Disneyland premiere of his 3-D George Lucas short, *Captain EO,* disguised as an old lady.

9/14 Sitting on a couch in the White House living quarters, the Reagans urge a "national crusade" against the "cancer of drugs." Afterward, the President—who will cut funding for anti-drug programs as soon as the election is over—squeezes his wife's hand reassuringly.

9/15 Welcoming a group of Soviet children to City Hall, Ed Koch is compelled to tell them their government "is the pits." Says one 14-year-old, "I want to get on the bus and go far away from this place."

Observes *The New York Times,* "He sounded like a cranky old man who needs a stray Airedale to kick."

■

Michael Jackson's manager Frank DiLeo reveals that the singer has installed a hyperbaric oxygen chamber in his home, which he thinks will help him live to 150. Says DiLeo, "I can't figure him out sometimes."

■

Kitty Kelley's Sinatra biography, *His Way,* reports Peter Lawford's comment that, before it became necessary to suck up to the Reagans, Frank thought Ronnie was "a real right-wing John Birch Society nut—dumb and dangerous" and called Nancy "a dope with fat ankles who could never make it as an actress."

9/16 Former Delaware governor Pierre S. (Pete) du Pont IV announces his candidacy for the 1988 Republican presidential nomination.

9/17 William Rehnquist is confirmed as Chief Justice, 65–33—the highest negative vote ever received by a confirmed justice.

Then, having exhausted themselves, members debate for about five minutes before confirming the equally conservative Antonin Scalia, 98–0.

9/19 NOW PLAYING: *Shanghai Surprise*, starring Sean Penn and Madonna. Said a hostile Penn to a publicist during the filming, "This film doesn't need publicity. The people will go to see it because we're in it." The $15 million movie goes on to gross $2.3 million.

9/21 Imelda Marcos explains that the reason there were so many shoes in her closets was, "Everybody kept their shoes there. The maids . . . everybody."

9/23 On the premiere of his newest late-night show, Dick Cavett tells Lily Tomlin he has not yet seen her brilliant Broadway show *The Search for Signs of Intelligent Life in the Universe* (which has been running for almost a year) and talks to her instead about the time 15 or so years ago when she walked off his show, which reminds him of the time Lester Maddox walked off his show, and of something rather clever that he said to Maddox, back then.

9/26 President Reagan vetoes a bill that would impose mild economic sanctions against South Africa. The veto is soundly overridden.

∎

After months of speculation about how Patrick Duffy would rejoin the cast of *Dallas*, the producers boldly reveal that Bobby Ewing wasn't really killed after all. His death, and the entire last season, turn out to have been Pam's bad dream. Meanwhile, on the *Dallas* spinoff *Knots Landing*, where grief over Bobby's demise

was a major plot point last season, he remains dead.

9/30 Eighty-five minutes after Soviet spy Gennadi Zakharov is allowed to fly home to Moscow, a plane carrying Nicholas Daniloff lands in Washington. The President claims there is "no connection" between the two events.

OCTOBER 1986

In which the President stumbles, and the First Lady tumbles

10/2 Bob Woodward reveals the US strategy, devised by National Security Adviser John Poindexter, of lying to the media about Libya in order to undermine Qaddafi.

"We are not telling lies," says President Reagan, "or doing any of these disinformation things." A more candid George Shultz defends the scheme. "If I were a private citizen . . . and read that my government was trying to confuse somebody who was . . . murdering Americans, I'd say, 'Gee, I hope it's true.' "

Woodward also reports that President Reagan livened up a recent meeting by asking, "Why not invite Qaddafi to San Francisco, he likes to dress up so much?"

Quipped Shultz, "Why don't we give him AIDS?"

10/3 "Mystery guest" Nicholas Daniloff inexplicably turns up at the celebration of Disney World's 15th anniversary, though he rushes off stage before he can be embraced by someone in a Mickey Mouse costume. "We didn't force anything," says a Disney PR man. "If he didn't want his picture taken with Mickey, that's okay."

∎

TV PREMIERE: *L.A. Law*, basically *Hill Street Blues* without the uniforms. The lesson

HERE'S WHAT THE CRITICS ARE SAYING ABOUT PRESIDENT REAGAN

"A high-powered cheerleader for our worst instincts, a nasty man whose major talent is to make us feel good about being creepy and who lets us pretend that tomorrow will never come."
—Activist Roger Wilkins

"The President's answers totter forwards, as if supported by a walking frame, never quite reaching the question, sometimes never even starting out. When he hasn't got a prepared response, which is usually, he has a trick of turning his head away from the question halfway through the answer, as if hoping the query will go away . . .

"His errors glide past unchallenged. At one point . . . he alleged that almost half the population gets a free meal from the government each day. No one told him he was crazy. The general message of the American press is that, yes, while it is perfectly true that the emperor has no clothes, nudity is actually very acceptable this year."
—Simon Hoggart in the London *Observer*

"His answer to any questions about young men being killed for some vague and perhaps non-existent reason in Central America has been to smile, nod, wave a hand and walk on. And America applauds, thus proving that senility is a communicable disease."
—Columnist Jimmy Breslin

"Probably the least knowledgeable of any President I've ever met, on any subject."
—Tip O'Neill

"Reagan swaggering around. Poor old thing! He's about as masculine as Marjorie Main. He was never a symbol of masculinity—though he sort of plays it. Actually, if he were, he'd be too threatening. . . . All the major stars are slightly androgynous—otherwise, they'd be unbearable. There is something rather grandmotherly about Reagan. And then again, he's rather boyish. Between the two, he comes off as non-threatening."
—Gore Vidal

of this paean to the yuppie ethic: if you work real hard and dress for success, you get to live in a nice place and sleep with Harry Hamlin or Susan Dey.

10/4   Dan Rather is accosted on Park Avenue by two well-dressed men who beat him up while repeatedly demanding, "Kenneth, what is the frequency?" The incident is never explained.

10/5   Three American mercenaries die on a supply run to the contras when their cargo plane is shot down by Nicaraguan government forces. Survivor Eugene Hasenfus is captured in the jungle. The White House, the State Department, the Defense Department and the CIA all claim non-involvement.

■

Sitting next to pianist Vladimir Horowitz as President Reagan thanks him for his White House concert, Nancy Reagan—on the edge of a three-foot-high stage—shifts in her chair and tumbles into a box of potted chrysanthemums.

"Honey," quips the President, "I told you to do that only if I didn't get any applause." Everyone laughs.

10/8   A *Ladies' Home Journal* poll finds that while Bill Cosby is the "most admired" man in America, President Reagan is considered the "most interesting."

10/9   Though President Reagan has stated that the downed cargo plane had "absolutely" no connection to the US government, Eugene Hasenfus—imprisoned in Managua—says his mission was supervised by the CIA.

10/10   Sen. John Kerry (D-MA) suggests that the Foreign Relations Committee question Lt. Col. Oliver North, a National Security Council member reportedly close to the Nicaraguan rebels, in connection with White House involvement in the private arming of the contras.

10/11   In Reykjavik, Iceland, President Reagan reprises his I'm-so-vigorous-I-don't-need-an-overcoat act as he greets Mikhail Gor-

bachev at Hofdi House, where they hold their first summit session. Raisa—who has shown up despite Nancy's understanding that the wives were staying home—comments on the First Lady's absence. "Maybe she had something else to do," she suggests. "Or maybe she is sick."

10/12   The summit collapses in Reykjavik amid mutual charges of intransigence and confusion about just which and how many weapons President Reagan suggested getting rid of.

"I don't know what else I could have done," Gorbachev reportedly says, as the two leaders walk grimly to their limousines.

"You could have said yes," Reagan reportedly says.

"The Soviets are the ones that refused to make the deal," barks Donald Regan. "It shows them up for what they are. . . . The Soviets refused to trade. Would you please get it straight? The President didn't refuse to trade."

Observes George Shultz, "The President's performance was magnificent."

■

George Bush denies any involvement in contra resupply efforts, despite having met twice with former CIA agent Felix Rodriguez, whose job that resupply has been.

10/15   MICHAEL JACKSON'S NAME IS NOW AVAILABLE FOR LICENSING
 —Two-page ad in *Women's Wear Daily*

10/17   George Shultz releases the text of President Reagan's arms control proposal to prove that he did *not* suggest getting rid of all nuclear weapons. Larry Speakes says the President may have been—as, despite his reputation as the Great Communicator, he seems so often to be—"misunderstood."

■

Staking out the little-explored territory of "adversarial portraiture," guerrilla artist Robbie Conal goes out in the middle of the night and posts copies of his latest work, *MEN WITH NO LIPS*—which depicts President Reagan, Donald Regan, Caspar Weinberger and James Baker as putrescent figures rotting from the corruption of power—on traffic light boxes and construction sites around Los Angeles. Its companion piece, *WOMEN WITH TEETH*—Nancy Reagan, Margaret Thatcher, Jeane Kirkpatrick and Joan Rivers, all grinning rapaciously—appears four months later.

10/18 "They've taken the pot, there is no more pot. You can't get any more pot. If you give us back the pot, we'll forget about the crack."
—Comic Sam Kinison attacking government drug policies on *Saturday Night Live*, from which timid NBC censors bleep the joke for West Coast viewers

10/19 "I used to play poker with him, and any guy who could screech over losing 40 bucks I always thought shouldn't be President of the United States."
—Tip O'Neill on Richard Nixon

10/20 BUSH AWARE OF CONTRA OPERATION, HASENFUS SAYS
—*The Washington Post*

10/21 TV evangelist and presidential hopeful Pat Robertson files a $35 million libel suit against former California congressman Pete McCloskey, who served with him in the Marines and has been more than happy to share his "single distinct memory" of Robertson: waving goodbye from the dock in Japan as the others were going off to combat in Korea, explaining "with a big grin on his face" that his father—a US senator—had pulled some strings to keep him safe.

10/22 "I was in such a hurry, I wrote my last name first."
—President Reagan, after signing his tax reform bill "Reagan Ronald"

10/23 MEESE SAYS HIGH COURT DOESN'T SET 'LAW OF LAND'
ASSERTS RULINGS OF TOP JUSTICES

BIND ONLY THOSE IN CASE
—*The New York Times*

10/24 Campaigning for the re-election of Oklahoma senator Don Nickles, President Reagan calls him "Don Rickles."

10/30 Ed Meese urges employers to begin spying on workers in "locker rooms, parking lots, shipping and mail room areas and even the nearby taverns" to try to catch them using drugs.

■

Nancy Reagan appears as a guest on *The Late Show Starring Joan Rivers*. "You're such a warm person," says Rivers, who called the President a "turkey neck" in a recent *Playboy*. "There's such a warmth coming out of you, it's incredible!"

10/31 "In a seeming paradox, those who approve of lying were much more likely to believe the Administration tells the truth. . . . The paradox was explained by the fact that almost all of those who approved of not telling the whole truth were supporters of the Administration."
—*The New York Times*, in a story headlined "Most Resent Lies by White House"

■

Campaigning in Spokane for the re-election of Washington senator Slade Gorton, President Reagan calls state GOP chairwoman Jennifer Dunn "Dunn Jennifer."

NOVEMBER 1986

In which the plot begins to unravel

11/1   Appearing in a Manhattan court to answer a weapons charge, Floyd Flow, 24, is arrested when a bag stuffed with 76 vials of crack is found on his person. Says Flow, "I forgot I had it with me."

■

A Texas hospital takes its phone off the hook after a computer glitch in the Dallas GOP's get-out-the-vote drive results in a four-hour barrage of recorded messages from President Reagan.

11/2   Hostage David Jacobsen is released in Beirut. When a reporter asks whether President Reagan might try to use his release to boost the chances of GOP Senate candidates, the query upsets Larry Speakes. "You're within one inch of getting your head lopped off with a question like that," he says.

11/3   In Lebanon, the pro-Syrian magazine *Al Shiraa* reports that the US has secretly been supplying arms to Iran.

11/4   Ali Akbar Hashemi Rafsanjani, speaker of the Iranian Parliament, says that former NSC adviser Robert McFarlane and four other Americans, carrying Irish passports and posing as members of a flight crew, recently traveled to Iran on a secret diplomatic mission to trade military equipment for Iran's help in curbing terrorism. Rafsanjani says the men brought a Bible signed by President Reagan and a cake in the shape of a key, which was said to be "a key to open US–Iran relations."

■

Despite President Reagan's careening around the country on behalf of Republican candidates, the Democrats pick up eight seats and reclaim the Senate, 55–45. Clearly a referendum on Reagan's second term—12 of the 16 would-be senators he appeared with lost—this effectively serves notice that America has gone as far right as it's going on this swing of the pendulum.

Except, possibly, for California, where voters remove state Supreme Court Justice Rose Bird and two colleagues for being too liberal.

11/5   "Washington ain't seen nothing yet!" —President Reagan addressing a White House post-election pep rally, still unaware of the double-edged nature of this phrase

11/7   "In the name of God, would you please just be responsible and back off?" —Recently released hostage David Jacobsen at the White House, berating reporters for asking President Reagan questions about the secret Iran arms deal

11/10   Bruce Springsteen's live album arrives in stores, selling over a million instantly. Because it sells so many copies so fast, it does not enjoy a particularly long chart life, leading to the absurd industry perception that it's sort of a failure when in fact it's the best-selling five-record set ever.

11/13   "For 18 months now, we have had under way a secret diplomatic initiative to Iran. That initiative was undertaken for the simplest and best of reasons: to renew a relationship with the nation of Iran; to bring an honorable end to the bloody six-year war between Iran and Iraq; to eliminate state-sponsored terrorism and subversion, and to effect the safe return of all hostages . . ." —President Reagan addressing the nation on the Iran arms deal, hoping that if he mentions the hostages last, people won't think their release was the prime motivation for the deal

"Now, my fellow Americans, there is an old saying that nothing spreads so quickly as a rumor. So I thought it was time to speak with you directly—to tell you first-hand about our dealings with Iran. As Will Rogers once said, 'Rumor travels faster, but it don't stay put as long as truth.' So let's get to the facts."
—President Reagan preparing to embellish the truth

"During the course of our secret discussions, I authorized the transfer of small amounts of defensive weapons and spare parts for defensive systems to Iran. . . . These modest deliveries, taken together, could easily fit into a single cargo plane. . . . We did not—repeat—did not trade weapons or anything else for hostages, nor will we."
—President Reagan claiming that the arms for hostages swap wasn't really a swap because we didn't give them too much stuff, and besides, the stuff we did give them hardly counts as weapons

11/14　"Stupefyingly incredible."
—British Labour Party member Denis Healey on President Reagan's speech

"He has damaged his credibility everywhere. And if the American people buy this one, God help us."
—Sen. J. James Exon (D-NE) on the speech

■

Donald Regan is asked if it isn't hypocritical to ask other nations not to ship arms to Iran while we do just that. "Hypocrisy," he explains, "is a question of degree."

■

Risk arbitrager Ivan Boesky—who recently told a Berkeley commencement, "Greed is healthy. You can be greedy and still feel good about yourself"—agrees to pay $100 million in fines and repayments for insider stock trading. Since, considering his profits, this is actually a lenient assessment—even with his eventual three-year jail sentence—he shows his gratitude by secretly recording incriminating conversations with colleagues.

11/15　A Nicaraguan court sentences Eugene Hasenfus to 30 years in jail. The Sandinistas, having gotten considerable PR mileage out of him, magnanimously let him go home in time for Christmas.

■

"Some of us are like a shovel brigade that follow a parade down Main Street cleaning up. We took Reykjavik and turned what was really a sour situation into something that turned out pretty well. Who was it that took this disinformation thing and managed to turn it? Who was it took on this loss in the Senate and pointed out a few facts and managed to pull that? I don't say we'll be able to do it four times in a row. But here we go again, and we're trying."
—Donald Regan defending himself in *The New York Times* against charges of incompetence, oblivious to what someone else—Nancy Reagan, say—might think of his manure metaphor

11/16　George Shultz appears on *Face the Nation* to distance himself from the Iran arms deal. Asked directly whether he can assure the public that no more arms will be sent, the Secretary of State—the nation's chief architect of foreign policy—says, "No."

11/18 79% REJECT PRESIDENT'S EXPLANATION OF IRAN DEAL
—*Los Angeles Times*

■

Discussing President Reagan's upcoming press conference, Larry Speakes tells reporters, "We can guess 99 out of 100 times the questions that you guys pose."

"Yeah," says Sam Donaldson, "but you can never guess what he's gonna answer."

11/19 At his 39th press conference, President Reagan describes the arms shipment as "really minuscule," again claiming that "everything that we sold them could be put in one cargo plane and there would be plenty of room left over." He also states—four times—that Israel had no involvement in the Iran arms deal, but later issues a correction: "There may be some misunderstanding of one of my answers tonight. There was a third country involved in our secret project with Iran." How there could have been a "misunderstanding" of something he said *four times* is not explained.

11/20 Donald Regan places the blame for the arms deal squarely on Robert McFarlane, whom he has long despised. "Let's not forget whose idea this was," he tells his staff. "It was Bud's idea. When you give lousy advice, you get lousy results."

■

"He's got to throw some of those babies out of the sleigh."
—Watergate felon John Ehrlichman advising President Reagan to fire some people

11/21 The shredding machine in White House aide Oliver North's office jams.

11/22 Mike Tyson, 20, defeats Trevor Berbick in Las Vegas and becomes the youngest heavyweight champion in history. "Look at me," he says. "I'm just a boy, and I got this belt on my waist."

11/23 "Mrs. Reagan. There is the smiling mamba in all of this."
—Sam Donaldson suggesting that the First Lady might effect the necessary personnel changes at the White House

11/24 REAGAN REJECTED AIDES' ADVICE TO ADMIT IRAN DEAL A MISTAKE
—*The Washington Post*

11/25 A grim President Reagan appears in the White House briefing room to say he "was not fully informed on the nature of one of the activities" undertaken as an off-shoot of the Iran arms deal. He announces that National Security Adviser John Poindexter has resigned and NSC staffer Oliver North has been fired, then introduces Ed Meese to explain why.

"Certain monies which were received in the transaction between representatives of Israel and representatives of Iran were taken and made available to the forces in Central America which are opposing the Sandinista government there," says Meese. "We don't know the exact amount yet. Our estimate is that it is somewhere between $10 and $30 million. . . . The President knew nothing about it."

As Meese talks, his head is positioned in front of the White House logo (THE WHITE HOUSE/WASHINGTON) in such a way that the only letters that can be seen on TV spell out WHITE WASHING.

Later, Reagan calls North and tells him, "This is going to make a great movie one day."

■

"If he knew about it, then he has willfully broken the law; if he didn't know about it, then he is failing to do his job. After all, we expect the President to know about the foreign policy activities being run directly out of the White House."
—Sen. John Glenn neatly summarizing the President's predicament

■

"The scandal of dealing with terrorists has

turned into a political disaster."
—NBC's John Chancellor on the day's revelations

"A bombshell of a story."
—CBS' Dan Rather

"The Iran affair is now a scandal."
—ABC's Peter Jennings

11/26   Ed Meese appears on TV to assure viewers that "the President knows what's going on."

■

"Does the bank president know whether a teller in the bank is fiddling around with the books? No."
—Donald Regan explaining why his total ignorance of the diversion of funds to the contras is completely justified

11/27   Oliver North—who reportedly shredded documents while the Justice Department inquiry was underway—is refused entrance to the White House.

11/28   "100 percent pure urine suitable for unanticipated urine demand."
—Ad in Austin newspaper by Byrd Laboratories, which is selling drug-free urine at $49.95 a bag

DECEMBER 1986

In which the First Couple goes on the defensive

12/1   A Gallup poll shows President Rea-

gan's popularity to have suffered the largest one-month decline ever recorded, plummeting from 67% to 46%.

■

"When the flak gets heavy out there, the wingman doesn't go peeling off and pull away from the flight leader, especially when the flight leader is known to the wingman to have total ability and a good record. So there's no hiding out on my part, and no pulling away from support for a President who has been so fantastically good to Barbara and to me and opened up a whole new dimension in our lives, and in whose word of honor I have total trust."
—George Bush "arfing" to *Time*

■

In a *Time* interview, President Reagan:

● Calls Oliver North "a national hero"
● Dismisses the furor over the growing scandal as "a Beltway bloodletting"
● Blames the press for interfering with the release of more hostages.

"There is bitter bile in my throat," he says. "This whole thing boils down to great irresponsibility on the part of the press."

■

President Reagan appears on national television with his newly appointed Tower Commission so Americans will know he's really serious about getting to the bottom of the whole affair, though not so serious that he would just call in North and Poindexter and, being the most powerful man on the planet, demand that they tell him everything.

■

The National Archives releases 1.5 million documents from the Nixon White House, among them a memo from aide Egil Krogh describing Elvis Presley's 1970 meeting with Nixon. "Presley indicated that he had been playing Las Vegas," wrote Krogh, "and the President indicated that he was aware of how difficult it is to perform in Las Vegas." After buttering Nixon up by calling the Beatles "anti-American," the singer—stoned on speed and scratching at his face—convinced the Pres-

ident to get him a federal drug agent's badge to certify his commitment to the anti-drug war — and to exempt him from inconvenient airport searches.

12/2 President Reagan names Frank Carlucci as his fifth National Security Adviser.

■

"Tonight the vault is full!"
—Geraldo Rivera hosting his second special, *American Vice: The Doping of a Nation,* which features a drug test of the studio audience and eight live drug busts in which doors are knocked down and suspects—innocent or guilty, what's the difference?—are hauled off to jail on national TV

12/3 "The President is absolutely convinced that he did not swap arms for hostages."
—George Bush, apparently believing that an affirmation of Reagan's detachment from reality will be somehow reassuring

12/4 REAGAN SLOW TO REALIZE EXTENT OF CRISIS
—*Los Angeles Times*

■

"The sky is black with chickens coming home to roost."
—Columnist Alexander Cockburn on the Iran-contra scandal

"Ha. Ha. Ha."
—*New Republic* editor Michael Kinsley expressing his "glee" at the President's recent misfortune, prompting the more sober David Broder to attack those "juveniles" gauche enough to gloat

■

"If I could write my epitaph, it would read, 'He told the truth. Always.'"
—Larry Speakes—who is leaving the White House at the end of January to take a high-paying job with Merrill Lynch—on how he wants to be remembered

12/5 MEESE BROUGHT IN FBI FOUR DAYS AFTER KEY DOCUMENT WAS FOUND
—*The Washington Post*

12/6 *The Washington Post* reports that Nancy Reagan's nagging about the need to fire Donald Regan became so intense that the President finally told her to "get off my goddamn back!"

■

President Reagan finally concedes that "mistakes were made," though he does not suggest who made them and implies that it certainly wasn't him.

12/7 President Reagan is reported to have had three "long, rambling conversations" over the past 10 days with a noted expert on White House scandal containment: Richard Nixon.

12/8 "When a mob shows up in the yard, howling that the head of the household be produced, the sons do not force the Old Man to sit down at a table and write up a list of his 'mistakes.' You start firing from the upper floors."

—White House communications director Pat Buchanan attacking the Republican party establishment, which he claims has "headed for the tall grass" by failing to defend the President

■

"If Colonel North ripped off the Ayatollah and took $30 million and gave it to the contras, then God bless Colonel North!"
—Pat Buchanan addressing a pro-Reagan rally in Miami

12/9   Oliver North and John Poindexter invoke their Fifth Amendment rights and refuse to testify before the House Foreign Affairs Committee. Says the jug-eared North earnestly, "I don't think there is another person in America that wants to tell this story as much as I do."

■

Reporters ask President Reagan if he's watching the House Foreign Affairs Committee hearings. "Oh, now and then when I can't find a ball game," he quips, leaving them to wonder what kind of ball game he expects to find early on a weekday morning in mid-December.

■

Richard Nixon tells President Reagan's critics, "It is time to get off his back." Says New Hampshire governor John Sununu of Nixon's speech, "I wish someone had videotaped that so it could be shown at every high school in the country."

12/10   "There seems to be an inordinate amount of information he was not aware of. He would say, 'I don't know.' It evoked laughter a number of times."
—Unnamed congressman describing William Casey's testimony before the House Foreign Affairs Committee

12/11   The Reagans are reportedly "stunned" by his allies' refusal to defend him on the Iran-contra matter. Explains Robert Dornan, normally one of the President's most rabid supporters, "When someone says, 'But he was giving arms to people he knew had killed our Marines,' it's hard to respond to that."

12/12   "There might be something—though not much—to be said for a President who at political risk wrongheadedly ordered an

action that he was convinced served the national interest. But there's *nothing* to be said for a President so inattentive to duty that middle-rank Navy and Marine officers on his staff were able to embark unimpeded on a course almost certain to undermine the foreign policy of the United States in some of its most important concerns. . . . Presidents are elected to watch such matters, not to nap after lunch."
—Columnist Tom Wicker

12/15   A *Los Angeles Times* poll shows that 78% of Americans perceive a cover-up by the White House, while only 33% believe President Reagan to be "very familiar" with complex issues.

12/16   Daniel Inouye (D-HI) and Warren Rudman (R-NH) are chosen to head the 11-member Senate committee investigating the Iran-contra scandal. The House, determined to create a panel even more unwieldy, appoints Lee Hamilton (D-IN) to chair a 15-member group.

■

President Reagan meets with Republican congressional leaders to get their input on his upcoming State of the Union message. Urged by one to support a federal health insurance plan for catastrophic illnesses, the President responds by complaining about a welfare family being put up at a ritzy New York hotel.

12/17   Nancy Reagan denies that the President told her to "get off my goddamn back." Says the First Lady, "They happened to pick the one word that Ronnie never ever uses, ever." This comes as a surprise to anyone familiar with outtakes from Reagan's movies, in which "goddamn" turns up with numbing regularity.

12/18   A malignant tumor is removed from William Casey's brain.

■

"There have been a number of people who have suggested that I abandon my individual rights under the Constitution of the United

States. The President has not asked that I do that. I don't believe the President really wants me to abandon my individual rights under the Constitution. People have died face down in the mud all over the world defending those individual rights."
—Oliver North, annoyed by Nancy Reagan's incessant demands that he "talk"

12/19 Lawrence E. Walsh is named independent counsel—the new nice name for a special prosecutor—for the Iran-contra scandal.

12/20 A dozen white youths, wielding baseball bats and other weapons, attack three black men in the Howard Beach section of Queens, chasing one of them, Michael Griffith, onto a nearby highway where he is killed by a

passing car, after which the beating of the others is resumed.

◾

MEESE NOW SAYS REAGAN, UNDER SEDATION AFTER SURGERY, MAY HAVE OKD 1ST ARMS DEAL
—*New York Newsday*

12/21 Sen. Paul Laxalt announces that President Reagan "is going to be in high visibility" in coming days "to demonstrate to the country that he's fully in charge." Says a White House aide of Laxalt's statement, "When we heard it, we all cracked up."

12/22 "We should brush this under the carpet real quick for the good of the country."
—Palm Springs mayor Frank Bogert suggesting the proper method of dealing with the scandal

12/23 "The President ordered this whole operation on Iran. He ordered his Administration not to tell the intelligence committees what he was doing. Now he wants the intelligence committee to tell him what his Administration was doing during the time they were under his orders not to tell the intelligence committee. Even Alice in Wonderland doesn't get this twisted around."
—Sen. Patrick Leahy (D-VT) on President Reagan's eagerness to receive the Senate Intelligence Committee's report on the arms deal

12/24 CASEY HAS NOT RECOVERED ALL NORMAL BRAIN FUNCTIONS
PROSPECTS FOR IMPROVEMENT ARE UNCLEAR
—*The Washington Post*

◾

"When one talks about what Reagan 'knew,' one could be dealing in metaphysics."
—Elizabeth Drew in *The New Yorker*

◾

VOYAGER SUCCEEDS IN HISTORIC FLIGHT

1986

WORLD CIRCUIT, ON ONE LOAD OF FUEL, ENDS IN CALIFORNIA
—*The New York Times*

12/28 "You can draw your own conclusion."
—Charles Z. Wick responding to a reporter's query as to whether Nancy Reagan is upset about the Iran-contra scandal

∎

Terry Dolan, 36, inappropriately homophobic co-founder of the National Conservative Political Action Committee (NCPAC), dies of AIDS.

12/31 A disgruntled employee at a San Juan hotel sets a fire that kills 96.

∎

The Wall Street Journal reports that when Oliver North, as a Naval Academy midshipman, suffered serious knee and back injuries in a 1964 car crash, he recuperated with a Liddy-like regimen of strengthening his body by repeatedly jumping off the roof of the family garage. ∎
Gary Hart attends rock star Don Henley's New Year's party in Aspen, where he makes the casual acquaintance of would-be Miami model Donna Rice.

POP QUIZ

1 True or false? When Donald Regan was asked if he only really respects other self-made millionaires, he replied indignantly, "Not true! The people I respect are the ones that do their jobs well, no matter how menial the task."

2 Which network newsman introduced coverage of the Reykjavik summit with the cry, "Ready, set, Gorbachev!"?
a David Brinkley
b Dan Rather
c Peter Jennings
d Tom Brokaw

3 True or false? According to Kitty Kelley's book, Frank Sinatra once demonstrated his love for a friend by saying, "Bill, if anybody ever does anything to hurt you, I'll kill them."

Match the newsmaker with his/her news.
4 J. Z. Knight
5 C. J. Rapp
6 Bill Cosby
7 Bill Buckner
8 Dennis Hopper
9 Ted Turner
10 David Cronenberg

___**a** Created Jolt cola, which boasted "all the sugar and twice the caffeine" of other colas
___**b** Chose inopportune moment to let baseball roll between legs
___**c** Channeled 35,000-year-old man named Ramtha
___**d** Rejuvenated career with performance as sexual psychopath in *Blue Velvet*
___**e** Had best-selling non-fiction book of the year and made stupid faces on TV

___**f** Sold MGM and said, "I wept because I had no movie studio until I met a man who had no sports teams"

___**g** Directed smartest horror movie of the decade, *The Fly*

11 True or false? Though it was commonly known, even by young children, that Iran was ruled by a man named Khomeini whose title was the Ayatollah, President Reagan persisted in calling him "the Khomeini."

12 How was Ed Meese described by a friend of 20 years?

a "His passion for law enforcement is rare in a man with so little respect for actual law."

b "He loves going after goldfish with a cannon."

c "He was an Oakland prosecutor who was lucky enough to know Ronald Reagan."

d "He has a big square head, several chins, a really fishy mouth and his eyes are way too close together."

13 What show did George Bush's aides think would be appropriate for him to make a guest appearance on, though he never actually did?

a *Miami Vice*

b *Cheers*

c *L.A. Law*

d *The Golden Girls*

14 Which of the Reagan offspring appeared in an American Express commercial?

a Maureen

b Michael

c Ron

d Patti

15 True or false? Drivers purporting to be con-cerned about the safety of their infant passengers plastered signs to that effect on rear windows, thus obstructing their vision and increasing the chances for an accident.

16 Which of these actually appeared on TV?

a *The Ironic Woman*, a Linda Ellerbee review of the century

b *The Search for Helga*, a live Geraldo Rivera special in which he claimed to have located Andrew Wyeth's secret model but when he got to her house nobody was there

c *Kate's Secret*, a TV movie starring Meredith Baxter-Birney as a binging and purging bulimic

d "There She Goes Again," a *60 Minutes* segment examining the First Lady's disturbing tendency to lose her balance

17 True or false? White House efforts to prevent President Reagan from answering unrehearsed questions by drowning them out with unnecessary helicopter noise were quickly thwarted by an indignant press corps that pointed out how humiliating it was to have a national leader—a Great Communicator!—who was afraid to open his mouth without a script.

ANSWERS

1-False (He said he also has "great respect for people of inherited wealth"), 2-b, 3-False (What he actually said was, "Bill, sometimes I wish someone would really hurt you so I could kill them"), 4-c, 5-a, 6-e, 7-b, 8-d, 9-f, 10-g, 11-True, 12-b, 13-a, 14-c, 15-True, 16-c, 17-False (Reporters merely acquiesced in the charade, shouting louder and contributing to the President's image as a nice guy bedeviled by boors)

1/2 Heading back to Washington after their annual New Year's at the Annenberg estate, the Reagans are asked, "What will 1987 be like?"

"Great," says Nancy.

"Better than '86," ad-libs the President.

1/4 Sixteen people are killed and 175 injured when a Conrail locomotive crashes into an Amtrak train outside Baltimore. It turns out that the Conrail engineer and brakeman had shared some marijuana not long before the accident.

■

Rev. Oral Roberts tells viewers, "God will call me home" if they don't help him raise $4.5 million in three months. "I need some very quick money," says the preacher. "I mean, I need it now." He gets his money and does not die.

■

President Reagan enters Bethesda Naval Hospital for minor prostate surgery and the removal of four more polyps from his colon. Larry Speakes—who described the President as "champing at the bit" to go home during his last hospital stay—reveals that he is now "chomping at the bit."

1/6 Former *New York Times* editor A. M. ("Abe") Rosenthal, forced out of power against his will because of the paper's mandatory retirement policy, begins writing a twice-weekly column that quickly establishes itself as a source for much unintended mirth among segments of the journalistic community.

1/7 CASEY IS DESCRIBED AS TOO IMPAIRED TO STAY ON AT C.I.A.

HOSPITAL CITES HIS DIFFICULTY IN SPEAKING AND MOVING SINCE BRAIN SURGERY
—*The New York Times*

1/8 Former NASA Administrator James Beggs reveals that Michael Deaver became extremely upset when he learned that his client, Coke, would be sharing "First Cola on a Space Shuttle" honors with Pepsi.

■

NBC reports that John Poindexter told Donald Regan he'd condoned the diversion of funds because he "felt sorry for the contras."

1/9 The White House releases the finding—signed by President Reagan on January 17, 1986—authorizing the sale of arms to Iran and ordering the CIA not to tell Congress. Also released is the 2½-page memo justifying the policy, which the President had not bothered to read.

1/10 "If the big spenders want a fight on the budget, they'd better strap on their helmets and shoulder pads. In this fourth and final quarter, I'm determined to go out there and win one for the American people and, yes—and one for the Gipper."
—President Reagan, recovering from surgery and assuring radio listeners that it won't be long before he's "suited up and back on the playing field"

1/12 The White House announces that George Bush's press secretary, Marlin Fitzwater, will replace Larry Speakes.

■

Agent Scott Meredith announces that Zebra Books will publish Michael Reagan's childhood memoir, *On the Outside Looking In.* Says Meredith, "You can tell from the title that he isn't happy with the relationship."

■

TV PREMIERE: *The Morning Program.* The floundering CBS News surrenders 90 daily minutes of prime A.M. time to the network's entertainment division. Actress Mariette Hartley and local news anchor Rolland Smith preside over a giddy amalgam that includes stand-up comics, a "Personals" segment (videodate pleas) and several appearances by Hartley's golden retriever. It lasts 11 months.

1/13 Rachel Abrams says she "would like to take a machine gun and mow [columnist] Anthony Lewis down" for attacking her husband Elliott's McCarthyite tactics as Assistant Secretary of State. Says the perpetually scowling Elliott, "I wouldn't waste the bullets. I would rather have them go to the contras."

■

"It wasn't a sustaining issue. It was the epitome of the fad issue, a classic really. It came and went in three weeks, max."
—GOP consultant Lee Atwater on the Reagans' anti-drug campaign

1/14 Larry Speakes scoffs at a *New York Times* account of President Reagan's recent stronger-than-usual detachment from reality, urging reporters to "bug off." And what about the Senate report that Reagan thought would exonerate him but that in fact reveals the howling depths of his ignorance? "Phooey," says Speakes. "P-H-O-O-E-Y."

1/16 "The President has absolutely convinced himself that what happened has absolutely nothing to do with hostages. . . . No one is going to talk him out of it, and it's not clear that anyone is even going to try."
—White House source

"The President has crawled into his shell."
—White House source

1/19 *Time* reports that a White House aide defended President Reagan's work habits by revealing that he sent a secretary a hand-written thank-you note for a get-well poem. "It shows he's up there doing things," said the aide. "It shows that he's extremely responsive and willing to get down into the details."

1/20 George Bush says President Reagan "is certain to this very day that he did not authorize arms-for-hostages."

■

CONTRA ARMS CREWS SAID TO SMUGGLE DRUGS
—*The New York Times*

■

Robert "Bud" McFarlane goes on *Nightline* to separate himself from the decision to bring the Iranians a cake. "Simply put, there was a cake on the mission," he says. "I didn't buy it, bake it, cook it, eat it, present it or otherwise get involved with it. . . . The cake was the product of a spontaneous idea of Col. North. . . . I didn't get involved with it."

1/22 An ABC News/*Washington Post* poll shows that 62% of the public think President Reagan is lying about the Iran-contra scandal.

■

On the day before he is to be sentenced on a bribery conviction, Pennsylvania state treasurer R. Budd Dwyer calls a press conference where he pulls out a .357 Magnum, inserts it in his mouth and blows the back of his head off. The entire sequence, notable for the quantity of blood that pours from his nose, is broadcast on two local stations.

1/24 A spokesman for Liberace denies a report that the pianist has AIDS.

1/25 Four university professors are kidnapped in Beirut, bringing to 14 the number of Americans taken hostage under President Reagan, who once promised "swift and effective retribution" for such incidents. In fact, though the media has seen no need to make a big thing of it, several hostages have languished in captivity far longer than any under President Carter.

1/26 The Tower Commission interviews President Reagan about the Iran-contra scandal. Though he is said by a source to lack a "highly detailed recollection," he acknowledges having authorized the arms sale to Iran in August 1985. This corroborates Robert McFarlane's testimony and directly contradicts Donald Regan's.

1/27 Delivering his State of the Union address, President Reagan finds himself being openly mocked by Democrats who—emboldened at last by his plunge in the polls—applaud sarcastically at inappropriate times during his speech.

1/28 "On the surface, selling arms to a country that sponsors terrorism, of course, clearly, you'd have to argue it's wrong, but it's the exception sometimes that proves the rule."
—George Bush on *Good Morning America*

Excerpts from a videotape of Ferdinand Marcos jogging, weight-lifting and shadow-boxing—recorded to demonstrate to his supporters at home that he is in good health and ready to return to power at any moment—make their American television debut on a Hawaiian news broadcast.

1/30 Larry Speakes says that President Reagan was "pleased" by a Senate Intelligence Committee report that he knew nothing about the diversion of funds to the contras—the only example on record of a President reveling in his ignorance of his own foreign policy initiatives. And did Reagan actually read the report? Of course not.

Desperate to demonstrate that he is in charge, President Reagan vetoes—of all things —a clean water bill. "I *just said no,*" catchphrases the President emphatically, putting on his stern face. The veto is overridden.

In his last speech as White House spokesman, Larry Speakes—without a scintilla of irony—tells the National Press Club it's time to "decide policy on the basis of what's good for the people, not what's good for television. . . . Let's not write a TV script and then create an event designed for the evening news." He receives a Presidential Citizens Medal, with a citation praising him as "a man whom the American people could always count on to tell them the truth."

FEBRUARY 1987

In which the President has trouble remembering his lines

2/2 Incapacitated CIA Director William Casey resigns. He is replaced by FBI chief William Webster.

James C. McKay is named independent counsel to investigate allegations of illegal lobbying on behalf of the Wedtech Corporation— a minority-owned Bronx defense contractor— by former White House aide Lyn Nofziger.

2/4 Liberace, 67, dies in Palm Springs. He had AIDS.

"If that student wants to say the world is flat, the teacher doesn't have the right to try to prove otherwise."

—Jim Cooper—lobbyist for Arizona governor Evan Mecham—telling Congress that "schools don't have any business telling people what to believe"

2/6 Walking into a roomful of aides assembled for a surprise 76th birthday party, President Reagan seems startled until his wife whispers to him, "It's your staff."

"Of all the 38 anniversaries of my 39th birthday," says the President incorrectly, "this is about the nicest."

■

Failing to "anticipate the perception of it," Lloyd Bentsen, new head of the Senate Finance Committee, offers lobbyists the pleasure of his company at a monthly breakfast in exchange for a $10,000 contribution to his re-election campaign. Public outcry forces his quick abandonment of the plan.

2/7 Despite insistence by the administration that its Iranian contacts were "moderates," an aide to George Bush acknowledges that the Vice President was told last summer by Israeli official Amiram Nir that "we are dealing with the most radical elements" in Iran because "we've learned they can deliver and the moderates can't."

2/9 Marlin Fitzwater explains that the difference between "moderates" and "radicals" is a "semantic" one that would be difficult to sort out. So, will the administration stop referring to its Iranian contacts as "moderates"? Says Fitzwater, "We'll probably use it and probably, maybe, not use it."

■

"Even though there may be some misguided critics of what we're trying to do, I think we're on the wrong path."

—President Reagan, launching his welfare reform program

■

Greeting the America's Cup winners at the White House, President Reagan puts on a *Croc-*

odile Dundee hat and misquotes that movie's catchphrase. "I just know," he says, "that whenever I put that on I'm going to find myself turning to Nancy and saying, 'G'bye, mate.'"

■

On the eve of his testimony before the Tower Commission, Robert McFarlane takes upwards of 20 Valiums in a failed suicide attempt.

2/11 President Reagan tells the Tower Commission that after discussing it with Don Regan, he now remembers that he did *not* authorize the arms sale in advance. Commission members are disheartened when, while reciting his recollection from a staff-supplied memo, he mistakenly reads his stage instructions aloud.

■

"We shouldn't have come here! I told you we shouldn't have come here!"

—Maria Alfano to her husband, Pietro—a key figure in the "Pizza Connection" heroin trial—as he lies on the sidewalk after being gunned down in Greenwich Village

2/12 "I think the key players around there know I expressed certain reservations on certain aspects."

—George Bush defending his Iran-contra inaction

■

"You know about the new fundamentalist group out there called LORD? What's it stand for? Let Oral Roberts Die."

—George Bush in Lansing, Michigan, telling a joke that plays better in northwest Washington than in the Republican heartland

■

President Reagan tells a group of junior high students about how Rex barks in front of Lincoln's bedroom and won't go in, which makes the President think Lincoln's ghost is there. "Well," he says, "I guess that's enough of a history lesson here for today."

2/13 NOW PLAYING: *Over the Top.* Though the public may love Sylvester Stallone as a bare-chested warrior, the audience for his portrait of an arm-wrestling trucker is—as it was in 1984 for his country-singing cabbie in *Rhinestone*—virtually non-existent. With even *Cobra* grossing far less than expected, it becomes clear that this is one actor people have no interest in seeing clothed.

■

President Reagan greets the Super Bowl–winning New York Giants at the White House, where he and the team captain dump popcorn on each other's heads.

Paul Hosefros/NYT Pictures

■

STREET BOMBSHELL
INSIDE-TRADING SCANDAL IMPLICATES HIGH AIDES AT GOLDMAN, KIDDER
TRADERS WATCH A HANDCUFFING
—*The Wall Street Journal*

2/16 TOWER PANEL PROBES WHETHER NORTH RAN ARRAY OF OTHER COVERT PROGRAMS
—*The Washington Post*

2/18 Sources reveal that Nancy Reagan is no longer speaking to Donald Regan. Asked if his chief of staff will be staying on, the President says, "Well, this is up to him"—as close to firing someone as he ever gets. "When I don't leave," Regan tells an aide, "they'll know I'm not leaving."

2/19 Chris Wallace reports that Nancy Reagan leaked the story about her feud with Donald Regan in an effort to force him out after he had the gall to hang up on one of her harangues. Her phone manners turn out to be no better. It is learned that in another conversation, it was *she*—furious at Regan for trying to subject her convalescing husband to reporters' questions—who shouted, "Have your damned news conference!" and hung up on *him*.

■

With media interest in his political future peaking, Mario Cuomo—aware that the next President could well be Hoover to Reagan's Coolidge—says he will not be a candidate in 1988. Speculation immediately turns to whether he'll accept a draft.

■

U.S. ISSUES RULES FOR DRUG TESTING
STEPS TO BAR CHEATING ALLOW
URINATION TO BE OBSERVED IN SOME
SITUATIONS
—*The Washington Post*

■

Retrieved computer messages show that Oliver North shared secret information with the Iranians. Says a source, "Ollie was running his own covert operation within the authorized covert operation."

■

"This column is about a large bunch of wonderfully hideous marine iguanas. . . ."
—A. M. Rosenthal in *The New York Times*

2/20 "I learned a lesson in my former profession. . . . We're saving the best stuff for the last act."
—President Reagan at a conservative pep rally

"The simple truth is, 'I don't remember—period.' "
—President Reagan—who, as a candidate, said he would resign at the slightest sign of senility—writing to the Tower Commission to set the record straight about whether he authorized the arms shipment in advance

2/22 "Nothing in his deplorable conduct of his office has been as contemptible as his clinging to it."
—George Will, frequent lunch partner of the First Lady, predicting the imminent departure of Donald Regan

Artist/voyeur Andy Warhol, 58, dies of a heart attack following gall-bladder surgery.

Oliver North's secretary, Fawn Hall—who has been granted immunity—admits helping her boss destroy documents last November.

2/23 Missouri congressman Richard Gephardt—whose indistinct eyebrows give his already smooth face an eerily androidal quality—becomes the first Democratic candidate in the 1988 presidential race.

The ultimate '80s protest song, the Beastie Boys' "(You Gotta) Fight for Your Right (to Party!)," begins a two-week stay in the Top Ten.

2/24 "One of my friends said Andy Warhol once said that everyone's famous for 15 minutes. I kind of feel like that right now."
—Fawn Hall providing a photo opportunity outside her lawyer's office

"People used to drop by to see Ollie just to sit outside his office and drool over Fawn."
—Unnamed White House aide

"I'd like to ask one question of everybody. Everybody that can remember what they were doing on August 8th of 1985, raise your hand.

I think it's possible to forget. Nobody's raised any hands."
—President Reagan, who would have gotten a different response from reporters had he asked, more pertinently, "Everybody that would remember approving the sale of arms to an enemy nation, raise your hand"

2/26 Pledging to "carefully study" it over the next several days, the President accepts his copy of the Tower Commission Report, which:

- Blames Regan for "the chaos that descended upon the White House"
- Says Shultz and Weinberger "simply distanced themselves from the program"
- Concludes that Casey "appears to have been informed in considerable detail"
- Euphemistically attacks Reagan's ignorance and sloth by faulting his "personal management style."

A paperback edition is an instant best seller.

2/27 Donald Regan storms out of the White House after hearing on CNN that Howard Baker is replacing him. Nancy Reagan, believed to have leaked the story to humiliate Regan, says she is "pleased" with the change, which takes Baker out of the 1988 presidential race and allows him—as many observers note—to be President now.

2/28 "When a national security adviser to the President attempts to commit suicide, when a secretary to a top presidential aide says she shredded and altered important White House documents, when the President says he can't remember if he authorized shipping arms to Iran and then changes his story, all of this becomes very disturbing to people."
—Democratic pollster Peter D. Hart

REAGAN'S IGNORANCE SHOCKED TOWER COMMISSION
—*The New York Times*

MARCH 1987

In which the Great Communicator fails to communicate

3/1 "We do not regard him as a mental patient. But we regard him as a President who didn't do his job."
—Tower Commission member Edmund Muskie on the Reagan "management style"

∎

"The record is that he was either absent or silent. I don't know what that does for him."
—Sen. Bob Dole attacking presidential rival George Bush's ineffectiveness in the Iran-contra scandal

∎

"Two things keep dynamic, complex societies like ours together: the strength of the leader's word and the reasonable rule of law. Here our leaders have forfeited credibility and flouted the rule of law. No matter what else you say, it's sad and dangerous."
—Mario Cuomo on the Tower Commission Report

3/2 A *New York Times*/CBS News poll shows that less than a quarter of the public thinks the President is running his own government. Howard Baker rejects this perception. "I have never seen Ronald Reagan more energetic, more fully engaged and more in command of difficult circumstances and questions," he burbles. "He has never been better."

∎

"At a time he most needs to appear strong, President Reagan is being weakened and made to appear wimpish and helpless by the political interference of his wife."
—William Safire on Nancy Reagan's ouster of Donald Regan

"When she gets her hackles up, she can be a dragon."
—Howard Baker on the First Lady

"I don't think most people associate me with leeches or how to get them off. But I know how to get them off. I'm an expert at it."
—Nancy Reagan gloating over the demise of Donald Regan during a speech to the American Camping Association

3/4 "That is fiction, and I think it is despicable fiction."
—President Reagan on reports of his wife's excessive influence

∎

US District Judge W. Brevard Hand bans the use of 44 textbooks in Alabama's public schools on the grounds that they unconstitutionally promote "the religion of secular humanism." The decision is reversed on appeal.

■

President Reagan responds to the Tower Commission with a 12-minute speech in which he:

- Acknowledges that the Iran-contra affair "happened on my watch"
- Says nobler aims of long-term peace "deteriorated . . . into trading arms for hostages"
- Calls the deal "a mistake" (though one that resulted from his excessive concern for the hostages).

As for his "management style," the problem was that "no one kept proper records of meetings or decisions," which led to his inability to recall approving the arms shipment. "I did approve it," says the President. "I just can't say specifically when." Lest anyone remain unnerved, he adds, "Rest assured, there's plenty of record-keeping now going on at 1600 Pennsylvania Avenue."

Says Indiana senator Dan Quayle after the speech, "The Gipper's back."

3/5 The Oliver North media stakeout—which has daily recorded the self-righteous Marine as, seat belt fastened, he drives off to work—asks his reaction to the Reagan speech. "If you came all the way out to Great Falls to find somebody to play President-bashing with," he says, "you came to the wrong driveway."

■

FAWN HALL GETS $500,000 BID FOR NUDE PHOTOS; NOT INTERESTED
—*Los Angeles Times*

3/6 Lobbyist Michael Deaver's last foreign client, the Saudi government, declines to renew its $500,000 contract. Lawyer Randall Turk says his client "wasn't able to perform a whole lot of services. . . . Anybody who Deaver talked to got interviewed by the FBI."

■

George Bush says he's "catching the dickens" from friends for not preventing the Iran arms deal.

■

"The business that I used to be in said, 'Save something for the third act.' And we will."
—President Reagan boarding a helicopter for a weekend at Camp David

■

TV evangelist Jim Bakker's wife, Tammy Faye, announces that she is currently undergoing treatment for her 17-year prescription drug addiction at the Betty Ford Center. She claims she didn't know she had a problem until she saw people and cats on the wing of an airplane.

3/10 Former governor Bruce Babbitt—who shares fellow Arizonan Morris Udall's vote-getting handicaps of keen intelligence and genuine wit—declares his candidacy for the Democratic presidential nomination.

■

Asked about the Iran-contra scandal at a photo opportunity, President Reagan feigns laryngitis. "I lost my voice," he says, grinning. "I can't talk."

3/11 Asked again about Iran-contra, President Reagan again feigns laryngitis. "I've lost my voice," he says. Explains Marlin Fitzwater, "This is a new tactic of his."

3/14 Sources reveal that, despite his recent speech, President Reagan still sees nothing wrong with the Iran arms deal. Says a GOP strategist, "I bet that if you get him aside and put a beer into him, he'd say he didn't make a mistake."

"I think you should take a look at the difference between point of view and facts."
—John Wayne in a newly discovered 1977 letter to Ronald Reagan, in which he claimed Reagan was spreading lies in his battle against the Panama Canal treaty

3/15 Interviewing George Bush on *60 Minutes*, Diane Sawyer raises the issue of what reporter Michael Kramer has called "the wimp factor."

Kramer, says Bush, will "never play linebacker for the Chicago Bears. You ever seen him?"

Sawyer brings up George Will's "lapdog" quote.

Will, says Bush, will "never play linebacker for the Chicago Bears. Have you ever seen him?"

As proof of his own non-wimpdom, he cites having been "shot down two months after my 20th birthday, fighting for my country. I didn't detect any wimp factor there."

3/18 Michael Deaver is indicted on five counts of perjury. He is the seventh senior administration official to be indicted, and the first under the provisions of the 1978 Ethics in Government Act.

Sen. Alan Simpson (R-WY) lashes out at

the press after an audacious reporter disturbs a photo opportunity by asking President Reagan a question. "You're not asking him things so you can get answers," he says. "You're asking him things because you know he's off-balance and you'd like to stick it in his gazoo." The *Los Angeles Times* erroneously reports the word as "bazoo."

3/19 At his first press conference in four months, President Reagan—who yesterday couldn't wait for his rehearsal to end so he could tell a dirty joke about a chimpanzee and a bus crash—assures the public that he won't be forgetting any more important things because "we now have quite a system installed of people taking notes, you know, at all our meetings and all our doings." As for his shattered credibility, he declares that he's "not going to tell falsehoods to the American people. I'll leave that to others."

The *Charlotte Observer* reports that TV evangelist Jim Bakker paid $115,000 to hush up a 1980 sexual encounter with 21-year-old church secretary Jessica Hahn. Bakker admits the charge, claiming that he was set up by former colleagues, and resigns for what he expects will be a brief period of penitence. The multimillion-dollar PTL ("People That Love" and "Praise The Lord") empire, which includes South Carolina's Heritage USA theme park, is taken over at his request by Jerry Falwell, whose fundamentalist contempt for the charismatic Pentecostalism of the PTL was summed up in his observation that people who speak in tongues "ate too much pizza last night."

3/22 The *Mobro 4,000*, a barge piled with 3,168 tons of New York garbage, begins a 162-day, 6,000-mile search for a port willing to dispose of its load. The boat—a surreal symbol of man's inability to clean up his own mess—is rebuffed by six states and three countries before New York City agrees to burn the trash.

3/24 Alexander Haig throws his "helmet

AT LONG LAST, THE PRESIDENT MEETS THE PRESS

After four months of silence, the President opened himself to questioning on the Iran-contra scandal, demonstrating his usual firm grasp of the subject at hand:

"...I don't know...I don't know whether we would have gotten more out...I don't know. I wouldn't be surprised if he was...I did not know at that time that there was any money involved. I only knew that...All we'd learned...Helen, I don't know. I only know that...All that I know...Sam, all I know is that...I can't remember just when...There are other people that don't remember either...I did not know that I had said it in such a way...I didn't realize that I had said that...We didn't know...I didn't know how far we could go...I still do not have the answer...It was a complete surprise to me...We're still waiting for that to be explained...I don't know...I don't know..."

into the ring" and announces his candidacy for the Republican presidential nomination.

■

"I've always been sort of partial to a big finish. You should have a good third-act curtain."
—President Reagan addressing a group of business executives

■

Rival TV preacher Jimmy Swaggart admits initiating the investigation of Jim Bakker's sexual misconduct.

3/25 "Jim has very seldom seen me without makeup and hardly ever in my life without my eyelashes. I think every woman ought to wear eyelashes, because I think the eyes are such an important part of the face."
—Tammy Faye Bakker, as quoted in the book *Christian Wives*, revealing that she wears makeup—and lots of it—to bed

3/26 FIGHT ERUPTS IN BABY M CASE OVER BOOK AND MOVIE RIGHTS
—*The New York Times*

3/27 Jessica Hahn says her sexual encounter with Jim Bakker, which she blames on drugged wine, made her feel "like a piece of hamburger somebody threw out in the street." Bakker responds that she was the aggressor, and that, despite her claims of innocence, she knew "all the tricks of the trade."

■

"Nice to see you, Mr. Ambassador."
—President Reagan greeting British Labour Party leader Denis Healey, while the actual ambassador—whom he has met—stands nearby

■

Failing to understand that the dynamics of his relationship with Congress have changed, President Reagan vetoes a popular highway bill. He is again overridden.

3/30 "My friends, we're not about to fall on the ball and wait for the clock to run out. Instead, we're going to have the greatest fourth quarter in presidential history."
—President Reagan delivering a pep talk to staffers

■

Vincent van Gogh's *Sunflowers* sells for $39.9 million, almost four times the previous record paid for a single work of art. During his lifetime, van Gogh sold one painting.

RON *MOTS*

Match the provocation with the wildly amusing response from the man William F. Buckley, Jr., called "the wittiest man to serve as President during this century."

1 President is heckled
2 President is interrupted mid-speech by loud noise
3 President receives applause
4 President commemorates anniversary of venerable American institution
5 President receives honorary college degree
6 President is asked about his hearing
7 President is introduced after a tardy arrival
8 President quotes long-dead historical figure

a "I'm delighted to celebrate anything that's older than I am."
b "What?"
c "Is there an echo in here?"
d "If I'd gotten a hand like that in Hollywood, I never would have left."
e "Missed me."
f "And ever since he told me that . . ."
g "I always thought the first one was honorary."
h "I guess that should have been the *late* President."

ANSWERS
1-c, 2-e, 3-d, 4-a, 5-g, 6-b, 7-h, 8-f

Bonus Question: Does President Reagan's joke that he's really not that old because "they mixed up the babies in the hospital" make any sense? Why?

[ANSWER: No, because any babies at the hospital at the time would have been the same age.]

APRIL 1987

In which the front-runner makes his first campaign promise

4/1   A White House official admits that President Reagan has never discussed AIDS with Surgeon General C. Everett Koop and has yet to read Koop's six-month-old report, which predicted 180,000 deaths from the disease by 1991.

■

Mets pitcher Dwight Gooden goes on the disabled list after testing positive for cocaine.

4/2   During a break in the filming of the gang movie *Colors*, Sean Penn punches extra Jeffrey Klein in the face for taking a few snapshots of him. He is booked for violating probation.

4/5   Fox Broadcasting takes its first baby step toward networkdom, providing Sunday night viewers with a new alternative: smutty comedies. Unsurprisingly, the Murdoch network soon finds its niche in "tabloid TV": cheap "reality-based" shows (*America's Most Wanted, A Current Affair, The Reporters*) that titillate viewers with grainy slow-motion re-enactments of violent crimes—in which the victims occasionally play themselves.

4/6   Buffalo congressman—and former football star—Jack Kemp declares his candidacy for the Republican presidential nomination.

■

"He also told me Tammy was very big and that he couldn't be satisfied by her. Those were his words exactly."
—Jessica Hahn in a 1985 statement describing how, as a virgin, she was raped by Jim Bakker, and then by their mutual friend Rev. John Fletcher

■

Convicted Watergate burglar G. Gordon Liddy begins a week-long stint as celebrity guest on *Super Password*.

■

Dodger vice president Al Campanis appears on *Nightline* to discuss the progress of blacks in baseball 40 years after Jackie Robinson broke the color barrier. Asked why there are no black managers in the major leagues, Campanis suggests that they may not be smart enough. "How many quarterbacks do you have?" he asks. "How many pitchers do you have, that are black?" Though he apologizes, he is fired after 43 years with the team.

■

Former Gary Hart adviser John McEvoy tells *Newsweek* that the candidate runs the risk of having the sex issue raised "if he can't keep his pants on."

4/7   MEESE ACKNOWLEDGES INTERCEDING FOR WEDTECH
  —*The Washington Post*

ATTORNEY GENERAL MEESE FACES RISING CRITICISM OVER HIS LEGAL ADVICE IN IRAN-CONTRA SCANDAL
  —*The Wall Street Journal*

4/8   Ed Meese—whose close ties to the principals in the growing Wedtech scandal have become increasingly public—finally removes himself from the investigation.

4/9   President Reagan tells reporters the Soviet bugging of the US embassy in Moscow was "outrageous." But, wasn't the US bugging of the Soviet embassy in Washington equally outrageous? The President says further discussion "wouldn't be useful."

4/13   John W. Hinckley, Jr., loses his bid for a 12-hour Easter pass after a psychiatrist reveals that he's established a pen-pal relationship with Florida Death Row inmate Ted Bundy and a search of his room turns up 20 photos of Jodie Foster.

Gary Hart travels to a Colorado park where, standing alone on a big rock, he calls for a "higher standard of public ethics" as he announces for the Presidency. "As a candidate," he promises, "I can almost guarantee that I'm going to make some mistakes."

4/15 A star-studded Hollywood fundraiser for the Hart campaign takes an unhappy turn when federal marshals seize $30,000 to satisfy one of his many outstanding 1984 debts.

To the delight of Book of Revelations fans, *Washington Post* reporter Lloyd Grove reveals that the address of the home the Reagans' friends have bought for them in Bel Air is 666 St. Cloud. Though Nancy has the address changed to the less satanic 668, city documents continue to list it as 666.

4/17 MEESE INVESTED OVER $50,000 WITH FIGURE IN WEDTECH CASE
—*The New York Times*

NEW ANIMAL FORMS WILL BE PATENTED
BUT POLICY FACES CHALLENGES OVER MORAL IMPLICATIONS
—*The New York Times*

15 EMPLOYEES OF WALL STREET FIRMS ARE ARRESTED ON COCAINE CHARGES
—*The New York Times*

4/20 THE CONFESSIONS OF A COKE ADDICT BY DAVID CROSBY
'There are four ways it can go—you can go crazy, you can go to prison, you can die or you can kick. Anything else is bull'
—*People*

4/21 Arrested for public drunkenness at a Florida nightclub, Judd Nelson repeatedly bangs his face against the police car window. "My face is my business and you guys are responsible!" he screams. "I'm going to sue you!" In jail, he bangs his head against the cell door.

4/22 Joe Hunt, leader of the Billionaire Boys Club—a group of well-connected young men who want to make big bucks fast and aren't too choosy about how—is convicted of first-degree murder in a bizarre revenge killing resulting from a bad business deal. Hunt suffers the further misfortune of being portrayed in the inevitable TV movie by Judd Nelson.

4/23 Donald Regan gets a $1 million advance from Harcourt Brace Jovanovich for his White House memoir, which his agent says will be "very sexy."

CRITICS ACROSS AMERICA ARE RAVING ABOUT JUDD NELSON

"The conspicuously mediocre Nelson . . . overplays as much as he did in *The Breakfast Club*. . . . You're reminded of high school Strindberg."
—*People* critic Scot Haller on *St. Elmo's Fire*

"All pout and strut, his face contorting around what seems to be a sea anemone but purports to be his nose."
—*Washington Post* critic Paul Attanasio on *St. Elmo's Fire*

"That camera hog Judd Nelson . . . can't figure out how to get our attention and looks miserable about it."
—*Village Voice* critic David Edelstein on *St. Elmo's Fire*

"Nelson gives a performance with flare: his eyes flare, his nostrils flare, his hair—if such a thing is possible—flares. His tonsils may have been flaring, too, but at least you can't see them."
—*Washington Post* critic Tom Shales on *Billionaire Boys Club*

"The smirkiest actor in current movies. . . . Please, someone make him stand in the corner."
—*USA Today* critic Mike Clark on *Blue City*

".008 charisma rating on the Richter scale."
—*Los Angeles Herald Examiner* critic Peter Rainer on *Blue City*

"You look at this kid with his doleful, superior expression and his hair hanging in his eyes, and you wonder if Paramount's executives aren't running the studio from the nuthouse."
—*New York* critic David Denby on *Blue City*

"Watching him act is like listening to the neighborhood boor at a cocktail party: You can't believe anyone has so little awareness of how he comes off."
—*People* critic Scot Haller on *From the Hip*

"Thoroughly unlikeable."
—*Variety* critic Har. on *Blue City*

"Judd Nelson, who always appears ready to burst into tears, reads his lines with a sneer—Nelson is both pompous and self-pitying, a ghastly combination."
—*New York* critic David Denby on *St. Elmo's Fire*

■

PHYSICISTS EXPRESS 'STAR WARS' DOUBT; LONG DELAYS SEEN
    STUDY DOUBTS WHETHER SPACE-BASED SYSTEM CAN SURVIVE ATTACK
    —*The New York Times*

4/24   Jim Bakker's rehabilitation suffers a setback when rival TV preacher John Ankerberg accuses him of engaging in sex with prostitutes and homosexuals, condoning wife-swapping among his employees, and misappropriating millions of dollars in ministry funds.

4/25   Gary Hart is asked if rumors of womanizing will hurt him in the Bible Belt. "Not at all," he says, "because they're not true."

4/27   "He implied that I made some kind of deal with him, which I did not, to give it back to him."
    —Jerry Falwell countering Jim Bakker's claim that his surrender of PTL was intended to be temporary

4/28   Benjamin Linder, an American volunteer working in Nicaragua, is shot to death by the contras.

4/29   It is reported that Michael Deaver may cite his previously unrevealed "serious alcohol problem" as an excuse in his perjury trial.

■

Massachusetts governor Michael Dukakis declares his candidacy for the Democratic presidential nomination, mentioning five times in his 13-minute speech that he is the son of immigrants. "DUKAKIS FOR *WHAT*?" bumper stickers begin appearing on Boston cars.

4/30   *Penthouse* reveals that, according to his book outline, Michael Reagan was repeatedly molested as a child by an older man he sought out as a father figure after being ignored by his own adoptive parents—so ignored, he writes, that until he was 10 he believed the family's black cook was his mother.

MAY 1987

In which the Nation experiences a scandal glut

5/1   With his wife weeping at his side, Jim Bakker emerges from his Palm Springs estate to deny charges of sexual indiscretions. "I have never been involved with wife-swapping," he says.
    "Never!" says Tammy.
    "I am not a homosexual," he says.
    "Right!" says Tammy.
    "And I've never been to a prostitute."
    As for their future, Tammy says, "We have to get a job," adding that she'd "love to work in a doctor's office."

5/3   In a *New York Times Magazine* profile, Gary Hart dismisses the womanizing issue. "Follow me around. I don't care," he says defiantly. "I'm serious. If anybody wants to put a tail on me, go ahead. They'd be very bored."
    Meanwhile, *The Miami Herald*—which staked out his Washington townhouse, albeit imperfectly, after receiving an anonymous tip—was not bored to find that the candidate spent "Friday night and most of Saturday" with a young blonde from Miami. A jittery Hart told reporters on the scene that he had "no personal relationship" with the woman.

5/4   With the Hart story on front pages around the world—except for *The New York*

Times, which plays it on page 16, under the snooze-inducing headline "Paper and Hart in Dispute Over Article"—actress/model Donna Rice, 29, is identified as the mystery woman. Rice—who says the candidate frequently called her from the campaign trail to complain about his image as a "womanizer"—claims to have stayed with her friend Lynn Armandt at the home of Hart's pal Bill Broadhurst. She denies having slept with Hart, and explains that when reporters saw her at his house, she was merely stopping by to pick up a book.

Oh, and the four of them recently took an overnight cruise to Bimini.

■

"This morning I had planned to clear up US-Soviet differences on intermediate-range nuclear missiles . . . but I decided to clean out Ronnie's sock drawer instead."
—Nancy Reagan attempting to defuse her power-behind-the-throne image

5/5 Appearing before a convention of newspaper publishers, Gary Hart accuses *The Miami Herald* of running a "misleading and false" story about his relationship with Donna Rice, whom he refers to as "the woman in question." Though he acknowledges putting himself

in "circumstances that could be misconstrued," he "absolutely" denies doing "anything immoral."

As for that trip to Bimini—aboard a chartered yacht called the *Monkey Business*—well, they hadn't meant to stay overnight but Customs had closed, and anyway the men and women slept on separate boats.

■

The Iran-contra hearings get underway in Washington, with the Brobdingnagian 26-man panel unleashing hours of self-serving introductory speeches. The first witness, arms profiteer Gen. Richard Secord, claims the administration approved his pro-contra activities with Oliver North who, he reveals, stood at attention while talking to the President on the phone.

Says Reagan of the hearings, "I hope I'm finally going to hear some of the things I'm still waiting to learn."

5/6 Less than 24 hours after Richard Secord implicates him in the Iran-contra scandal, William J. Casey, 74, dies of pneumonia. His funeral is notable for the anti-contra eulogy given—in the presence of the Reagans—by Bishop John McGann, who, it is said, "came to bury, not praise" Casey.

■

After three days of silence, Lee Hart joins her husband in New Hampshire. Though she claims to believe him, she does observe, "If I could have been planning his weekend schedule, I think I would have scheduled it differently." Asked directly if he has "ever committed adultery"—the first time this query has been posed to a candidate—Hart says, "I do not have to answer that question."

5/7 Amid reports that *The Washington Post* is about to break the story of another extramarital affair, Gary Hart suspends his campaign and heads home to Troublesome Gulch, Colorado. Hours later, CBS airs recent footage of the candidate relaxing on the *Monkey Business* with a contestant (not Donna Rice) in a "Miss Hot Bod" beauty pageant.

Rep. Stewart B. McKinney (R-CT) becomes the first congressman to die of AIDS.

5/8 Shifting the blame for his downfall from his own rampant libido to those who reported on it, an "angry and defiant" Gary Hart ends his candidacy with a bitter diatribe against the press that offers no apology to his betrayed supporters. So ill-considered is this attack—eerily reminiscent of Richard Nixon's famous "Last Press Conference" of 1962—that it earns him a congratulatory letter from the former President, who tells Hart he "handled a very difficult situation uncommonly well."

5/11 Ed Meese—examined in 1984 by Jacob Stein and currently a target of Lawrence Walsh's Iran-contra probe—comes under the bailiwick of Wedtech independent counsel James McKay, making him the first man to be investigated by three special prosecutors. Says President Reagan of his embattled aide, "I have always known him to be a man of honesty and integrity."

Senate counsel Arthur Liman questions Robert McFarlane about Oliver North's destruction of documents as the Iran-contra scandal unraveled. "What did he tell you about a 'shredding party'?" Liman asks.
"Well," says McFarlane, "just that there had to be one."

5/12 Investigators discover that the $10 million solicited for the contras by Elliott Abrams from the Sultan of Brunei—which had been missing for nine months—was mistakenly deposited to the account of a Swiss businessman after Oliver North transposed two digits in his arms network's secret account.

5/14 Robert McFarlane is asked why he failed to protest foolhardy administration policy. "If I'd done that," he explains, "Bill Casey, Jeane Kirkpatrick and Cap Weinberger would have said I was some kind of Commie."

5/15 President Reagan says he was "very definitely involved in the decisions about support to the freedom fighters. It was my idea to begin with." Asked about the conflict between this statement and previous claims of abject ignorance, Marlin Fitzwater says, "They're going to stay in conflict."

Joan Rivers is fired from her low-rated late-night show. Fox Broadcasting denies rumors that Jim and Tammy Faye Bakker have been asked to be the new hosts.

NOW PLAYING: *Ishtar*. Elaine May *is* Michael Cimino! With the media focusing on the salaries of its stars and the self-indulgence of its director—She built her own sand dune because the real ones didn't look right! She needed a *blind camel!*—people have been ready to hate this $40 million road movie for weeks, and hate it they do. Set in the African desert and boasting a soundtrack of intentionally terrible songs sung by Dustin Hoffman and Warren Beatty, it replaces *Heaven's Gate* in the pop pantheon as the latest Worst Movie Ever. Hollywood observers gleefully call it *Howard the Camel*.

Sen. Howell Heflin (D-AL) claims that Fawn Hall smuggled papers out of the White House in her underwear. "She had stuffed documents in her brassiere," he says. "I think that's been in the papers, hasn't it? . . . I thought I'd seen this. Hasn't this been in the papers or something?" Now it has.

5/16 PANTYSCAM FUROR!
ANGRY FAWN: 'I NEVER SMUGGLED SECRETS IN MY UNDIES FOR OLLIE'
—*New York Post*

5/17 Thirty-seven sailors are killed aboard the USS *Stark* when the ship—in the Persian Gulf to protect Iraq's ally Kuwait's oil tankers from Iranian attack—is hit by an Exocet missile idiotically fired by an Iraqi fighter jet. President Reagan later refers to the *Stark* as "the plane."

Jim Bakker asks Jerry Falwell if he can have his ministry back. Falwell says no, Bakker has done some very bad things and he can't come back.

Observes Jimmy Swaggart, who now fears Falwell and is publicly lobbying for the Bakkers' return, "If I tell you I'm going to keep your truck for five days and then I'm going to give it back to you, and then someone finds out you're a homosexual, I still owe you your truck."

5/18 Sen. Paul Simon (D-IL) declares his candidacy for the Presidency. He becomes famous for his bow ties and huge earlobes, though not for his vote-getting abilities.

5/19 Oliver North's courier, Rob Owen—code name "TC" (The Courier)—tells the Iran-contra committee about traveling to a Chinese market in New York and meeting a man who rolled up his pant leg and handed over a wad of 95 $100 bills after Owen uttered the code phrase, "Mooey sent me." He concludes his testimony with an ode to North, whom he loves "like a brother."

5/20 Contra leader Adolfo Calero tells the committee he had "developed an affection" for William Casey and "used to refer to him as 'Uncle Bill.' "

5/22 "There were birthday bonuses, Christmas bonuses, Valentine's Day bonuses, Saturday morning bonuses. . . . Usually you get bonuses for success, but at the time they took the bonuses, this ministry was going down $1 million to $4 million per month."
—Jerry Nims, new CEO of PTL, revealing that the Bakkers received an extra $1.9 million in the past year

5/23 With $12 million in PTL funds unaccounted for, auctioneers begin selling off various Bakker possessions, among them an air-conditioned doghouse.

5/25 The *National Enquirer* publishes photographs—reportedly obtained for a sizable fee from her "friend" Lynn Armandt—of Donna Rice cavorting with Gary Hart in the Bahamas.

"Which office do I go to to get my reputation back?"
—Raymond Donovan on being acquitted of charges brought against him 32 months earlier, though his reputation had its unsavory side even before his indictment

5/27 CIA operative Felix Rodriguez (aka Max Gomez) testifies that Oliver North once said of a congressional investigating committee, "These people want me, but they cannot touch me because the old man loves my ass."

Though the precise nature of President Reagan's fondness for the North posterior is unclear, *The New York Times* protects its readers from the rawness of the quote. "Colonel North pointed to the Congressional debate on television," reports the *Times*, "and remarked that 'those people want me, but they can't touch me' because he was in favor with 'the old man.' "

"I have sat across the table from men who have told me of your homosexual advances."
—Jerry Falwell at a 90-minute press confer-

ence where he calls Jim Bakker a greedy, unrepentant sexual deviant, all the while unctuously professing his "love" for him

"I've been married to this man for 26 years, and I can tell you one thing: he's not homosexual, or is he bisexual. He's a wonderful, loving husband."
—Tammy Faye Bakker, patting Jim's knee on *Nightline*, which gets its highest rating ever

"Ted, can I say something? I just want to say, remember, God loves you. He really, really does."
"I want to say that, too. . . . God loves you, He really does."
"He really, really does."
"Bye bye."
—Tammy and Jim signing off on *Nightline*

5/29   Interior Secretary Donald Hodel is reported to be backing away from strict controls on fluorocarbons to protect the ozone layer. The new plan calls for a PR campaign to encourage people to protect *themselves* by wearing sunglasses, hats and sun-screen lotion. How the planet's lotionless creatures are to avoid skin cancer is not addressed.

■

Sepulchral Los Angeles prosecutor Lea D'Agostino's political prospects are dimmed with the acquittal of all five defendants in the *Twilight Zone* trial. "My wife and I are still in

Los Angeles Times

a daze," exults John Landis two days later to *USA Today*. "I'm having lox and bagels by the pool."

■

The National Archives releases more Nixon documents, including a list of songs he wanted played at his state funeral if he died in office (culminating in "California Here I Come"), and a list of "goals for '71–'72." Among them: "1. End War," "8. Hard Work" and, last on the list, "11. Family."

■

The London Hospital Medical College rejects a $500,000 offer by Michael Jackson to buy the remains of John Merrick, the Elephant Man. He doubles his bid, but the bones, it turns out, are simply not for sale.

JUNE 1987

In which a secretary offers a novel interpretation of the Constitution

6/1   Washington police don large yellow rubber gloves to arrest 64 demonstrators protesting Reagan AIDS policies, while at an international AIDS conference, George Bush is booed by several scientists when he endorses increased AIDS testing. "Who was that?" he asks, thinking his mike is off. "Some gay group out there?"

6/2   Hatchet-faced assistant secretary of state Elliott Abrams acknowledges to the Iran-contra committee that it was "a mistake" for him to have misled Congress in earlier testimony. He explains that he answered "No" when asked if he'd discussed contra fundraising because he had been involved in fundraising *for* the contras, not *by* them. Rep. Jack Brooks (D-TX) observes that Abrams is a "lying son of a bitch."

6/3   Rep. Jack Brooks tells Elliott Abrams he takes "more pride in not knowing anything than anybody I ever saw." Replies Abrams, "I

never said I had no idea about most of the things you said I said I had no idea about."

6/6   U.S. PLANNING RANDOM BLOOD TESTS FOR AIDS VICTIMS
      AIDS PRECAUTIONS TAKEN BY DENTISTS
      FEAR OF AIDS PROMPTS SHERIFF TO ORDER OFFICERS' JUMP SUITS
      —*The New York Times*

6/8   In Venice for the economic summit, President Reagan is asked why he's using a side entrance rather than the front entrance used by other world leaders. "I just wait until somebody points me in the direction I'm supposed to go," says the President, "and I don't ask any questions about it."

■

Lynn Armandt makes some more money off Donna Rice, telling *People*—for a reported $200,000—that her friend indeed spent the night with Gary Hart in Washington, as well as on the *Monkey Business*.

6/9   Describing Oliver North as "every secretary's dream of a boss," Fawn Hall defends him against charges of illegality. "Sometimes," she observes, "you have to go above the written law, I believe."

CONTRA AID

What happened to all those millions in contra aid? According to a letter from a State Department official, here's where almost $22,000 of it went:

Electric stoves (2)	$1,572.38	Boxing gloves (2 pair)	195.00
Dining room set (1)	654.94	Baseballs (4)	46.80
Living room sets (2)	1,283.63	Baseball bats (2)	127.40
Sofa sleeper (1)	477.75	Volleyball equipment (4 sets)	1,071.68
Electric coffee makers (5)	487.50	Domino sets (12)	132.18
19″ Admiral color TVs (3)	2,949.20	Boxes of candy (620)	6,570.00
TV antennas (3)	541.40	Deodorants (2,317)	5,760.53
Cable (300 feet)	108.00	Total	$21,978.39

■

Delaware senator Joseph R. Biden, Jr., announces his candidacy for the Democratic presidential nomination.

6/11   At a press conference following the Venice economic summit, President Reagan says "there could still be some lowering" of the dollar, a comment that causes a brief fluctuation in world currency markets before it's corrected. He is also unable to recall the name of the UN body taking up a resolution on the Persian Gulf—the hardly obscure UN Security Council.

6/12   "Mr. Gorbachev, open this gate! Mr. Gorbachev, tear down this wall!"
—President Reagan, seeking to dispel his growing aura of irrelevance by staging a macho photo op at the Berlin Wall

■

"Schroeder's passed more legislation than Joe Biden. She's been in Congress longer than Gephardt. . . . I could add that she's got a better haircut than Al Gore, but that would sound tacky."
—Democratic adviser Ann Lewis defending the potential presidential campaign of Colorado congresswoman Pat Schroeder

6/16   Bernhard Goetz is acquitted of attempted murder but convicted of illegal gun possession. He gets six months in jail, appeals, and winds up with a full year sentence.

■

"I can't wait to use it!"
—President Reagan holding up a very big pen with the word "VETO" on it

■

Fox Broadcasting changes its mind about letting Frank Zappa host an edition of *The Late Show,* deeming his plans for the hour too unconventional. Noting Fox executives' "deep-seated belief" that the show is basically fine as it is, Zappa says, "They seemed to think, 'This is what the public wants. It's just an accident the ratings are in the toilet.' "

6/17   Tammy Faye Bakker accuses Jerry Falwell of trying "to take our home away," selling her son's toys and giving her dogs to the pound, not to mention burying unsold copies of her albums with a bulldozer. "I wake up every morning wishing they had killed me," she says, "and Jim does, too." Whose murder Jim wishes for is unclear.

THE PRESIDENT JUST SAYS NO

"Legislation like the $88 billion boon-doggle of a highway bill sort of gives me a case of heartburn. How do I spell relief? V-E-T-O."

"If any tax hike ever comes across my desk, my handling of the veto pen will make the way Eliot Ness went after Al Capone look like child's play."

"Any tax increase that reaches my desk will be headed on . . . a one-way cruise to nowhere on the S.S. *Veto.*"

"If a tax hike makes it to my desk, I'll veto it in less time than it takes Vanna White to turn the letters V-E-T-O."

VANNA SPEAKS

Just a taste of what Vanna spoke on the abridged audiocassette version of her non-best-selling autobiography, *Vanna Speaks:*

"I never get bored, because there's always different puzzles, I'm wearing different clothes, there's different contestants, there's different prizes."
—On the endless fascination of *Wheel of Fortune*

"My biggest embarrassment was when I fell flat on my face. The guy had just won a brand-new car in a bonus round. I was clapping so hard, I was so excited for him, I missed the last step and fell right on my face. It was terrible. I was so embarrassed. So I picked myself up and dusted myself off and went over to the winner to congratulate him, and he said, 'Did you have a nice trip?' I was so embarrassed."
—On an embarrassing moment

"It's not as easy as it looks, being on all the time. I mean, what happens if I'm in a bad mood?"
—On the difficulties of her line of work

6/18 DETECTION TEST SHOWS AIRLINES DIDN'T FIND 20% OF WEAPONS
—*The New York Times*

■

A Delta jet in Nashville begins taxiing down a runway where another plane has been cleared for takeoff. Tragedy is narrowly averted.

■

"It's a question of dignity. Whether I did, whether I didn't—with Gary Hart or anybody else—I wouldn't answer it one way or the other."
—Donna Rice refusing to tell Barbara Walters what she wants to know

6/22 *Newsweek* publishes a letter from George W. Bush, oldest son of the Vice President, denying rumors of his father's adultery. "The answer to the Big A question," writes Bush, "is N.O."

■

The *National Enquirer* reports details of Michael Jackson's obsession with Elizabeth Taylor. Among them: he has a room in his home dominated by a huge video screen that plays her movies round the clock, he sent her a life-size inflatable doll of himself for her birthday, and he proposed marriage to her. Says record producer Quincy Jones, "The biggest misconception about him is that he's weird."

■

The BESS MYERSON Scandal
MISS AMERICA & MR. WRONG
The shocking story of how her love for a criminal led our most famous beauty queen to disgrace
—*People*

6/23 "Some said that I was singing golden oldies. . . . Well, the line-item veto and the balanced-budget amendment may be oldies but they're goodies. And those who think they don't stand a chance on the charts had better keep their dial tuned to this station. It's rock 'n' roll time again at the White House."

—President Reagan trying to distract public attention from the Iran-contra hearings with a PR campaign for the line-item veto (which he claims to have used "943 times" as governor) and a balanced-budget amendment (not that he has ever submitted one, or could, even if the law demanded it)

■

Pentagon official Noel Koch tells the Iran-contra committee about the code names used in discussions about hostage negotiations: Koch was "Aaron," Ollie was "Paul," the Israeli functionary was "the Bookkeeper," missiles were "Dogs," the airport was "the Swimming Pool," Iran was "Apple," Israel was "Banana," the US was "Orange" and hostages were "Zebras."

Says a Senate lawyer, "I take it . . . there never came a time when Col. North said that Paul was sending Aaron and the Bookkeeper to the Swimming Pool to get a price so that Orange could send some Dogs through Banana to Apple for some Zebras. Is that correct?"

"Well," says Koch, "you would sort of start down that road and get so self-conscious you couldn't do it."

■

Sean Penn gets 60 days for violating his probation by driving recklessly and beating up a movie extra. He spends much of his summer in jail, while his wife takes her concert tour around the world.

6/25 Pope John Paul II meets with Kurt Waldheim at the Vatican, just as if the Austrian president wasn't a former Nazi.

6/26 Reagan defender Alan Simpson denies reports of increasing presidential out-of-itness. "I even saw him do a cowboy doodle the other day," he says. "He used to do that when he was in his prime."

■

Two more polyps are removed from President Reagan's colon.

6/27 POWELL LEAVES HIGH COURT; TOOK KEY ROLE ON ABORTION AND ON AFFIRMATIVE ACTION
PRESIDENT GAINS CHANCE TO CHANGE THE SHAPE OF COURT'S FUTURE
—*The New York Times*

■

Ailing *Hustler* co-publisher Althea Leasure Flynt, 33, drowns in her bathtub in Los Angeles. "The sad part of this story is that no one will ever know Althea for the wonderful person she was," widower Larry tells the *National Enquirer*. "They will know her for being a junkie who had AIDS and married a porn publisher—and I think that's a tragedy. She was a beautiful person."

6/29 Tennessee senator Albert Gore, Jr., 39, enters the Democratic presidential race. Though he hopes to win the yuppie vote, this turns out to be precisely the group most offended by the grandstanding of his wife, Tipper, against dirty rock lyrics. As the campaign progresses, his relentless pandering—to southern rednecks on defense, to New York Jews on Israel—prompts muckraker Jack Newfield to call Gore the first candidate to "run for President by pretending to be worse than he is."

■

"We don't care about the political or ideological allegiance of a prospective judge."
—Ed Meese on the Supreme Court vacancy, causing his audience to burst into laughter

6/30 Following takeoff from Los Angeles, a Delta pilot pushes the wrong buttons and cuts off fuel to his engines, causing the jet to plunge to within 600 feet of the Pacific before he can restart them.

JULY 1987

In which the patriot defends big ideas and petty cash

7/1   President Reagan names Robert Bork—famous for carrying out Nixon's order to fire Archibald Cox during Watergate's Saturday Night Massacre—to Lewis Powell's Supreme Court seat. "Conservatives have waited over 30 years for this day," says fundraiser Richard Viguerie. The President urges the Senate to "keep politics out of the confirmation process," though it seems hardly to have been absent from the nomination process.

■

MEESE DID NOT FOLLOW ETHICS LAW IN BLIND INVESTMENT, OFFICIAL SAYS
—*The New York Times*

■

"We went from the Seven Dwarfs to the Magnificent Seven."
—Richard Gephardt giving himself and his fellow candidates too much credit for their performances in the first debate of the 1988 campaign

■

Sixteen Mexican illegal aliens heading for Dallas in a boxcar die from lack of oxygen and heat that reaches more than 120 degrees. "I asked God to help me out," says the only survivor, "but I'm pretty sure the others did the same thing."

7/2   Political extremist Lyndon LaRouche is indicted in Boston in connection with credit card fraud by his fundraisers.

7/5   A Delta jet landing in Washington smashes into a van while taxiing to the terminal.

7/6   A movement is started to recall Arizona governor Evan Mecham, who in his first six months in office:

- Cancelled the state celebration of Martin Luther King, Jr.'s, birthday, saying, "He's been blown up by others, and doesn't deserve a holiday"
- Asked for a list of all homosexuals in the state government
- Endorsed a book in which black children were called "pickaninnies," explaining that blacks themselves used the term affectionately
- Spoke at a John Birch Society convention
- Nominated a man to investigate government corruption who was revealed to have been twice court-martialed.

Says Mecham, "I'm doing things that hasn't been done before."

■

Nancy Reagan, 66, celebrates her 64th birthday.

7/7   Lt. Col. Oliver North, medals gleaming from his Marine uniform and certified as a "national hero" by his commander in chief, begins six nationally televised days before the Iran-contra committee. "I came here to tell you the truth," he says, "the good, the bad and the ugly." Though President Reagan has repeatedly expressed his eagerness to find out what happened, his spokesman claims that he is too busy to watch TV.

■

A Delta jet scheduled to land in Lexington, Kentucky, instead comes down 19 miles away in Frankfort. Says an FAA spokesman, "The pilot stated he was on the ground, but he didn't know where."

7/8 A Delta jet flying 60 miles off course over the Atlantic is involved in a near miss with a Continental jet.

■

Oliver North testifies that conveniently dead William Casey helped run the secret contra program, and says of the plan to use Iranian money to support the rebels, "I think it was a neat idea." Less neat, though, are the implications "that Ollie North might have been doing a little hanky-panky with his secretary," fueled by speculation on why he cashed a traveler's check at a hosiery shop.

"Ollie North has been loyal to his wife since the day he married her," Ollie North declares. "And the fact is I went to my best friend and I asked her, 'Did I ever go to Park Lane Hosiery?' And you know what she told me? 'Of course you did, you old buffoon, you went there to buy leotards for our two little girls.'"

As for his improper acceptance of a free security gate, "I'll be glad to meet Abu Nidal on equal terms anywhere in the world. Okay? There's an even deal for him. But I am not willing to have my wife and my four children meet Abu Nidal or his organization on his terms." But, really, how much protection against the world's most vicious terrorists can a fence provide? No one asks.

■

President Reagan is unable to watch Oliver North's testimony because he is busy holding up a very big saw with the words "BUDGET CUTTER" on it.

7/9 With Oliver North turning out to be as good a bad actor as the President himself, wife

Betsy accompanies him to Day Three of his testiony, where:

- He swaggeringly boasts that he shredded documents in the presence of Justice Department officials
- He says he is so committed to following orders that if the President tells him to "go stand in the corner and sit on his head, I will do so," leaving unclear whose head will be sat on and how it will be accomplished while standing
- His lawyer, Brendan Sullivan, gets even more prickly than usual and snaps, "I'm not a potted plant!"
- Dan Rather accidentally refers to him as "Oliver Nark."

Meanwhile, fearful that Reagan's lack of interest in the proceedings seems aberrational, White House aides report that he *is* paying attention, inspiring the *New York Times* headline, "REAGAN IS 'AWARE' OF NORTH HEARING."

7/10 Manucher Ghorbanifar denies Oliver North's story that they negotiated the Iran arms

deal in a men's room. "Imagine it!" he says. "I'm supposed to have taken a man who is chief of operations for the National Security Council and said, 'Come to the bathroom, screw me, overcharge for the weapons, finish me in Iran, and then send the money to your friends, the contras.' Honest to God, this is the biggest joke I have ever heard in my life. I was never alone with him."

■

MEESE TELLS PANEL HE DIDN'T VIOLATE U.S. LAW ON ETHICS
'APPEARANCE OF IMPROPRIETY' IN HIS ACTIVITIES IS FOUND BY SENATOR AT HEARING
—*The New York Times*

MEESE KNEW ADVISER HAD WEDTECH TIES
BUT ATTORNEY GENERAL SAYS THAT HE AND CONSULTANT NEVER DISCUSSED FIRM
—*The Wall Street Journal*

MEESE SAYS FAILURE TO DISCLOSE TRUST ASSETS WAS INADVERTENT
—*The Washington Post*

7/12 Two Delta jets are forced to return to Cincinnati after takeoff due to equipment failure, while in Boston, a Delta jet lands on the wrong runway—though the right airport.

7/13 After four days of Oliver North's using the hearings as a soapbox for his version of democracy, several lawmakers give him their views. "Although he is regularly asked to do so," says Sen. George Mitchell (D-ME), "God does not take sides in American politics, and in America, disagreement with the policies of the government is not evidence of lack of patriotism."

Not everyone is so disapproving. Says Orrin Hatch of the contra funding scheme, "I have to confess I kind of think it's a neat idea, too."

7/14 "The second slide is a photograph of Andrei Gromyko."
—Oliver North, presenting his contra fundraising slide show at the hearings where, since security prevents the room from being darkened, he can't actually show the slides but must hold them up to the light and describe them

■

President Reagan says he'll wait until the hearings are over to offer any comments. "Then," he warns, "you won't be able to shut me up."

7/15 Unaware that Olliemania has already peaked, would-be profiteers rush paperback and home video versions of his testimony to the marketplace. Business consultant John Hudson says he'll manufacture an Oliver North doll, explaining, "It's impossible for it not to sell."

■

Preternaturally bland John Poindexter claims that he kept the President uninformed of the fund diversion—though he was sure he would "approve if asked"—in order to "provide some future deniability." Says the pipe-puffing admiral, "On this whole issue, you know, the buck stops here with me." This revelation ends the suspense and, with no danger of impeachment, the nation abandons its interest in the hearings.

Dan Rather tells former CIA chief William Colby that he's heard several committee members speculate that William Casey isn't really dead.

"I attended his funeral," says Colby.

"He's dead, no question?" asks Rather.

"Yes."

7/16 In their first major action since Oliver North's efforts to make them folk heroes, the contras kill three children and a pregnant woman.

A Delta flight to Salt Lake City returns to Los Angeles not long after takeoff because an improperly closed galley door interferes with cabin pressurization.

"JOAN, YOU HAVE *OUR* $2.5M 13,000 SQ. FT. HOME WHICH WE BOUGHT FOR *CASH* DURING OUR MARRIAGE. I AM NOW HOMELESS. HELP!"

—Picket sign carried by former Swedish rock star Peter Holm outside Joan Collins' Beverly Hills mansion as her divorce proceedings against him are about to begin

7/17 Lyn Nofziger pleads not guilty to six counts of illegal lobbying on behalf of the Wedtech Corporation.

7/19 Two Delta jets—which are supposed to be at least five miles apart—come within 1.3 miles of each other over northern Virginia.

7/23 John Poindexter is reported to have used the phrase "I can't recall," or some variation thereof, 184 times during his five days of testimony.

7/25 "I am a card-carrying member of the ACLU."

—Michael Dukakis campaigning in Iowa

7/26 French explorers retrieve the first artifacts—some dishes—from the *Titanic*.

Survivor Eva Hart, 82, calls the salvagers "vultures."

7/27 "I reject a potted plant Presidency. I'm here to do a job."

—President Reagan picking up his newest prop, an oversized pair of scissors, and cutting a big credit card labelled "CONGRESSIONAL EXCESS"

7/28 A careless speech writer includes the word "paradigm" in President Reagan's speech on superconductivity. Yes, he pronounces it "paradijum."

7/29 Sen. George Mitchell tells Ed Meese he finds it "hard to accept" his explanation that he took no notes during his early questioning of key officials—and didn't even ask the most obvious questions—because he didn't realize the fund diversion was a criminal case.

"I take offense at the idea that it's hard to accept," says Meese.

Insists Mitchell, "It's hard to accept."

During two days of testimony, Meese utters the phrase "I don't recall," or some variation thereof, about 340 times.

Los Angeles police begin spending more time on local freeways after the 13th in a six-week series of highway shootings—many triggered by hot-tempered traffic disputes—that have killed four and injured two. Observes University of California professor Raymond W. Novaco, who studies driver stress, "There is a highly significant decrease in tolerance."

7/30 "How many times do we put up with this rug merchant type of stuff?"
—Donald Regan testifying that he recommended breaking off the Iran arms deal after being "snookered" once too often

7/31 Another skin cancer is removed from President Reagan's nose.

AUGUST 1987

In which the rock recluse re-emerges with a brand-new look

8/3 The Iran-contra hearings come to an end. The award for most unusual closing statement goes to Idaho senator James McClure, who cites a passage from *Butterflies Are Free* concerning diarrhea.

8/5 "We were not in the loop."
—George Bush explaining that he "didn't attend the meeting" at which objections to the Iran arms deal were raised because "I was off at the Army–Navy football game"

■

MEESE FAILED TO FOLLOW ETHICS RULES, GAO SAYS
PARTNERSHIP WITH WEDTECH FIGURE IS CITED
—*The Washington Post*

8/7 The Reagan administration's peace plan for Nicaragua—widely perceived as an excuse to resume military aid to the contras—is ignored by five Central American leaders who opt instead for a plan suggested by Costa Rican president Oscar Arias. House Speaker Jim Wright endorses the Arias plan and suggests

SPEAK LOUDLY AND CARRY A BIG SHTICK

"Shut up!"
—President Reagan to a GOP congressional candidate who has been heckling him during a White House meeting

"Over my dead body!"
—Talking tough about tax increases

"Never!"
—On whether the US owes Egypt an apology for intercepting the jet with the *Achille Lauro* hijackers on board

"Forgive me if I say, hell, no."
—On whether Moscow has a veto over American deployment of SDI

"Hell, no."
—On whether he plans to fire Caspar Weinberger

"Let him try."
—On Abul Abbas' threat to launch attacks in the US

that, despite Ollie's best efforts, further military aid is unlikely.

8/12 After boasting for months about how much he'll have to say when the Iran-contra hearings end, President Reagan goes on TV and devotes less than six minutes to the subject, repeating what he's said many times before and ignoring hundreds of specific charges and questions that have been raised.

8/16 New Age cultists gather at various "sacred sites" and "power points" around the world for the Harmonic Convergence, an effort to prevent a predicted quarter century of catastrophe by holding hands, humming and, in the words of one participant, "meditating our buns off."

8/20 Two Gary Hart associates suggest that a recent poll showing him still leading the Democratic field might lead him to re-enter the race. "If this is a trial balloon," says a former Hart aide, "it's the *Hindenburg* of trial balloons."

8/24 New York plastic surgeon Howard Bellin assesses Michael Jackson's evolving physiognomy. "I believe he's had three rhinoplasties (nose jobs) and two operations on his chin," he says. "I think he had a chemical face peel, cheekbone implants, his upper lip thinned and a fat suction from his cheek." If the singer had come to him in the first place and told him that this is what he wanted to look like, says Bellin, he would have told him, "That's going to look awful."

8/25 The Dow Jones industrial average closes at a record 2,722.42.

8/28 The Arcadia, Florida, home of Clifford and Louise Ray, who have gone to court to get their three young boys—all of whom contracted AIDS from contaminated blood-clotting drugs—admitted to public school, is destroyed by arson.

8/31 With the release of Michael Jackson's new album, *Bad*, CBS devotes a prime time special to the premiere of the 16-minute video of the title cut (directed by Martin Scorsese). An embalmed-looking Jackson—encased in buckles and sporting a new chin cleft in a face that seems no longer able to move—plays a prep school student who comes home to the ghetto and proves he's still "bad" by grabbing his crotch a lot.

The album, though hugely successful, does not come close to fulfilling his goal of outselling *Thriller*.

SEPTEMBER 1987

In which the candidates expose some rough edges

9/1 "She was a beautiful young model on the brink of a promising career when her face was brutally slashed with a razor . . ."
—Geraldo Rivera beginning the taping of the first episode of his daily talk show

■

Protesting American arms shipments to the contras by blocking a military train, San Francisco activist S. Brian Willson loses both legs below the knees when the train fails to stop. He is later sued by civilian members of the train crew for the "humiliation, embarrassment [and] emotional distress" the incident caused them.

9/7 Gary Hart says his treatment by the media has won him "the victims' vote," claiming that, for the first time in his life, "black people come up to me on the street and want to shake hands with me."

9/8 "I make No Excuses—I only wear them."
—Donna Rice endorsing No Excuses jeans in a commercial premiering on MTV

"This attractive lady, whom I had only recently been introduced to, dropped into my lap. I chose not to dump her off."
—Gary Hart explaining the origin of that *Enquirer* photo on *Nightline*, where, while offering no details, he acknowledges not having been "absolutely and totally faithful to my wife"

9/10 Jerry Falwell—who has vowed that there will be "no more sideshows" connected with the PTL—fulfills a fundraising promise by hurtling fully clothed down a Heritage USA water slide. The reverend, obviously in over his head with his entire PTL involvement, resigns within a month.

9/11 With presidential hopeful Joe Biden about to preside over the Bork hearings, video excerpts of a highly personal speech by British politician Neil Kinnock—intercut with nearly identical (and unattributed) passages from a Biden speech—begin circulating among reporters. Though Biden says he usually credits Kinnock, his seeming appropriation of another man's life does little for his credibility. Speculation begins about which rival campaign compiled the "attack video."

∎

Asked for an example of George Bush's having been "a pivotal player" in policy-making, President Reagan says he "can't answer in that context." He adds that he thinks the best preparation for the Presidency is being a governor.

∎

Furious over a CBS decision to delay his newscast to show the end of a women's semifinal tennis match, Dan Rather—in Miami for the Pope's visit—walks off the set, causing the network to "go black" for six minutes after the final set. The incident prompts a wave of speculation about his sanity.

9/14 BUSH, BLUE-BLOOD, TEXAS OIL MAN, WASHINGTONIAN, STILL MUST CONFRONT THE QUESTION: WHO ARE YOU?
—*The Wall Street Journal*

∎

STALLONE'S BODYGUARD REVEALS:
THE SHAMELESS SEXCAPADES OF SLY'S BEDHOPPING WIFE
HE TELLS HOW BRAZEN BRIGITTE WAS A FLIRT EVEN ON THEIR HONEYMOON . . . AND WENT MAN-CRAZY AFTERWARDS
—*Star*

9/15 Rejecting advice that he lose the unsightly beard, Robert Bork testifies at his Senate confirmation hearings. Though supporters have been counting on his warmth and intelligence to win over critics—whose concerns include his insistence that there is no Constitutional right to privacy—he instead comes across as a cold, angry man with no evident humor. His nomination is understood to be in trouble.

■

Fawn Hall—now signed with the William Morris Agency—tells Barbara Walters that running for office has "definitely crossed my mind." She says her ordeal over the past several months has "made me realize that probably I'm a lot deeper person than I thought I was." A month later, she receives a $10 ticket for eating a banana in a Washington subway station.

9/18   In Japan for a concert tour, Michael Jackson visits the mayor of Osaka accompanied by his pet chimp Bubbles, who sips Japanese green tea. "We were surprised to see the chimpanzee," says a city official, "but we understand he is his good friend."

■

NOW PLAYING: *Fatal Attraction*. The ultimate yuppie horror movie plays on all the basic fears of the age—infidelity, AIDS, child safety—to teach a suddenly popular lesson: if you fool around, a monster may come and boil your kid's bunny.

9/23   Amidst charges of plagiarism dating back to law school, Joe Biden—whose presidential hopes have been staked on his reputation for inspiring oratory—withdraws from the race. Since it soon turns out he has a brain aneurysm requiring surgery, this move in all likelihood saves his life.

■

"They've unleashed a tiger now."
—George Bush reacting to his third-place finish in an Iowa straw poll

9/27   *The Washington Post* publishes excerpts from Bob Woodward's *Veil: The Secret Wars of the CIA, 1981–1987*. Media attention focuses on the scene in which the author sneaked into the dying William Casey's hospital room and asked if he knew about the diversion of funds. Casey is reported to have nodded.

For some reason, this titillating but hardly surprising tidbit—who thinks he *didn't* know? —is considered more newsworthy than the revelation that Casey was *personally responsible* for the deaths of 80 innocent people in Beirut, victims of a malfunctioning car bomb intended to assassinate a Hezbollah terrorist.

9/28   Jessica Hahn—who is reported to have received $1 million from *Playboy*—begins

GREAT MOMENTS IN DENIALS

"I am not a wimp."
—Illinois gubernatorial candidate Adlai Stevenson III

"I am not a Communist and have not joined the Communist Party and was never asked to join the Communist Party."
—Billy Graham defending his observation that he'd seen no evidence of religious repression in the USSR

"I am not a lesbian and I am not a slut."
—Vanessa Williams

"I am not a felon."
—Lyn Nofziger pleading not guilty to charges of illegal lobbying

"I am not a wild man nor a schmuck."
—Ed Koch explaining that he will stick to his diet (in fact, he doesn't) after suffering a minor stroke

a publicity tour to promote the new issue, in which, declaring, "I am not a bimbo," she poses for 10 pages of topless photos.

■

Pat Schroeder bursts into tears as she announces that she will not run for President in 1988. Hostile media reaction to this display of emotion certifies a reversal in public standards: it is now only permissible for a *man* to cry in public.

9/29 Defending a fundraising letter attacking the "homosexual lobby" trying to recall him, Evan Mecham is asked for the "true version" of several different explanations about the letter. Says the angry Arizona governor, "Don't ever ask me for a true statement again."

■

"How many relatives does he have in Iowa? That's the only thing I want to know."
—George Bush on being lavishly praised in Warsaw by Lech Walesa

"Boy, they were big on crematoriums, weren't they?"
—George Bush after a tour of the Auschwitz death camp

■

TV PREMIERE: *thirtysomething*. Realistic yuppies with realistic yuppie problems, and all the drama that implies.

9/30 Dukakis campaign manager John Sasso resigns after admitting that he was the source of the Biden "attack video." Why he is penalized for disseminating accurate information goes unexplained.

■

DOCUMENTS SHOW FBI COMPILED FILES ON MORE THAN 100 TOP U.S. WRITERS
—*The Washington Post*

■

President Reagan complains to the arch-conservative *Washington Times* that a Soviet "disinformation campaign" has made anti-Communism in the US "unfashionable." He speaks nostalgically of the good old days when Sen. Joseph McCarthy and the House Un-American Activities Committee would investigate suspected subversives. "They've done away with those committees," says the President. "That shows the success of what the Soviets were able to do in this country."

■

Employing his unvarying review of any book that contains truths he doesn't like, President Reagan dismisses *Veil* as "an awful lot of fiction." Asked if Casey engaged in covert activities without his knowledge, the President replies, "Not that I know of."

OCTOBER 1987

In which a bubble bursts

10/1 Los Angeles anchorman Kent Schocknek dives under his desk when the studio starts shaking while he's reporting on the biggest earthquake to hit the area—6.1 Richter—since 1971. He earns the sobriquet "Kent Aftershock-nek."

■

TV evangelist Pat Robertson—who stayed at a friend's house there for three months in 1959—returns to his "roots" in the Brooklyn ghetto of Bedford-Stuyvesant to announce his candidacy for the Republican presidential nomination. "Bigot!" local residents chant, proving that you can't go home again. "Bigot!"

10/2   George Bush continues his loose-lipped trek across Europe, telling a Brussels audience that Soviet tanks are so well built that the mechanics should be sent to Detroit "because we could use that kind of ability." Motown auto workers are predictably unamused.

10/6   The Senate Judiciary Committee votes 9–5 against the Bork nomination.

■

The stock market drops 91.55 points—the biggest one-day plunge in history.

10/7   Pat Robertson acknowledges a *Wall Street Journal* report that he's been less than candid about his wedding date, and that his first child was born only ten weeks after the marriage. Complains the candidate, "I have never had this kind of precision demanded of me before."

10/10   Jesse Jackson enters the race for the Democratic presidential nomination.

10/12   On the day that George Bush announces his candidacy, *Newsweek* runs a cover story on him with the headline "Fighting the 'Wimp Factor.' " He is reportedly so upset that he counts the number of times the word "wimp" appears in the article. (Nine.)

10/13   "If I have to appoint another one, I'll try to find one that they'll object to just as much as they did to this one."
—President Reagan, bitter about the impending defeat of the Bork nomination

HERE'S WHAT THE CRITICS ARE SAYING ABOUT PRESIDENT REAGAN

"So shockingly dumb that by his very presence in the office he numbs an entire country."
—Jimmy Breslin

"I dig the cat. He's spontaneous. A lot of times he'll blurt stuff out—I can relate to that."
—Van Halen lead singer Sammy Hagar

"He isn't popular. There isn't anything about his policies anybody likes. The pollsters' questions are so dumb: 'Do you find him a nice old thing who makes you feel good when he honks away on the box?' 'Yes, he's a nice old thing who makes me feel good when he honks away on the box.' Well, that isn't an endorsement of war in Nicaragua."
—Gore Vidal

At a state dinner for El Salvador's president José Napoleón Duarte, entertainer Lionel Hampton forgets where the guest of honor is from, calling it "that great foreign country down there." Meanwhile, the President discusses Armageddon with Duarte's wife.

10/14 The stock market drops 95.46 points —the biggest one-day plunge in history.

■

The Bakkers announce a 25-city "Farewell for Now" tour featuring Tammy's singing and Jim's "sharing from his heart." The tour is cancelled when only 32 tickets are sold for its Nashville opening.

■

"A lot of the people that support me, they were ... at their daughters' coming-out parties ..."
—George Bush, vastly overestimating the Iowan debutante population to explain his third-place finish in a state straw poll

10/15 Los Angeles residents awaken to find that Robbie Conal has plastered the city with his newest homage to the President, *CONTRA DICTION*. "In this one, I think of him as a little paranoid, a little hurt and maybe a little confused," says the artist of the new portrait, "and that's the way *he's* made *me* feel for years."

10/16 U.S., FACING CRITICISM, DROPS PLAN TO CUT BENEFITS FOR POOR
  —*The New York Times*

■

The stock market drops 108.36 points—the biggest one-day plunge in history.

■

The decade's child-in-a-well story comes to a happy ending as 18-month-old Jessica McClure of Midland, Texas, is rescued from the 22-foot-deep shaft she tumbled into 58½ hours earlier.

10/17 Nancy Reagan's left breast is re-

moved after it is found to be cancerous. As if this isn't bad enough, her mother dies nine days later. As if that isn't bad enough, daughter Patti—citing "other travel plans"—does not attend the funeral.

10/19 The stock market drops 508 points —the biggest one-day plunge in history—with an estimated total loss of $503 billion. Shouts the President above the noise of his helicopter as he heads off to visit Nancy, "There is nothing wrong with the economy!"

"You don't understand. The wife expects a new Jaguar every year, and the two houses aren't paid for yet."
—Yuppie complaining to *Newsweek* about the stock market collapse

■

George Steinbrenner fires Lou Piniella and names Billy Martin manager of the Yankees for the fifth time.

10/20 Galleys of former Education Secretary T. H. Bell's forthcoming White House memoir reveal that, to President Reagan's "mid-level right-wing staffers," Martin Luther King, Jr., was "Martin Lucifer Coon," Arabs were "sand niggers" and a law prohibiting discrimination against women was "the lesbians' bill of rights."

10/22 "What went wrong?"
"What went wrong with what?"
—President Reagan responding to questions about the unprecedented stock plunge, which he calls "a long overdue correction"

"The Secretary General."
—President Reagan referring to Secretary of State George Shultz

10/23 Despite terrifying rumors that his replacement will be Orrin Hatch, Robert Bork is rejected by the largest Senate margin ever, 58–42. Says one observer of Bork's failure to win over undecided senators in private meetings, "The dogs just didn't like the food."

10/27 Michael Deaver's perjury trial gets underway in Washington. Says a former aide, "I think if he had it to do over again, he would probably have handled his media differently."

10/28 At the first Republican debate, George Bush takes the advice of former Nixon media guru Roger Ailes and calls Pete du Pont by his given name, "Pierre," in order to make viewers think du Pont is the real wimp because of his sissy moniker.

10/29 President Reagan, who claims that the time has come "to put the national interest ahead of partisan political interests," ignores aides urging a moderate Court appointment and nominates Ed Meese's extremely partisan 41-year-old choice, bearded Borklet Douglas H. Ginsburg. At the White House ceremony, Ginsburg's young daughter, Hallee, topples over.

10/31 Supreme Court nominee Douglas Ginsburg confirms that his wife, Hallee Morgan, performed abortions during her medical training in Boston.

NOVEMBER 1987

In which a lot of important people confess to using drugs

11/1 Further details emerge about the background of Douglas Ginsburg: as a Justice Department lawyer, he "personally handled" a cable TV case while he had close to $140,000 invested in a Canadian cable company with major US holdings.

11/2 New York lawyer Joel Steinberg brings his unconscious, illegally adopted six-year-old Lisa to the hospital, where he is told that she has suffered permanent brain damage as a result of a blow to the head. "What you are saying is she's not going to be an Olympic athlete, but she'll survive," says Steinberg. Told that his child is probably brain dead, he asks, "Have you found anything else wrong with her?"

When Lisa dies, and the public finds that Steinberg's common-law wife, Hedda Nussbaum, is one of the most brutally battered spouses anyone has ever seen, Joel Steinberg instantly becomes one of the most despised New Yorkers of the decade—so reviled that fellow prisoners on his trips to and from court take the opportunity to spill urine on him.

11/4 Students of Douglas Ginsburg's courses at Harvard Law School describe them as "worthless" and "rock bottom."

11/5 Douglas Ginsburg confirms another rumor: "Once as a student in the 1960s and on a few occasions in the '70s," while he was a Harvard law professor, he smoked marijuana. He calls it a "mistake."

11/6 With Douglas Ginsburg's survival—already in doubt before the pot revelation—in serious jeopardy, conservatives fearful that a third nominee will be less ideologically pure are thrust into the surreal position of downplaying his drug use. "He was not an addict," says the President, not previously known for condoning recreational usage. "He was nothing of that kind."

Meanwhile, aware that this question will now be asked of all baby-boom politicians, Georgia congressman Newt Gingrich admits that he smoked marijuana once, 19 years ago, but it had no effect on him.

■

WEINBERGER DEPARTS; PENTAGON TRANSITION BEGINS
REAGAN NAMES CARLUCCI DEFENSE SECRETARY, POWELL SECURITY ADVISER
—*The Washington Post*

■

In a PBS AIDS special hosted by Ron Reagan, singer Ruben Blades uses a banana to demonstrate how to put on a condom. The International Banana Association protests, claiming that the "unsavory" combination will damage the industry, but no decline in banana consumption is noted.

■

"How are you, Miss Piggy, on the subject of pork bellies?"
—Ted Koppel on a special edition of *Nightline* that employs the Muppets to explain Wall Street to the layman

11/7 Douglas Ginsburg asks President Reagan to withdraw his nomination.

Meanwhile, Albert and Tipper Gore announce that they smoked grass in their youth (though they now regret it), Bruce Babbitt says he smoked it 20 years ago, and Sen. Claiborne Pell (D-RI) says he took "several puffs" off a joint years ago and "didn't like it."

■

WHITE HOUSE DEFENDS MRS. MEESE'S LETTER TO JUDGE
ATTORNEY GENERAL'S WIFE URGED LENIENCY IN SENTENCING LAWMAKER'S SON FOR TAX FRAUD
—*The Washington Post*

11/8 Rep. Connie Mack III (R-FL) tells a reporter he smoked marijuana "more than once, but not often" when he was in his 30s, "but I have not done it in years." Sen. Lawton Chiles (D-FL) says he smoked it once, 17 years ago.

■

Appearing on *Face the Nation*, Ginsburg defender Orrin Hatch is asked why he—of all people—thinks it's okay that a pot smoker was teaching students the law. Hatch points out that it happened a decade ago.

"But," says Lesley Stahl, "he was a professor *of the law.*"

"So what?" shouts Hatch. "I mean—I think that's—no, wait a minute, I . . . I think that's a factor to be considered."

■

White House aides—trying, in the wake of the Ginsburg disaster, to head off another round of stories about President Reagan's increasing irrelevance—claim he was "very active and very animated" at a recent budget meeting and that he even pounded the table for emphasis.

11/9 Bob Dole goes home to Russell, Kansas, to announce his candidacy for the Republican presidential nomination. "I offer a record," he says in his first official tweak at despised rival George Bush, "not a resume."

11/10 The *New York Post* conducts a survey of the drug use of various politicians, among them Richard Nixon. "He has never smoked pot," says spokesman John Taylor. And how does he know? "I just feel absolutely certain about it. Don't you?"

■

"He's no embarrassment to me."
—President Reagan responding to a query about whether Ed Meese has, perhaps, become something of an, er, embarrassment

11/11 Claiming that his recent judicial fiascos have "made all of us a bit wiser," President Reagan names clean-shaven conservative Anthony Kennedy as his third choice for the Powell seat. Reaffirming his support for Ed Meese—whom columnist James J. Kilpatrick, a former ally, has called "that consummate bungler"—he embraces his Attorney General, who then returns to the US Courthouse to resume his sixth appearance before a federal grand jury.

■

Attending a Veterans Day service at the Vietnam War Memorial, Bob Hope says the day "brings back a lot of memories to me 'cause, you know, I saw nine years of . . . those kids laughing and cheering . . . but I never realized till I saw *Platoon* what really went on with the serious stuff."

11/12 VAN GOGH'S "IRISES" SELLS FOR $53.9 MILLION
—*The New York Times*

11/15 Jessica Hahn reveals that she has taken up temporary residence in the Playboy mansion, where she will spend the next several months recuperating from a series of cosmetic surgeries.

11/17 "Caribou like the pipeline. They lean up against it, have a lot of babies, scratch on it. There's more damn caribou than you can shake a stick at."
—George Bush scoffing at environmentalists who had feared the Alaska oil pipeline would cut into the caribou population

11/18 The Iran-contra committee's final report says President Reagan bears ultimate responsibility for the scandal because he failed to carry out his oath to "take care that the laws be faithfully executed." Ed Meese is singled out for having "poorly served" the President—first, with his advice on the legality of the arms deal, and then when he "departed from standard investigative techniques" in conducting his probe.

Eight of the panel's most rabid Reaganites—among them, of course, Orrin Hatch—issue a minority report labelling the hearings a "witch hunt" and the findings of the majority "hysterical."

■

With foreign ownership of US communications conglomerates on the rapid increase, CBS sells its records division to Sony for $2 billion.

11/20 The administration announces an immigration agreement that will send more than 2,500 Cuban prisoners in US jails home against their wishes. For some reason, Ed Meese fails to anticipate prisoner reaction, and is surprised when inmates in Atlanta and Louisiana, with nothing really to lose, seize hostages. Though Meese agrees to a moratorium on deportations, the uprising continues for more than a week.

11/26 Howard Baker reveals that the Iran-contra committee's report was "personally hurtful" to President Reagan. "He really, really did not like it," says Baker, "and really, really feels personally put upon by many of the implications and many of the assertions."

11/30 TV PREMIERE: *CBS This Morning*. CBS News tries again, this time teaming actual reporters Kathleen Sullivan and Harry Smith as hosts. How will this show differ from its predecessor? Says news president Howard Stringer, "No dog, no kitchen, no fireplace."

■

Tycoon Donald Trump proves you can be TOO DARN RICH
A billionaire at 41, he has four casinos, umpteen jets, limos and mansions—and the ego that ate Manhattan. He *says* he's too busy to run for the White House, but he's bought everything else.
—*People*

■

"No, I don't resent his popularity or anything else. Good Lord, I co-starred with Errol Flynn once."

—President Reagan on Mikhail Gorbachev, whose charming smile and attractive wife make him much harder to hate than those unlovable old men before him

■

Michael Deaver's White House memoir, *Behind the Scenes*, is excerpted in *Life*. The highlight involves a 1980 incident in which the Reagans found themselves taking part in a communion service. Nancy "hissed, 'Are those people drinking out of the same cup?'" and was assured that all she had to do was dip her wafer into the chalice. Unfortunately, she dropped it in by mistake and prompted her husband—who had been told to follow her lead—to toss his wafer in as well, leaving the pastor "shaking his head as these blobs of gunk floated in the chalice."

DECEMBER 1987

In which the President repeats himself, and a pariah re-appears

12/1 Joan Rivers files a $50 million libel suit against *GQ*, which has run a pseudonymous article by a supposed longtime friend who claims to have been privy to her cruel attacks on her husband, Edgar, both before and after his recent suicide.
The author—who in fact has never met Rivers—is revealed as Nixon apologist Ben Stein, whose vapid writing under his own name tends to focus more on his grotesque fondness for air-headed teenage girls and expensive cars. Stein compares his "reporting" techniques to those of Woodward and Bernstein and claims that his use of a pseudonym ("Bert Hacker") places him "in the tradition of Alexander Hamilton and Samuel Johnson."

12/3 With Mikhail Gorbachev having gone one-on-one with Tom Brokaw, President Reagan demonstrates his own "vitality" by sitting for an interview with four news anchors. The President criticizes opponents of the arms treaty he is about to sign—though their objections are not unlike those he has raised against previous treaties—leading to his denunciation by far-right activist Howard Phillips as a "useful idiot for Soviet propaganda."

12/4 MEESE NOT YET IN COMPLIANCE WITH ETHICS RULES

FIVE MONTHS AFTER PROMISE, FINANCIAL DISCLOSURES REMAIN INSUFFICIENT —*The Washington Post*

12/7 On the eve of the third US-Soviet summit, Rona Barrett complains to Soviet spokesman Vladimir Posner that Americans don't see nearly enough "attractive" Russians, and that they should stop wearing those ugly "fur hats." Posner explains that the hats are worn as protection against the extreme cold.

12/8 Before signing the arms treaty, President Reagan once again cites his favorite Russian proverb, *"Doveryai, no proveryai*—trust, but verify." An exasperated Mikhail Gorbachev says, "You repeat that at every meeting!"

Afterward, the President claims to have "an entirely different relationship" with Gorbachev "than I had with his predecessors," none of whom he ever met.

12/9 Dismissing reports of their mutual loathing as "so silly, so silly," Nancy Reagan gives Raisa Gorbachev a tour of the White House. She is stymied by several of her guest's questions, such as, "When was it built?"

■

Columnist Jack Anderson reports that Gorbachev's decision to stay at the Soviet embassy has thwarted CIA plans to collect a specimen of his stool.

12/10 Mikhail Gorbachev suddenly lunges out of his limousine in front of Duke Zeibert's Washington restaurant, where he is mobbed by well-wishers while George Bush

stands by unmobbed. Observes Jack Kemp's press secretary, John Buckley, "When George Bush stands next to Reagan, he looks smaller than life. When he stands next to Gorbachev, he looks like a bonsai tree."

12/11 TV PREMIERE: *Wilton North Report.* Given a blank check by a desperate Fox Broadcasting to come up with the late-night show of his dreams, producer Barry Sand comes up with a terrible title, constructs a set that looks like a jail and hires two medium-market drive-time deejays—described by more than one observer as "geeks"—to make witless cracks about the physical unsightliness of famous others. The show lasts four weeks.

12/13 *The Orange County Register* reports that a test of 24 bills of various denominations— collected at random in California's staunchest conservative enclave—shows that all of them contain traces of cocaine.

12/14 In its annual Dubious Achievements issue, *Esquire* transfers its "Why Is This Man Laughing?" award—traditionally given to Richard Nixon—to Gary Hart.

■

Having lost $30,000 marketing his Ollie North doll, John Lee Hudson announces that he is padding them with extra stuffing and revamping them as Gorbachev dolls. "The birthmark will be there," says Hudson. "It'll be tricky. You don't want to make him look like a weirdo."

12/15 "Let the people decide. I'm back in the race!"
—Gary Hart, with Lee at his side, announcing his re-entry into the presidential race

"We are moving into a new year with a new image."
—Spokesperson for No Excuses jeans explaining that Donna Rice will no longer be appearing on behalf of the product

■

President Reagan is asked how he responded to Mikhail Gorbachev's offer to cut aid to the Sandinistas. He consults a note card and says, "This is a subject we are going to be discussing for quite some time."

12/16 "When I disagreed with him he heard it from me. I didn't sit there at his side to say 'yeah' to every cockamamie idea that came before the President and then claim I didn't know about it afterwards unless it was a winner."
—Al Haig describing the difference between

his relationship with President Reagan and George Bush's

■

Michael Deaver is convicted of three counts of perjury. A journalist, on the phone with one White House aide when another aide bursts into the room with the news, reports that both aides "roared with laughter."

12/19 LARGE DISCREPANCY IN MEESE TRUST FUND
ADVISER INVESTED MORE THAN ACCOUNT HELD
—*The Washington Post*

12/22 Ed Meese's lawyer—and friend of 30 years—E. Robert Wallach (who prefers to spell his name sans capital letters) is indicted on racketeering, fraud and conspiracy charges in connection with the Wedtech scandal, as is Ed Meese's financial consultant, W. Franklyn Chinn.

12/28 Gary Hart is declared eligible for the federal matching funds he was entitled to when he withdrew in May. Many observers think the money—needed to pay off outstanding debts—is the entire reason for Hart's re-entry.

12/30 An unusually heavy demand for non-smoking seats aboard a TWA flight from Boston to Los Angeles leads to a complete smoking ban. Toward the end of the flight, 11 passengers protest by lighting cigarettes, and the flight attendant who demands that they be extinguished is physically assaulted.

POP QUIZ

1 Who did *Spy* magazine say "seems to be running a private tutorial in the Art of the Sullen, Dopey Literary Stare"?
a Jay McInerney
b David Leavitt
c Bret Easton Ellis
d Tama Janowitz

2 According to his book *Trump: The Art of the Deal*, what did Donald Trump do the day after meeting that "man of great warmth," Cardinal John O'Connor?
a He volunteered to renovate three churches of the Cardinal's choosing
b He went to confession for the first time

in years and spent several hours in the booth

c He used him as a character reference on his application for a Nevada gambling license

d He tried to enlist the Cardinal in his campaign to jail street peddlers who spill condiments on the sidewalk

3 Who claimed to be "the only network correspondent in history who ever voluntarily took a dope test on television"?

a Charles Kuralt
b Bernard Shaw
c Ron Reagan
d Geraldo Rivera

4 Which former Watergate felon appeared briefly as one of Dreyer's Ice Cream's "Unbelievable Spokesmen for an Unbelievable Product"?

a H. R. ("Bob") Haldeman
b John Ehrlichman
c John Mitchell
d John Dean

5 Which of these actually appeared on TV?

a *Wake Up and Smell the Corpses*, a Geraldo special on necrophilia
b *Jokes by Jake*, a Joe Piscopo body-building/comedy special
c *Amerika*, an anti-Soviet mini-series commissioned by ABC as penance to the far right for *The Day After*
d *Full Medal Jackass*, a docudrama about Oliver North

6 True or false? George Bush claimed that when he was shot down during World War II, one of the things he thought about as he floated in the ocean was the "separation of church and state."

Match the product with the consumer complaint.

7 Bic lighter
8 Audi 5000
9 Suzuki Samurai
10 Beech-nut Apple Juice
___**a** Lurches forward unexpectedly
___**b** Contains unadvertised ingredients
___**c** Explodes without warning
___**d** Tips over

11 What do Michael Jackson and President Reagan have in common?

a They both keep a llama in the backyard
b They both love the same joke about horse manure
c They both bid for the Elephant Man's remains
d They both have been publicly linked to monkeys

12 Which allegedly comic performance prompted one critic to write, "By the end of the film, I felt that I'd spent an hour and a half at the lowest level where human life can still be called human"?

a Bill Cosby in *Leonard Part 6*
b Chevy Chase in *Three Amigos*
c Jim Varney in *Ernest Goes to Camp*
d Eddie Murphy in *Eddie Murphy Raw*

13 Which novel received the fewest good reviews?

a *The White House Mess* by Christopher Buckley
b *Postcards from the Edge* by Carrie Fisher
c *The Strategies of Zeus* by Gary Hart
d *The Bonfire of the Vanities* by Tom Wolfe

14 Which movie was famous for its sweating scene?

a *Broadcast News*
b *Hannah and Her Sisters*
c *Full Metal Jacket*
d *Dirty Dancing*

Match the newsmaker with his/her news.
15 Walter Hudson
16 Eddie Murphy
17 Robert Gottlieb
18 Allan Bloom

19 Lawrence ("L.T.") Taylor
20 Tom Fiedler
21 Woody Allen
22 Kitty Dukakis

___a Railed against rock 'n' roll in a book that sold far better than expected

___b Became new editor of *The New Yorker* amidst considerable media coverage

___c Began diet after ballooning to over 1,000 pounds

___d Spent the night outside Gary Hart's house

___e Testified before Congress against odious colorization of black-and-white movies

___f Proposed as a solution to the South Africa situation "bloodshed for two or three days, then I think they should just party for the rest of the week"

___g Revealed 26-year amphetamine addiction that spouse was unaware of

___h Justified drunk driving by saying, "If I don't care what happens to me now, can I really think about what might happen to others?"

23 How did Orrin Hatch distinguish himself in the Senate?

a He took sycophancy to new heights during the Rehnquist hearings

b He took sycophancy to new heights during the Iran-contra hearings

c He took sycophancy to new heights during the Bork hearings

d All of the above

Who said what?
24 Brigitte Nielsen
25 Pat Robertson
26 Bruce Willis
27 Roseanne Barr
28 Judd Nelson
29 Evan Mecham
30 Donna Rice
31 Geraldo Rivera

___a "The ultimate cool is not being concerned, it's not worrying about whether you are cool or not. I guess people think I'm cool, I don't know."

___b "We ought to close Halloween down. Do you want your children to dress up like witches? They are acting out satanic rituals."

___c "Of course, that's nothing to be proud of, getting a divorce and leaving your child somewhere else, but it doesn't mean you're not a good mother."

___d "I'm not sure but what maybe we have become a bit too much of a democracy."

___e "What I would say to Joan [Rivers] is, 'Yeah, I eat the same as you. I just don't puke when I'm through.'"

___f "My life is a vehicle to explore the media and ethics. . . . It's a woman's story. It's about trying to maintain a balance in life between marriage and a career. Any stupid publisher who doesn't want it has his head up his butt!"

___g "I think a lot of the criticism is based on men, mostly, in their 30s and 40s mostly, measuring themselves against me."

___h "This career might be a stepping stone to the governorship of California and then to the presidency. There's a precedent, and it's been done by lesser men."

32 How did *Village Voice* critic Mim Udovitch characterize the fictional subgenre encompassing such authors as Jay McInerney, Bret Easton Ellis and Tama Janowitz?

a "F. Scott Fitzbratpack"

b "Lit Lite"

c "Anomie of the People"

d "White Dopes on Punk"

ANSWERS

1-a, 2-c, 3-d, 4-b, 5-c, 6-True, 7-c, 8-a, 9-d, 10-b, 11-d, 12-d, 13-c, 14-a, 15-c, 16-f, 17-b, 18-a, 19-h, 20-d, 21-e, 22-g, 23-d, 24-c, 25-b, 26-a, 27-e, 28-h, 29-d, 30-f, 31-g, 32-d

JANUARY 1988

In which the gloves come off

1/4 Jesse Jackson reveals that he was once dependent on a painkiller, though it happened more than a quarter century ago and lasted for less than a day.

■

With increasing numbers of homeless people sleeping in the winter streets, Ed Koch directs his energies toward a boycott of New York movie theaters charging $7 admission.

1/7 BUSH REGULARLY ATTENDED MEETINGS ON IRAN SALES
    RECORDS INDICATE KNOWLEDGE UNDERSTATED
    —*The Washington Post*

1/10 "If I am elected I won't be the first adulterer in the White House. I may be the first one to have publicly confessed."
    —Gary Hart employing the Nixonian tactic of downplaying bad deeds by citing others similarly guilty

"One could argue—I wouldn't—that Ronald Reagan walked away from a marriage."
    —Gary Hart employing the Nixonian tactic of pointing out something unpleasant while seeking credit for not pointing it out

1/11 Exclusive: Liz tells the whole emotional story
    WHY I GOT FAT—AND HOW I LOST 60 LBS.
    "It's a wonder I didn't explode," says Taylor in an excerpt from her revealing new book
    —*People*

1/12 MEESE'S ACTIONS ON PHONE REGULATION PROBED
    INDEPENDENT COUNSEL MCKAY STUDYING POSSIBLE CONFLICT-OF-INTEREST VIOLATION
    —*The Washington Post*

1/15 Michael Deaver—in need of cash to pay his legal bills—holds a tag sale to sell off the contents of his offices.

■

Oddsmaker Jimmy (the Greek) Snyder celebrates Martin Luther King, Jr.'s, birthday by discussing civil rights in the world of sports. "If they take over coaching like everybody wants them to," he says of blacks, "there's not going to be anything left for white people. . . .
    "I'm telling you that the black is the better athlete. . . . This goes all the way to the Civil War when, during the slave trading, the owner, the slave owner, would breed his big black with his big woman so that he would have a big black kid, see. That's where it all started."
    CBS fires him.

1/16 "Voodoo economics . . . that's the only memorable thing I ever said."
    —George Bush, still haunted by his rare blurt of truth

1/18 Questioned about abortion by an Iowa high school student, George Bush grabs a paper out of her hand, finds that it's a Jack Kemp flyer, holds it up and, with a considerable flourish, tears it into pieces. *"Finis!"* he cries.

■

CHER
She's made *Moonstruck* a megahit, her lover is 23 & she's tough enough to say: 'Mess with me and I'll kill you'
—*People*

■

The *National Enquirer* reports that Nancy Reagan issued a White House edict—"No more Sinatra"—after reading what Frank had to say about her and Ronnie in *His Way.*

1/20 President Reagan begins his last year in office with a pep rally for his staff. "As they say in show biz," he says, "let's bring them to their feet with our closing act."

© 1988 Craig T. Mathew

1/23 Gossip columnist Suzy reports that Sylvester Stallone and former Deb of the Year Cornelia Guest are getting married. "Sylvester proposed to Cornelia Thursday night in Beverly Hills," writes Suzy, "and she said yesyesyes. They are deliriously in love." No wedding takes place.

1/25 GARY HART'S 15 YEARS OF ADULTERY
WHY HIS WIFE TOLERATED HIS ESCA-

PADES WITH TOPLESS STARLETS, A SKI BUNNY . . . AND AN AIRLINE STEWARDESS
GET SHIRLEY MACLAINE OUT OF THAT ROOM!
THAT WAS THE PANIC ORDER AS AIDES SPOTTED LEE HART ENTERING THE HOTEL LOBBY
—*Star*

■

President Reagan's final State of the Union address is overshadowed by a live TV encounter between George Bush and Dan Rather. Bush—who has been psyched into a near-frenzy by media guru Roger Ailes—petulantly dismisses Rather's questions about his still-murky involvement in the Iran-contra scandal. "It's not fair to judge my whole career by a rehash on Iran," whines Bush. "How would you like it if I judged your career by those seven minutes when you walked off the set in New York?" Rather (whose six-minute tantrum occurred in Miami) shouts back, "Mr. Vice President, you've made us hypocrites in the face of the world! How could you?"

Afterward, Bush crows, "The bastard didn't lay a glove on me."

1/26 "I need combat pay for last night, I'll tell you. . . . You know, it's Tension City when you're in there."
—George Bush offering a morning-after postmortem on the Rather interview

"Macho!"
—George W. Bush at campaign headquarters, raising both fists in tribute to his big brave dad

1/27 "I wasn't there. Well, maybe I was there but I didn't hear anything. Well, maybe I heard something but I don't remember what. Anyway, after all this time, nobody cares what I did."
—Columnist Lars-Erik Nelson summing up the Bush Iran-contra defense

1/29 MEESE PROBE FOCUSING ON ALLEGED BRIBE PLAN
HE REPORTEDLY WAS TOLD OF SCHEME TO ASSURE IRAQ PIPELINE CONSTRUCTION BY PAYING OFF HIGH ISRAELI
—Los Angeles Times

1/30 ABORTION ADVICE BARRED AT FEDERALLY AIDED CLINICS
VAST REVERSAL OF POLICY, AFFECTING MILLIONS OF PEOPLE, FACES BATTLE
—The New York Times

FEBRUARY 1988

In which the President's script is published

2/2 Courting the gun owners of New Hampshire, George Bush pulls out a tiny little gun—significantly smaller than even Nancy Reagan's famous weapon.

∎

"I do not recall having read the specific words that have now mushroomed into importance."
—Ed Meese, again citing his trusty selective memory to explain his failure to take action after receiving a memo telling of the planned bribing of Israeli officials in connection with an Iraqi oil pipeline

2/3 MEESE VAGUE IN NOFZIGER TESTIMONY

29 TIMES HE ASSERTS NOT RECALLING ACTS IN LOBBYING CASE
—Los Angeles Times

∎

FBI CHIEF DENIES SURVEILLANCE OF DISSIDENTS WAS 'MASSIVE'
—The Washington Post

2/4 Anthony Kennedy, 51, is confirmed as a Supreme Court Justice, 97–0. Liberals who note his potential longevity wonder if maybe they wouldn't have been better off with the 60-year-old, overweight, chain-smoking Bork.

∎

Furious at what he perceives as the Bush campaign's unfair attacks on his wife, Liddy, Bob Dole gives vent to his lifetime loathing of the George Bushes of the world. Storming onto the Senate floor, he confronts the Vice President in full view of TV cameras, waving a piece of paper in his face. Bush—dealing with an angry adult male instead of a teenage girl—does not grab the page and scream, *"Finis!"*

2/5 Mario Cuomo says the weakest GOP ticket would be "Bush and Bush."

∎

At a surprise party for the President's upcoming 77th birthday, Marvin Hamlisch introduces "He's Our Man (The Ronald Reagan March)," a song commissioned by the First Lady: "He's our man/And he's giving his best/He's our man/And he's up to the test/He has done the job the best that anyone can." Reagan observes that the event is "the 38th anniversary of my 39th birthday."

∎

Arizona governor Evan Mecham—already facing a special election as a result of the hugely successful recall movement—is impeached by the state House of Representatives for obstruction of justice. Though he suggests that his accusers will be torn "to bits" by his lawyers, what actually happens is that he's convicted and removed from office.

∎

"It's gotten to the point where I think some

1988

HERE'S WHAT THE CRITICS ARE SAYING ABOUT GEORGE BUSH

"People would say, 'We need a man on the ticket.' "
—Rep. Pat Schroeder explaining why Bush won't pick a female running mate

"A do-nothing lackluster wherever he sat."
—Alexander Haig

"A cross between Rambo and Mary Poppins."
—Peter Fenn, Democratic media consultant

"Bush carves an image of a friendly—though not a favorite—uncle."
—Los Angeles Herald Examiner editorial

"The national twit."
—Michael Kinsley

"Bush has gone about it all with a gusto that borders on the unseemly. . . .

It's not the fetching and heeling but the excessive tail-wagging that grates."
—Jody Powell on the Bush vice presidency

"[He] has the look about him of someone who might sit up and yip for a Dog Yummie."
—Mike Royko

"Anybody who has to spend all his time demonstrating his manhood has somehow got to know he ain't got it."
—Al Haig

"Bush always smiles like he's hoping to get a better grade from a teacher."
—Mike Royko

"Poor George is hopelessly inarticulate. He never finishes a sentence or puts in a verb."
—Nancy Ellis, sister

of the people are embarrassed saying at a cocktail party that they work for the Justice Department. You see the person you're talking to jump back in alarm."
—Justice Department official describing morale under the tenure of Ed Meese

2/6 NORIEGA INDICTED BY U.S. OVER LINKS TO ILLEGAL DRUGS
    EXTRADITION ISN'T LIKELY
—The New York Times

2/7 Heavyweight champion Mike Tyson marries TV actress Robin Givens, a Sarah Law-

rence alumnus who had the distinction of being the only person booed at her graduation.

2/8 Neighboring congressman Richard Gephardt edges past neighboring senator Paul Simon to win the Iowa caucus, with Michael Dukakis third. Finishing last, with .3% of the vote: Gary Hart.

Neighboring senator Bob Dole wins Iowa's GOP primary, drawing twice as many votes as George Bush, who finishes third behind Pat Robertson. Dan Rather happily describes Bush's defeat as a "humiliation."

1988

2/11 "It's a lousy law."
—Lyn Nofziger on being convicted of three counts of illegal lobbying in the Wedtech case, for which he gets 90 days and a $30,000 fine, later reversed on appeal.

2/12 "I've done all the damage I can, Bob."
—Alexander Haig withdrawing from the race and endorsing Bob Dole, while Haig's intended victim, George Bush, is seen driving several large vehicles to prove . . . something

2/13 "Bob says when Ronald Reagan wants something important he calls Bob Dole. That's funny—when he wanted somebody to be Vice President of the United States he called me."
—George Bush, not mentioning that when Reagan wanted somebody to be Vice President, he first called Gerald Ford

2/14 At the Republican debate in New Hampshire, Pat Robertson claims to be in possession of information about Soviet missiles hidden in Cuban caves. "Nobody can say for certain," he points out, "that those missiles aren't there."

■

George Bush is asked whom he'd pick as his running mate. "I haven't selected *her*," he says. "But let me tell you, this gender thing is history. You're looking at a guy who sat down with Margaret Thatcher across the table and talked about serious issues."

2/15 Countering Bob Dole's proposal for a one-year, across-the-board spending freeze, George Bush suggests an alternate plan, delightfully called a "leadership freeze."

2/16 Officials of Augsburg College in Minneapolis decide not to name a wing of a new building after alumnus Elroy Stock—who donated $500,000 to the school—when they learn that he has sent approximately 100,000 hate letters to interracial couples.

■

Bob Dole's efforts to put his 1976 slasher

image behind him suffer a setback when he tells a du Pont supporter to "get back in your cave." His mood is not improved when George Bush beats him in New Hampshire, 38%–29%. Tom Brokaw, interviewing them both by satellite, asks if they have any messages for each other. "Just wish him well and we'll meet him in the South," says Bush. And Senator Dole, any message for the winner? "Yeah," snarls Dole, "tell him to stop lying about my record."

As expected, neighboring governor Michael Dukakis wins the New Hampshire Democratic primary. Gary Hart finishes last with 4%.

2/18 Bruce Babbitt—whose popularity among members of the media inspired his slogan, "Let the press decide!"—pulls out of the race, as does Pete du Pont.

2/19 Bob Dole is asked once too many times about his bad mood. "I don't think I'm dispirited," he snaps. "I've got a bad cold. Maybe you'll get one, one day."

2/20 Rupert Murdoch—labelled "the Number One dirt bag" in the communications industry by Sen. Lowell Weicker—sells the *New York Post*.

2/21 POLL FINDS LESS OPTIMISM IN U.S. ON FUTURE, A FIRST UNDER REAGAN
—*The New York Times*

■

Jimmy Swaggart, whose visits to a Louisiana prostitute have been exposed by rival evangelist Marvin Gorman (whose own adultery had been previously exposed by Swaggart), temporarily steps down from his ministry after a gasping and sobbing TV confession. The prostitute, Debra Jo Murphree, soon appears naked in *Penthouse*, where she supplies the seedy details of their trysts—she assumed lewd poses while he masturbated.

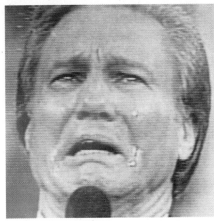

2/23   ROBERTSON   CLAIMS   BUSH LEAKED SWAGGART SCANDAL
—*The Washington Post*

■

MEMO TO MEESE DESCRIBES PIPELINE PAYMENTS
    WALLACH WROTE OF 'ARRANGEMENT' TO BENEFIT ISRAEL AND LABOR PARTY
    ATTORNEY GENERAL TELLS FRIENDS HE WON'T QUIT
—*The Washington Post*

2/24   The Supreme Court rules 8–0 that even though Jerry Falwell really, really didn't like it, Larry Flynt had the right to jokingly claim that the porcine reverend lost his virginity to his own mother in a drunken outhouse tryst.

2/25   ROBERTSON: KNEW LOCATION OF HOSTAGES
    CANDIDATE CLAIMS WHEREABOUTS WERE BROADCAST ON CBN IN '85
—*The Washington Post*

■

Sam Donaldson broadcasts excerpts from President Reagan's private schedule for the day—a document that includes a complete script for everything he is to say in private meetings. Among the "talking points" suggested: "Bob, I appreciate you and your colleagues

SETTING THE RECORD STRAIGHT

"Goofy greeting children outside French pavilion."
—*New York Times* caption for photo accompanying article about a restaurant at Epcot Center

"A picture caption . . . misidentified the Disney character greeting visitors. It was Pluto."
—*New York Times* correction

"Katzenberg and his son David with Mickey, at Disneyland."
—*New York Times* caption for photo accompanying article about Disney's resurgence in the film industry

"A picture caption . . . misidentified the costumed character shown with him and his son. It was Minnie Mouse, not Mickey."
—*New York Times* correction

coming down today," "I want to thank all of you for your input," "God bless you all" and "Otis, what are your thoughts?"

2/26 "I believe in Jesus Christ as my personal savior. Always will."
—George Bush telling a group of evangelical ministers what he knows they want to hear

MARCH 1988

In which the President's son's book is published

3/1 George Bush attacks Congress for cutting off aid to the contras, claiming it "pulls the plug out from under the President of the United States."

■

With his seemingly doomed libel suit against Paul McCloskey coming to trial on Super Tuesday, Pat Robertson uses his fast-fading campaign as an excuse to drop the case. The judge rules McCloskey the "prevailing party," and says no further action can be brought against him in the matter. Robertson incongruously declares this "a tremendous victory."

3/3 A two-day meeting of NATO leaders ends in Brussels with a 19-point communiqué that President Reagan praises. Later, asked by reporters if he is pleased with the document, he replies, "No, haven't read it."
"We saw it last night," says Howard Baker. "No problems and it's very good."
"Yes," says the President. "Very good. No problems."

3/4 20/20 airs a Barbara Walters chat with Nancy Reagan. Does the First Lady have any thoughts on the occasion of her 36th wedding anniversary? She does: "It seems like 36 minutes."

3/6 Jesse Jackson is asked if he would accept the vice presidency. "It would be illegal," he explains. "You cannot be the nominee of the party and its vice presidential nominee."

■

"I'll tell you something. If this country ever loses its interest in sports or ever loses its interest in fishing, we got real trouble . . ."
—George Bush campaigning in Missouri at the World's Fishing Fair

3/7 "We're going to heavy-up the speeches."
—Press secretary Peter Teeley announcing the new Bush strategy

3/8 DIVINE, TRANSVESTITE FILM ACTOR, FOUND DEAD IN HOLLYWOOD AT 42
—*The New York Times*

■

George Bush beats Bob Dole in 16 Super Tuesday primaries. Dole wisely avoids live TV interviews. On the Democratic side, Al Gore wins six states, though no one really notices.

3/9 President Reagan presides over the unveiling of the Knute Rockne stamp at Notre Dame, where he flubs the line he's probably recited more often than any other. "Win just one," he misreads the teleprompter, "for the Gippet." He does not correct himself.

3/10 "The unbearable lightness of Bush's campaign may be incurable. . . . We are going to test the proposition of the Democrat who said of his party, 'If we can't beat Bush, we should pick another country.' "
—George Will

■

Jack Kemp withdraws from the race and begins a losing campaign for the vice presidency.

3/11 Having received 3% of the Super Tuesday vote, Gary Hart—conceding that the people have pretty much decided—pulls out of the 1988 race for the second time. And how will he earn a living now? "It's none of your business."

3/13 "Gore? You mean Dore, the Republican?"
—Chicago construction worker displaying unfamiliarity with the candidates as the Illinois primary approaches

■

Porn star John ("Johnny Wadd") Holmes dies in Los Angeles of AIDS.

■

Rat Pack members Frank Sinatra, Dean Martin and Sammy Davis, Jr., reunite for a farewell concert tour. Martin distinguishes himself on opening night by forgetting lyrics and tossing a lit cigarette into the $40-a-ticket audience. He is soon dropped from the tour.

3/14 On the eve of certain defeat in Illinois, Bob Dole insists that only he will decide when it's time to quit, though he adds, "If you're out there and you've been twisting in the wind for six or eight months and you start to smell a little, *then* maybe somebody has to cut the rope just for your own good." Two weeks later, he decides it's time.

3/16 Desperate for a renewal of military aid to the contras, President Reagan claims Nicaragua has invaded Honduras—just as he claimed two years earlier—and sends 3,200 US troops as a show of support. Even so, Congress passes no aid.

■

President Reagan—who still can't understand why he's perceived as insensitive to minorities—vetoes a major civil rights bill that would restore anti-discrimination laws removed by a Supreme Court decision. The veto is soundly overridden.

■

Oliver North, John Poindexter, Richard Secord and Albert Hakim plead not guilty to charges of conspiracy, theft and fraud in connection with the Iran-contra scandal. North—

who calls the indictment a "badge of honor"— retires from the Marines to defend himself more freely. Says President Reagan of the indictments, "I have no knowledge of anything that was broken."

3/20 Michael Reagan begins the promotional tour for his autobiography, *On the Outside Looking In*, described by reviewer Barbara Lippert as "a peculiar memoir that seems to include every time he vomited and wet his pants." Among the highlights—besides the previously noted child molestation:

- His delight, as a teenager, when Nancy's Lincoln Continental rolled down a hill and was totalled—"I laughed and was only sorry she wasn't in it"
- His taking a hammer to a bicycle given him by mom Jane Wyman—"With every smashing blow I thought of that bike as my mother, hoping if I destroyed it I was also destroying her"
- Nancy's response to his bad report card— "You're not living up to the Reagan name or image, and unless you start shaping up, it would be best for you to change your name"
- Jane Wyman's reaction when he told her he was writing the book—"I can't believe you have anything to say at this time in your life that's worth reading"
- The last words in the book—"Thanks, Mom and Dad! Love, Mike."

3/21 ROB LOWE & FAWN HALL IN WHIRLWIND ROMANCE
'FAWN'S THE GREATEST! SHE'S FUNNY, BEAUTIFUL AND LOYAL. NO WONDER OLIVER NORTH THOUGHT SHE WAS TERRIFIC.'
—*National Enquirer*

3/24 BABY JESSICA'S RESCUERS FIGHTING OVER TV RIGHTS
—*The New York Times*

3/25 With the jury at his murder trial in its

ninth day of deliberations, Robert Chambers pleads guilty to first-degree manslaughter in the death of Jennifer Levin. He gets five to 15 years, becoming eligible for parole in 1993.

3/26 Jesse Jackson beats Michael Dukakis by a 2–1 margin in Michigan, throwing a serious scare into party regulars that lasts until Dukakis wins in Wisconsin 10 days later. Richard Gephardt—whose attacks on foreign car makers can't even earn him a victory in Detroit—drops out of the race.

3/30 HIGH JUSTICE AIDES QUIT AMID CONCERN OVER MEESE'S ROLE
NO. 2 OFFICIAL OUT
ATTORNEY GENERAL'S LEGAL WOES ARE CITED AS 6 LEAVE THEIR POSTS
—*The New York Times*

3/31 "I've never been on Air Force One. I've never even spent so much time with Dad alone. Being next to him on a whole flight means I'll have spent more time with him in the air than I ever have on the ground."
—Michael Reagan, heading to California with the folks on their jet

■

Ed Meese wakes up to a *Washington Post* editorial that says he "leaves a smudge wherever he goes." At the Justice Department, he is greeted at his private entrance by hostile graffiti ("RESIGN" and "SLEAZE"). In the Senate, right-wing elder statesman Strom Thurmond says of Meese, "That boy's got to go."
Meese says he sees "no reason" to step down.

4/1 "Don't vote for that fuckin' Bush!"
—Bruce Springsteen, taking a stand at New York's Nassau Coliseum

■

With attention shifting to the New York primary, Ed Koch takes advantage of the national media spotlight to deliver a harangue against Jesse Jackson, who he says would put the country "in bankruptcy in three weeks." As for his Middle East policies, says Koch, any Jews who support Jackson "have got to be crazy!"

4/2 MCKAY NOT SEEKING INDICTMENT OF MEESE
DECISION BASED ON EVIDENCE NOW IN HAND BUT GRAND JURY WILL CONTINUE ITS PROBE
—*Los Angeles Times*

JUSTICE REOPENING MEESE PROBE
ETHICS INQUIRY WAS SUSPENDED AFTER SPECIAL COUNSEL'S APPOINTMENT
—*The Washington Post*

4/3 Campaigning in Wisconsin, Michael Dukakis shows off his rapport with infants.

4/4 "Hi, Bush."
—Unimpressed child greeting the Vice President at the White House Easter Egg Roll

4/7 Paul Simon drops out of the presidential race. No one notices.

■

Another White House memoir appears: Larry Speakes' *Speaking Out.* Among the juicier tidbits:

- Nancy Reagan was "likely to stab you in the back"
- George Bush was "the perfect yes man"
- Caspar Weinberger was "a small man, a whiny type of guy"
- The President's children rarely called, even when he was seriously ill, "and he and Mrs. Reagan didn't call them"
- Preparing the President for a press conference was "like re-inventing the wheel."

Confesses Speakes, "Some of the business about his lack of attention to detail was true."

4/9 John Zaccaro, Jr., is convicted of selling cocaine in Vermont. He gets four months, which he is allowed to serve under house arrest in a $1,500-a-month apartment that includes maid service, cable TV and access to a gym.

4/10 Appearing on *Meet the Press* to plug his latest book, *1999: Victory Without War,* Richard Nixon says the biggest mistake of his Presidency was waiting too long "to bomb and mine North Vietnam." He also suggests that Henry Kissinger be named as special Mideast negotiator. "Now, Henry is devious," he says, "Henry is difficult, some people think he's obnoxious—but he's a terrific negotiator."

4/11 "Okay, Michael, let's go!"
—Olympia Dukakis ending her acceptance speech for her Best Supporting Actress Oscar for *Moonstruck* with a message to her cousin

"If this picture wins any more awards, the Academy's gonna have to see it."

—Albert Brooks, Best Supporting Actor nominee for *Broadcast News,* giving host Chevy Chase a line about *The Last Emperor*'s Oscar sweep that Chase is too chicken to use

■

The media suddenly discovers the hidden gem in Larry Speakes' book: his confession that, during the 1985 Geneva summit, he twice made up quotes and attributed them to President Reagan, whose utterances had in fact been "very tentative and stilted." He also admits having assigned words actually spoken by George Shultz during the Korean air liner crisis to Reagan, "since the President had had almost nothing to say." Speakes—who notes that his creativity "played well"—explains that fabricating quotes "is not lying" because "I knew those quotes were the way he felt."

4/12 The day after Cher wins the Best Actress Oscar, Sonny Bono is elected mayor of Palm Springs.

4/13 "I was never a volunteer anything. Who had the time? . . . Find the time, my favorite magazine said. You're needed. . . . So here I am every Tuesday night in the soup kitchen, making sandwiches. I think I am a better person. I know I'm a happier one. I love that magazine. I guess you could say I'm That COSMOPOLITAN GIRL."
—Magazine ad appearing in *The New York Times*

■

"Tonight you'll be looking at some horrible scenes and meeting some horrible people."
—Geraldo Rivera welcoming viewers to his latest special, *Murder: Live from Death Row*

"We are told, Tommy, and this may come as a surprise to you, that you have a 13-year-old son who is watching this program right now, who has just been told that you are his father and that you are a murderer."
—Geraldo interviewing Alabama death row inmate Tommy Arthur, who killed his wife's sister

"Your wife wants you to die. Your reaction, quickly."
—Geraldo ending his interview with Tommy Arthur

". . . horrible . . . tragic . . . awful . . . senseless . . . murdering frenzy . . . mad with jealousy . . . sexual psychopath . . . sickest of the sick . . . homicidal monsters . . . grisly . . . battered, bloody bodies . . . stabbed, strangled, ravaged . . . savage . . . brutally murdered—grotesque aberration . . . raped her corpse . . ."
—Excerpts from Geraldo's observations

"It oozes out of our television sets and into our living rooms."
—Geraldo Rivera discussing murder, though he could as easily be describing his brand of journalism

"You're a murderin' dog, Charlie. You're a mass-murderin' dog."
—Geraldo Rivera during the requisite interview with Charles Manson

■

"I find it entirely fiction."
—President Reagan offering a familiar review to Larry Speakes' book

4/14 An increasingly strident Ed Koch announces his support for Al Gore—the only candidate who made a point of telling the mayor he'd read his memoirs—in the New York primary.

■

MEESE WIFE WAS GIVEN JOB BY SEEKER OF U.S. CONTRACT
—The New York Times

■

PATENT FOR MOUSE ISSUED TO HARVARD
RIGHTS ARE FIRST IN THE WORLD FOR HIGHER FORM OF LIFE
—The New York Times

4/15 With his credibility in tatters, Larry Speakes loses his $400,000-a-year job as chief

spokesman for Merrill Lynch. He re-enters the job market with considerably less heat than he had when last there.

4/17 Appearing on *This Week with David Brinkley*, Ed Koch insists he wants to discuss "substantive matters . . . I want to talk about Jesse Jackson's character flaws." He attacks Jackson for allegedly lying about his actions during the moments after the King assassination, then denies calling him a liar. "I just say under stress he will do what's convenient," brays His Shrillness, "and if lying is convenient, that's what he will do."

4/18 "Hi, everybody, it's us! Al Gore and me!"
—Ed Koch campaigning in Manhattan with his chosen candidate, who by now seems to be straining to put as much physical distance as possible between himself and his patron

■

U.S. STRIKES 2 IRANIAN OIL RIGS, HITS 6 NAVY VESSELS IN BATTLES OVER MINING SEA LANES IN GULF
BIG IRAQI PUSH, TOO
A HELICOPTER MISSING—RAIDS ARE A WARNING, PRESIDENT DECLARES
—The New York Times

4/19 Michael Dukakis wins the New York primary, with Jesse Jackson a strong second. "Koch made hysteria," says Jackson. "I made history." Al Gore gets 10% of the vote and pulls out of the race.

■

The Senate Labor Committee is told that George Bush recently pressed for easing requirements for toxic gas ventilation in the workplace. The Bush plan—which had the advantage of being cheaper—was to make the workers wear personal respirators, an unquestionably less effective method of protection.

4/21 Former Justice Department officials Arnold Burns and William Weld explain to President Reagan how a prosecutor more aggressive than James McKay could justify indicting Ed Meese. The President seems visibly upset—one aide describes him as "gray"—but he calms down when Meese comes by and assures him there's "no problem."

4/24   HILL TOLD SDI WOULD BE 'CATASTROPHIC FAILURE'
  —*The Washington Post*

4/25   GREEDY GREEDY GREEDY
  'Queen of the Palace' LEONA HELMSLEY & billionaire hubby HARRY face jail. His charge: tax fraud. Hers: extortion. But that's nothing compared with their despotic, skinflint ways with employees and family. Here's how some of the rich get richer.
  —*People*

4/26   Defending his personal style, George Bush asks, "What's wrong with being a boring kind of guy?" He says it would be a bad idea "to kind of suddenly get my hair colored, and dance up and down in a miniskirt," adding, "I kind of think I'm a scintillating kind of fellow."
  Later, he kind of wins the Pennsylvania primary and has kind of enough delegates for the nomination.

4/27   President Reagan is asked if he could imagine any circumstances that would prompt him to demand Ed Meese's resignation. "Well," he says, "maybe if he had a complete change of character."

4/28   MEESE WANTS BROADER DRUG TESTING
  EVERYONE ARRESTED WOULD BE SUBJECT TO TESTS
  —*The New York Times*

MAY 1988

In which the President's ex-chief-of-staff's book is published

5/2   Campaigning in Indiana, George Bush asks Gov. Robert Orr, "What kind of a guy is Dan Quayle?" Orr assures him the state's junior senator is "a fine, fine person."

5/3   Madonna makes her Broadway debut in David Mamet's *Speed-the-Plow*, attracting many more teenagers to the theater than might otherwise have turned out for a play about two obnoxious Hollywood schmucks.

5/4   "The policies that both Dukakis and Jackson are espousing would take us back to the malaise days. I'll be making that point over and over, and they'll be running for cover like a bunch of quails."
  —George Bush offering an early clue as to the direction of his vice presidential thinking

  ■
  TRAVEL PLANS FOR MEESE'S JAPAN TRIP UNDER SCRUTINY
  ETHICS REGULATION RAISES QUESTIONS ABOUT USE OF PUBLIC OFFICE FOR OTHERS' PROFIT
  —*The Washington Post*

5/5   With its most famous teacher, Jamie Escalante, immortalized in a Hollywood film, East L.A.'s Garfield High School gets a visit from George Bush. "You don't have to go to college to be a success," the would-be Education President says, seemingly unaware that the school sends 70% of its mainly Hispanic students to college. "We need the people who run the offices, the people who do the hard physical work of our society." It becomes known among snide aides as his "You, too, can be a janitor" speech.

5/6   "We have had triumphs, we have made mistakes, we have had sex . . ."
  —George Bush, meaning to say that he and the President had "setbacks"

5/7   Billy Martin requires 40 stitches to close a gash in his left ear after an altercation at a Texas topless bar. He is soon fired for the fifth time, and vows not to return for a sixth. "I'm sick and tired of being accused of being a drunkard," he says. "I haven't had a drink in two days."

5/8 OFFICIALS SAY BUSH HEARD '85 CHARGE AGAINST NORIEGA
    SEEMING CONTRADICTION
    VICE PRESIDENT HAS SAID THAT HE DIDN'T KNOW OF REPORTS ON DRUG ROLE UNTIL '88
    —*The New York Times*

■

Donald Regan's memoir, *For the Record*, exposes Nancy Reagan's secret obsession with astrology, which led her to consult a stargazing "friend," San Francisco heiress Joan Quigley, before approving her husband's schedule. "Feb 20–26 be careful," Quigley would warn. "March 19–25 no public exposure . . . April 21–28 stay home." Among the other highlights:

- Nancy's comment about Raisa Gorbachev after an evening in which she held forth on Marxist-Leninist theory—"Who does that dame think she is?"
- Her efforts to keep abortion out of Presidential speeches—"I don't give a damn about those right-to-lifers!"
- Her insistence that Casey be fired as he lay dying of cancer—"He's dragging Ronnie down!"
- The President's reaction when fire broke out in his study—"He continued reading . . . until guards asked if he wouldn't like

to move while they put out the fire. He hadn't wanted to bother anybody."

5/9 "I was taken aback by the vengefulness of the attack. It comes through to me that Don Regan doesn't really like me."
    —Brief statement issued by Nancy Reagan, who lets it be known that she will continue consulting Ms. Quigley

"I'll be damned if I'll just stand by and let them railroad my wife."
    —President Reagan, telling a reporter that Nancy is "very upset" about Don's book, which he calls "a bunch of falsehoods," without refuting any of them

5/11 With Pat Robertson officially out of the race, President Reagan finally declares his support for George Bush, mentioning his name only three times and once mispronouncing it to rhyme with "rush."

5/16 Maury Povich, host of Fox Broadcasting's sleazy *A Current Affair*, presents a home videotape—recorded just before the Robert Chambers murder trial began—showing the defendant cavorting with several lingerie-clad teenage girls. In the tape's key moment, Chambers amuses himself by pretending to strangle a doll. "Oops," he says, "I think I killed it." The girls—some of whom knew Jennifer Levin—find this quite funny.

■

Ed Meese fires Justice Department spokesman Terry Eastland for conducting an ineffective PR campaign on his behalf. Since Eastland is highly regarded among conservatives, his dismissal upsets a group Meese can ill afford to alienate. Claiming he has "destroyed the department," the *Washington Times* joins the hordes demanding his resignation.

5/17 NOT A SLAVE TO THE ZODIAC, REAGAN SAYS
    —*The New York Times*

SEVEN REVELATIONS FROM MICHAEL JACKSON'S AUTOBIOGRAPHY, *MOONWALK*

"I felt that one glove was cool; wearing two gloves seemed so ordinary."

"Trying to fire your Dad is not easy."

"My relationships with girls have not had the happy ending I've been hoping for."

"I know in my heart that I'm not funny."

"I'm one of the loneliest people in the world."

"I have never had my cheeks altered or my eyes altered. I have not had my lips thinned, nor have I had dermabrasion or a skin peel. I have had my nose altered twice and I recently added a cleft to my chin, but that's it. Period. I don't care what anyone else says—it's my face and I know."

"I didn't invent plastic surgery. It's been around for a long time."

5/19 MEESE SAYS RESIGNATION WOULD SUGGEST GUILT
—*The Washington Post*

■

Donald Regan knocks Michael Jackson's autobiography, *Moonwalk*, out of the Number One slot on the *New York Times* list.

5/25 George Shultz concedes that the three-month US effort to ease Manuel Noriega out of power—which had degenerated to the point where he wouldn't have to leave Panama until August, or maybe never—has failed.

■

NOW PLAYING: *Rambo III*. Sylvester Stallone does his part to keep the Cold War alive, battling cartoonishly brutal Russians in Afghanistan even as, in real life, the personable Gorbachev is withdrawing Soviet troops. Writes *L.A. Weekly* critic John Powers, "His diction (always bad) is now incomprehensible, as if his ego has grown so big that it now fills his mouth like a cup of mashed potatoes." The $60 million film does not make back its cost, sending the rapidly fading box-office attraction scurrying back to the sanctuary of *Rocky V*.

5/26 "What did you start out on, just for the heck of it?"
—George Bush chatting with a patient at a Newark drug rehab

"Did you come here and say, 'The heck with it, I don't need this darn thing'? Did you go through a withdrawal thing?"
—George Bush chatting with another patient

■

With a Gallup poll showing their man 16 points behind, top Bush aides tell a group of pro-Dukakis voters some things they don't know about their candidate:

● His prisoner furlough program let a first-degree murderer out to commit rape
● He vetoed a bill that would have forced teachers to recite the Pledge of Allegiance

THE THING THING

"I feel a little . . . uncomfortable sometimes with the elevation of the religion thing."
—George Bush on religion

"You know, the civil disobedience thing."
—On civil disobedience

"The feminist thing."
—On women

"I've never felt stronger politically in my life. It's hard to tell, but I just can't accept the tarnished-image thing."
—On the effects of the Iran-contra scandal

"The women thing."
—On his unpopularity with female voters

"The roots thing."
—On the compilation of campaign footage of his family and his Maine home

"I'm not going to get into the Meese thing."
—On the troubles of the Attorney General

"We're in a kind of balancing thing here."
—On the negotiations to remove Noriega

"The drought thing."
—On the drought

"Oh, the vision thing."
—On where he wants to take the country

• His own Boston Harbor is really polluted.

Half of them become undecided voters, and the Bush campaign has found its themes.

5/28 ANOTHER TOP MEESE AIDE QUITS JUSTICE DEPT.
—*The New York Times*

5/29 While their husbands hold their first summit session in Moscow, Nancy Reagan and Raisa Gorbachev have tea and tour a cathedral. Is it true, Nancy is asked, that she said of Raisa, "Who does that dame think she is?" No, she says coldly.

Then, determined to match Mikhail Gorbachev's spontaneous limo sprint in Washington, the Reagans take a surprise 10-minute stroll down a Moscow street. Unfortunately, this would-be PR coup leads to a mob scene in which their Soviet bodyguards assault reporters, bystanders and some US officials.

5/30 Attending the Memorial Day parade in Kennebunkport, Maine, George Bush twice refers to the holiday as "Veterans Day."

■

At a state dinner at the Kremlin, the President nods off during Gorbachev's toast, then offers his own remarks, which are dominated by a long-winded synopsis of the 1956 Civil War film *Friendly Persuasion*. "It has fun," says the

President, who gives his hosts a copy. "It has humor. There's a renegade goose, a mischievous young boy, a nosy neighbor, a love-struck teenager in love with a gallant soldier . . ." He goes on for several minutes, as Soviet eyes glaze over.

5/31 In a speech to students at Moscow State University, President Reagan explains the American Indian situation: the US has "provided millions of acres" for "preservations—or the reservations, I should say" so the Indians could "maintain their way of life," though he now wonders, "Maybe we should not have humored them in that, wanting to stay in that kind of primitive lifestyle. Maybe we should have said, 'No, come join us. Be citizens along with the rest of us.'"

For the record, Indians have been citizens since 1924, and few would say they've been "humored" by being allowed to maintain the culture they created before their land was taken from them.

JUNE 1988

In which a new scandal prompts a familiar response

6/1 Bob Dole is asked to comment on President Reagan's seemingly warmer endorsement of Gorbachev than of his own man George Bush. "Gorbachev," Dole happily observes, "has more of a future."

■

"I want to say something. I want to say something now, okay?"
—Nancy Reagan insisting on pointing out the religious significance of the art treasures she's being shown by Raisa Gorbachev, who stares at her watch

■

"If I can make Willie Horton a household name, we win the election."
—Bush campaign manager Lee Atwater preparing to turn Michael Dukakis' furloughed rapist into the national bogeyman

6/6 Fundamentalist media watchdog Donald Wildmon claims to have seen Mighty Mouse snorting cocaine in a recent Saturday morning cartoon. Though animator Ralph Bakshi explains that the rodent was sniffing flowers, the scene is cut from future broadcasts.

6/7 Primary victories in California and New Jersey give Michael Dukakis the delegates he needs for nomination. Declares the winner, who enjoys a double-digit lead over Bush in national polls, "Name-calling and labels don't work and aren't going to work."

6/8 "You know, if I listened to him long enough, I would be convinced that we're in an economic downturn, and that people are homeless, and people are going without food and

medical attention, and that we've got to do something about the unemployed.''
—President Reagan accusing Michael Dukakis of misleading campaign rhetoric

6/9   George Bush (Yale '48) attacks Michael Dukakis' foreign policy views as having been "born in Harvard Yard's boutique.''

■

Appearing on *Nightline*, George Bush repeatedly calls Ted Koppel "Dan.''
"No,'' says Koppel, "Dan's the other fellow.''
"It's Freudian, hey, listen, it's Freudian,'' says Bush. "I promise you, it is Freudian.''
After the fourth "Dan,'' media consultant Roger Ailes tapes a sign next to the camera that reads, "TED.'' Says Bush afterward, "Somewhere between going ballistic with Dan Rather and being benign and pleasant with Ted Koppel is the real me.''

6/10   A bicycle messenger is prevented from entering the Justice Department because he's wearing a T-shirt that proclaims, "Experts Agree! MEESE IS A PIG.''

6/14   POSTAL CHIEF TO SEEK END TO MAILINGS OF DEADLY VIRUSES
    —*Los Angeles Times*

6/15   "Did you have anal sex?''
—Pugnacious gay-bashing talk show host Morton Downey, Jr., interviewing his brother Tony, who has AIDS

6/17   Texas Democrats rent—and throw a party in—the Intercontinental Hotel suite that George Bush cites as his Houston residence.

6/19   "I didn't know anything about it.''
—Former Defense Secretary Caspar Weinberger employing the traditional Reagan administration excuse as a huge Pentagon bribery scandal begins to unfold

6/20   "If you think it was an accident, applaud.''
—Geraldo Rivera asking his studio audience to vote about Natalie Wood's drowning

■

The *National Enquirer* reports that Michael Jackson, who owns the Beatles song catalogue, only sold "Revolution'' to Nike after John Lennon's ghost came to him and said, "Let my music live.'' Says Jackson, "I'd been thinking about the Nike ad all day. I immediately understood what he was telling me.''

6/21   At a press conference following his last economic summit in Toronto, President Reagan says that neither he nor Cap Weinberger could have been expected to have known about the burgeoning Pentagon scandal. "It should be understandable how such things can happen in something as big as our government is,'' says the President, who clearly husbands his anger for poor people who wangle a few extra food stamps.

■

FRAUD EVIDENCE IGNORED, SENATOR SAYS
MEESE DEFENDS HANDLING OF PENTAGON CASES, DISPUTES GRASSLEY
    —*The Washington Post*

6/22   "Some people just know her a little bit/Some people know her a lot/Some people just read the headlines/Some people know what they've got/Some people say she's kinda terrific/ All that has been said/At one more luncheon, one more dinner/Let's hear it for the lady in red."

—Marvin Hamlisch composing an original song for a Washington tribute to Nancy Reagan

6/23 "I'm opposed to these unsupervised weekend furloughs for first-degree murderers who are not eligible for parole. Put me down as against that."

—George Bush disproving critics who claim he's basing his entire campaign on the Pledge of Allegiance

6/25 John Landis invites the jury that acquitted him of involuntary manslaughter to a private screening of his new Eddie Murphy movie, *Coming to America*. He does not offer to fly them in by helicopter.

6/27 "This is it. In two months, it's pee-in-a-bottle time."

—Meese spokesman Patrick Korten giving Justice Department employees 60 days' warning before starting random drug testing

■

Mike Tyson—who says he wants to hit his opponent "so hard that I make the nose bone go into his brain and kill him"—earns $20 million by defeating Michael Spinks in 91 seconds of the first round of their championship fight in Atlantic City. Robin Givens is booed.

6/29 The Supreme Court votes 7–1 to uphold the law authorizing special prosecutors to investigate government officials. Antonin Scalia dissents.

■

With three White House guards suspended for suspected off-duty cocaine use, a random drug-testing policy is announced for all executive office employees.

JULY 1988

In which the nation's top cop is embarrassed by premature exoneration

7/3 The battleship *Vincennes*—one of the Navy's ultra-sophisticated computer-supported Aegis cruisers—mistakes Iran Air Flight 655 for a fighter plane and blasts it out of the sky, killing 290. President Reagan calls the incident an "understandable accident." Though reliable reports say the Soviet downing of KAL 007 was also inadvertent, he insists there is "no comparison" between the events.

Says George Bush, "I will never apologize for the United States of America! I don't care what the facts are!"

7/4 Jesse Jackson, who has stopped short of demanding the vice presidency but clearly wants something for his second-place finish, arrives with his wife for dinner at the Dukakis home in Brookline. Unfortunately, the meal (clam chowder and poached salmon) is not to his liking, leading him to have take-out food delivered to him at the Boston Pops concert the foursome attends afterward.

7/5 Ed Meese claims that James McKay's decision not to indict him has "completely vindicated" him and, with the cloud over his head lifted, says he is now free to resign and will soon do so.

7/6 The first of many syringes, blood vials and other hospital souvenirs—some contaminated with the AIDS virus—washes ashore on Long Island, forcing the closing of miles of beaches in the midst of the worst East Coast heat wave of the decade. Officials downplay the risk to bathers, pointing out that these items make up only a small percentage of beach debris. "People are living in an age of fear," says a health department spokesperson. "People are afraid when they hear the words 'infectious waste.' "

■

Nancy Reagan, 67, celebrates her 65th birthday.

7/7 Jesse Jackson is asked whether his plan to bring his supporters to the Democratic convention on a bus is designed to "steal the thunder" from his opponent. "Mr. Dukakis," says Jackson, "has no intention of bringing any thunder to Atlanta."

7/8 MEESE SAYS HE MET HIS ETHICAL GOAL
—*The New York Times*

7/10 REAGAN HAILS MEESE HONESTY
—*The New York Times*

7/12 "I'm too controlled. I'm too clear. I'm too mature to be angry."
—An obviously furious Jesse Jackson after learning from reporters—rather than from the candidate personally, who claims he couldn't contact him—that he will not be Michael Dukakis' running mate, and that Texas senator Lloyd Bentsen will be

7/13 Nancy Reagan's office has no comment on reports that her ghostwriter, William Novak—who co-authored the memoirs of Lee Iacocca and Tip O'Neill—has called marijuana an "intellectual stimulant."

7/17 "It's not over until it's over—and then it's not over."
—Jesse Jackson on the eve of his summit meeting with Michael Dukakis, where he faces the reality that he has no future in the party if he fails to support its nominee

7/18 KITTY & THE DUKE
He mows, he cooks, he shops—he even *does the dishes!* Barbara Bush, eat your heart out
—*People*

■

Independent counsel James McKay reports that though he thinks prosecution is unwarranted, he has concluded that Ed Meese "probably violated the criminal law" four times since becoming America's chief law enforcement officer. McKay says Meese filed a false income tax return, failed to pay capital gains taxes on time, and participated in decisions about matters in which he had a financial interest.

A furious Meese responds, "McKay doesn't know beans about criminal law, let alone taxes. I've had a reputation all my life for scrupulous honesty and integrity, and frankly I'm outraged by this sort of report. The only person who says there is a criminal violation is Mr. McKay and he's wrong."

■

"Poor George, he can't help it—he was born with a silver foot in his mouth."
—Texas state treasurer Ann Richards delivering the keynote speech in Atlanta, getting Democrats all excited about what an easy target Bush is

7/19 "A toothache of a man."
—Texas agriculture commissioner Jim Hightower on George Bush

"Where was George?"
—Ted Kennedy bringing the mocking of the Vice President to its crescendo by leading a giddy refrain about his famed invisibility

■

"His foreparents came to America on immigrant ships. My foreparents came to America on slave ships. But whatever the original ships, we are both in the same boat now."
—Jesse Jackson switching the convention to a more serious mode, exhorting his supporters to find "common ground" with the uninspiring nominee

■

Having heard enough of Ed Meese's self-righteous pronouncements, the Justice Department opens an investigation into his possible violation of federal ethics laws.

7/20   Traveling in Amsterdam, Ed Koch attacks local officials for tolerating the open sale of marijuana and hashish. "That," declares the mayor, "couldn't take place in New York City."

■

Far-right fundamentalist preacher R. L. Hymers protests Martin Scorsese's *The Last Temptation of Christ*—which he proudly refuses to see, lest he discover it's one of the few truly religious movies made in the past decade—by leading an anti-Semitic demonstration outside the home of MCA chairman Lew Wasserman, whose company is distributing the film.

■

Following a comically endless nominating speech by Arkansas governor Bill Clinton (who parlays his public humiliation into a guest shot with Johnny Carson), Michael Dukakis receives his party's presidential nomination. Cameras in his suite record the candidate's exuberant reaction: he waves away a glass of champagne.

7/21   "This election is not about ideology—it's about competence."
—Michael Dukakis accepting the nomination, exhibiting a dismaying misunderstanding of what *every* election is about

WAS IT MONDALE OR WAS IT DUKAKIS?

Many people have remarked on the dismaying similarities between the Democratic presidential candidates of 1984 and 1988. Perhaps Jay Leno put it best when he said, "Dukakis is Greek for Mondale." In each of the instances below, was it Mondale, or was it Dukakis?

1 His media director boasted that the candidate "dares to be cautious."

2 Tip O'Neill said he had to "stop acting like a gentleman and come out fighting."

3 Interviewing him was compared to "popping a quarter into a jukebox."

4 Andrew Young called his campaign team "a bunch of smart-assed white boys who think they know it all."

5 He was described as "a candidate who, when a match was lit in the vicinity, poured gasoline all over himself."

6 His performance at his second debate prompted Bill Moyers to observe, "He kept going for the jugular with a feather."

7 He was described as "the kind of guy you'd like to have in your foxhole—if you wanted to study soil erosion."

8 Murray Kempton said he'd "risen up as the fighting liberal he would have been too sensible to be if he felt there was a chance of victory left."

9 He explained his wussiness by saying, "I'm slow to anger."

10 He was referred to as a "tourniquet of a man."

11 He said there was a public image of him as a "kind of slug."

12 He was described by Murray Kempton as "so pathetically terminal a case that to keep on noticing his limitations is a kind of cruelty."

[MONDALE: 1, 2, 4, 6, 8, 11
DUKAKIS: 3, 5, 7, 9, 10, 12]

7/22   WEDTECH PROSECUTOR ASSAILS MEESE AS 'A SLEAZE'
—*The New York Times*

■

PEE-WEE HERMAN: IS HE HILARIOUS OR TOO CREEPY FOR WORDS?
—*The New York Times*, reviewing (unfavorably) *Big Top Pee-wee*

7/26   A Gallup poll shows Michael Dukakis leading George Bush 55% to 38%.

■

Former Justice Department official Arnold Burns tells the Senate Judiciary Committee that Ed Meese turned the department into "a world of Alice in Wonderland" in which "up was down and down was up, in was out and out was in, happy was sad and sad was happy, rain was sunshine and sunshine was rain, hot was cold and cold was hot." His colleague William Weld says he thinks Meese should have been prosecuted.

■

"We may be incompetent, we may be stupid, we may have bad taste. . . . But we are not crooks."
—Disney's Jeff Katzenberg telling striking writers—whose 22-week walkout is coming to a not particularly successful end—why they should be more trusting of producers

7/27   "How do we make equality of opportunity a reality in America? We can start by supporting the Equal Rights Amendment, and I support the R.E.A.!"
—Lloyd Bentsen campaigning in Albuquerque

7/28   George Bush is asked if the public perception of him is at odds with reality. "Much different," he says. "For example, I like pork rinds, but that doesn't fit the mold."

7/30   "A fish rots from the head first."
—Michael Dukakis citing a perhaps too pungent proverb in response to a question about whether President Reagan should be held re-

sponsible for the shoddy ethics of so many in his administration

AUGUST 1988

In which the Future is haunted by the past

8/1   Jessica Hahn's rebuilt body—"I had my nose done, I had my teeth recapped . . . I had my breasts done"—goes on display in *Playboy*. Posing nude, she explains, was "probably the best time of my life—except for when I found God."

■

America's last Playboy Club closes in Lansing, Michigan.

■

A *National Enquirer* excerpt from a Secret Service agent's memoir reveals that Richard Nixon has been known to put on a hospital gown backward "and tramp down the hall with the front flying open."

8/3   "He called me a bleached-blond idiot, and I called him a wart-faced phony."
—Right-wing L.A. talk show host Wally George recounting an exchange with Morton Downey, Jr., who George thinks stole his act

■

"Look, I'm not going to pick on an invalid."
—President Reagan coyly refusing to demand that Michael Dukakis release his medical records in the wake of completely false rumors that he twice *got depressed and consulted a psychiatrist!*

8/4   On the 24th anniversary of the discovery of the bodies of three civil rights workers in Mississippi, Michael Dukakis campaigns nine miles from the site and—fearful of offending white southerners whose votes he doesn't have a prayer of getting anyway—does not mention the event.

■

Director Franco Zeffirelli denies that he called *The Last Temptation of Christ* "a product of that Jewish cultural scum in Los Angeles." The comment is reported to exist on tape.

8/6 With Treasury Secretary James A. Baker III quitting to take over his friend George Bush's campaign, a CBS News/*New York Times* poll shows Michael Dukakis ahead by 17 points. The governor interprets this as a mandate to take the rest of the month off, secure in the knowledge that his opponent's efforts to paint him as a man who lets murderers out of jail and won't let kids say the pledge is doomed to failure.

8/7 Rupert Murdoch—who owns a movie studio, a movie magazine (*Premiere*) and a TV network—buys a TV magazine, paying Walter Annenberg $3 billion for *TV Guide.*

8/8 Talk show host Sally Jessy Raphael devotes an hour to "sexual confusion," with guests including a man born with male and female organs, a married man who wishes he had female organs so he could go to bed with a man, and a man who claims to be in the process of acquiring female organs. "It is very difficult," says Raphael, thanking her guests, "to come on and describe your private parts."

8/9 With black teenager Tawana Brawley's claim of being raped by a group of whites under serious question, conservative black leader Roy Innis—who says Brawley made the whole thing up—shoves Brawley defender (and all-around racial ambulance chaser) Rev. Al Sharpton to the floor during the taping of a Morton Downey, Jr., show.

■

"When he . . . makes an allusion to the President about a fish rotting from the head down, I won't call that very positive campaigning."
—George Bush denying responsibility for the negative tone of the campaign

■

The Chicago Cubs beat the New York Mets, 6–4, in the first night game at 74-year-old Wrigley Field.

8/10 Ed Koch—who has urged New Yorkers not to give to beggars, saying, "If you feel guilty, see a priest"—announces plans for an anti-beggar ad campaign.

8/12 Ed Meese serves his long-awaited last day as Attorney General. His replacement, former Pennsylvania governor Richard Thornburgh, declines several opportunities to say he will emulate his predecessor.

■

Brigitte Nielsen and football star Mark Gastineau announce their engagement. Each claims to have the name of the other tattooed on his/her posterior.

8/13 BUSH OVERTAKES DUKAKIS IN ABC POLL
— *Los Angeles Times*

BUSH AND TOP AIDES PRUNE RUNNING-MATE LIST TO 6
ONE IS A DARK HORSE FROM INDIANA
—*The New York Times*

George Bush pats his wife's posterior during an otherwise civilized interview with Dan Rather.

8/14 Bush aides are reported to be talking up Indiana senator Dan Quayle, 41—a darling of the far right—as a possible running mate. Quayle appears on *This Week with David Brinkley*, where he mentions the name "George Bush" 10 times in two minutes. "George Bush is going to make this decision by himself," he says, "and whoever can help George Bush get elected President I'm sure will accept the nod, and that is the goal, because it is so important that we have George Bush as the next President of the United States." He also says the ongoing drought has been hard on the "coyn and sorbean" crops.

President Reagan arrives in New Orleans, where he calls the Democrats "liberal" 22 times in his arrival speech. "It's time to talk issues, to use the dreaded 'L' word," he says. "Liberal, liberal, liberal." He is presented with an enormous "Gipper's Gavel" to add to his vast collection of oversized props.

8/15 Russian comic Yakov ("What a country!") Smirnoff opens the Republican convention in New Orleans with the Pledge of Allegiance. Other notable first-day events:

* Bob Dole—who has displayed a perverse eagerness to serve as running mate to a man he despises—fatally damages his cause by describing the vice presidential selection process as "demeaning"
* Al Haig likens the Democratic party to a blind bat "hanging upside down in dark, damp caves up to its navel in guano"
* Nancy Reagan grits her teeth and says, "The time has come for the Bushes to step into the limelight and the Reagans to step into the wings"
* President Reagan delivers his farewell speech to the convention, misstating his catchphrase of the evening, "Facts are stubborn things," as a more-appropriate-for-him "Facts are stupid things."

■

UNDER YOKO'S SPELL
From the explosive new biography of JOHN LENNON, scenes of despair, drugs and domination by his wife

    —*People* excerpt from Albert Goldman's necrophiliac exhumation

8/16 After seeing the Reagans off at the airport—where he points out his half-Mexican grandkids as "the little brown ones"—George Bush, finally his own man, announces his first presidential decision: Dan Quayle, a "Man of the Future," will be his running mate. Quayle's youth and alleged good looks—he is billed as a Redford lookalike, though he in fact resembles Pat Sajak—are expected to blind women and baby boomers to his immaturity and hard-right views.

Quayle leaps out of the crowd and up to the podium, bouncing around as he waves his arms and shouts, "Believe me, we will win because America cannot afford to lose!" He grabs Bush's shoulder, almost punching him in the stomach as he brays, "Let's go get 'em!" Bush looks ill.

8/17 George Bush loses the parents-of-mauled-children vote by pledging that he and his running mate will campaign like "pit bulls." Meanwhile, Dan Quayle's debut on the national stage is an inauspicious one, as reporters focus in on several touchy areas. Among them:

* His connection to a 1980 sex scandal involving lobbyist Paula Parkinson—"It's been fully gone into," he says peevishly, "and if you don't know that, you should"

- His neanderthal voting record on civil rights, the environment and other progressive issues
- His embarrassing scholastic record
- His decision, despite vociferous support for the Vietnam War, to avoid the draft by joining the National Guard—"I did not know in 1969 that I would be in this room today, I'll confess"—and the question as to whether his rich, influential parents pulled any strings on his behalf.

Democratic analyst Robert Squier notes that the GOP "could end up with a ticket [of] Wimp and War Wimp, and that's a tough one to try to campaign with."

8/18   ". . . accept your nomination . . . going to win . . . proud to have Dan Quayle . . . hold my charisma in check . . . don't hate government . . . scandal to give a weekend furlough to a hardened first-degree killer . . . Read! My! LIPS! No! New! Taxes! . . . kinder and gentler nation . . . go ahead, make my 24-hour time period . . . quiet man . . . hear the quiet people others don't . . . I am that man! . . . a thousand points of light . . . I pledge allegiance to the flag of the United States of America . . ."
—George Bush, who, as did Michael Dukakis a month ago, succeeds in lowering expectations to the point where a competent speech is exalted as a dazzling display of oratorical pyrotechnics

8/19   A mob scene ensues in Dan Quayle's home town of Huntington when campaign aides pipe the sound from a contemptuous press interrogation of the candidate out to a rally of his supporters. Why, he is asked, if no influence was necessary, did he ask his parents to help him get into the National Guard?
    "I do—I do—I do—I do what any normal person would do at that age," says Quayle. "You call home. You call home to mother and father and say, 'I'd like to get in the National Guard.'" Despite his barely passing grades, he claims eagerness to pursue his law school education, rather than fear for his safety, led to his deci-

sion. The response seems to satisfy his townsfolk, who chant, "BOR-ING! BOR-ING!" at reporters.

8/20   Campaigning with his running mate at the Ohio State Fair, George Bush compares reporters at the Quayle press conference to bluefish. "There was a flurry, there was a feeding flurry in the water out there," he says. "Have you ever seen them when they are just squirming all around and feeding in a frenzy. That's exactly what was happening."
    Quayle, who warns that the US is "naked, absolutely nude to attack" by the Soviets, faces his first hecklers, who chant, "Quayle, Quayle called his mom/Everybody else went to Nam." They also shout "Chicken!" as hundreds of live fowl can be heard squawking nearby.

8/21   After coming face to face with a furious World War II vet who snarls, "You're a draft dodger," Dan Quayle is sent home for a crash course in campaigning, or, as the press dubs it, "Vice President school."

■

"This was a PR outfit that became President and took over the country."

—Former Reagan press aide Leslie Janka, as quoted by Mark Hertsgaard in *On Bended Knee: The Press and the Reagan Presidency*, a book that convincingly points up the media's inadequacies and is therefore poorly reviewed by said media

8/22 "He did not go to Canada, he did not burn his draft card and he *damn sure* didn't burn the American flag! And I am proud to have him at my side!"

—George Bush assuring a Veterans of Foreign Wars convention in Chicago that his running mate is innocent of a series of unmade charges

"My National Guard unit was never called up to active duty, but after the last 72 hours no one can say I never faced combat."

—Dan Quayle, making amends with the Veterans of Foreign Wars by trivializing their experiences

■

"Don't let him fool you, America. He's about as close to Ronald Reagan in the area of national security as Winnie the Pooh is to Refrigerator Perry in the area of bears."

—George Bush attacking Michael Dukakis in Chicago

■

FOREST FIRES RAGE IN WESTERN PARKS

YELLOWSTONE HAS ITS WORST DAY— ARMY SENDING TROOPS

—*The New York Times*

8/23 "If the Vice President is saying he'd sign an unconstitutional bill, then in my judgment he's not fit to hold the office."

—Michael Dukakis, trailing in post-GOP convention polls, but confident that this is all he has to say to put an end to that pesky Pledge of Allegiance issue

■

Playboy reveals that Paula Parkinson told lawyers seven years ago that Dan Quayle "said he wanted to make love" and "flirted a lot and

THE WORLD IS RUN BY C STUDENTS

"He was as vapid a student as I can ever recall. . . . Nothing came out of his mouth that was worth remembering."

—Dan Quayle's political science professor, Robert Sedlack, who said he would "inevitably think of Dan Quayle" when he heard the phrase, "The world is run by C students"

"Girls, golf and alcohol."

—Dan Quayle's classmate describing his majors

"Dan Quayle was one of the few people able to get from the Deke house to the golf course without passing through a classroom."

—Dan Quayle's English professor

"He received a D in political science, which was his major, and his record was pretty much Cs."

—Robert Sedlack

GREAT MIND'S THINK ALIKE

danced extremely close and suggestively" during that 1980 golf weekend in Florida. Quayle stages a taking-out-the-trash photo op to demonstrate what he thinks of such stories, demanding "some respect and dignity for things I did not do."

Meanwhile, James Quayle says his son Dan's main interests in school were "broads and booze."

8/25 "I don't know what his problem is with the Pledge of Allegiance. . . . His fervent opposition to the pledge is symbolic of an entire attitude best summed up in four little letters: ACLU. . . . He says—here's an exact quote—he says, 'I am a card-carrying member of the ACLU.' Well, I am not and I never will be."
—George Bush, uncowed by his opponent's cries of "Unconstitutional!"

■

Dan Quayle cites, among his qualifications to be President, his eight years on the Senate Armed Services Committee, where his work with cruise missiles involved "getting them

more accurate so that we can have precise precision."

Asked by a farmer about a local pork issue, Quayle says, "Whatever you guys want, I'm for," explaining that he knows "quite a bit about farm policies" because "I come from Indiana, a farm state." And what, then, is his message to farmers? "My message?" says Quayle, looking confused. He smiles and says nothing.

■

Right-wing Idaho senator Steve Symms claims to have heard that there are photographs of Kitty Dukakis "burning the American flag" in the '60s, though he, of course, has not actually seen them.

8/26   Though the release of school records is a normal requirement for any number of positions, Dan Quayle—seeking to place himself a chicken bone away from the Presidency—refuses to divulge his. He concedes that his resume contains an inflated description of his job with the Indiana attorney general's office, though the error is blamed, oddly enough, on his staff.

8/27   "Although in public I refer to him as Mr. Vice President, in private I call him George. When he called, when I talked to him on the phone yesterday, I called him George rather than Mr. Vice President. But in public, it's Mr. Vice President because that's who he is."
—Dan Quayle explaining the "intra-personal" relationship he has developed with George Bush

8/28   Asked what qualifications he would bring to the role of anti-drug czar, should he be so assigned, Dan Quayle claims to be familiar with the National Narcotics Border Interdiction System "in a general sense." He is asked who runs it. "Who is the head of it? I don't know who the head of it is," says Quayle. The answer? George Bush.

8/29   Michael Dukakis serenely embarks on a two-day tour of his home state, as if wresting the "Wimp" label away from George Bush hasn't just cost him 15–20 points in the national polls.

■

Jessica Hahn, the first celebrity to parlay a nude spread in *Playboy* into a radio job, starts work at Phoenix's KOY-FM as the "Morning Zoo Y95 Weather and Prize Bunny." One of the first listeners to phone in calls her a "slut."

8/30   Dan Quayle addresses a convention of fire chiefs, where he holds a fireman's hat over his head for cameras, but doesn't actually put it on, lest he disturb his coiffure.

8/31   Sen. Orrin Hatch calls the Democrats "the party of homosexuals," then denies he said it. A radio station produces the comment on tape.

■

At a Lake Erie campaign stop, George Bush declares, "I am an environmentalist," a statement Michael Dukakis finds so patently absurd that he sees no need to make sure the voters understand how truly Orwellian it is.

MICHAEL DUKAKIS SOLVES THE DEFICIT

"There are only two ways to reduce the budget deficit. . . . We must do both."
—Michael Dukakis (April 1987)

"There are only three ways to reduce the deficit. . . . We must do all three."
—Michael Dukakis (September 1987)

"There are only four ways to reduce the federal budget deficit. . . . We must do all four."
—Michael Dukakis (August 1988)

SEPTEMBER 1988

In which the Future seems anything but bright

9/1 George Bush arrives in Boston for a ferry ride in what he calls "the dirtiest harbor in America"—a devastating invasion of their home turf that Dukakis aides have known about for days yet failed to combat. A local poll shows that the governor of Massachusetts has blown a 14-point lead in his home state.

9/2 "My opponent expressing concern about the environment is like George Steinbrenner expressing concern for managers."
—George Bush campaigning at a New Jersey beach

"Eeek! Eeek! Eeek!"
—George Bush being nipped repeatedly as he empties traps aboard a Delaware crab boat, after which he claims the Democrats remind him of "what I brought out of that river—blue crabs"

■

"There's two men running for President. . . . Michael Dukakis [is] a liberal, and he doesn't want to admit it. . . . George Bush [is] a pure opportunist, who's pretending he's an arch-conservative. . . . They're the Duke and the Dauphin, the two characters in *Huckleberry Finn.* . . . These are guys who are charlatans. Neither one of them is telling the truth."
—Political analyst Christopher Matthews

■

With a growing sense of doom settling on his campaign, Michael Dukakis rehires manager John Sasso, who says—because what else can he say?—"I think the campaign is going incredibly well." Adds Dukakis campaign chairman Paul Brountas, "The fact is, this campaign is in excellent shape."

9/4 "Perestroika is nothing more than refined Stalinism."
—Dan Quayle displaying his unrefined comprehension of the Soviet political system

9/5 Tammy Faye Bakker describes her last night in her PTL mansion before being evicted by Jerry Falwell. "As I lay on the floor in the dark, empty room," she says, "Tuppins, my puppy, licked at the tears running down my face. 'Oh, Tuppins,' I sobbed. 'Why has God forsaken me?'"

■

With both candidates fond of fish metaphors, George Bush officially kicks off his campaign by struggling to fillet a freshly caught bass, while his tie dips into a bin of seafood. Afterward, he attacks his opponent's defense positions, claiming, "He thinks a naval exercise is something you find in Jane Fonda's workout book."

Meanwhile, at the Statue of Liberty, Dan Quayle's mind-numbing word-by-word analysis of the Pledge of Allegiance is interrupted by angry protesters who hoist hostile signs and shout, "40,000 dead from AIDS—where was Dan?" Says Quayle uneasily, "Who are these folks?"

9/6 "Dan Quayle's idea of a naval exercise is getting golf balls out of a water hazard."
—Dukakis aide Mark Gearan

9/7 "Today, you remember—I wonder how many Americans remember—today is Pearl Harbor Day. Forty-seven years ago to this very day we were hit and hit hard at Pearl Harbor. . . . Did I say September 7th? Sorry about that. December 7th, 1941."

—George Bush, who twice called Memorial Day "Veterans Day," promising voters a very special kind of continuity

9/8 "I could have been an atheist. I could have been a polygamist. I could have been anything else and questions wouldn't have been asked."

—Bush campaign worker Jerome Brentar, fired when his oft-voiced doubts about the existence of the Holocaust come to light

■

The two campaigns reach an agreement on debates: there will be two (Dukakis wanted three or four), the first will be September 25th (Dukakis wanted September 14th), the second will be October 13th or 14th (Dukakis wanted the end of October) and both will be general in subject matter (Dukakis wanted the first devoted solely to foreign policy).

Says Paul Brountas of the pact, "I'm pleased with it."

■

After the taping of a *Geraldo* about violent men and the battered women who kill them, a feminist and a wife-beater get into a brawl. "I see why your wife shot you!" screams the feminist. "You deserve to be shot in the head!" shouts the wife-beater. Rivera locks himself in his dressing room and drinks a gin and tonic until police arrive.

■

Believing himself to be at his best off the cuff, Dan Quayle dismays his advisers by abandoning his prepared text and delivering a rambling, incoherent speech that leaves his Chicago audience baffled. Among the highlights: his citing of the Tom Clancy novel *Red Storm Rising* as justification for building an anti-satellite weapon, and his citing of the philosophy of basketball coach Bobby Knight to support in-

creased defense spending. Says an aide of this ad-libbing, "We didn't think he would deviate that far."

On the domestic front, he declares that Republicans "understand the importance of bondage between parent and child," though, of course, he means "bonding."

■

Dan Quayle's toothy, retro-coiffed wife, Marilyn, observes six times in the course of a single plane ride that she's "not getting paid" for serving as her husband's chief adviser. "Well, I'm working, but I'm still not getting paid," she says. "I'm still a lawyer, I'm just not paid." "I have no different role for Dan than his administrative assistant. It's just I don't get paid." Etc.

She also defends her spouse's much-maligned intellect, claiming that he "really is the studious sort" who "tries to read Plato's *Republic* every year" (though she does not reveal if he has ever succeeded), and points out that "Franklin Roosevelt was a lousy student. He failed the bar exam seven times." In fact, FDR took the test *once*, as a second-year law student, and passed.

9/9 Surrendering to Republican pressure, Jim Wright announces that the Pledge of Allegiance will be recited in the House twice a week.

■

Addressing a sweaty, T-shirted audience at an Ohio steel plant, a suit-clad Dan Quayle declares, "I can identify with steelworkers. I can identify with workers that have had a difficult time." He claims to have defended steel quotas in a face-to-face encounter with President Reagan, looking him "right across the eyes." Says one worker of Quayle's appeal, "It's a long way off yet."

■

"I got into law school fair and square. Nothing improper was done and no rules were broken."

—Dan Quayle responding to a report that his college grades were so low that his entry into law school was dependent on a special "equal opportunity" program primarily intended to increase minority admissions

9/11 Bush campaign aide Fred Malek resigns after the resurfacing of a previously reported revelation that, in 1971, he followed President Nixon's orders and compiled a list of Jews at a government bureau.

9/12 Six more Bush campaign advisers quit amid charges of anti-Semitism.

■

TV PREMIERE: *USA Today: The Television Show*—a daily TV version of the newspaper that set out to be a print version of TV. "We're taking television into the next decade," says producer Steve Friedman. "Twenty-five years from now, people will look back at this show and call it one of the most influential shows in television."

9/13 Touring the General Dynamics plant in Michigan, Michael Dukakis puts on an enormous green helmet and rides around in the turret of an M-1 Battle Tank, evoking unhelpful media comparisons to Snoopy and Rocky the Flying Squirrel. Explains an aide, "He said he wanted to hear what the other guys in the tank were saying. Fine. But he looked like an idiot."

THE QUAYLE WIT

"I understand you have a balloon festival here. Well, you ought to invite Michael Dukakis. He's got a lot of hot air."
—Dan Quayle campaigning in Albuquerque

"I can understand why Michael Dukakis doesn't fit in too well down here. He thinks a longhorn is something you play in the Boston Symphony."
—Campaigning across Texas

"The only thing that zigs and zags more than the Rio Grande is our opponent's positions on the issues."
—Campaigning in El Paso

"He thinks an oilman is someone who just went swimming in Boston Harbor."
—Campaigning in Wisconsin

"His idea of farm production is growing flowers in Harvard Yard."
—On the agricultural policies of Michael Dukakis

"You have even more snow here than comes out of the mouth of the man from Massachusetts."
—Campaigning at an Ohio ski lodge

■

"Want to hear a sad story about the Dukakis campaign? The governor of Massachusetts, he lost his top naval adviser last week. The rubber duck drowned in his bathtub."
—Dan Quayle campaigning in Milwaukee

9/14 "Back under the previous Administration, things were rough in the flag business. . . . Well, since we began restoring pride in the United States of America, business has been booming. Flag sales have taken off."
—George Bush campaigning in Orange County

■

Landslide: The Unmaking of the President: 1984–88, by White House correspondents Jane Mayer and Doyle McManus, reveals that Reagan was so detached during the Iran-contra scandal that aides signed his initials to documents without his knowledge. Says an aide to Howard Baker of Reagan's underlings, "They told stories about how inattentive and inept the President was. . . . They said he wouldn't come to work —all he wanted to do was to watch movies and television at the residence."

9/15 Howard Baker confirms that when he became chief of staff, there was some concern about the President's ability to remain in office. But, he says, he instantly found Reagan to be "the most presidential man I've ever known," and that was that.
Says the President of the *Landslide* report, "No truth at all." In other words, fiction.

■

Asked about the Holocaust during a rare news conference, Dan Quayle calls it "an obscene period in our nation's history." Reminded that the Holocaust did not take place in America, he explains that "in this century's history" is what he meant to say. "We all lived in this century," he says, adding cryptically, "I didn't live in this century."

9/16 Defending his campaign against charges of ethnic prejudice, George Bush says,

"I hope I stand for anti-bigotry, anti-Semitism, anti-racism." He goes on to misquote, of all things, the Pledge of Allegiance: "And to the liberty for which it stands, one nation under God with freedom and justice for all."
Meanwhile, Dan Quayle repeatedly calls Belgian endive "Belgium endive."

■

The 1988 Summer Olympics begin in Seoul, South Korea. Among the highlights:

- US middleweight Anthony Hembrick is eliminated when his coaches misread the schedule and he arrives 12 minutes late for his match
- Greg Louganis smashes his head on the diving board but goes on to win a gold medal
- A referee is attacked in the ring by the coaches of a losing South Korean boxer
- Two US gold-medal swimmers are arrested for stealing a marble lion's head from a hotel
- Canadian track star Ben Johnson is stripped of his gold medal for using steroids.

NBC broadcasts a numbing 179½ hours of competition—less a considerable chunk for commercials—which, given the serious lack of interest among US viewers, is overkill of a high order.

9/17 "There's a lot of things we can refer to the man from Massachusetts as. We can call him 'Mr. Tax Increase.' We can call him 'Mr. Polluter.' We can call him 'Mr. Weak on National Defense.' But let me tell you something. Come November 8th, there's one thing we'll never call the governor of Massachusetts, and that is 'Mr. President.' "
—Dan Quayle, described by an adviser as "the future standing right up there"

9/19 MICHAEL JACKSON'S PLASTIC FACE IS MELTING—SAYS SURGEON
—*Star*

■

A CRY FOR HELP
Fearing for her life, friends of Robin Givens leak a frightening story of Mike Tyson's private

1988

THE QUOTABLE QUAYLE

"The real question for 1988 is whether we're going to go forward to tomorrow or past to the—to the back!"

"We will invest in our people, quality education, job opportunity, family, neighborhood, and yes, a thing we call America."

"We'll let the sunshine come in and shine on us, because today we're happy and tomorrow we'll be even happier."

"We're going to have the best-educated American people in the world."

"This election is about who's going to be the next President of the United States!"

violence and his threat to kill them both
—*People*

■

Bobby McFerrin's "Don't Worry, Be Happy"—adopted, with no irony, as the Bush campaign's theme song—begins two weeks as the nation's Number One song.

9/20 "I've never been to a flag factory!"
—George Bush in New Jersey, visiting his first one

"Wouldn't working here lift your spirits?"
—Senate candidate Pete Dawkins to Bush as they leave the actually quite grim workplace

"We took it exactly one day too far."
—Bush aide responding to the "Enough with the flag, already!" stories on all three network newscasts

9/21 "Go back and tell George Bush to start talking about the issues."
—Barry Goldwater stunning Dan Quayle at an Arizona campaign stop

9/23 Michael Deaver gets three years in prison (suspended), 1,500 hours of community service, and a $100,000 fine. "It was a very fair sentence," he says, "if I had been guilty."

■

An MTV poll finds that by a 42%–27% margin, its viewers think Michael Dukakis would be the "most fun on a cross-country road trip." Dukakis also ekes out a 37%–36% victory on the question of who "would throw the best parties," though more viewers (43%–36%) want to have dinner at George Bush's house.

9/25 Billy Carter, 51, dies of pancreatic cancer in Plains, Georgia.

■

Marilyn Quayle and her parents are reported to be followers of Col. Robert B. Thieme, Jr., a far, far right-wing preacher who has been

257

known to wear his Air Force uniform in the pulpit. His specialty is Armageddon.

◾

At their first debate in Winston-Salem, North Carolina, Michael Dukakis:

- Unconvincingly claims to "resent" the slurs on his patriotism
- Attempts to soften his "Zorba the Clerk" image by emotionlessly declaring, "I care deeply about people, all people"
- Finds himself laughed at when he says he's "very tough on violent crime"
- Can be seen smirking toothily whenever his opponent speaks.

George Bush, meanwhile:

- Says "there's plenty" of weapons systems he opposes, naming three that have already been cut
- Complains about the cocaine scene in *Crocodile Dundee* and refers to a drug addict as "a narcotics-wrapped-up guy."
- Refers to Dukakis as the "Ice Man"
- Admits he has not yet "sorted out" what the penalties should be if abortion is again made illegal, leaving open the possibility that he would jail women who have them.

9/26   James Baker says that after the debate George Bush decided that women shouldn't go to jail for having abortions after all, but maybe the doctors who perform them should.

◾

Time runs a photo of Dan Quayle with a fly resting between his eyebrows.

9/27   "Bush skitters like a waterbug on the surface of things, strewing fragments of thoughts, moving fast lest he linger so long that he is expected to show mastery of, or even real interest in, anything."
—Columnist George Will on the debate

"What also came through . . . is the utter banality of Bush's intellect. His mind is organized like a factory-outlet store—everything scattered around and nothing worth more than $49.95."
—Columnist Ross K. Baker

"The debate sharpened the choice . . . a man who can't express his thoughts or a man who can't express his feelings."
—Columnist Mary McGrory

◾

"I would think very exciting."
—Lloyd Bentsen on what life would be like under President Quayle

9/28   Country singers Loretta Lynn, Crystal Gayle and Peggy Sue travel on George Bush's bus tour across central Illinois. "He's country and I love him," Lynn tells a crowd. "George Bush. Phew!" And just how much does she dislike Michael Dukakis? "Why, I can't even pronounce his name!"

9/29   No longer taken for granted, the space shuttle *Discovery* is the center of attention as it blasts off without blowing up, ending a 32-month US absence from space.

◾

"Hello, everybody, I'm Dan Quayle."
—Robert Redford campaigning with Michael Dukakis in New Jersey

◾

Fawn Hall's agent says she's writing her autobiography.

◾

The Nobel Peace Prize, which the First Lady was known to covet as the perfect going-away present for her husband, goes to the UN peacekeeping forces. Says one former Reagan aide, "They had very, very high hopes. Nancy must be wearing black."

9/30   Delivering his standard speech in Texas, Michael Dukakis suddenly refers to his father as "my daddy."

◾

The Dukakis campaign begins broadcasting "The Packaging of George Bush," an incomprehensible series of ads purporting to depict cynical Bush aides thinking up ways to manipulate the voters. Observes one political consultant, "It took me 10 seconds before I realized it wasn't a Bush spot."

■

"He had a great time. I didn't think we were ever going to get him out of the booth."
—Marlin Fitzwater on President Reagan's visit to Wrigley Field, where he did the play-by-play of the first inning of a Cubs-Pirates game, taking the opportunity to tell some of his favorite sportscasting stories

■

Mike Tyson sits calmly beside wife Robin Givens as she tells Barbara Walters that he's a violent manic depressive and life with him is "torture . . . pure hell . . . worse than anything I could possibly imagine." Two days later police are called to their New Jersey estate after the champion begins throwing large objects through the windows. Givens files for divorce within days.

OCTOBER 1988

In which the Nation suffers from Future shock

10/3   BRUCE'S NEW LOVE
Here's the lowdown on SPRINGSTEEN'S mystery woman, PATTI SCIALFA, the 35-year-old *Jersey Girl* who displaced actress Julianne Phillips, 29, and brought the Boss back to his roots
—*People*

10/4   The Bush campaign begins airing a stark black-and-white spot featuring prisoners going through a revolving door. An ominous voice-over talks about "weekend furloughs to first-degree murderers" while misleading statistics about Dukakis' record on crime are flashed on the screen.

■

"The liberal governor of Massachusetts—I love calling him that!"
—George Bush campaigning in Albuquerque

"You are such a weenie."
—University of Pennsylvania student greeting Dan Quayle

■

Stephen Mernick, an Orthodox Jew, buys PTL for $115 million.

10/5   On the morning of his debate with Lloyd Bentsen, Dan Quayle visits the Omaha Civic Auditorium to check out the debate site. "You're going to see Dan Quayle as he really is," he tells reporters. Inside, an ABC camera crew catches him rehearsing with Bush media adviser Roger Ailes. "Hey, Roger," he says nervously, "does . . . on, on this, you know, if I'm gonna, if I, if I decide on my gesture over there . . . is that all right . . . you don't mind?"

Leaving the hall after a sound check, he declares, "The mike works. That's very important to make sure the mike works and ours is working well."

DANNY, WE HARDLY KNEW YE

"I've had that stigma since I first ran for the Senate. It's stuck ever since. I think I have a feeling of what Jack Kennedy went through."

—Dan Quayle on his resemblance to Robert Redford

"I'm very close to the same age as Jack Kennedy when he was elected, not Vice President, but President."

—Dan Quayle campaigning in Boonville, Missouri

"I would point out that he has held elective Federal office for 12 years, virtually the same as John F. Kennedy when he ran for President."

—Dan Quayle's dad writing in *The New York Times*

"I've had 12 years of service, the same years of service that John Kennedy had before he ran for President, and I'd be glad to compare my legislative accomplishments . . . with his accomplishments."

—Dan Quayle

■

Asked three times at the debate what he would actually do if he suddenly became President—and three times robotically reciting his meager qualifications—Dan Quayle testily observes, "I have as much experience in the Congress as Jack Kennedy did when he sought the Presidency."

"Senator," says Lloyd Bentsen somberly, delivering what is instantly recognized as the sound bite of the night, "I served with Jack Kennedy. I knew Jack Kennedy. Jack Kennedy was a friend of mine. Senator, you're no Jack Kennedy."

"That was really uncalled for, Senator," whimpers Quayle, affecting the look of a wounded fawn.

"*You're* the one who was making the comparison, Senator," Bentsen shoots back, "and I'm one who knew him well. And frankly I think you're so far apart in the objectives you choose for your country that I did not think the comparison was well taken."

"After seeing Quayle, I could not vote for Bush."

—Toledo carpenter Greg Kretz, a member of the national 2–1 majority that thinks Lloyd Bentsen wiped the floor with his opponent

"When you think about what might have happened, we have to be pretty happy."

—Campaign chief James Baker assessing the Quayle performance

10/6 "I think that remark was a cheap shot unbecoming a senator of the United States."

—President Reagan—who not too long ago called Michael Dukakis an "invalid"—complaining about Lloyd Bentsen's assault on Quayle

■

"Clint Eastwood's answer to violent crime is, 'Go ahead, make my day.' My opponent's answer is slightly different. His motto is, 'Go ahead, have a nice weekend.'"

—George Bush campaigning in Texas

10/7 Michael Dukakis travels to a Missouri automotive parts plant to decry foreign ownership of American businesses, blissfully unaware that the plant is owned by Italians. "Maybe the Republican ticket wants our children to work for foreign owners and owe their future to foreign owners," he declares, "but that's not the kind of future Lloyd Bentsen and I want for America." Crowd response is muted.

■

Dan Quayle, whose handlers are struggling to fool people into thinking he's not an immature brat, sprays water on reporters during a campaign stop. "This is for all the articles you've written about me," he says.

■

"Dan Quayle can no longer be dismissed as a public man incapable of enlarging his stature. On Wednesday afternoon, he was only a vague misfortune for the Republicans, and overnight, he swelled himself close to the proportions of a disaster."
—Murray Kempton

10/10 Dan Quayle is again asked what he would do if he had to assume the Presidency. "Certainly, I know what to do," he says angrily, "and when I am Vice President—and I will be—there will be contingency plans under different sets of situations and I tell you what, I'm not going to go out and hold a news conference about it. I'm going to put it in a safe and keep it there! Does that answer your question?"

10/12 Humiliated by Bush aides who describe their job as having to "potty train" him, Dan Quayle declares his independence from his handlers. "Lookit," he says, "I've done it their way this far and now it's my turn. I'm my own handler. Any questions? Ask me. . . . There's not going to be any more handler stories because I'm the handler. . . . I am Doctor Spin." Speculation begins instantly that his handlers told him to say this.

■

On the eve of the second Bush/Dukakis debate, ABC's evening news devotes more than half its broadcast to a new poll showing George Bush with a virtually guaranteed electoral vote landslide.

10/13 Scientific tests prove that the Shroud of Turin—believed by Catholics to be Christ's burial cloth—was a fake created no earlier than the mid-13th century.

■

"Most alarming is his staunch refusal to inform the public about his performance in college and law school—or to provide his academic and his disciplinary records. He has admitted 'mediocre grades,' but he won't release the records. If he has nothing to hide, why has he permitted rumors to persist, not only about poor grades, but disciplinary actions for plagiarism and the hiring of surrogates to take his exams?"
—Full-page ad in major US newspapers demanding, "RELEASE DAN QUAYLE'S COLLEGE RECORDS *NOW*"

■

"It's everything he's ever done, basically."
—UCLA anti-Bush protester Liela Rand explaining her distaste for the candidate

■

Michael Dukakis arrives at UCLA with one goal for the second debate: act like a normal human. He wastes no time demonstrating his inability to do so, answering Bernard Shaw's unusually blunt first question—"If Kitty Dukakis were raped and murdered, would you favor an irrevocable death penalty for the killer?"—with a bloodless recital of his opposition to capital punishment and the importance of fighting drugs. The race is understood to be over.

For his part, Bush again reminds viewers that Dukakis "equated the President to a *rotting fish!* He said that!" Afterward, Dukakis quickly scurries off stage, leaving Bush alone to bask in his triumph.

10/14 Welcoming the crew of the space shuttle *Discovery* to the White House, President Reagan wonders aloud how long it will be be-

HERE'S WHAT THE CRITICS ARE SAYING ABOUT DAN QUAYLE

"This kid Quayle is a firecracker. . . . He is potentially the sharpest, best-looking, most engaging young politician to come along since Jack Kennedy."

—*New York Post* columnist Ray Kerrison

"A boisterous speaker whose face turns red and arms flap wildly when he gets excited about the issue being debated. . . . Frequently talks at length about issues whether he completely understands them or not."

—Sara Fritz/Henry Weinstein, *Los Angeles Times*

"Dan Quayle with his shiny cheekbones looks less like a movie star than like a ratings stud on the local news."

—James Wolcott

"Bit of a quiz show host."

—John O'Sullivan, editor, *National Review*

"There's something chilling about a hawk on defense who pronounces the word 'nuclear' as 'nucular.' "

—David Gritten, *Los Angeles Herald Examiner*

"I'd like to see him spend just one night in the jungle. Don't even throw in the enemy. Just the elements."

—Chicago Vietnam vet John LaPenta

"He doesn't have the greatest smarts in the world."

—James Quayle, Dan's dad

fore "the children of America turn to their parents and say, 'Gee, Mom and Dad, can I borrow the spaceship tonight?' " No one hazards a guess.

■

NOW PLAYING: *The Accused,* starring Jodie Foster as a gang-rape victim. St. Elizabeths does not suggest a field trip for John W. Hinckley, Jr.

10/15 "I'm picking up Bush vibrations/ He's the best guy to lead this nation."

—Beach Boys Mike Love and Bruce Johnston serenading Bush rallies in California

■

NUCLEAR HAZARDS AT OHIO WEAPON PLANT WERE ALLOWED BY U.S. FOR DECADES

—*The New York Times*

10/16 "Now, I'm having trouble with these questions, because they are putting me beyond where I want to be. . . . I am focusing on November 8th, and I don't want to be dragged beyond that."

—George Bush taking reporters' questions for the first time in 18 days, annoyed that they keep asking what he'd do as President

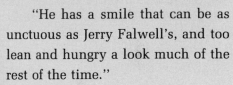

"He seems like a figure fixed in time and place: a Friday afternoon in the late 1960s at the 'Deke' house at DePauw University. The beer keg has been tapped and Quayle and his fraternity brothers are leaning out of the second-story window leering at coeds. This is the man George Bush presents to us to fill the place once occupied by Theodore Roosevelt, Harry Truman and Hubert Humphrey."
—Columnist Ross K. Baker

"He is not a ruminating creature. His nesting place is the mindless crowd, and his native woodnote the barbaric yawp. . . . The back of Dan Quayle's head is beginning to bald and his pale eyes sit upon a balcony

of crow's feet and there is the alarming suspicion that he will too soon be wrinkled and yet still be callow and too early grown old before he has really grown up."
—Murray Kempton

"He has a smile that can be as unctuous as Jerry Falwell's, and too lean and hungry a look much of the rest of the time."
—Tom Shales

"The impression he gave—of maturity, a becoming modesty, and a certain resourcefulness—were in rather refreshing contrast to the good-old-boy street smartness of Bentsen."
—Columnist William F. Buckley, Jr., offering a unique perspective on the debate

Jose R. Lopez/NYT Pictures

DUKAKIS PLOTS STRATEGY TO WIN WITH 18 STATES
CAMP SEEKS TO DISPEL NOTION BUSH HAS WON
—*The Washington Post*

10/17 Michael Dukakis meets with a supporter in a Cleveland diner. "Let's kick some ass out there, okay?" the man says. "Okay," says Dukakis dully. "Very good. We'll do it."

"I hope this means our liberal congressional friends are dropping their nostalgia for

the 'do your own thing in your own time, baby' 1960s."
—President Reagan on efforts to pass a bill mandating the death penalty for drug kingpins

Lisa Marie Presley
LOVE ME TENDER
Elvis's little girl, now 20 and pregnant with his first grandchild, comes out of the shadows to marry her Scientologist boyfriend
—*People*

Elaine Crispen confirms that, despite her

1982 announcement that she would not do it anymore, Nancy Reagan has continued to receive free designer clothing over the past six years. "She made a promise not to do this again and she broke her little promise," says Crispen, who points out—as Reagan aides so often seem to do—that no actual laws were broken.

10/18   "Our hearts are with you."
—President Reagan, whose tolerance for the suffering of poor humans is boundless, phoning the Alaskan National Guard to offer his support in the effort to rescue three whales trapped under ice

■

"I am the future."
—Dan Quayle

■

Children's Express reporter Suki Chong, 11, interviews Dan Quayle for a PBS show about the candidates. "Let's suppose I was sexually molested by my father and I became pregnant," she begins. "Would you want me to carry that baby to term?"

"My answer would be yes," says the visibly uncomfortable candidate, who looks younger than his inquisitor.

"But, don't you think this would *ruin my whole life?*" asks the girl.

"I would just like to see the baby have an opportunity."

"So," says Chong, with a directness infuriatingly lacking in her older colleagues, "although you're not actually killing me, you would sacrifice my prospects for the future for that baby."

"See, I've gotten to know you just a little bit," says Quayle, "and you're a very strong woman. You're a strong person. And . . . though this would be a traumatic experience that you would never forget, I think that you would be very successful in life."

Later, she asks Bush campaign manager Lee Atwater if the message the choice of Quayle sends is that "kids should get average grades in schools." Atwater claims Quayle "wasn't an average student." Replies Chong contemptuously,

"Of course he was."

10/19   "Friends, this is garbage. This is political garbage."
—Michael Dukakis finally fighting back, attacking an Illinois GOP flier claiming, "All the murderers and rapists and drug pushers and child molesters in Massachusetts vote for Michael Dukakis"

10/20   "For a public official's spouse to be 'on the take' is wrong, plain and simple. Nancy Reagan knew it, hid it for years, lied when caught, and now seeks to have a flock of taxpayer-paid press agents explain her ethical lapse away . . ."
—William Safire on the First Lady's inability to just say no when it comes to her clothing addiction

■

"We have gold and yellow and some red and, believe me, those are Republican colors. Bold colors, bright colors, future colors! You know what our opponents' colors are? Gray and dark gray!"
—Dan Quayle talking about the fall colors in rural Ohio

■

NBC agrees to pull an ad for *Favorite Son*, a six-hour mini-series about kinky sex in Washington, after Bush campaign aides complain that the promotional copy—"He's a handsome, charismatic young senator. He's campaigning for a place in the White House. But something in his past could cost him the election"—could reflect badly on Dan Quayle.

10/21   "If I'm elected President, if I'm remembered for anything, it would be this: a complete and total ban on chemical weapons. Their destruction forever. That's my solemn mission."
—George Bush, who cast several tie-breaking votes in the Senate to resume production of nerve gas

■

"George Bush says he hears the quiet peo-

WHAT'S QUAYLE'S SIGN?

Among the placards and banners greeting the candidate on the campaign trail:

"Quayle: Intensely Mediocre"

"War Hero? Rich Boy"

"VPs Should Be Better than C Students"

"Honk if you're smarter than Dan Quayle"

"Did your daddy get you this job, too"

"Spoiled Rich Sissy"

"Dan, Call Me!" (girl w/phone number on sign)

"Definition of a Quayle: Two right wings and no backbone"

"Dan, who took your law exam for you?"

"Vote for Quayle or Manson gets out of jail"

"Quayle's no J.F.K."

"He's not Quayleified."

"Dan Quayle is an Awesome Dude"

---

ple others don't. I have a friend in Los Angeles who hears the quiet people others don't, and he has to take a lot of medication for it."
—Albert Brooks campaigning for Michael Dukakis

10/24   Convicted killer John Wayne Gacy objects to his name being used "to scare people into voting for George Bush" in a campaign flier claiming he'd be eligible for weekend furloughs if he'd committed his 33 murders in Massachusetts.

■

Dan Quayle is asked whether he'd want his wife to have the baby if she were raped and became pregnant. In the event of such a "tragic" situation, he says, he would hope that she "would have the child." And how he would feel about raising, say, Willie Horton's child? He is not asked.

■

Okay, our focus: Are Babies Being Bred for Satanic Sacrifice? Controversial, to say the least. Unbelievable, to say the least. Disgusting, to say the least. We'll be right back."
—Geraldo Rivera cutting to a commercial on his daily talk show

10/25   ". . . Drinking blood . . . grave robbing . . . mutilated animals . . . drinking her 15-year-old victim's blood . . . gouged out his victim's eyes . . . butchered his mother . . . cut the ears off . . . drinking his own blood. . . . The acts . . . are so horrible that the question could fairly be raised again: why are we doing this broadcast?"
—Geraldo Rivera presenting his first—and last—NBC special, *Devil Worship: Exposing Satan's Underground*, which *The New York*

Times calls "pornography masquerading as journalism"

"What must it be like to a father to think that his own son was disposed of in bits and pieces and thrown in the garbage?"
—Geraldo to the parent of a victim, needing to know

"That man is *so* repugnant. All of these satanic murderers are."
—Geraldo making it clear that, though he loves to recycle excerpts from his interview with "today's top satanic celebrity," Charles Manson, personally he can't stand him

"Geraldo should be arrested for exposing himself."
—Former NBC News president Reuven Frank on the Rivera oeuvre

■

"What is it about the Bush campaign that has absolutely nailed you to the wall?"
—Ted Koppel to Michael Dukakis during a stultifying appearance on *Nightline,* where the candidate uses his precious time to remind voters why his election is even more unthinkable than Bush's

10/27   Continuing his free media blitz, Michael Dukakis tells Dan Rather that he might not have responded to Bush's attacks "as quickly as I should have."

■

"I would guess that there's adequate low-income housing in the country."
—Dan Quayle offering a very uneducated guess about the homeless situation

10/28   *The Philadelphia Daily News* says it "could have endorsed the 1979–80 George Bush," but not the 1988 version "who pretends, despite all the evidence, that J. Danforth Quayle is not a callow moron."

10/29   "My only hope for those whales is

that they don't end up in Boston Harbor."
—George Bush doing shtick about the two surviving creatures, who are heading back to the open sea

10/30   DUKAKIS MAY BE STAGING COMEBACK
    LONGTIME DEMOCRATS IN KEY BIG STATES LEAVE BUSH AS POLLS SHOW GAP CLOSING
—*Los Angeles Times*

■

"I'm a liberal in the tradition of Franklin Roosevelt and Harry Truman and John Kennedy."
—Former moderate technocrat Michael Dukakis discovering the joys of populism as he goes into the last full week of the campaign 10 points behind

10/31   "Miracle of miracles! Headlines! Read all about it! My opponent finally, after knocking me in the debate, called himself the big 'L,' called himself a liberal."
—George Bush, reverting to hysteria as the clock runs out

■

The Islamic Jihad releases a taped statement by Terry Anderson—held in Lebanon since March 1985—in which he accuses the US of blocking efforts to free him and the other hostages. "I don't think that was Terry speaking," says President Reagan. "I think he had a script that was given to him. When I was given a script, I always read the lines."

■

Dan Quayle crashes through a paper pumpkin at a Halloween rally in a Michigan high school.

NOVEMBER 1988

In which the Nation overcomes its fear of the Future

11/1   Campaigning in California, President

DID YOU HEAR THE ONE ABOUT THE MALE BIMBO?

"What were Dan Quayle's three toughest years? Second grade."

"What do you get when you cross a chicken and a hawk? A Quayle."

"Why did the chicken cross the road? To join the National Guard."

"This looks like the kind of group that would buy Dan Quayle a tape of *Good Morning, Vietnam*."
—Johnny Carson

"I was just back in the newsroom there—saw Pat Robertson and Dan Quayle swapping war stories."
—Jay Leno

"*Full Dinner Jacket*."
—Jay Leno on the new Vietnam movie starring Dan Quayle

"I don't like to deal in rumors, but I heard that the guy who took Dan Quayle's law boards for him, *he* cheated."
—Albert Brooks

Reagan quotes that well-known character from fiction, "Huckleferry Binn."

11/2 "It seemed like he appeared on every television show except *Wheel of Fortune*. You see, he was afraid that Vanna might turn over the 'L' word."
—George Bush attacking Michael Dukakis for going on TV

"If he's Harry Truman, I'm Roger Rabbit."
—President Reagan, attacking Dukakis while demonstrating that when it comes to inane pop-culture references, he still has no peer

■

Asked if the woman raped by Willie Horton should have had his baby if she'd become pregnant, Dan Quayle says yes. He goes on to display his continuing gynecological ignorance, claiming that rape victims wouldn't need to worry about abortions if they'd just submit to the "normal medical procedure" of a "D & C" (dilation and curettage) right afterward. In fact, uterus scraping is never part of post-rape care, since a

fertilized egg takes several days to enter the womb.

11/3 "I only play the Terminator in my movies. But let me tell you, when it comes to the American future, Michael Dukakis will be the real Terminator!"
—Arnold Schwarzenegger campaigning for George Bush

■

"Respond to the attacks immediately. Don't let them get away with a thing."
—Michael Dukakis revealing what he's learned from the campaign, though not explaining why he needed to learn it again, having been beaten by a similar campaign 10 years earlier

■

Geraldo Rivera gets a long-overdue come-uppance during the taping of a sweeps-month segment on "Teen Hatemongers" when talk show brawler Roy Innis, with the host's blessing, attempts to throttle a white supremacist. During the resulting melee—the logical culmination of a year of increasingly confronta-

tional TV programming—a chair lands in the sensation-mongering host's face, demolishing his nose.

11/4 Oklahoma prison inmate Brett Kimberlin, who has been trying to call a press conference to claim that he used to sell marijuana to Dan Quayle, is placed in solitary confinement.

■

'VIRUS' IN MILITARY COMPUTERS DISRUPTS SYSTEMS NATIONWIDE
   EXPERTS CALL IT THE LARGEST ASSAULT EVER ON THE NATION'S SYSTEMS
—*The New York Times*

11/5 AUTHOR OF COMPUTER 'VIRUS' IS SON OF N.S.A. EXPERT ON DATA SECURITY
—*The New York Times*

■

"If you ask me, as Robert Palmer has been singing recently, you are simply irresistible."
—President Reagan responding to cheers from college students

11/6 George Bush rejects poll results showing most voters blame him for the negative tone of the campaign, citing instead "those personal attacks night after night on me, on my character

at that idiotic Democratic convention."

■

"He's slipping and sliding, we're rocking and rolling."
—Michael Dukakis, ending his campaign with a marathon 48-hour, nine-state blitz

■

"In the primaries . . . it was enough for him then not to be Jesse Jackson, and he seems to have taken it for granted that it would be enough thereafter not to be George Bush. Not being Jesse Jackson worked but not being George Bush apparently hasn't, and now he must try to arise and say in thunder just who Michael Dukakis is, and the gifts of nature and the allotment of time look too small to equip him for that job."
—Murray Kempton on Michael Dukakis

11/7 "So, if I could ask you one last time, tomorrow, when mountains greet the dawn, will you go out there and win one for the Gipper?"
—President Reagan making his last campaign appearance on behalf of George Bush, whose half-hour election-eve TV ad omits any mention of a Mr. Dan Quayle

11/8 Dan Quayle celebrates Election Day with a bizarrely ritualistic visit to the dentist. Though he and George Bush are elected by a 54%–46% margin, polls show that Quayle cost the ticket at least 2% of the vote. The Democrats win 10 states and 112 electoral votes, their best showing since 1976. Voter turnout—50.16%—is the lowest since 1924.

11/9 George Bush names campaign chief James Baker Secretary of State.

11/10 John Mitchell, the only US Attorney General to do time in jail, dies of a heart attack at 75.

11/14 "As we sat in front of our TV set, we realized that something *had* changed. No longer did the programming include, at regular intervals, footage of violent criminals going

1988

through revolving doors, recitations of the horrors that might be visited on peace-loving Americans if a 'card-carrying member of the ACLU' became President, or bursts of talk about Boston Harbor and 'Taxachusetts.' George Bush was not even President yet, and the United States was already a kinder and gentler place, because the Bush campaign was over."
—*The New Yorker*'s Talk of the Town

■

THE FIRST LADY

No fancy Nancy, loyal, unflappable BARBARA BUSH brings a simpler Yankee style, 10 lively grandchildren and the first man she ever kissed to the White House
—*People*, reflecting a deep national relief at the imminent departure of Mrs. Reagan

11/15 "The Secret Service is under orders that if Bush is shot, to shoot Quayle."
—Massachusetts senator John Kerry telling a joke for which he will quickly apologize

■

Talk show host Oprah Winfrey—the nation's most renowned dieter—brings out a wheelbarrow loaded with 65 pounds of fat, the better to demonstrate exactly how much weight she's lost.

11/16 Despite his claim during the debate that he knows her, Dan Quayle is not invited to the Reagan administration's state dinner for Margaret Thatcher.

11/17 George Bush pays off some more campaign debts, naming New Hampshire governor John Sununu as White House chief of staff and campaign manager Lee Atwater as the new Republican party head.

11/18 Marilyn Quayle gives up her quixotic quest to take over Dan's Senate seat. Observes one relieved Indiana Republican, "That was very smart. I think the only person pushing her was her."

11/21 The Reagans break ground for his presidential library near Los Angeles. Nancy, as she is apt to do in such situations, almost falls down.

■

Richard Nixon—who was 40 when he became Vice President—meets with Dan Quayle. "I was very surprised," he says afterward. "He is a very different man from the intellectual midget who has been portrayed among the media."

11/22 The national hoopla surrounding the 25th anniversary of the assassination of JFK peaks with the Arts and Entertainment Network's minute-by-minute replay of NBC's original coverage of the event, providing an eerie glimpse into the past.

11/24 REAGAN POCKET-VETOES STRICTER ETHICS RULES
—*The Washington Post*

11/28 George Bush holds a fence-mending meeting with Bob Dole. "The race is over. I'm a big boy," says Dole afterward. "We'll say the Pledge of Allegiance every day and go to work."

HERE'S WHAT THE CRITICS ARE SAYING ABOUT PRESIDENT REAGAN

"He believes he's above it all. He believes it. That's why *they* believe it. I can't believe it. But they do."
—1984 campaign aide Stu Spencer marvelling at President Reagan's ability to fool others by fooling himself, as reported in *Landslide*

"If we told Reagan to walk outside, turn around three times, pick up an acorn, and throw it out to the crowd, we'd be lucky to get a question from him asking, 'Why?'"
—Unnamed White House source

"He demonstrated for all to see how far you can go in this life with a smile, a shoeshine and the nerve to put your own spin on the facts."
—*Boston Globe* columnist David Nyhan

"Poor dear, there's nothing between his ears."
—Margaret Thatcher, as quoted in *Mrs. Thatcher's Revolution* by Peter Jenkins

"Why do the Reagans always fly together?"
"Because if they flew separately, and one crashed, the other would have to talk to the children."
—Source unknown

11/30 Dan Quayle says one of the lessons he learned from the campaign was not to talk so much. "Verbosity," he explains, "leads to unclear, inarticulate things."

DECEMBER 1988

In which the President absolves himself of all blame

12/1 New York's network affiliates preempt their soaps and game shows to present Hedda Nussbaum's testimony in Joel Steinberg's trial for the murder of six-year-old Lisa. She sums up the depravity of the situation by revealing that while the girl lay comatose on the bathroom floor, she and Joel freebased cocaine. He is convicted of manslaughter.

12/2 "The thing is if you control the Senate meetings, you control the gavel. And the gavel is a very important instrument . . . an instrument of power. An instrument that establishes the agenda."
—Dan Quayle suggesting that he's considering presiding over the Senate, a notion he has not yet discussed with newly elected Majority Leader George Mitchell or Minority Leader Bob Dole

12/6 "We have people making hundreds of

dollars a week living in our shelters. We have people who go to work with briefcases, rather nice, spiffy."
—Ed Koch proposing that homeless people taking refuge in city shelters be charged rent, explaining, "It's all part of character building"

■

With his first new album in years about to be released, Roy Orbison—rock's greatest white singer—dies at 52 of a heart attack.

■

The Gorbachevs arrive in New York for his speech to the UN. Disappointed that they have decided against a visit to Trump Tower, Donald Trump rushes downstairs when he hears the Soviet leader has dropped by after all. The man outside his building turns out to be a Gorbachev look-alike.

Their visit to New York is cut short when a devastating earthquake destroys Soviet Armenia.

12/8 President Reagan holds his 44th and final news conference, for an average of one every 66.4 days. As he has at almost every previous one, he blames the Congress and previous Democratic Presidents for his budget deficits. *The New York Times* calls him "a defensive old man."

12/9 The last Presidential polyp is removed from Reagan's large intestine, for a total of 15.

12/13 With five weeks left in office, President Reagan delivers his farewell address on domestic policy, in which he continues to deny that his defense spending increases and tax cuts were in any way responsible for the $155 billion deficit, blaming instead an "iron triangle" of congressmen, lobbyists and journalists.

12/14 Market consultant Faith Popcorn says she expects Barbara Bush to usher in a new acceptance of the Older Lady. "What's wrong with looking 60," she asks, "instead of looking like an anorexic 12-year-old?"

12/16 After making high ethical standards one of the mainstays of his campaign, George Bush nominates John Tower—whose personal life has been the subject of considerable media scrutiny—to run the Pentagon. "I woke up every morning and laughed myself silly over what I was reading in the newspapers," says the nominee, no doubt exaggerating his glee at reports of his drinking, womanizing and coziness with defense contractors.

■

Texas judge Jack Hampton says he gave an 18-year-old killer a lighter sentence because his two victims were gay. "These two guys who got killed wouldn't have been killed if they hadn't been cruising the streets picking up teenage boys," he explains.

■

Right-wing extremist Lyndon LaRouche is convicted of conspiracy to defraud the Internal Revenue Service and mail fraud.

12/19 The *National Enquirer* says that Nancy Reagan is in a state of panic over reports that "daughter Patti is telling all to sizzling biography writer Kitty Kelley!"

12/20 The *World News Tonight* curse strikes again: former co-anchor Max Robinson, 49—the first black network anchor—dies of AIDS, leaving Peter Jennings as the only survivor of the original three-man ABC team.

12/21 Judge Gerhard Gesell sets January 31 as the starting date for Oliver North's trial.

12/22 Publicists for *E.T.* star Drew Barrymore report that the 13-year-old actress has completed treatment for alcohol abuse, and will start filming a TV movie in which she plays a drug-dependent teen who enters a rehab.

■

President Reagan—whose tenure has coincided with a huge increase in the homeless population—uses his last interview with David

DAN QUAYLE TALKS ABOUT THE FAMILY

"Don't forget the importance of the family. It begins with the family. We're not going to redefine the family. Everybody knows the definition of the family. [Meaningful pause] A child. [Meaningful pause] A mother. [Meaningful pause] A father. There are other arrangements of the family, but that is a family and family values."

"I've been very blessed with wonderful parents and a wonderful family, and I am proud of my family. Anybody turns to their family. I have a very good family. I'm very fortunate to have a very good family. I believe very strongly in the family. It's one of the things we have in our platform, is to talk about it."

"I suppose three important things certainly come to my mind that we want to say thank you. The first would be our family. Your family, my family—which is composed of an immediate family of a wife and three children, a larger family with grandparents and aunts and uncles. We all have our family, whichever that may be. . . . The very beginnings of civilization, the very beginnings of this country, goes back to the family. And time and time again, I'm often reminded, especially in this Presidential campaign, of the importance of a family, and what a family means to this country. And so when you pay thanks I suppose the first thing that would come to mind would be to thank the Lord for the family."

Brinkley to again claim that many of these unfortunates are homeless by "their own choice," as must be many of the jobless, since he again points out that the Sunday papers are full of want ads. Asked how an actor could handle the Presidency, Reagan says he's wondered "how you could do this job and not be an actor."

■

JETLINER CARRYING 258 TO U.S. CRASHES IN SCOTTISH TOWN
    ALL BELIEVED DEAD
    SYRACUSE UNIVERSITY HAD 38 PEOPLE ABOARD—CAUSE IS UNKNOWN
    —*The New York Times*

12/23   PAN AM WAS TOLD OF TERROR THREAT

U.S. EMBASSY IN FINLAND WAS TIPPED OFF 2 WEEKS AGO
    —*The New York Times*

12/26   "These aren't 'animals,' these are wild quail. . . . I don't think I could shoot a deer. Quail—that's something else again."
    —George Bush embarking on a hunting trip in Texas, displaying a unique perspective on biology and becoming the second politician to publicly link the words "shoot" and "Quayle"

12/27   President Reagan visits his new office in the penthouse of the Fox Plaza, the Los Angeles high-rise used as the location for the terrorist movie *Die Hard*.

1 How did Dan Quayle seek to reassure voters about him during his debate with Lloyd Bentsen?

a He said he understands complicated defense matters like "telemetry and acryption," though the word is actually "encryption"

b He said he has a "commitment to preserving the environment" because "I take my children hiking and fishing, walking in the woods"

c He said he has a "commitment to the poor" that once led him to visit people at a food bank who were incredibly grateful that "I took time out of my schedule" to do so

d He said he knows Margaret Thatcher and Helmut Kohl and "they know me," though in fact he's had only a single brief meeting with each

e He said that if he became President, he would know the people he had to work with "on a firsthand basis"

f He said he read three books—including Richard Nixon's latest—"over the last spring vacation"

g He said his grandmother once told him, "You can do anything you want to if you just set your mind to it and go to work"

h He pointed out that he once authored a piece of legislation

i He said he would never have "another Jimmy Carter grain embargo, Jimmy, Jimmy Carter, Jimmy Carter grain embargo, Jimmy Carter grain embargo"

j All of the above

2 What advice did George Bush's mother, Dorothy, offer about his presidential campaign?

a She said he was "talking about yourself too much"

b She said he was "talking about fish too much"

c "For God's sake, George, stop dropping Margaret Thatcher's name!"

d "Whatever you do, George, don't pick a callow moron as your running mate."

3 Which aspect of George Bush's version of his role in the Iran-contra affair troubled his critics?

a His insistence that though he knew we were selling arms to Iran and trying to get back our hostages, he never put the two together, despite his attendance at over 30 meetings on the subject, despite his claim that concern for tortured CIA station chief William Buckley ("I wanted Mr. Buckley out of there") led him to go along with the plan, and despite the existence of documents showing that the White House already knew Buckley had been killed

b His insistence that he never discussed contra resupply efforts with contra-aid manager and former CIA agent Felix Rodriguez, despite the existence of a memo saying he did

c His insistence that he had no idea Shultz and Weinberger opposed the plan—if he'd known, he said, he probably would have been against it himself—despite his well-documented presence at the meeting where Shultz was said to have become "apoplectic" in his opposition

d All of the above, plus too many others to list

4 Which revelation appeared in Michael Deaver's book?

a Jackie Onassis called him "a young Fred Astaire" and he "just melted"

b President Reagan was so interested in neurosurgery that he "could diagnose a brain tumor just by hearing the symptoms on a soap opera"

c The author once ran through a glass door in his haste to retrieve Nancy's makeup kit from an airplane

d All of the above

5 Which famous dead star was reportedly seen alive several times in 1988?

a John Belushi
b Elvis Presley
c Jackie Gleason
d Karen Carpenter

6 How did Dan Quayle refer to George Bush on the campaign trail?

a "Mr. Next President"
b "The President of Vice"
c "George the Bush"
d "Borge Gush"

7 What did George Bush call for on the campaign trail?

a A better life for "inner ghetto city youth"
b "A kitchen in every pot"
c Policies that will allow people to "send your college to children"
d All of the above, plus the death penalty for "those narked-up terrorist kind of guys"

8 Which 1988 non-candidate exulted, "We don't have to do what the candidates do—talk about huge issues in 30 seconds in a field somewhere, trying to make sure cows don't urinate on our shoes"?

a Sam Nunn
b Paul Laxalt
c Bill Bradley
d Mario Cuomo

9 Complete comic Sam Kinison's bewilderment at a fellow performer's success: "_____—a nation decides not to hurt somebody's feelings."

a Tom Hanks
b Chevy Chase
c Howie Mandel
d Whoopi Goldberg

10 Which Bush campaign aide was described by TV critic Emily Prager as "a guy with a turned-up nose and the sadistic look of a bad boyfriend"?

a Lee Atwater
b Craig O. Fuller
c Roger Ailes
d Rich Bond

11 True or false? President Reagan made such a pest of himself by injecting himself into televised sporting events that, by his last year in office, the networks made it clear that they had no intention of giving his post-game shenanigans any air time.

12 What was Brandon Tartikoff's idea for minimizing the effects of the 22-week writers' strike?

a Take scripts from old failed shows and reshoot them with today's stars
b Compile a special consisting of his own cameo appearances on NBC shows
c Create a series about professional women who spend an inordinate amount of time in their underwear
d Turn two hours a night over to Geraldo Rivera

13 Which of these statements about Dan Quayle is untrue?

a After working for four years writing National Guard press releases, he still managed to test well below average in categories like "fundamentals of writing" and "Army information"
b His newspaper-publishing parents were members of the John Birch Society
c His IQ was tested at 165
d He was inspired by the film *The Candidate*—though its irony was lost on him—and claimed in a campaign slogan to be "better looking than Robert Redford"

14 Which film failed to gross $100 million at the box office?

a *Who Framed Roger Rabbit*

b *Three Men and a Baby*
c *Big*
d *Arthur 2 On the Rocks*

15 What did James Baker say during a debate planning meeting when told that Dan Quayle had a preference for particular dates?
a "We'll try to accommodate him, but everyone has his own priorities."
b "We don't care what Dan Quayle wants."
c "Dan Quayle. Dan Quayle. Atwater, do we know a Dan Quayle?"
d "Quayle, Schmayle."

16 Which of George Bush's potential running mates did Paula Parkinson claim to have spent an evening making love with?
a Bob Dole
b Jack Kemp
c Elizabeth Dole
d Alan Simpson

Match the newsmaker with his/her news.
17 Duffey Strode
18 Sen. Chic Hecht
19 Carl Rowan
20 Don DeLillo
21 Ed Joyce
22 Joyce Brown
23 Donald Rochon
24 Michael Reagan
___**a** Pledged opposition to the placement of a "nuclear suppository" in his state
___**b** Complained about harassment by white FBI co-workers that included the pasting of an ape's head over his son's head on a family photo
___**c** Strongly supported gun control laws, yet shot backyard intruder with unlicensed handgun
___**d** Hosted a cable talk show promoting the $39.95 "diet patch," a direct-mail device to be stuck on the "appetite control center" on the wrist
___**e** Enjoyed brief New York media celebritydom as former—and future— homeless person
___**f** Was repeatedly suspended from North Carolina elementary school for screaming biblical verses at classmates
___**g** Wrote novel about Lee Harvey Oswald
___**h** Wrote CBS memoir revealing that a flustered Dan Rather once kissed him on the cheek

Who said what?
25 Phil Donahue
26 Gary Hart
27 Sylvester Stallone
28 Roger Ailes
29 Pat Robertson
30 Susan Estrich
___**a** "I used to be called cold and aloof. Now I'm just enigmatic. Give me another 25 years and I'll be transparent."
___**b** "Look, I'm trying to run for President. I can't sit here and debate free trade vs. fair trade."
___**c** "The only question is whether we depict Willie Horton with a knife in his hand or without it."
___**d** "I'd rather be called 'sleazy' than to be identified as 'intelligent.'"
___**e** "If Bush thinks he's going to get anywhere with this Pledge stuff, he's crazy."
___**f** "My life is perhaps one of the great cruel jokes ever perpetrated on the American public."

31 Which did *Time* pick as Planet of the Year?
a Saturn
b Uranus
c Pluto
d Earth

32 Which unfortunate trend dominated the late '80s?
a The fading out of vinyl records
b The greenhouse effect
c Perfumed magazine ads
d Ads for office systems peopled by hostile business types

e The verbization of nouns (e.g., "parenting")

f The initial fetish ("The A-word," "The B-word," etc.)

g All of the above

33 Which of these did *not* appear on TV?

a Phil Donahue in a dress

b Two TV movies about Liberace in eight days

c Vanna White in her dramatic debut

d An effective Dukakis spot

34 According to Patricia Seaton Lawford in her book *The Peter Lawford Story*, what

was Nancy Davis known for before she married Ronald Reagan?

a "For giving the best parties in Hollywood."

b "For giving the best directions in Hollywood."

c "For giving the best head in Hollywood."

d "For having the biggest head in Hollywood."

ANSWERS

1-j, 2-a, 3-d, 4-d, 5-b, 6-c, 7-d, 8-d, 9-d, 10-a, 11-True, 12-a, 13-c, 14-d, 15-b, 16-b, 17-f, 18-a, 19-c, 20-g, 21-h, 22-e, 23-b, 24-d, 25-d, 26-a, 27-f, 28-c, 29-b, 30-e, 31-d, 32-g, 33-d, 34-c

1989

JANUARY 1989

In which the First Couple play their final scenes

1/3   Michael Dukakis announces that he will not seek re-election as governor of Massachusetts in 1990. He does not rule out another race for the Presidency, though millions of Democrats rule it out for him.

1/4   With tension mounting over the possible production of chemical weapons in Libya, US Navy warplanes shoot down two Libyan fighter jets. President Reagan, it is announced, was awakened at 2:53 A.M. with the news.

1/5   The Reagans return to the White House for the last time, with the President having spent a total of 458 days of his reign in California.

■

Madonna files for divorce from Sean Penn.

1/9   President Reagan delivers his final budget. Though the nation's 17 nuclear weapons plants have been so carelessly maintained as to present a public health threat, he calls for under $1 billion to start their $138 billion rehabilitation.

1/11   "All great change in America begins at the dinner table. So tomorrow night in the kitchen, I hope the talking begins. And children, if your parents haven't been teaching you what it means to be an American, let 'em know and nail 'em on it. That would be a very American thing to do."
—President Reagan taking the opportunity in

his farewell speech to the nation to suggest that children should monitor their parents for sufficient patriotism

1/15   In a *60 Minutes* interview airing on Martin Luther King, Jr.'s, birthday, President Reagan—again citing his half-century-old support for desegregation of baseball as proof of his commitment to equality—suggests that many civil rights leaders are just using racism to promote themselves. "Sometimes I wonder if they really want what they say they want," he says, pointing out that they are "doing very well leading organizations based on keeping alive the feeling that they're victims of prejudice."

■

Roger Sandler, who claims he is owed $1,500 for the unauthorized and uncredited use of two of his photos in Michael Reagan's book, finds a message from the President's son on his answering machine. Says Reagan, "I hope your family dies in a plane crash with you in it."

1/17   "We found that the independent counsel's report far from vindicates Mr. Meese; rather, it details conduct which should not be tolerated by any government employee, especially not the attorney general of the United States."
—Justice Department report on the ethics of Ed Meese

1/18   REAGAN REJECTS JUSTICE DEPT. CRITICISM OF MEESE
PRESIDENT BELIEVES REPORT MAY BE WORK OF 'POLITICAL ENEMIES,' WHITE HOUSE SAYS
—*The Washington Post*

■

President Reagan—aka "the Gipper"—greets the undefeated Notre Dame team at the White House, where he is presented with

George Gipp's actual monogrammed sweater, to the fury of alumni who feel it belongs at the university and not in the possession of an actor.

■

Oliver North learns that although he did not receive one of President Reagan's last 10 pardons, George Steinbrenner—convicted of making illegal contributions to the 1972 Nixon campaign—did.

■

REAGAN'S RATING IS BEST SINCE 40'S FOR A PRESIDENT
FINAL APPROVAL IS AT 68%
POPULARITY OF 8-YEAR TENURE HAS MARKEDLY INCREASED TRUST IN GOVERNMENT
—*The New York Times*

1/19 The Reagans spend their last night in the White House. So, despite Nancy's long-ago offer, they didn't move out early, after all. (And so much for the zero-year jinx!)

1/20 As his wife—decked out in a little blue sailor's hat—looks on, Dan Quayle takes as much of the vice presidential oath of office as Justice Sandra Day O'Connor (who leaves out six words) remembers. He assumes office nonetheless, assuring the nation of, at best, four years of vague unease.

George Bush, who has spent the past eight years "blindly" supporting his President, implies in his inaugural address that maybe the greed and materialism has gotten a bit out of hand. "A new breeze is blowing," says the new President. "The new breeze blows."

As the Reagans depart, the backwash of their helicopter blows the little blue sailor's hat right off Marilyn Quayle's head.

At 3:30 P.M., the Reagans' last official flight on a presidential jet landed at Los Angeles International Airport. As a fitting ending to their glamorous reign, they were welcomed home by megastar Rich Little. When Little claimed that imitating Reagan gave him a "terrible urge to run off with Nancy," the former First Lady threw her head back in would-be helpless laughter.

The former President joked that he'd been asked to appear in "a remake of *Bedtime for Bonzo*—only this time they wanted me to play Bonzo." He promised to "keep on campaigning out there on the mashed potato circuit" for those same causes that had so captivated the voters during his tenure: the line-item veto and the balanced-budget amendment. Little then presented them with enormous California license plates—"THE PREZ" and "F L NANCY" —to add to their collection of absurdly oversized props.

Finally, after eight years as a President and his First Lady, the Reagans waved to their fans, climbed into their limo, and headed for the Bel Air home their friends had bought for them— at 666 St. Cloud.

"What a waste it is to lose one's mind, or not to have a mind. . . . How true that is."
—Dan Quayle addressing the United Negro College Fund, whose slogan is "A mind is a terrible thing to waste," 1989

ACKNOWLEDGMENTS

Besides me and the President, there are two people without whom *The Clothes Have No Emperor* would not exist: my agent and friend Geri Thoma, whose steadfast support for my work spans the decade, and my editor Tim McGinnis, whose understanding of this project was crucial to its initiation, and whose death of heart failure at 34 was a loss not just to his family and friends but to everyone who cares about smart books and good writing. For knowing what's funny and what's not, they both have my love and gratitude.

I also want to thank Edward Walters, who brought the kind of enthusiasm to the book that editors usually reserve for projects they think up themselves. For his sympathetic and intelligent editing, I am wildly grateful.

Thanks, too, to photo researcher Lucy Handley for tracking down all my favorites, to designer Bonni Leon for making it look so good, to Liz Cunningham, Steve Messina and Renée Rabb for their attention to the details, and to Dick Baxter for his patient computer lessons. My gratitude also extends to each of the columnists, critics and observers quoted herein, without whose witty insights this book would be a much-diminished work; to CNN and C-SPAN, for showing what the broadcast networks didn't; and to my parents, who got me hooked on newsprint at the age of seven.

This would have been a much lonelier undertaking had I not had so many wonderful friends who shared my perceptions. For their periodic reassurance that this stuff was worth collecting, I thank Andy Aaron, Kurt Andersen, Michael Baumayr, Leon Bing, Bob Brienza, Nancy Cain, Caroline Carney, Joan Chu, Richard Clurman, Shirley Clurman, Robbie Conal, Norman Cook, Stuart Cornfeld, Beverly D'Angelo, Marnie Delaney, Jamie Diamond, Brenda Dillon, Lee Eisenberg, Teri Garr, Greg Gigilioli, Meg Greenfield, Lloyd Grove, Lisa Grunwald, David Handelman, Carol Hatfield, Barbara Hershey, David Hirshey, Doug Ireland, Maren Jensen, Judy Jones, Judy Kessler, Noah Kimerling, Michael Kinsley, Beverly Kopf, Paul Krassner, John Long, Sharon Long, Michael Longacre, Vanessa Longacre, Patty Marx, Gerald Marzorati, Jaren Millard, Holly Morris, Susan Morrison, Janine Nichols, Nils Nichols, Mark O'Donnell, Michael O'Donoghue, Andy Port, Steve Radlauer, Muney Rivers, Devie Rosenbloom, Lane Sarasohn, Barry Secunda, Debbie Siebers, Ann Slichter, Penelope Spheeris, Penny Stallings, Judy Telander, Rick Telander, Gig Thompson, Audrey Walker, Philip Waters, John Wilbur, John Wilburn, David Wild, Arthur Zich and Janet Zich.

My love and special thanks go to Lynne Aston, Ivan Bernstein, Albert Brooks, Christopher Buckley, Carol Caldwell, Leslee Dart, Carrie Fisher, Rob Fleder, Marilyn Johnson, Monica Johnson, Peter W. Kaplan, Jerry Lazar, John Lombardi, Penny Marshall, Peter Occhiogrosso, Mary Kay Place, Michael Searles, Harry Shearer, Arleen Sorkin and Danny Zuker for their generous indulgence of (and contributions to) my obsession, and to my dear friend Sarah Longacre, whose wisdom and humor helped keep me sane through insane times.

Finally, I thank several people whose brilliance served as inspiration for this work: Murray Kempton, whose stunning columns—often cited herein—deserve several books of their own; Paul Conrad and Mark Alan Stamaty, whose savage cartoons provided the most accurate reporting of the decade; Harold Hayes, who, as editor of *Esquire* in the '60s, raised the chronicling of the idiotic public moment into an art form, and John Lennon, who insisted on the truth.

INDEX